ANNUAL EDITIONS

American Government
Thirty-Second Edition

EDITOR

Bruce Stinebrickner
DePauw University

Professor Bruce Stinebrickner teaches American politics in the Department of Political Science at DePauw University in Greencastle, Indiana. He has also taught American politics at Lehman College of the City University of New York, at the University of Queensland in Brisbane, Australia, and in a DePauw program for Argentine students in Buenos Aires. He received his Ph.D. from Yale University in 1974. In his courses and publications on American politics, Professor Stinebrickner brings valuable insights gained from living, teaching, and lecturing abroad.

McGraw-Hill/Dushkin
530 Old Whitfield Street, Guilford, Connecticut 06437

Visit us on the Internet
http://www.dushkin.com

Credits

1. **Foundations of American Politics**
   Unit photo—Courtesy of the Library of Congress.
2. **Structures of American Politics**
   Unit photo—Courtesy of K. Jewell/U.S. House of Representatives.
3. **Process of American Politics**
   Unit photo—AP/World Wide Photo by Ron Edmonds.
4. **Products of American Politics**
   Unit photo—Northrop Corporation photo.

Copyright

Cataloging in Publication Data
Main entry under title: Annual Editions: American Government. 2002/2003.
1. U.S.—Politics and government—1945—Periodicals. I. Stinebrickner, Bruce, *comp*. II. Title: American government.
ISBN 0–07–250708–X   320.9'73'0924'05   76-180265   ISSN 0891–3390

Thirty-Second Edition

Cover image © 2002 PhotoDisc, Inc.
Printed in the United States of America   234567890BAHBAH5432   Printed on Recycled Paper

Editors/Advisory Board

Members of the Advisory Board are instrumental in the final selection of articles for each edition of ANNUAL EDITIONS. Their review of articles for content, level, currentness, and appropriateness provides critical direction to the editor and staff. We think that you will find their careful consideration well reflected in this volume.

To the Reader

In publishing ANNUAL EDITIONS we recognize the enormous role played by the magazines, newspapers, and journals of the public press in providing current, first-rate educational information in a broad spectrum of interest areas. Many of these articles are appropriate for students, researchers, and professionals seeking accurate, current material to help bridge the gap between principles and theories and the real world. These articles, however, become more useful for study when those of lasting value are carefully collected, organized, indexed, and reproduced in a low-cost format, which provides easy and permanent access when the material is needed. That is the role played by ANNUAL EDITIONS.

Annual Editions: American Government 02/03 is the thirty-second edition of a book that has become a mainstay in many introductory courses on the American political system. The educational goal is to provide a readable collection of up-to-date articles that are informative, interesting, and stimulating to students beginning their study of the American political system.

The inauguration of President George W. Bush in January, 2001, seemed to mark a new beginning for the American political system after the tumultuous events of the preceding few years. Receding into the past were the 2000 presidential election controversy that engulfed the nation for 5 long weeks before Bush emerged as president-elect; the Clinton-Lewinsky scandal that in 1998 led to the impeachment of an American president for only the second time in history; and the meteoric rise and fall of Speaker of the House Newt Gingrich, who was at the forefront of American politics from 1994, when he led his Republican party to majority control of the House for the first time in 40 years, to late 1998, when he announced his decision to resign after disappointing results for his party in midterm House elections.

When President Bush took office, his Republican party controlled the presidency and both houses of Congress, albeit by narrow margins. The Senate was split 50-50 between Republicans and Democrats, but Vice President Dick Cheney's tie-breaking vote allowed Republicans to name the majority leader and the chairs of all committees. That arrangement changed abruptly in May, when Republican Senator Jim Jeffords of Vermont announced that he was becoming an independent, thus giving Democrats control of the Senate. In turn, Democrat Tom Daschle of South Dakota replaced Republican Trent Lott of Mississippi as Senate majority leader and every Senate committee chairmanship also changed hands.

As of early September, President Bush was still working to establish himself in his new political surroundings. Democrats remained buoyed by the turn of events in the Senate, and a host of critical budgetary and other decisions faced Congress and the president as Congress reconvened in Washington after its normal late summer recess. September promised to be a month in which Democrats and Republicans locked horns in Washington. The start of a new fiscal year on October 1 approached amid signs of a continuing economic slowdown, growing uncertainty about the wisdom of long-term tax cuts pushed through Congress by the Bush administration in spring 2001, and increasingly partisan disagreement about how to spend the anticipated, though dwindling, budgetary surplus.

Then came the September 11, 2001, terrorist attacks on the World Trade Center and the Pentagon! The world-and the world of American politics-turned topsy-turvy. Republican and Democratic members of Congress joined hands on Capitol Hill and sang "God Bless America" with tears in their eyes. President George W. Bush seized the reins of leadership in America's new "war on terrorism" and his public approval ratings soared above 90 percent, figures rivaled only once before, when his own father served as commander-in-chief during the Persian Gulf War in 1991.

The immediate aftermath of the shocking events of September 11 resulted in the start of U.S. military activities in Afghanistan in October. The ruling Taliban and the associated Al Qaeda terrorist network resisted briefly before giving way to the military onslaught. On the domestic front, anthrax mailings to several locations, including the Capitol Hill office of Senate Majority Leader Daschle, resulted in several deaths, the illness of others, and widespread fears among Americans. Concerns about maintaining a balanced budget, protecting Social Security, and passing year-end appropriations bills virtually disappeared. American unity and bipartisanship were the order of the day.

As this book goes to press in early 2002, President Bush's popularity remains at extraordinarily high levels. But differences between Democrats and Republicans on how to help the ailing economy are being aired, with Democrats loudly wondering about the long-term tax cuts enacted almost a year ago and Republicans hewing to the traditional line that helping businesses helps all Americans. In addition, the Enron bankruptcy and potential scandals associated with it are making headlines. With both houses of Congress closely divided between the two parties, American voters will have their say at mid-term Congressional elections in November, 2002.

The systems approach provides a rough organizational framework for this book. The first unit focuses on ideological and constitutional underpinnings of American politics, from both historical and contemporary perspectives. The second unit treats the major institutions of the national government. The third covers the "input" or "linkage" mechanisms of the system: political parties, elections, interest groups, and media. The fourth and concluding unit shifts the focus to policy choices that confront the government in Washington and resulting "outputs" of the political system. Also included in the book is a list of related *World Wide Web* sites and a *Topic Guide,* which can be used to explore particular areas in greater depth.

Each year thousands of articles about American politics are published, and deciding which to reprint in a collection of readings such as this can be difficult. Since no position on the political spectrum has a monopoly on truth, articles are chosen with an eye toward providing viewpoints from left, right, and center. Substantially more than half of the selections in this book are new to this year's edition, and a good number of them factor the events of September 11 into attempts to describe and understand contemporary American politics.

Next year will bring another opportunity for change, and you, the reader, are invited to participate in the process. Please complete and return the postpaid *article rating form* on the last page of the book, and let us know your reactions and your suggestions for improvement.

Bruce Stinebrickner
Editor

Contents

UNIT 1
Foundations of American Politics

The sixteen selections in this unit outline the foundations of American politics. In addition to primary documents, there are discussion of contemporary political ideals and viewpoints as well as recent commentaries on constitutional issues.

Part A.   *Basic Documents*

1. **The Declaration of Independence, 1776,** Thomas Jefferson, *The Declaration of Independence,*
   This document formally announces that 13 former British colonies have become the free and independent United States of America. It eloquently identifies certain **historic principles** on which their claim to independence rests.

2. **The Constitution of the United States, 1787,** *The Constitution of the U.S.,*
   The Constitution provides an organizational blueprint for the national government and for the **federal** relationship between the national government and the states. In addition, the first 10 amendments, commonly known as the **Bill of Rights,** spell out limits on what the government can do. A commentary accompanying the actual document provides a brief account of the writing of the Constitution and also notes some of its significant features.

3. **The Size and Variety of the Union as a Check on Faction,** James Madison, *The Federalist Papers,* No. 10, 1787
   James Madison argues in support of the union of the 13 states under the new **Constitution.** According to Madison, a system of **representative democracy** governing a large territory and many people will help control the undesirable effects of **"faction."**

4. **Checks and Balances,** James Madison, *The Federalist Papers,* No. 51, 1787
   According to James Madison, both the **separation of powers** among three branches of government and the **division of powers** between the states and the central government will help preserve **representative democracy** under the new **Constitution.**

Part B.   *Contemporary Views and Values*

5. **Why Don't They Like Us?,** Stanley Hoffmann, *The American Prospect,* November 19, 2001
   In the wake of September 11, 2001, Stanley Hoffmann explores the factors that have led to various strands of **anti-Americanism** around the globe. He also suggests ways of addressing legitimate grievances against the contemporary world's sole **superpower.**

6. **Which America Will We Be Now?,** Bill Moyers, *The Nation,* November 19, 2001
   In the context of September 11, 2001, Bill Moyers argues for improving democracy in the United States by **campaign finance reform,** more penetrating coverage of politics by **news media,** a fairer tax system, and recognition of the important contributions of firefighters, police officers, and other **public servants.**

The concepts in bold italics are developed in the article. For further expansion, please refer to the Topic Guide and the Index.

The concepts in bold italics are developed in the article. For further expansion, please refer to the Topic Guide and the Index.

UNIT 2
Structures of American Politics

Eighteen articles in this unit examine the structure and present status of the American presidency, Congress, the judiciary, and bureaucracy.

The concepts in bold italics are developed in the article. For further expansion, please refer to the Topic Guide and the Index.

The concepts in bold italics are developed in the article. For further expansion, please refer to the Topic Guide and the Index.

UNIT 3
Process of American Politics

In this unit, sixteen articles review how political parties, voters, election processes, interest groups, and the media work within the process of American politics.

The concepts in bold italics are developed in the article. For further expansion, please refer to the Topic Guide and the Index.

The concepts in bold italics are developed in the article. For further expansion, please refer to the Topic Guide and the Index.

UNIT 4
Products of American Politics

Four selections in this unit examine the domestic, economic, foreign, and defense policies that American government produces.

The concepts in bold italics are developed in the article. For further expansion, please refer to the Topic Guide and the Index.

Topic Guide

This topic guide suggests how the selections in this book relate to the subjects covered in your course. You may want to use the topics listed on these pages to search the Web more easily.

On the following pages a number of Web sites have been gathered specifically for this book. They are arranged to reflect the units of this *Annual Edition*. You can link to these sites by going to the DUSHKIN ONLINE support site at *http://www.dushkin.com/online/*.

ALL THE ARTICLES THAT RELATE TO EACH TOPIC ARE LISTED BELOW THE BOLD-FACED TERM.

Appointment process
23. Fixing the Appointment Process

Bill of Rights
2. The Constitution of the United States, 1787
30. A Judge Speaks Out

Bureaucracy
32. Turkey Farm
33. Reforming U.S. Intelligence After the Terrorist Attack
34. Police Blotter

Bush, George W.
21. The Art of Compromise
22. Leakproof?
36. Family Tree, Party Roots

Campaign finance reform
6. Which America Will We Be Now?
26. Feingold's Crusade
40. Follow the Money
42. Soft Money Unleashed

Clinton, Bill
18. Hooked on Polls
19. When Presidents Speak

Congress
2. The Constitution of the United States, 1787
3. The Size and Variety of the Union as a Check on Faction
12. Insurance Against the Once Unthinkable
13. Overruling the Court
17. Gone Are the Giants
24. Crackup of the Committees
25. Can It Be Done?
26. Feingold's Crusade
27. John Dingell's Staying Power
28. Of Judges and Senators
29. Uninsured Americans Linger on Congress' Waiting List

Constitution
2. The Constitution of the United States, 1787
3. The Size and Variety of the Union as a Check on Faction
4. Checks and Balances
12. Insurance Against the Once Unthinkable
14. The 28th Amendment
15. Immigrants for President

Declaration of Independence
1. The Declaration of Independence, 1776

Elections
25. Can It Be Done?
26. Feingold's Crusade
31. Reconsidering "Bush v. Gore"
35. Running Scared
39. Making Every Vote Count

40. Follow the Money
41. No Need to Repeal the Electoral College
47. The Media and Politics: It's More Than the News
49. Echo Chamber of Horrors

Electoral college
25. Can It Be Done?
41. No Need to Repeal the Electoral College

Federal government
2. The Constitution of the United States, 1787
4. Checks and Balances

Federalism
2. The Constitution of the United States, 1787
3. The Size and Variety of the Union as a Check on Faction

Health care issues
29. Uninsured Americans Linger on Congress' Waiting List

Historic perspectives
1. The Declaration of Independence, 1776
2. The Constitution of the United States, 1787
3. The Size and Variety of the Union as a Check on Faction
4. Checks and Balances

Homeland and national security
33. Reforming U.S. Intelligence After the Terrorist Attack
34. Police Blotter
53. *Now* Do You Believe We Need a Draft?
54. Immigration and Terrorism

Interest groups
3. The Size and Variety of the Union as a Check on Faction
43. Government's End
44. Associations Without Members
45. The World According to AARP

Judicial system
2. The Constitution of the United States, 1787
16. Guns and Tobacco: Government by Litigation
30. A Judge Speaks Out

Media
30. A Judge Speaks Out
46. Journalism and Democracy
47. The Media and Politics: It's More Than the News
48. The Making of a Movement: Getting Serious About Media Reform
49. Echo Chamber of Horrors
50. The Two-Bucks-a-Minute Democracy

Nominations
25. Can It Be Done?
28. Of Judges and Senators
35. Running Scared
39. Making Every Vote Count

World Wide Web Sites

The following World Wide Web sites have been carefully researched and selected to support the articles found in this reader. The easiest way to access these selected sites is to go to our DUSHKIN ONLINE support site at *http://www.dushkin.com/online/*.

AE: American Government 02/03

The following sites were available at the time of publication. Visit our Web site—we update DUSHKIN ONLINE regularly to reflect any changes.

General Sources

The Federal Web Locator
http://www.infoctr.edu/fwl/

Use this site as a launching pad for the Web sites of U.S. federal agencies, departments, and organizations. It is well organized and easy to use for informational and research purposes.

John F. Kennedy School of Government
http://www.ksg.harvard.edu

Starting from Harvard University's KSG page, you will be able to click on a huge variety of links to information about American politics and government, ranging from political party and campaign data to debates of enduring issues.

Library of Congress
http://www.loc.gov

Examine this Web site to learn about the extensive resource tools, library services/resources, exhibitions, and databases available through the Library of Congress in many different subfields of government studies.

UNIT 1: Foundations of American Politics

American Studies Web
http://www.georgetown.edu/crossroads/asw/

This eclectic site provides links to a wealth of Internet resources for research in American studies, including agriculture and rural development, government, and race and ethnicity.

Federalism: Relationship Between Local and National Governments
http://www.infidels.org/~nap/index.federalism.html

Federalism versus states' rights has always been a spirited debate in American government. Visit this George Mason University site for links to many articles and reports on the subject.

Opinion, Inc.: The Site for Conservative Opinion on the Web
http://www.opinioninc.com

Open this site for access to political, cultural, and Web commentary on a number of issues from a conservative political viewpoint. The site is updated frequently.

Scanned Originals of Early American Documents
http://www.law.emory.edu/FEDERAL/

Through this Emory University site you can view scanned originals of the Declaration of Independence, the Constitution, and the Bill of Rights. The transcribed texts are also available, as are *The Federalist Papers*.

Smithsonian Institution
http://www.si.edu

This site provides access to the enormous resources of the Smithsonian, which holds some 140 million artifacts and specimens in its trust for "the increase and diffusion of

knowledge." Here you can learn about American social, cultural, economic, and political history from a variety of viewpoints.

The Written Word
http://www.mdle.com/WrittenWord/

This is an online journal of economic, political, and social commentary, primarily from a center or left-of-center viewpoint. The site provides links to governmental and political Web resources.

UNIT 2: Structures of American Politics

Department of State
http://www.state.gov

View this site for understanding into the workings of a major U.S. executive branch department. Links explain exactly what the Department does, what services it provides, and what it says about U.S. interests around the world, along with much more information.

Federal Reserve System
http://woodrow.mpls.frb.fed.us/info/sys/index.html

Consult this page to learn the answers to FAQs about the Fed, the structure of the Federal Reserve system, monetary policy, and more. It provides links to speeches and interviews as well as essays and articles presenting different views on the Fed.

National Archives and Records Administration (NARA)
http://www.nara.gov/nara/welcome.html

This official site, which oversees the management of all federal records, offers easy access to background information for students interested in the policy-making process, including a search of federal documents and speeces, and much more.

National Center for Policy Analysis
http://www.ncpa.org

Through this site access discussions on an array of topics that are of major interest in the study of American government, from regulatory policy and privatization to economy and income. The Daily Policy Digest is also available .

Supreme Court/Legal Information Institute
http://supct.law.cornell.edu/supct/index.html

Open this site for current and historical information about the Supreme Court. The LII archive contains many opinions issued since May 1990 as well as a collection of nearly 600 of the most historical decisions of the Court.

United States House of Representatives
http://www.house.gov

This Web page of the House of Representatives will lead you to information about current and past House members and agendas, the legislative process, and more. You can learn about events on the House floor as they happen.

United States Senate
http://www.senate.gov

This U.S. Senate Web page will lead to information about current and past Senate members and agendas, legislative activities, and committees.

www.dushkin.com/online/

UNIT 3: Process of American Politics

The Henry L. Stimson Center
http://www.stimson.org

The Stimson Center, a nonprofit and self-described nonpartisan organization, focuses on issues where policy, technology, and politics intersect. Use this site to find assessments of U.S. foreign and domestic policy and other topics.

Influence at Work
http://www.influenceatwork.com

This commercial site focuses on the nature of persuasion, compliance, and propaganda, with many practical examples and applications. Students of such topics as the roles of public opinion and media influence in policy making should find these discussions of interest. The approach is based on the research and methods of influence expert Dr. Robert Cialdini.

LSU Department of Political Science Resources
http://www.artsci.lsu.edu/poli/

This extensive site will point you to a number of resources for domestic and international political and governmental news, including LSU's Political Science WWW Server, which is maintained by a dedicated group of professionals.

Marketplace of Political Ideas/University of Houston Library
http://info.lib.uh.edu/politics/markind.htm

Here is a collection of links to campaign, conservative/liberal perspectives, and political party sites. There are General Political Sites, Democratic Sites, Republican Sites, Third Party Sites, and much more.

NationalJournal.com
http://nationaljournal.com

This is a major site for information on American government and politics. There is discussion of campaigns, the congressional calendar, a news archive, and more for politicians and policy makers. Membership is required, however, to access much of the information.

Poynter Online
http://www.poynter.org

This research site of the Poynter Institute for Media Studies provides extensive links to information and resources about the media, including media ethics and reportage techniques. Many bibliographies and Web sites are included.

RAND
http://www.rand.org

RAND is a nonprofit institution that works to improve public policy through research and analysis. Links offered on this home page provide for keyword searches of certain topics and descriptions of RAND activities and major research areas.

UNIT 4: Products of American Politics

American Diplomacy
http://www.unc.edu/depts/diplomat/

American Diplomacy is an online journal of commentary, analysis, and research on U.S. foreign policy and its results around the world.

Cato Institute
http://www.cato.org/research/ss_prjct.html

The Cato Institute presents this page to discuss its Project on Social Security Privatization. The site and its links begin from the belief that privatization of the U.S. Social Security system is a positive goal that will empower workers.

Foreign Affairs
http://www.foreignaffairs.org

This home page of the well-respected foreign policy journal is a valuable research tool. It allows users to search the journal's archives and provides indexed access to the field's leading publications, documents, online resources, and more. Links to dozens of other related Web sites are possible from here.

The Gallup Organization
http://www.gallup.com

Open this Gallup Organization home page for links to an extensive archive of public opinion poll results and special reports on a variety of topics related to American society, politics, and government.

International Information Programs
http://usinfo.state.gov

This wide-ranging page offered by the State Department provides definitions, related documentation, and a discussion of topics of concern to students of American government. It addresses today's hot topics as well as ongoing issues that form the foundation of the field. Many Web links are provided.

STAT-USA
http://www.stat-usa.gov/stat-usa.html

This essential site, a service of the Department of Commerce, contains daily economic news, frequently requested statistical releases, information on export and international trade, domestic economic news and statistical series, and databases.

Tax Foundation
http://www.taxfoundation.org/index.html

Ever wonder where your taxes go? Consult the site of this self-described "nonprofit, nonpartisan policy research organization" to learn the history of "Tax Freedom Day," tax burdens around the United States, and other information about your tax bill or taxes in general.

UNIT 1

Foundations of American Politics

Unit Selections

Key Points to Consider

• What do you think would surprise the Founders most about the values and ideals held by Americans today?

• Which ideals, ideas, and values seem likely to remain central to American politics, and which seem likely to erode and gradually disappear?

• To what rights do you think all Americans are entitled? Do all Americans have these rights now? If not, why not?

• What makes constitutional interpretation and reinterpretation necessary in the American political system?

• Do you consider yourself a conservative, a liberal, a socialist, a reactionary, or what? Why?

 **Links: www.dushkin.com/online/**
These sites are annotated in the World Wide Web pages.

American Studies Web
http://www.georgetown.edu/crossroads/asw/

Federalism: Relationship Between Local and National Governments
http://www.infidels.org/~nap/index.federalism.html

Opinion, Inc.: The Site for Conservative Opinion on the Web
http://www.opinioninc.com

Scanned Originals of Early American Documents
http://www.law.emory.edu/FEDERAL/

Smithsonian Institution
http://www.si.edu

The Written Word
http://www.mdle.com/WrittenWord/

This unit treats some of the less concrete aspects of the American political system—historic ideals, contemporary ideas and values, and constitutional and legal issues. These dimensions of the system are not immune to change. Instead, they interact with the wider political environment in which they exist, and they are modified accordingly. Usually this interaction is a gradual process, but sometimes events foster more rapid change.

Human beings can be distinguished from other species by their ability to think and reason at relatively high levels of abstraction. In turn, ideas, ideals, values, and principles can and do play important roles in politics. Most Americans value ideals such as democracy, freedom, equal opportunity, and justice. Yet the precise meanings of these terms and the best ways of implementing them are

the subject of much dispute in the political arena. Such ideas and ideals, as well as disputes about their "real" meanings, are important elements in the practice of American politics.

Although the selections in this unit span more than 200 years, they are clearly related to one another. Understanding contemporary political viewpoints is easier if the ideals and principles of the past are also taken into account. In addition, we can better appreciate the significance of historic documents such as the Declaration of Independence and the Constitution if we are familiar with contemporary ideas and perspectives. The interaction of different ideas and values plays an important part in the continuing development of the "foundations" of the American political system.

The first section of this unit includes several historic documents from the eighteenth century. The first is the Declaration of Independence. Written in 1776, it proclaims the Founders' views of why independence from England was justified and, in so doing, identifies certain "unalienable" rights that "all men" are said to possess. The second document, the Constitution of 1787, remains in effect to this day. It provides an organizational blueprint for the structure of American national government, outlines the federal relationship between the national government and the states, and expresses limitations on what government can do. Twenty-seven amendments have been added to the original Constitution in two centuries. In addition to the Declaration of Independence and the Constitution, the first section includes two

selections from *The Federalist Papers,* a series of newspaper articles written in support of the proposed new Constitution. Appearing in 1787 and 1788, *The Federalist Papers* treated various provisions of the new Constitution and argued that putting the Constitution into effect would bring about good government.

The second section treats contemporary political ideas and viewpoints. As selections in this section illustrate, efforts to apply or act on political beliefs in the context of concrete circumstances often lead to interesting commentary and debate. "Liberal" and "conservative" are two labels often used in American political discussions, but political views and values have far more complexity than can be captured by these two terms.

Selections in the third section show that constitutional and legal issues and interpretations are tied to historic principles as well as to contemporary ideas and values. It has been suggested that, throughout American history, almost every important political question has at one time or another appeared as a constitutional or legal issue.

The historic documents and the other selections in this unit might be more difficult to understand than the articles in other units. Some of them may have to be read and reread carefully to be fully appreciated. But to grapple with the important material treated here is to come to grips with a variety of conceptual blueprints for the American political system. To ignore the theoretical issues raised would be to bypass an important element of American politics today.

The Declaration of Independence

WHEN in the Course of human events, it becomes necessary for one people to dissolve the political bands which have connected them with another, and to assume among the powers of the earth, the separate and equal station to which the Laws of Nature and of Nature's God entitle them, a decent respect to the opinions of mankind requires that they should declare the causes which impel them to the separation.—We hold these truths to be self-evident, that all men are created equal, that they are endowed by their Creator with certain unalienable Rights, that among these are Life, Liberty and the pursuit of Happiness.—That to secure these rights, Governments are instituted among Men, deriving their just powers from the consent of the governed.—That whenever any Form of Government becomes destructive of these ends, it is the Right of the People to alter or to abolish it, and to institute new Government, laying its foundation on such principles and organizing its powers in such form, as to them shall seem most likely to effect their Safety and Happiness. Prudence, indeed, will dictate that Governments long established should not be changed for light and transient causes; and accordingly all experience hath shewn, that mankind are more disposed to suffer, while evils are sufferable, than to right themselves by abolishing the forms to which they are accustomed. But when a long train of abuses and usurpations, pursuing invariably the same Object evinces a design to reduce them under absolute Despotism, it is their right, it is their duty, to throw off such Government, and to provide new Guards for their future security.—Such has been the patient sufferance of these Colonies; and such is now the necessity which constrains them to alter their former Systems of Government. The history of the present King of Great Britain is a history of repeated injuries and usurpations, all having in direct object the establishment of an absolute Tyranny over these States. To prove this, let Facts be submitted to a candid world.—He has refused his Assent to Laws, the most whole-some and necessary for the public good.—He has forbidden his Governors to pass Laws of immediate and pressing importance, unless suspended in their operation till his Assent should be obtained; and when so suspended, he has utterly neglected to attend to them.—He has refused to pass other Laws for the accommodation of large districts of people, unless those people would relinquish the right of Representation in the Legislature, a right inestimable to them and formidable to tyrants only.—He has called together legislative bodies at places unusual, uncomfortable, and distant from the depository of their public Records, for the sole purpose of fatiguing them into compliance with his measures.—He has dissolved Representative Houses repeatedly, for opposing with manly firmness his invasions on the rights of the people.—He has refused for a long time, after such dissolutions, to cause others to be elected; whereby the Legislative powers, incapable of Annihilation, have returned to the People at large for their exercise; the State remaining in the meantime exposed to all the dangers of invasion from without, and convulsions within.—He has endeavoured to prevent the population of these States; for that purpose obstructing the Laws for Naturalization of Foreigners; refusing to pass others to encourage their migrations hither, and raising the conditions of new Appropriations of Lands.—He has obstructed the Administration of Justice, by refusing his Assent to Laws for establishing Judiciary powers.—He has made Judges dependent on his Will alone, for the tenure of their offices, and the amount and payment of their salaries.—He has erected a multitude of New Offices, and sent hither swarms of Officers to harass our people, and eat out their substance. He has kept among us, in times of peace, Standing Armies without the Consent of our legislatures.—He has affected to render the Military independent of and superior to the Civil power.—He has combined with others to subject us to a jurisdiction foreign to our constitution, and unacknowledged by our laws; giving his Assent to their Acts of pretended Legislation:—For quartering large bodies of armed troops among us:—For protecting them, by a mock Trial, from punishment for any Murders which they should commit on the Inhabitants of these States:—For cutting off our Trade with all parts of the world:—For imposing Taxes on us without our Consent:—For depriving us in many cases, of the benefits of Trial by Jury:—For transporting us beyond Seas to be tried for pretended offences:—For abolishing the free System of English Laws in a neighboring Province, establishing therein an Arbitrary government, and enlarging its Boundaries so as to render it at once an example and fit instrument for introducing the same absolute rule into these Colonies:—For taking away our Charters, abolishing our most valuable Laws and altering fundamentally the Forms of our Governments:—For suspending our own Legislatures, and declaring themselves invested with power to legislate for us in all cases whatsoever.—He has abdicated Government here, by declaring us out of his Protection and waging War against us.—He has plundered our seas, ravaged our Coasts, burnt our towns, and destroyed the lives of our people.—He is at this time transporting large Armies of foreign Mercenaries to compleat the works of death, desolation and tyranny, already begun with circumstances of Cruelty & perfidy scarcely paralled in the most barbarous ages, and totally unworthy the Head of a civilized nation.—He has constrained our fellow Citizens taken Captive on the high Seas to bear Arms against their Country, to become the executioners of their friends and Brethren, or to fall themselves by their Hands.—He has excited domestic insurrections amongst us, and has endeavoured to bring on the inhabitants of our frontiers, the merciless Indian Savages, whose known rule of warfare, is an undistinguished destruction of all ages, sexes and conditions. In every stage of these Oppressions We have Petitioned for Redress in the most humble terms: Our repeated Petitions have been answered only by repeated injury. A Prince, whose character is thus marked by every act which may define a Tyrant, is unfit to be the ruler of a free people. Nor have We been wanting in attentions to our British brethren. We have warned them from time to time of attempts by their legislature to extend an unwarrantable jurisdiction over us. We have reminded them of the circumstances of our emigration and settlement here. We have appealed to their native justice and magnanimity, and we have conjured them by the ties of our common kindred to disavow these usurpations, which would inevitably interrupt our connections and correspondence. They too have been deaf to the voice of justice and of consanguinity. We must, therefore, acquiesce in the necessity, which denounces our Separation, and hold them, as we hold the rest of mankind, Enemies in War, in Peace Friends.—

WE, THEREFORE, the Representatives of the UNITED STATES OF AMERICA, in General Congress, Assembled, appealing to the Supreme Judge of the world for the rectitude of our intentions, do, in the Name, and by Authority of the good People of these Colonies, solemnly publish and declare, That these United Colonies are, and of Right ought to be FREE AND INDEPENDENT STATES; that they are Absolved from all Allegiance to the British Crown, and that all political connection between them and the State of Great Britain, is and ought to be totally dissolved; and that as Free and Independent States, they have full Power to levy War, conclude Peace, contract Alliances, establish Commerce, and to do all other Acts and Things which Independent States may of right do.—And for the support of this Declaration, with a firm reliance on the protection of divine Providence, we mutually pledge to each other our Lives, our Fortunes and our sacred Honor.

The History of The Constitution of the United States

CONSTITUTION OF THE UNITED STATES. The Articles of Confederation did not provide the centralizing force necessary for unity among the new states and were soon found to be so fundamentally weak that a different political structure was vital. Conflicts about money and credit, trade, and suspicions about regional domination were among the concerns when Congress on February 21, 1787, authorized a Constitutional Convention to revise the Articles. The delegates were selected and assembled in Philadelphia about three months after the call. They concluded their work by September.

The delegates agreed and abided to secrecy. Years afterward James Madison supported the secrecy decision writing that "no man felt himself obliged to retain his opinions any longer than he was satisfied of their propriety and truth, and was open to the force of argument." Secrecy was not for all time. Madison, a delegate from Virginia, was a self-appointed but recognized recorder and took notes in the clear view of the members. Published long afterward, Madison's Journal gives a good record of the convention.

The delegates began to assemble on May 14, 1787, but a majority did not arrive until May 25. George Washington was elected President of the Convention without opposition. The lag of those few days gave some of the early arrivals, especially Madison, time to make preparations on substantive matters, and Gov. Edmund Jennings Randolph presented a plan early in the proceedings that formed the basis for much of the convention deliberations. The essentials were that there should be a government adequate to prevent foreign invasion, prevent dissension among the states, and provide for general national development, and give the national government power enough to make it superior in its realm. The decision was made not merely to revise the articles but to create a new government and a new constitution.

One of the most crucial decisions was the arrangement for representation, a compromise providing that one house would represent the states equally, the other house to be based on popular representation (with some modification due to the slavery question). This arrangement recognized political facts and concessions among men with both theoretical and practical political knowledge.

Basic Features. Oliver Wendell Holmes, Jr., once wrote that the provisions of the Constitution were not mathematical formulas, but "organic living institutions [sic] and its origins and growth were vital to understanding it." The constitution's basic features provide for a supreme law—notwithstanding any other legal document or practice, the Constitution is supreme, as are the laws made in pursuance of it and treaties made under the authority of the United States.

The organizational plan for government is widely known. Foremost is the separation of powers. If the new government were to be limited in its powers, one way to keep it limited would have been executive, legislative, and judicial power [given] to three distinct and non-overlapping branches. A government could not actually function, however, if the separation meant the independence of one branch from the others. The answer was a design to insure cooperation and the sharing of some functions. Among these are the executive veto and the power of Congress to have its way if it musters a super-majority to override that veto. The direction of foreign affairs and the war power are both dispersed and shared. The appointing power is shared by the Senate and the president; impeaching of officers and financial controls are powers shared by the Senate and the House.

A second major contribution by the convention is the provision for the judiciary, which gave rise to the doctrine of judicial review. There is some doubt that the delegates comprehended this prospect but Alexander Hamilton considered it in *Federalist* No. 78: "The interpretation of the laws is a proper and peculiar province of the Courts.... Wherever a particular statute contravenes the Constitution, it will be the duty of the judicial tribunals to adhere to the latter and disregard the former."

Another contribution is the federal system, an evolution from colonial practice and the relations between the colonies and the mother country. This division of authority between the new national government and the states recognized the doctrine of delegated and reserved powers. Only certain authority was to go to the new government; the states were not to be done away with and much of the Constitution is devoted to insuring that they were to be maintained even with the stripping of some of their powers.

It is not surprising, therefore, that the convention has been called a great political reform caucus composed of both revolutionaries and men dedicated to democracy. By eighteenth-century standards the Constitution was a democratic document, but standards change and the Constitution has changed since its adoption.

Change and Adaptation. The authors of the Constitution knew that provision for change was essential and provided for it in Article V, insuring that a majority could amend, but being restrictive enough that changes were not likely for the "light and transient" causes Jefferson warned about in the Declaration of Independence.

During the period immediately following the presentation of the Constitution for ratification, requiring assent of nine states to be effective, some alarm was expressed that there was a major defect: there was no bill of rights. So, many leaders committed themselves to the presentation of constitutional amendments for the purpose. Hamilton argued that the absence of a bill of rights was not a defect; indeed, a bill was not necessary. "Why," he wrote, in the last of *The Federalist Papers*, "declare things that shall not be done which there is no power to do?" Nonetheless, the Bill of Rights was presented in the form of amendments and adopted by the states in 1791.

Since 1791 many proposals have been suggested to amend the Constitution. By 1972 sixteen additional amendments had been adopted. Only one, the Twenty-first, which repealed the

Eighteenth, was ratified by state conventions. All the others were ratified by state legislatures.

Even a cursory reading of the later amendments shows they do not alter the fundamentals of limited government, the separation of powers, the federal system, or the political process set in motion originally. The Thirteenth, Fourteenth, Fifteenth, and Nineteenth amendments attempt to insure equality to all and are an extension of the Bill of Rights. The others reaffirm some existing constitutional arrangements, alter some procedures, and at least one, the Sixteenth, states national policy.

Substantial change and adaptation of the Constitution beyond the formal amendments have come from national experience, growth, and development. It has been from the Supreme Court that much of the gradual significant shaping of the Constitution has been done.

Government has remained neither static nor tranquil. Some conflict prevails continually. It may be about the activities of some phase of government or the extent of operations, and whether the arrangement for government can be made responsive to current and prospective needs of society. Conflict is inevitable in a democratic society. Sometimes the conflict is spirited and rises to challenge the continuation of the system. Questions arise whether a fair trial may be possible here or there; legislators are alleged to be indifferent to human problems and pursue distorted public priorities. Presidents are charged with secret actions designed for self-aggrandizement or actions based on half-truths. Voices are heard urging revolution again as the only means of righting alleged wrongs.

The responses continue to demonstrate, however, that the constitutional arrangement for government, the allocation of powers, and the restraints on government all provide the needed flexibility. The Constitution endures.

Adam C. Breckenridge, University of Nebraska-Lincoln

The Constitution of the United States

We the People of the United States, in Order to form a more perfect Union, establish Justice, insure domestic Tranquility, provide for the common defence, promote the general Welfare, and secure the Blessings of Liberty to ourselves and our Posterity, do ordain and establish this Constitution for the United States of America.

ARTICLE. I.

SECTION. 1. All legislative Powers herein granted shall be vested in a Congress of the United States, which shall consist of a Senate and House of Representatives.

SECTION. 2. The House of Representatives shall be composed of Members chosen every second Year by the People of the several States, and the Electors in each State shall have the Qualifications requisite for Electors of the most numerous Branch of the State Legislature.

No Person shall be a Representative who shall not have attained to the age of twenty five Years, and been seven Years a Citizen of the United States, and who shall not, when elected, be an Inhabitant of that State in which he shall be chosen.

Representatives and direct Taxes shall be apportioned among the several States which may be included within this Union, according to their respective Numbers, which shall be determined by adding to the whole Number of free Persons, including those bound to Service for a Term of Years, and excluding Indians not taxed, three fifths of all other Persons. The actual Enumeration shall be made within three Years after the first Meeting of the Congress of the United States, and within every subsequent Term of ten Years, in such Manner as they shall by Law direct. The Number of Representatives shall not exceed one for every thirty Thousand, but each State shall have at Least one Representative; and until such enumeration shall be made, the State of New Hampshire shall be entitled to chuse three, Massachusetts eight, Rhode-Island and Providence Plantations one, Connecticut five, New York six, New Jersey four, Pennsylvania eight, Delaware one, Maryland six, Virginia ten, North Carolina five, South Carolina five, and Georgia three.

When vacancies happen in the Representation from any State, the Executive Authority thereof shall issue Writs of Election to fill such Vacancies.

The House of Representatives shall chuse their Speaker and other Officers; and shall have the sole Power of Impeachment.

SECTION. 3. The Senate of the United States shall be composed of two Senators from each State, chosen by the Legislature thereof, for six years; and each Senator shall have one Vote.

Immediately after they shall be assembled in Consequence of the first Election, they shall be divided as equally as may be into three Classes. The Seats of the Senators of the first Class shall be vacated at the Expiration of the second Year, of the second Class at the Expiration of the fourth Year, and of the third Class at the Expiration of the sixth Year, so that one third may be chosen every second year; and if Vacancies happen by Resignation, or otherwise, during the Recess of the Legislature of any State, the Executive thereof may make temporary Appointments until the next Meeting of the Legislature, which shall then fill such Vacancies.

No Person shall be a Senator who shall not have attained to the Age of thirty Years, and been nine Years a Citizen of the United States, and who shall not, when elected, be an Inhabitant of that State for which he shall be chosen.

The Vice President of the United States shall be President of the Senate, but shall have no Vote, unless they be equally divided.

The Senate shall chuse their other Officers, and also a President pro tempore, in the Absence of the Vice President, or when he shall exercise the Office of President of the United States.

The Senate shall have the sole Power to try all Impeachments. When sitting for that Purpose, they shall be on Oath or Affirmation. When the President of the United States is tried the Chief Justice shall preside: And no Person shall be convicted without the Concurrence of two thirds of the Members present.

Judgment in Cases of Impeachment shall not extend further than to removal from Office, and disqualification to hold and enjoy any Office of honor, Trust or Profit under the United States: but the Party convicted shall nevertheless be liable and subject to Indictment, Trial, Judgment and Punishment, according to Law.

SECTION. 4. The Times, Places and Manner of holding Elections for Senators and Representatives, shall be prescribed in each State by the Legislature thereof; but the Congress may at any time by Law make or alter such Regulations, except as to the Places of chusing Senators.

The Congress shall assemble at least once in every Year, and such Meeting shall be on the first Monday in December, unless they shall by Law appoint a different Day.

SECTION. 5. Each House shall be the Judge of the Elections, Returns and Qualifications of its own Members, and a Majority of each shall constitute a Quorum to do Business; but a smaller Number may adjourn from day to day, and may be authorized to compel the Attendance of absent Members, in such Manner, and under such Penalties as each House may provide.

Each House may determine the Rules of its Proceedings, punish its Members for disorderly Behaviour, and, with the Concurrence of two thirds, expel a Member.

Each House shall keep a Journal of its Proceedings, and from time to time publish the same, excepting such Parts as may in their Judgment require Secrecy; and the Yeas and Nays of the Members of either House on any question shall, at the Desire of one fifth of those Present, be entered on the Journal.

Neither House, during the Session of Congress, shall, without the Consent of the other, adjourn for more than three days, nor to any other Place than that in which the two Houses shall be sitting.

SECTION. 6. The Senators and Representatives shall receive a Compensation for their Services, to be ascertained by Law, and paid out of the Treasury of the United States. They shall in all Cases, except Treason, Felony and Breach of the Peace, be privileged from Arrest during their Attendance at the Session of their respective Houses, and in going to and returning from the same; and for any Speech or Debate in either House, they shall not be questioned in any other Place.

No Senator or Representative shall, during the Time for which he was elected, be appointed to any civil Office under the Authority of the United States, which shall have been created, or the Emoluments whereof shall have been encreased during such time; and no Person holding any Office under the United States, shall be a Member of either House during his Continuance in Office.

SECTION. 7. All Bills for raising Revenue shall originate in the House of Representatives; but the Senate may propose or concur with amendments as on other Bills.

Every Bill which shall have passed the House of Representatives and the Senate, shall, before it become a Law, be presented to the President of the United States; If he approve he shall sign it, but if not he shall return it, with his Objections to that House in which it shall have originated, who shall enter the Objections at large on their Journal, and proceed to reconsider it. If after such Reconsideration two thirds of that House shall agree to pass the Bill, it shall be sent, together with the Objections, to the other House, by which it shall likewise be reconsidered, and if approved by two thirds of that House, it shall become a Law. But in all such Cases the Votes of both Houses shall be determined by Yeas and Nays, and the Names of the Persons voting for and against the Bill shall be entered on the Journal of each House respectively. If any Bill shall not be returned by the President within ten Days (Sundays excepted) after it shall have been presented to him, the Same shall be a Law, in like Manner as if he had signed it, unless the Congress by their Adjournment prevent its Return, in which Case it shall not be a Law.

Every Order, Resolution, or Vote to which the Concurrence of the Senate and House of Representatives may be necessary (except on a question of Adjournment) shall be presented to the President of the United States; and before the Same shall take Effect, shall be approved by him, or being disapproved by him, shall be repassed by two thirds of the Senate and House of Representatives, according to the Rules and Limitations prescribed in the Case of a Bill.

SECTION. 8. The Congress shall have Power To lay and collect Taxes, Duties, Imposts and Excises, to pay the Debts and provide for the common Defence and general Welfare of the United States; but all Duties, Imposts and Excises shall be uniform throughout the United States;

To borrow Money on the credit of the United States;

To regulate Commerce with foreign Nations, and among the several States, and with the Indian Tribes;

To establish an uniform Rule of Naturalization, and uniform Laws on the subject of Bankruptcies throughout the United States;

To coin Money, regulate the Value thereof, and of foreign Coin, and fix the Standard of Weights and Measures;

To provide for the Punishment of counterfeiting the Securities and current Coin of the United States;

To establish Post Offices and post Roads;

To promote the Progress of Science and useful Arts, by securing for limited Times to Authors and Inventors the exclusive Right to their respective Writings and Discoveries;

To constitute Tribunals inferior to the supreme Court;

To define and punish Piracies and Felonies committed on the high Seas, and Offences against the Law of Nations;

To declare War, grant Letters of Marque and Reprisal, and make Rules concerning Captures on Land and Water;

To raise and support Armies, but no Appropriation of Money to that Use shall be for a longer Term than two Years;

To provide and maintain a Navy;

To make Rules for the Government and Regulation of the land and naval Forces;

To provide for calling forth the Militia to execute the Laws of the Union, suppress Insurrections and repel Invasions;

To provide for organizing, arming, and disciplining, the Militia, and for governing such Part of them as may be employed in the Service of the United States, reserving to the States respectively, the Appointment of the Officers, and the Authority of training the Militia according to the discipline prescribed by Congress;

To exercise exclusive Legislation in all Cases whatsoever, over such District (not exceeding ten Miles square) as may, by Cession of Particular States, and the Acceptance of Congress, become the Seat of the Government of the United States, and to exercise like Authority over all Places purchased by the Consent of the Legislature of the State in which the Same shall be, for the Erection of Forts, Magazines, Arsenals, dock-Yards, and other needful Buildings;—And

To make all Laws which shall be necessary and proper for carrying into Execution the foregoing Powers, and all other Powers vested by this Constitution in the Government of the United States, or in any Department or Officer thereof.

SECTION. 9. The Migration or Importation of such Persons as any of the States now existing shall think proper to admit, shall not be prohibited by the Congress prior to the Year one thousand eight hundred and eight, but a Tax or duty may be imposed on such Importation, not exceeding ten dollars for each Person.

The Privilege of the Writ of Habeas Corpus shall not be suspended, unless when in Cases of Rebellion or Invasion the public Safety may require it.

No Bill of Attainder or ex post facto Law shall be passed.

No Capitation, or other direct, Tax shall be laid, unless in Proportion to the Census or Enumeration herein before directed to be taken.

No Tax or Duty shall be laid on Articles exported from any State.

No Preference shall be given by any Regulation or Commerce or Revenue to the Ports of one State over those of another; nor shall Vessels bound to, or from, one State, be obliged to enter, clear or pay Duties in another.

No Money shall be drawn from the Treasury, but in Consequence of Appropriations made by Law; and a regular Statement and Account of the Receipts and Expenditures of all public Money shall be published from time to time.

No Title of Nobility shall be granted by the United States: And no Person holding any Office of Profit or Trust under them, shall, without the Consent of the Congress, accept of any present Emolument, Office, or Title, of any kind whatever, from any King, Prince, or foreign State.

SECTION. 10. No State shall enter into any Treaty, Alliance, or Confederation; grant Letters of Marque and Reprisal; coin Money; emit Bills of Credit; make any Thing but gold and silver Coin a Tender in Payment of Debts; pass any Bill of Attainder, ex post facto Law, or Law impairing the Obligation of Contracts, or grant any Title of Nobility.

No State shall, without the Consent of the Congress, lay any Imposts or Duties on Imports or Exports, except what may be absolutely necessary for executing its inspection Laws: and the net Produce of all Duties and Imposts, laid by any State on Imports or Exports, shall be for the Use of the Treasury of the United States; and all such Laws shall be subject to the Revision and Controul of the Congress.

No state shall, without the Consent of Congress, lay any Duty of Tonnage, keep Troops, or Ships of War in time of Peace, enter into any Agreement or Compact with another State, or with a foreign Power, or engage in War, unless actually invaded, or in such imminent Danger as will not admit of delay.

ARTICLE. II.

SECTION. 1. The executive Power shall be vested in a President of the United States of America. He shall hold his Office during the Term of four Years, and, together with the Vice President, chosen for the same Term, be elected as follows

Each State shall appoint, in such Manner as the Legislature thereof may direct, a Number of Electors, equal to the whole Number of Senators and Representatives to which the State may be entitled in the Congress: but no Senator or Representative, or Person holding an Office of Trust or Profit under the United States, shall be appointed an Elector.

The Electors shall meet in their respective States, and vote by Ballot for two Persons, of whom one at least shall not be an Inhabitant of the same State with themselves. And they shall make a List of all the persons voted for, and of the Number of Votes for each; which List they shall sign and certify, and transmit sealed to the Seat of Government of the United States, directed to the President of the Senate. The President of the Senate shall, in the Presence of the Senate and House of Representatives, open all the Certificates, and the Votes shall then be counted. The Person having the greatest Number of Votes shall be the President, if such Number be a Majority of the whole Number of Electors appointed; and if there be more than one who have such Majority, and have an equal Number of Votes, then the House of Representatives shall immediately chuse by Ballot one of them for President; and if no Person have a Majority, then from the five highest on the List the said House shall in like Manner chuse the President. But in chusing the President, the Votes shall be taken by States, the Representation from each State having one Vote; a quorum for this Purpose shall consist of a Member or Members from two thirds of the States, and a Majority of all the States shall be necessary to a Choice. In every Case, after the Choice of the President, the Person having the greatest Number of Votes of the Electors shall be the Vice President. But if there should remain two or more who have equal Votes, the Senate shall chuse from them by Ballot the Vice President.

The Congress may determine the Time of chusing the Electors, and the Day on which they shall give their Votes; which Day shall be the same throughout the United States.

No Person except a natural born Citizen, or a Citizen of the United States, at the time of the Adoption of this Constitution, shall be eligible to the Office of President; neither shall any person be eligible to that Office who shall not have attained to the Age of thirty five Years, and been fourteen Years a Resident within the United States.

In Case of the Removal of the President from Office, or of his Death, Resignation, or Inability to discharge the Powers and Duties of the said Office, the Same shall devolve on the Vice President, and the Congress may by Law provide for the Case of Removal, Death, Resignation or Inability, both of the President and Vice President, declaring what Officer shall then act as President, and such Officer shall act accordingly, until the Disability be removed, or a President shall be elected.

The President shall, at stated Times, receive for his Services, a Compensation, which shall neither be encreased nor diminished during the Period for which he shall have been elected, and he shall not receive within that period any other Emolument from the United States, or any of them.

Before he enter on the Execution of his Office, he shall take the following Oath or Affirmation:—"I do solemnly swear (or affirm) that I will faithfully execute the Office of President of the United States, and will to the best of my Ability, preserve, protect and defend the Constitution of the United States."

SECTION. 2. The President shall be Commander in Chief of the Army and Navy of the United States, and of the Militia of the several States, when called into the actual Service of the United States; he may require the Opinion, in writing, of the principal Officer in each of the executive Departments, upon any Subject relating to the Duties of their respective Offices, and he shall have Power to grant Reprieves and Pardons for Offences against the United States, except in Cases of Impeachment.

He shall have Power, by and with the Advice and Consent of the Senate, to make Treaties, provided two thirds of the Senators present concur; and he shall nominate, and by and with the Advice and Consent of the Senate, shall appoint Ambassadors, other public Ministers and Consuls, Judges of the supreme Court, and all other Officers of the United States, whose Appointments are not herein otherwise provided for, and which shall be established by Law: but the Congress may by Law vest the Appointment of such inferior Officers, as they think proper, in the President alone, in the Courts of Law, or in the Heads of Departments.

The President shall have Power to fill up all Vacancies that may happen during the Recess of the Senate, by granting Commissions which shall expire at the End of their next Session.

SECTION. 3. He shall from time to time give to the Congress Information of the State of the Union, and recommend to their Consideration such Measures as he shall judge necessary and expedient; he may, on extraordinary Occasions, convene both Houses, or either of them, and in Case of Disagreement between them, with Respect to the Time of Adjournment, he may adjourn them to such Time as he shall think proper; he shall receive Ambassadors and other public Ministers; he shall take Care that the Laws be faithfully executed, and shall Commission all the Officers of the United States.

SECTION. 4. The President, Vice President and all civil Officers of the United States, shall be removed from Office on Impeachment for, and Conviction of, Treason, Bribery, or other high Crimes and Misdemeanors.

ARTICLE. III.

SECTION. 1. The judicial Power of the United States, shall be vested in one supreme Court, and in such inferior Courts as the Congress may from time to time ordain and establish. The Judges, both of the supreme and inferior Courts, shall hold their Offices during good Behaviour, and shall, at stated Times, receive for their Services, a Compensation, which shall not be diminished during their Continuance in Office.

SECTION. 2. The judicial Power shall extend to all Cases, in Law and Equity, arising under this Constitution, the Laws of the United States, and Treaties made, or which shall be made, under their Authority;—to all Cases affecting Ambassadors, other public Ministers and Consuls;—to all Cases of admiralty and maritime Jurisdiction;—to Controversies to which the United States shall be a Party;—to Controversies between two or more States;—between a State and Citizens of another State;—between Citizens of different States;—between Citizens of the same State claiming Lands under Grants of different States, and between a State, or the Citizens thereof, and foreign States, Citizens or Subjects.

In all Cases affecting Ambassadors, other public Ministers and Consuls, and those in which a State shall be Party, the supreme Court shall have original Jurisdiction. In all the other Cases before mentioned, the supreme Court shall have appellate Jurisdiction, both as to Law and Fact, with such Exceptions, and under such Regulations as the Congress shall make.

The Trial of all Crimes, except in Cases of Impeachment, shall be by Jury; and such Trial shall be held in the State where the said Crimes shall have been committed; but when not committed within any State, the Trial shall be at such Place or Places as the Congress may by Law have directed.

SECTION. 3. Treason against the United States, shall consist only in levying War against them, or in adhering to their Enemies, giving them Aid and Comfort. No Person shall be convicted of Treason unless on the Testimony of two Witnesses to the same overt Act, or on Confession in open Court.

The Congress shall have Power to declare the Punishment of Treason, but no Attainder of Treason shall work Corruption of Blood, or Forfeiture except during the Life of the Person attained.

ARTICLE. IV.

SECTION. 1. Full Faith and Credit shall be given in each State to the public Acts, Records, and judicial Proceedings of every other State. And the Congress may by general Laws prescribe the Manner in which such Acts, Record and Proceedings shall be proved, and the Effect thereof.

SECTION. 2. The Citizens of each State shall be entitled to all Privileges and Immunities of Citizens in the several States.

A Person charged in any State with Treason, Felony, or other Crime, who shall flee from Justice, and be found in another State, shall on Demand of the executive Authority of the State from which he fled, be delivered up, to be removed to the State having Jurisdiction of the Crime.

No Person held to Service or Labour in one State, under the Laws thereof, escaping into another, shall, in Consequence of any Law or Regulation therein, be discharged from such Service or Labour, but shall be delivered up on Claim of the Party to whom such Service or Labour may be due.

SECTION. 3. New States may be admitted by the Congress into this Union; but no new State shall be formed or erected within the Jurisdiction of any other State; nor any State be formed by the Junction of two or more States, or Parts of States, without the Consent of the Legislatures of the States concerned as well as of the Congress.

The Congress shall have Power to dispose of and make all needful Rules and Regulations respecting the Territory or other Property belonging to the United States; and nothing in this Constitution shall be so construed as to Prejudice any Claims of the United States, or of any particular State.

SECTION. 4. The United States shall guarantee to every State in this Union a Republican Form of Government, and shall protect each of them against Invasion; and on Application of the Legislature, or of the Executive (when the Legislature cannot be convened) against domestic Violence.

ARTICLE. V.

The Congress, whenever two thirds of both Houses shall deem it necessary, shall propose Amendments to this Constitution, or, on the Application of the Legislature of two thirds of the several States, shall call a Convention for proposing Amendments, which, in either Case, shall be valid to all Intents and Purposes, as Part of this Constitution, when ratified by the Legislatures of three fourths of the several States, or by Conventions in three fourths thereof, as the one or the other Mode of Ratification may be proposed by the Congress; Provided that no Amendment which may be made prior to the Year One thousand eight hundred and eight shall in any Manner affect the first and fourth Clauses in the Ninth Section of the first Article; and that no State, without its Consent, shall be deprived of its equal Suffrage in the Senate.

ARTICLE. VI.

All Debts contracted and Engagements entered into, before the Adoption of this Constitution, shall be as valid against the United States under this Constitution, as under the Confederation.

This Constitution, and the Laws of the United States which shall be made in Pursuance thereof; and all Treaties made, or which shall be made, under the Authority of the United States, shall be the supreme Law of the Land; and the Judges in every State shall be bound thereby, any Thing in the Constitution or Laws of any State to the Contrary notwithstanding.

The Senators and Representatives before mentioned, and the Members of the several State Legislatures, and all executive and judicial Officers, both of the United States and of the several States, shall be bound by Oath or Affirmation, to support this Constitution; but no religious Test shall ever be required as a Qualification to any Office or public Trust under the United States.

ARTICLE. VII.

The Ratification of the Conventions of nine States, shall be sufficient for the Establishment of this Constitution between the States so ratifying the Same.

Done in Convention by the Unanimous Consent of the States present the Seventeenth Day of September in the Year of our Lord one thousand seven hundred and Eighty seven and of the Independence of the United States of America the Twelfth In witness whereof We have hereunto subscribed our Names,

Go. WASHINGTON—Presidt. and deputy from Virginia

New Hampshire	JOHN LANGDON NICHOLAS GILMAN
Massachusetts	NATHANIEL GORHAM RUFUS KING
Connecticut	Wm. SAML JOHNSON ROGER SHERMAN
New York...	ALEXANDER HAMILTON
New Jersey	WIL: LIVINGSTON DAVID BREARLEY Wm. PATERSON JONA: DAYTON
Pennsylvania	B FRANKLIN THOMAS MIFFLIN ROBt MORRIS GEO. CLYMER THOs. FITZSIMONS JARED INGERSOLL JAMES WILSON GOUV MORRIS
Delaware	GEO: READ GUNNING BEDFORD jun JOHN DICKINSON RICHARD BASSETT JACO: BROOM
Maryland	JAMES McHENRY DAN OF St THOs. JENIFER DANL CARROLL
Virginia	JOHN BLAIR JAMES MADISON Jr.
North Carolina	Wm. BLOUNT RICHd. DOBBS SPAIGHT HU WILLIAMSON
South Carolina	J. RUTLEDGE CHARLES COTESWORTH PINCKNEY CHARLES PINCKNEY PIERCE BUTLER
Georgia	WILLIAM FEW ABR BALDWIN

In Convention Monday, September 17th 1787.

Present The States of

New Hampshire, Massachusetts, Connecticut, Mr. Hamilton from New York, New Jersey, Pennsylvania, Delaware, Maryland, Virginia, North Carolina and Georgia.

Resolved,

That the preceeding Constitution be laid before the United States in Congress assembled, and that it is the Opinion of this Convention, that it should afterwards be submitted to a Convention of Delegates, chosen in each State by the People thereof, under the Recommendation of its Legislature, for their Assent and Ratification; and that each Convention assenting to, and ratifying the Same, should give Notice thereof to the United States

in Congress assembled. Resolved, That it is the Opinion of this Convention, that as soon as the Conventions of nine States shall have ratified this Constitution, the United States in Congress assembled should fix a Day on which Electors should be appointed by the States which shall have ratified the same, and a Day on which the Electors should assemble to vote for the President, and the Time and Place for commencing Proceedings under this Constitution. That after such Publication the Electors should be appointed, and the Senators and Representatives elected: That the Electors should meet on the Day fixed for the Election of the President, and should transmit their Votes certified, signed, sealed and directed, as the Constitution requires, to the Secretary of the United States in Congress assembled, that the Senators and Representatives should convene at the Time and Place assigned; that the Senators should appoint a President of the Senate, for the sole Purpose of receiving, opening and counting the Votes for President; and, that after he shall be chosen, the Congress, together with the President, should, without Delay, proceed to execute this Constitution.

By the Unanimous Order of the Convention

Go. WASHINGTON—Presidt.

W. JACKSON Secretary.

RATIFICATION OF THE CONSTITUTION

State	Date of ratification
Delaware	Dec 7, 1787
Pennsylvania	Dec 12, 1787
New Jersey	Dec 19, 1787
Georgia	Jan 2, 1788
Connecticut	Jan 9, 1788
Massachusetts	Feb 6, 1788
Maryland	Apr 28, 1788
South Carolina	May 23, 1788
New Hampshire	June 21, 1788
Virginia	Jun 25, 1788
New York	Jun 26, 1788
Rhode Island	May 29, 1790
North Carolina	Nov 21, 1789

ARTICLES IN ADDITION TO, AND AMENDMENT OF, THE CONSTITUTION OF THE UNITED STATES OF AMERICA, PROPOSED BY CONGRESS, AND RATIFIED BY THE SEVERAL STATES, PURSUANT TO THE FIFTH ARTICLE OF THE ORIGINAL CONSTITUTION.

AMENDMENT I.

Congress shall make no law respecting an establishment of religion, or prohibiting the free exercise thereof; or abridging the freedom of speech, or of the press; or the right of the people peaceably to assemble, and to petition the Government for a redress of grievances.

AMENDMENT II.

A well regulated Militia, being necessary to the security of a free State, the right of the people to keep and bear Arms, shall not be infringed.

AMENDMENT III.

No Soldier shall, in time of peace be quartered in any house, without the consent of the Owner, nor in time of war, but in a manner to be prescribed by law.

AMENDMENT IV.

The right of the people to be secure in their persons, houses, papers, and effects, against unreasonable searches and seizures, shall not be violated, and no Warrants shall issue, but upon probable cause, supported by Oath or affirmation, and particularly describing the place to be searched, and the persons or things to be seized.

AMENDMENT V.

No person shall be held to answer for a capital, or otherwise infamous crime, unless on a presentment or indictment of a Grand Jury, except in cases arising in the land or naval forces, or in the Militia, when in actual service in time of War or public danger; nor shall any person be subject for the same offence to be twice put in jeopardy of life or limb; nor shall be compelled in any criminal case to be a witness against himself, nor be deprived of life, liberty, or property, without due process of law; nor shall private property be taken for public use, without just compensation.

AMENDMENT VI.

In all criminal prosecutions, the accused shall enjoy the right to a speedy and public trial, by an impartial jury of the State and district wherein the crime shall have been committed, which district shall have been previously ascertained by law, and to be informed of the nature and cause of the accusation; to be confronted with the witnesses against him; to have compulsory process for obtaining witnesses in his favor, and to have the Assistance of Counsel for his defence.

AMENDMENT VII.

In Suits at common law, where the value in controversy shall exceed twenty dollars, the right of trial by jury shall be preserved, and no fact tried by a jury, shall be otherwise re-examined in any Court of the United States, than according to the rules of the common law.

AMENDMENT VIII.

Excessive bail shall not be required, nor excessive fines imposed, nor cruel and unusual punishments inflicted.

AMENDMENT IX.

The enumeration in the Constitution, of certain rights, shall not be construed to deny or disparage others retained by the people.

AMENDMENT X.

The powers not delegated to the United States by the Constitution, nor prohibited by it to the States, are reserved to the States respectively, or to the people.

AMENDMENT XI.

(Adopted Jan. 8, 1798)
The Judicial power of the United States shall not be construed to extend to any suit in law or equity, commenced or prosecuted against one of the United States by Citizens of another State, or by Citizens or Subjects of any Foreign State.

AMENDMENT XII.

(Adopted Sept. 25, 1804)
The Electors shall meet in their respective states and vote by ballot for President and Vice-President, one of whom, at least, shall not be an inhabitant of the same state with themselves; they shall name in their ballots the person voted for as President, and in distinct ballots the person voted for as Vice-President, and they shall make distinct lists of all persons voted for as President, and of all persons voted for as Vice-President, and of the number of votes for each, which lists they shall sign and certify, and transmit sealed to the seat of the government of the United States, directed to the President of the Senate;—The President of the Senate shall, in the presence of the Senate and House of Representatives, open all the certificates and the votes shall then be counted;—The person having the greatest number of votes for President, shall be the President, if such number be a majority of the whole number of Electors appointed; and if no person have such majority, then from the persons having the highest numbers not exceeding three on the list of those voted for as President, the House of Representatives shall choose immediately, by ballot, the President. But in choosing the President, the votes shall be taken by states, the representation from each state having one vote; a quorum for this purpose shall consist of a member or members from two-thirds of the states, and a majority of all the states shall be necessary to a choice. And if the House of Representatives shall not choose a President whenever the right of choice shall devolve upon them, before the fourth day of March next following, then the Vice-President shall act as President, as in the case of the death or other constitutional disability of the President.—The person having the

greatest number of votes as Vice-President, shall be the Vice-President, if such number be a majority of the whole number of Electors appointed, and if no person have a majority, then from the two highest numbers on the list, the Senate shall choose the Vice-President; a quorum for the purpose shall consist of two-thirds of the whole number of Senators, and a majority of the whole number shall be necessary to a choice. But no person constitutionally ineligible to the office of President shall be eligible to that of Vice-President of the United States.

AMENDMENT XIII.

(Adopted Dec. 18, 1865)

SECTION 1. Neither slavery nor involuntary servitude, except as a punishment for crime whereof the party shall have been duly convicted, shall exist within the United States, or any place subject to their jurisdiction.

SECTION 2. Congress shall have power to enforce this article by appropriate legislation.

AMENDMENT XIV.

(Adopted July 28, 1868)

SECTION 1. All persons born or naturalized in the United States and subject to the jurisdiction thereof, are citizens of the United States and of the State wherein they reside. No State shall make or enforce any law which shall abridge the privileges or immunities of citizens of the United States; nor shall any State deprive any person of life, liberty, or property, without due process of law; nor deny to any person within its jurisdiction the equal protection of the laws.

SECTION 2. Representatives shall be apportioned among the several States according to their respective numbers, counting the whole number of persons in each State, excluding Indians not taxed. But when the right to vote at any election for the choice of electors for President and Vice President of the United States, Representatives in Congress, the Executive and Judicial officers of a State, or the members of the Legislature thereof, is denied to any of the male inhabitants of such State, being twenty-one years of age, and citizens of the United States, or in any way abridged, except for participation in rebellion, or other crime, the basis of representation therein shall be reduced in the proportion which the number of such male citizens shall bear to the whole number of male citizens twenty-one years of age in such State.

SECTION 3. No person shall be a Senator or Representative in Congress, or elector of President and Vice President, or hold any office, civil or military, under the United States, or under any State, who, having previously taken an oath, as a member of Congress, or as an officer of the United States, or as a member of any State legislature, or as an executive or judicial officer of any State, to support the Constitution of the United States, shall have engaged in insurrection or rebellion against the same, or given aid or comfort to the enemies thereof. But Congress may by a vote of two-thirds of each House, remove such disability.

SECTION 4. The validity of the public debt of the United States, authorized by law, including debts incurred for payment of pensions and bounties for services in suppressing insurrection or rebellion, shall not be questioned. But neither the United States nor any State shall assume or pay any debt or obligation incurred in aid of insurrection or rebellion against the United States, or any claim for the loss or emancipation of any slave; but all such debts, obligations and claims shall be held illegal and void.

SECTION 5. The Congress shall have power to enforce, by appropriate legislation, the provisions of this article.

AMENDMENT XV.

(Adopted March 30, 1870)

SECTION 1. The right of citizens of the United States to vote shall not be denied or abridged by the United States or by any State on account of race, color, or previous condition of servitude.

SECTION 2. The Congress shall have power to enforce this article by appropriate legislation.

AMENDMENT XVI.

(Adopted Feb. 25, 1913)

The Congress shall have power to lay and collect taxes on incomes, from whatever source derived, without apportionment among the several States, and without regard to any census or enumeration.

AMENDMENT XVII.

(Adopted May 31, 1913)

The Senate of the United States shall be composed of two Senators from each State, elected by the people thereof, for six years; and each Senator shall have one vote. The electors in each State shall have the qualifications requisite for electors of the most numerous branch of the State legislatures.

When vacancies happen in the representation of any State in the Senate, the executive authority of such State shall issue writs of election to fill such vacancies: Provided, That the legislature of any State may empower the executive thereof to make temporary appointments until the people fill the vacancies by election as the legislature may direct.

This amendment shall not be so construed as to affect the election or term of any Senator chosen before it becomes valid as part of the Constitution.

AMENDMENT XVIII.

(Adopted Jan. 29, 1919)

SECTION 1. After one year from the ratification of this article the manufacture, sale or transportation of intoxicating liquors within, the importation thereof into, or the exportation thereof from the United States and all territory subject to the jurisdiction thereof for beverage purposes is hereby prohibited.

SECTION 2. The Congress and the several States shall have concurrent power to enforce this article by appropriate legislation.

SECTION 3. This article shall be inoperative unless it shall have been ratified as an amendment to the Constitution by the legislatures of the several States, as provided in the Constitution, within seven years from the date of the submission hereof to the States by the Congress.

AMENDMENT XIX.

(Adopted Aug. 26, 1920)

The right of citizens of the United States to vote shall not be denied or abridged by the United States or by any State on account of sex.

Congress shall have power to enforce this article by appropriate legislation.

AMENDMENT XX.

(Adopted Feb. 6, 1933)

SECTION 1. The terms of the President and Vice President shall end at noon on the 20th day of January, and the terms of Senators and Representatives at noon on the 3d day of January, of the years in which such terms would have ended if this article had not been ratified; and the terms of their successors shall then begin.

SECTION 2. The Congress shall assemble at least once in every year, and such meeting shall begin at noon on the 3d day of January, unless they shall by law appoint a different day.

SECTION 3. If, at the time fixed for the beginning of the term of the President, the President elect shall have died, the Vice President elect shall become President. If a President shall not have been chosen before the time fixed for the beginning of his term, or if the President elect shall have failed to qualify, then the Vice President elect shall act as President until a President shall have qualified; and the Congress may by law provide for the case wherein neither a President elect nor a Vice President elect shall have qualified, declaring who shall then act as President, or the manner in which one who is to act shall be selected, and such person shall act accordingly until a President or Vice President shall have qualified.

SECTION 4. The Congress may by law provide for the case of the death of any of the persons from whom the House of Representatives may choose a President whenever the right of choice shall have devolved upon them, and for the case of the death of any of the persons from whom the Senate may choose a Vice President whenever the right of choice shall have devolved upon them.

SECTION 5. Sections 1 and 2 shall take effect on the 15th day of October following the ratification of this article.

SECTION 6. This article shall be inoperative unless it shall have been ratified as an amendment to the Constitution by the legislatures of three-fourths of the several States within seven years from the date of its submission.

AMENDMENT XXI.

(Adopted Dec. 5, 1933)

SECTION 1. The eighteenth article of amendment to the Constitution of the United States is hereby repealed.

SECTION 2. The transportation or importation into any State, Territory, or possession of the United States for delivery or use therein of intoxicating liquors, in violation of the laws thereof, is hereby prohibited.

SECTION 3. This article shall be inoperative unless it shall have been ratified as an amendment to the Constitution by conventions in the several States, as provided in the Constitution, within seven years from the date of the submission hereof to the States by the Congress.

AMENDMENT XXII.

(Adopted Feb. 27, 1951)

SECTION 1. No person shall be elected to the office of the President more than twice, and no person who has held the office of President, or acted as President, for more than two years of a term to which some other person was elected President shall be elected to the office of the President more than once. But this Article shall not apply to any person holding the office of President when this Article was proposed by the Congress, and shall not prevent any person who may be holding the office of President, or acting as President, during the term within which this Article becomes operative from holding the office of President or acting as President during the remainder of such term.

SECTION 2. This Article shall be inoperative unless it shall have been ratified as an amendment to the Constitution by the legislatures of three-fourths of the several States within seven years from the date of its submission to the States by the Congress.

AMENDMENT XXIII.

(Adopted Mar. 29, 1961)

SECTION 1. The District constituting the seat of Government of the United States shall appoint in such manner as the Congress may direct:

A number of electors of President and Vice President equal to the whole number of Senators and Representatives in Congress to which the District would be entitled if it were a State, but in no event more than the least populous State; they shall be in addition to those appointed by the States, but they shall be considered, for the purposes of the election of President and Vice President, to be electors appointed by a State; and they shall meet in the District and perform such duties as provided by the twelfth article of amendment.

SECTION 2. The Congress shall have power to enforce this article by appropriate legislation.

AMENDMENT XXIV.

(Adopted Jan. 23, 1964)

SECTION 1. The right of citizens of the United States to vote in any primary or other election for President or Vice President, for electors for President or Vice President, or for Senator or Representative in Congress, shall not be denied or abridged by the United States or any State by reason of failure to pay any poll tax or other tax.

SECTION 2. The Congress shall have the power to enforce this article by appropriate legislation.

AMENDMENT XXV.

(Adopted Feb. 10, 1967)

SECTION 1. In case of the removal of the President from office or of his death or resignation, the Vice President shall become President.

SECTION 2. Whenever there is a vacancy in the office of the Vice President, the President shall nominate a Vice President who shall take the office upon confirmation by a majority vote of both houses of Congress.

SECTION 3. Whenever the President transmits to the President pro tempore of the Senate and the Speaker of the House of Representatives his written declaration that he is unable to discharge the powers and duties of his office, and until he transmits to them a written declaration to the contrary, such powers and duties shall be discharged by the Vice President as Acting President.

SECTION 4. Whenever the Vice President and a majority of either the principal officers of the executive departments or of such other body as Congress may by law provide, transmit to the President pro tempore of the Senate and the Speaker of the House of Representatives their written declaration that the President is unable to discharge the powers and duties of his office, the Vice President shall immediately assume the powers and duties of the office as Acting President.

Thereafter, when the President transmits to the President pro tempore of the Senate and the Speaker of the House of Representatives his written declaration that no inability exists, he shall resume the powers and duties of his office unless the Vice President and a majority of either the principal officers of the executive department or of such other body as Congress may by law provide, transmit within four days to the President pro tempore of the Senate and the Speaker of the House of Representatives their written declaration that the President is unable to discharge the powers and duties of his office. Thereupon Congress shall decide the issue, assembling within forty-eight hours for that purpose if not in session. If the Congress within twenty-one days after receipt of the latter written declaration, or, if Congress is not in session, within twenty-one days after Congress is required to assemble, determines by two-thirds vote of both Houses that the President is unable to discharge the powers and duties of his office, the Vice President shall continue to discharge the same as Acting President; otherwise, the President shall resume the powers and duties of his office.

AMENDMENT XXVI.

(Adopted June 30, 1971)

SECTION 1. The right of citizens of the United States, who are 18 years of age or older, to vote shall not be denied or abridged by the United States or by any state on account of age.

SECTION 2. The Congress shall have the power to enforce this article by appropriate legislation.

AMENDMENT XXVII.

(Adopted May 7, 1992)

No law, varying the compensation for the services of the Senators and Representatives, shall take effect, until an election of Representatives shall have intervened.

THE SIZE AND VARIETY OF THE UNION AS A CHECK ON FACTION

FEDERALIST NO. 10

(MADISON)

To the People of the State of New York:

AMONG the numerous advantages promised by a well-constructed Union, none deserves to be more accurately developed than its tendency to break and control the violence of faction. The friend of popular governments never finds himself so much alarmed for their character and fate, as when he contemplates their propensity to this dangerous vice. He will not fail, therefore, to set a due value on any plan which, without violating the principles to which he is attached, provides a proper cure for it. The instability, injustice, and confusion introduced into the public councils, have, in truth, been the mortal diseases under which popular governments have everywhere perished; as they continue to be the favorite and fruitful topics from which the adversaries to liberty derive their most specious declamations. The valuable improvements made by the American constitutions on the popular models, both ancient and modern, cannot certainly be too much admired; but it would be an unwarrantable partiality, to contend that they have as effectually obviated the danger on this side, as was wished and expected. Complaints are everywhere heard from our most considerate and virtuous citizens, equally the friends of public and private faith, and of public and personal liberty, that our governments are too unstable, that the public good is disregarded in the conflicts of rival parties, and that measures are too often decided, not according to the rules of justice and the rights of the minor party, but by the superior force of an interested and overbearing majority. However anxiously we may wish that these complaints had no foundation, the evidence of known facts will not permit us to deny that they are in some degree true. It will

be found, indeed, on a candid review of our situation, that some of the distresses under which we labor have been erroneously charged on the operation of our governments; but it will be found, at the same time, that other causes will not alone account for many of our heaviest misfortunes; and, particularly, for that prevailing and increasing distrust of public engagements, and alarm for private rights, which are echoed from one end of the continent to the other. These must be chiefly, if not wholly, effects of the unsteadiness and injustice with which a factious spirit has tainted our public administrations.

By a faction, I understand a number of citizens, whether amounting to a majority or minority of the whole, who are united and actuated by some common impulse of passion, or of interest, adverse to the rights of other citizens, or to the permanent and aggregate interests of the community.

There are two methods of curing the mischiefs of faction: the one, by removing its causes; the other, by controlling its effects.

There are again two methods of removing the causes of faction: the one, by destroying the liberty which is essential to its existence; the other, by giving to every citizen the same opinions, the same passions, and the same interests.

It could never be more truly said than of the first remedy, that it was worse than the disease. Liberty is to faction what air is to fire, an aliment without which it instantly expires. But it could not be less folly to abolish liberty, which is essential to political life, because it nourishes faction, than it would be to wish the annihilation of air, which is essential to animal life, because it imparts to fire its destructive agency.

The second expedient is as impracticable as the first would be unwise. As long as the reason of man continues fallible, and he is at liberty to exercise it, different opinions will be formed. As long as the connection subsists between his reason and his self-love, his opinions and his passions will have a reciprocal influence on each other; and the former will be objects to which the latter will attach themselves. The diversity in the faculties of men, from which the rights of property originate, is not less an insuperable obstacle to a uniformity of interests. The protection of these faculties is the first object of government. From the protection of different and unequal faculties of acquiring property, the possession of different degrees and kinds of property immediately results; and from the influence of these on the sentiments and views of the respective proprietors, ensues a division of the society into different interests and parties.

The latent causes of faction are thus sown in the nature of man; and we see them everywhere brought into different degrees of activity, according to the different circumstances of civil society. A zeal for different opinions concerning religion, concerning government, and many other points, as well of speculation as of practice; an attachment to different leaders ambitiously contending for pre-eminence and power; or to persons of other descriptions whose fortunes have been interesting to the human passions, have, in turn, divided mankind into parties, inflamed them with mutual animosity, and rendered them much more disposed to vex and oppress each other than to co-operate for their common good. So strong is this propensity of mankind to fall into mutual animosities, that where no substantial occasion presents itself, the most frivolous and fanciful distinctions have been sufficient to kindle their unfriendly passions and excite their most violent conflicts. But the most common and durable source of factions has been the various and unequal distribution of property. Those who hold and those who are without property have ever formed distinct interests in society.

Those who are creditors, and those who are debtors, fall under a like discrimination. A landed interest, a manufacturing interest, a mercantile interest, a moneyed interest, with many lesser interests, grow up of necessity in civilized nations, and divide them into different classes, actuated by different sentiments and views. The regulation of these various and interfering interests forms the principal task of modern legislation, and involves the spirit of party and faction in the necessary and ordinary operations of the government.

No man is allowed to be a judge in his own cause, because his interest would certainly bias his judgment, and, not improbably, corrupt his integrity. With equal, nay with greater reason, a body of men are unfit to be both judges and parties at the same time; yet what are many of the most important acts of legislation, but so many judicial determinations, not indeed concerning the rights of single persons, but concerning the rights of large bodies of citizens? And what are the different classes of legislators but advocates and parties to the causes which they determine? Is a law proposed concerning private debts? It is a question to which the creditors are parties on one side and the debtors on the other. Justice ought to hold the balance between them. Yet the parties are, and must be, themselves the judges; and the most numerous party, or, in other words, the most powerful faction must be expected to prevail. Shall domestic manufactures be encouraged, and in what degree, by restrictions on foreign manufactures? are questions which would be differently decided by the landed and the manufacturing classes, and probably by neither with a sole regard to justice and the public good. The apportionment of taxes on the various descriptions of property is an act which seems to require the most exact impartiality; yet there is, perhaps, no legislative act in which greater opportunity and temptation are given to a predominant party to trample on the rules of justice. Every shilling with which they overburden the inferior number, is a shilling saved to their own pockets.

It is in vain to say that enlightened statesmen will be able to adjust these clashing interests, and render them all subservient to the public good. Enlightened statesmen will not always be at the helm. Nor, in many cases, can such an adjustment be made at all without taking into view indirect and remote considerations, which will rarely prevail over the immediate interest which one party may find in disregarding the rights of another or the good of the whole.

The inference to which we are brought is, that the *causes* of faction cannot be removed, and that relief is only to be sought in the means of controlling its *effects*.

If a faction consists of less than a majority, relief is supplied by the republican principle, which enables the majority to defeat its sinister views by regular vote. It may clog the administration, it may convulse the society; but it will be unable to execute and mask its violence under the forms of the Constitution. When a majority is included in a faction, the form of popular government, on the other hand, enables it to sacrifice to its ruling passion or interest both the public good and the rights of other citizens. To secure the public good and private rights against the danger of such a faction, and at the same time to preserve the spirit and the form of popular government, is then the great object to which our inquiries are directed. Let me add that it is the great desideratum by which this form of government can be rescued from the opprobrium under which it has so long labored, and be recommended to the esteem and adoption of mankind.

By what means is this object attainable? Evidently by one of two only. Either the existence of the same passion or interest in a majority at the same time must be prevented, or the majority, having such coexistent passion or interest, must be rendered, by their number and local situation, unable to concert and carry into effect schemes of oppression. If the impulse and the opportunity be suffered to coincide, we well know that neither moral nor religious motives can be relied on as an adequate control. They are not found to be such on the injustice and violence of individuals, and lose their efficacy in proportion to the number combined together, that is, in proportion as their efficacy becomes needful.

From this view of the subject it may be concluded that a pure democracy, by which I mean a society consisting of a small number of citizens, who assemble and administer the government in person, can admit of no cure for the mischiefs of faction. A common passion or interest will, in almost every case, be felt by a majority of the whole; a communication and concert result from the form of government itself; and there is nothing to check the inducements to sacrifice the weaker party or an obnoxious individual. Hence it is that such democracies have ever been spectacles of turbulence and contention; have ever been found incompatible with personal security or the rights of property; and have in general been as short in their lives as they have been violent in their deaths. Theoretic politicians, who have patronized this species of government, have erroneously supposed that by reducing mankind to a perfect equality in their political rights, they would, at the same time, be perfectly equalized and assimilated in their possessions, their opinions, and their passions.

A republic, by which I mean a government in which the scheme of representation takes place, opens a different prospect, and promises the cure for which we are seeking. Let us examine the points in which it varies from pure democracy, and we shall comprehend both the nature of the cure and the efficacy which it must derive from the Union.

The two great points of difference between a democracy and a republic are: first, the delegation of the government, in the latter, to a small number of citizens elected by the rest; secondly, the greater number of citizens, and greater sphere of country, over which the latter may be extended.

The effect of the first difference is, on the one hand, to refine and enlarge the public views, by passing them through the medium of a chosen body of citizens, whose wisdom may best discern the true interest of their country, and whose patriotism and love of justice will be least likely to sacrifice it to temporary or partial considerations. Under such a regulation, it may well happen that the public voice, pronounced by the representatives of the people, will be more consonant to the public good than if pronounced by the people themselves, convened for the purpose. On the other hand, the effect may be inverted. Men of factious tempers, of local prejudices, or of sinister designs, may, by intrigue, by corruption, or by other means, first obtain the suffrages, and then betray the interests, of the people. The question resulting is, whether small or extensive republics are more favorable to the election of proper guardians of the public weal; and it is clearly decided in favor of the latter by two obvious considerations:

In the first place, it is to be remarked that, however small the republic may be, the representatives must be raised to a certain number, in order to guard against the cabals of a few; and that, however large it may be, they must be limited to a certain number, in order to guard against the confusion of a multitude. Hence, the number of representatives in the two cases not being in proportion to that of the two constituents, and being proportionally greater in the small republic, it follows that, if the proportion of fit characters be not less in the large than in the small republic, the former will present a greater option, and consequently a greater probability of a fit choice.

In the next place, as each representative will be chosen by a greater number of citizens in the large than in the small republic, it will be more difficult for unworthy candidates to practise with success the vicious arts by which elections are too often carried; and the suffrages of the people being more free, will be more likely to centre in men who possess the most attractive merit and the most diffusive and established characters.

It must be confessed that in this, as in most other cases, there is a mean, on both sides of which inconveniences will be found to lie. By enlarging too much the number of electors, you render the representative too little acquainted with all their local circumstances and lesser interests; as by reducing it too much, you render him unduly attached to these, and too little fit to comprehend and pursue great and national objects. The federal Constitution forms a happy combination in this respect; the great and aggregate interests being referred to the national, the local and particular to the State legislatures.

The other point of difference is, the greater number of citizens and extent of territory which may be brought within the compass of republican than of democratic government; and it is this circumstance principally which renders factious combinations less to be dreaded in the former than in the latter. The smaller the society, the fewer probably will be the distinct parties and interests composing it; the fewer the distinct parties and interests, the more frequently will a majority be found of the same party; and the smaller the number of individuals composing a majority, and the smaller the compass within which they are placed, the more easily will they concert and execute their plans of oppression. Extend the sphere and you take in a greater variety of parties and interests; you will make it less probable that a majority of the whole will have a common motive to invade the rights of other citizens; or if such a common motive exists, it will be more difficult for all who feel it to discover their own strength, and to act in unison with each other. Besides other impediments, it may be remarked that, where there is a consciousness of unjust or dishonorable purposes, communication is always checked by distrust in proportion to the number whose concurrence is necessary.

17

Hence, it clearly appears, that the same advantage which a republic has over a democracy, in controlling the effects of faction, is enjoyed by a large over a small republic,—is enjoyed by the Union over the States composing it. Does the advantage consist in the substitution of representatives whose enlightened views and virtuous sentiments render them superior to local prejudices and to schemes of injustice? It will not be denied that the representation of the Union will be most likely to possess these requisite endowments. Does it consist in the greater security afforded by a greater variety of parties, against the event of any one party being able to outnumber and oppress the rest? In an equal degree does the increased variety of parties comprised within the Union, increase this security. Does it, in fine, consist in the greater obstacles opposed to the concert and accomplishment of the secret wishes of an unjust and interested majority? Here, again, the extent of the Union gives it the most palpable advantage.

The influence of factious leaders may kindle a flame within their particular States, but will be unable to spread a general conflagration through the other States. A religious sect may degenerate into a political faction in a part of the Confederacy; but the variety of sects dispersed over the entire face of it must secure the national councils against any danger from that source. A rage for paper money, for an abolition of debts, for an equal division of property, or for any other improper or wicked project, will be less apt to pervade the whole body of the Union than a particular member of it; in the same proportion as such a malady is more likely to taint a particular county or district, than an entire State.

In the extent and proper structure of the Union, therefore, we behold a republican remedy for the diseases most incident to republican government. And according to the degree of pleasure and pride we feel in being republicans, ought to be our zeal in cherishing the spirit and supporting the character of Federalists.

PUBLIUS

Federalist No. 10 from *THE FEDERALIST papers,* 1787.

CHECKS AND BALANCES

FEDERALIST NO. 51

(MADISON)

To the People of the State of New York:

To what expedient, then, shall we finally resort, for maintaining in practice the necessary partition of power among the several departments, as laid down in the Constitution? The only answer that can be given is, that as all these exterior provisions are found to be inadequate, the defect must be supplied, by so contriving the interior structure of the government as that its several constituent parts may, by their mutual relations, be the means of keeping each other in their proper places. Without presuming to undertake a full development of this important idea, I will hazard a few general observations, which may perhaps place it in a clearer light, and enable us to form a more correct judgment of the principles and structure of the government planned by the convention.

In order to lay a due foundation for that separate and distinct exercise of the different powers of government, which to a certain extent is admitted on all hands to be essential to the preservation of liberty, it is evident that each department should have a will of its own; and consequently should be so constituted that the members of each should have as little agency as possible in the appointment of the members of the others. Were this principle rigorously adhered to, it would require that all the appointments for the supreme executive, legislative, and judiciary magistracies should be drawn from the same fountain of authority, the people, through channels having no communication whatever with one another. Perhaps such a plan of constructing the several departments would be less difficult in practice than it may in contemplation appear. Some difficulties, however, and some additional expense would attend the execution of it. Some deviations, therefore, from the principle must be admitted. In the constitution of the judiciary department in particular, it might be inexpedient to insist rigorously on the principle: first, because peculiar qualifications being essential in the members, the primary consideration ought to be to select that mode of choice which best secures these qualifications; secondly, because the permanent tenure by which the appointments are held in that department, must soon destroy all sense of dependence on the authority conferring them.

It is equally evident, that the members of each department should be as little dependent as possible on those of the others, for the emoluments annexed to their offices. Were the executive magistrate, or the judges, not independent of the legislature in this particular, their independence in every other would be merely nominal.

But the great security against a gradual concentration of the several powers in the same department, consists in giving to those who administer each department the necessary constitutional means and personal motives to resist encroachments of the others. The provision for defence must in this, as in all other cases, be made commensurate to the danger of attack. Ambition must be made to counteract ambition. The interest of the man must be connected with the constitutional rights of the place. It may be a reflection on human nature, that such devices should be necessary to control the abuses of government. But what is government itself, but the greatest of all reflections on human nature? If men were angels, no government would be necessary. If angels were to govern men, neither external nor internal controls on government would be necessary. In framing a government which is to be administered by men over men, the great difficulty lies in this: you must first enable the government to control the governed; and in the next place oblige it to control itself. A dependence on the people is, no doubt, the primary control on the government; but experience has taught mankind the necessity of auxiliary precautions.

This policy of supplying, by opposite and rival interests, the defect of better motives, might be traced through the whole system of human affairs, private as well as public. We see it particularly displayed in all the subordinate distributions of power, where the constant aim is to divide and arrange the several offices in such a manner as that each may be a check on the other—that the private interest of every individual may be a sentinel over the public rights. These inventions of prudence cannot be less requisite in the distribution of the supreme powers of the State.

But it is not possible to give to each department an equal power of self-defence. In republican government, the legislative authority necessarily predominates. The remedy for this inconveniency is to divide the legislature into different branches; and to render them, by different modes of election and different principles of action, as little connected with each other as the nature of their common functions and their common dependence on the society will admit. It may even be necessary to guard against dangerous encroachments by still further precautions. As the weight of the legislative authority requires that it should be thus divided, the weakness of the executive may require, on the other hand, that it should be fortified. An absolute negative on the legislature appears, at first view, to be the natural defence with which the executive magistrate should be armed. But perhaps it would be neither altogether safe nor alone sufficient. On ordinary occasions it might not be exerted with the requisite firmness, and on extraordinary occasions it might be perfidiously abused. May not this defect of an absolute negative be supplied by some qualified connection between this weaker department and the weaker branch of the stronger department, by which the latter may be led to support the constitutional rights of the former, without being too much detached from the rights of its own department?

If the principles on which these observations are founded be just, as I persuade myself they are, and they be applied as a criterion to the several State constitutions, and to the federal Constitution, it will be found that if the latter does not perfectly correspond with them, the former are infinitely less able to bear such a test.

There are, moreover, two considerations particularly applicable to the federal system of America, which place that system in a very interesting point of view.

First. In a single republic, all the power surrendered by the people is submitted to the administration of a single government; and the usurpations are guarded against by a division of the government into distinct and separate departments. In the compound republic of America, the power surrendered by the people is first divided between two distinct governments, and then the portion allotted to each subdivided among distinct and separate departments. Hence a double security arises to the rights of the people. The different governments will control each other, at the same time that each will be controlled by itself.

Second. It is of great importance in a republic not only to guard the society against the oppression of its rulers, but to guard one part of the society against the injustice of the other part. Different interests necessarily exist in different classes of citizens. If a majority be united by a common interest, the rights of the minority will be insecure. There are but two methods of providing against this evil: the one by creating a will in the community independent of the majority—that is, of the society itself; the other, by comprehending in the society so many separate descriptions of citizens as will render an unjust combination of a majority of the whole very improbable, if not impracticable. The first method prevails in all governments possessing an hereditary or self-appointed authority. This, at best, is but a precarious security; because a power independent of the society may as well espouse the unjust views of the major, as the rightful interests of the minor party, and may possibly be turned against both parties. The second method will be exemplified in the federal republic of the United States. Whilst all authority in it will be derived from and dependent on the society, the society itself will be broken into so many parts, interests and classes of citizens, that the rights of individuals, or of the minority, will be in little danger from interested combinations of the majority. In a free government the security for civil rights must be the same as that for religious rights. It consists in the one case in the multiplicity of interests, and in the other in the multiplicity of sects. The degree of security in both cases will depend on the number of interests and sects; and this may be presumed to depend on the extent of country and number of people comprehended under the same government. This view of the subject must particularly recommend a proper federal system to all the sincere and considerate friends of republican government, since it shows that in exact proportion as the territory of the Union may be formed into more circumscribed Confederacies, or States, oppressive combinations of a majority will be facilitated; the best security, under the republican forms, for the rights of every class of citizens, will be diminished; and consequently the stability and independence of some member of the government, the only other security, must be proportionally increased. Justice is the end of government. It is the end of civil society. It ever has been and ever will be pursued until it be obtained, or until liberty be lost in the pursuit. In a society under the forms of which the stronger faction can readily unite and oppress the weaker, anarchy may as truly be said to reign as in a state of nature, where the weaker individual is not secured against the violence of the stronger; and as, in the latter state, even the stronger individuals are prompted, by the uncertainty of their condition, to submit to a government which may protect the weak as well as themselves; so, in the former state, will the more powerful factions or parties be gradually induced, by a like motive, to wish for a government which will protect all parties, the weaker as well as the more powerful. It can be little doubted that if the State of Rhode Island was separated from the Confederacy and left to itself, the insecurity of rights under the popular form of government within such narrow limits would be displayed by such reiterated oppressions of factious majorities that some power altogether independent of the people would soon be called for by the voice of the very factions whose misrule had proved the necessity of it. In the extended republic of the United States, and among the great variety of interests, parties, and sects which it embraces, a coalition of a majority of the whole society could seldom take place on any other principles than those of justice and the general good; whilst there being thus less danger to a minor from the will of a major party, there must be less pretext, also, to provide for the security of the former, by introducing into the government a will not dependent on the latter, or, in other words, a will independent of the society itself. It is no less certain than it is important, notwithstanding the contrary opinions which have been entertained, that the larger the society, provided it lie within a particular sphere, the more duly capable it will be of self-government. And happily for the *republican cause,* the practicable sphere may be carried to a very great extent, by a judicious modification and mixture of the *federal principle.*

PUBLIUS

Federalist No. 51 from *THE FEDERALIST papers,* 1787.

Why Don't They Like Us?

How America Has Become the Object of Much of the Planet's Genuine Grievances—and Displaced Discontents

BY STANLEY HOFFMANN

It wasn't its innocence that the United States lost on September 11, 2001. It was its naïveté. Americans have tended to believe that in the eyes of others the United States has lived up to the boastful clichés propagated during the Cold War (especially under Ronald Reagan) and during the Clinton administration. We were seen, we thought, as the champions of freedom against fascism and communism, as the advocates of decolonization, economic development, and social progress, as the technical innovators whose mastery of technology, science, and advanced education was going to unify the world.

Some officials and academics explained that U.S. hegemony was the best thing for a troubled world and unlike past hegemonies would last—not only because there were no challengers strong enough to steal the crown but, above all, because we were benign rulers who threatened no one.

But we have avoided looking at the hegemon's clay feet, at what might neutralize our vaunted soft power and undermine our hard power. Like swarming insects exposed when a fallen tree is lifted, millions who dislike or distrust the hegemon have suddenly appeared after September 11, much to our horror and disbelief. America became a great power after World War II, when we faced a rival that seemed to stand for everything we had been fighting against—tyranny, terror, brainwashing—and we thought that our international reputation would benefit from our standing for liberty and stability (as it still does in much of Eastern Europe). We were not sufficiently marinated in history to know that, through the ages, nobody—or almost nobody—has ever loved a hegemon.

Past hegemons, from Rome to Great Britain, tended to be quite realistic about this. They wanted to be obeyed or, as in the case of France, admired. They rarely wanted to be loved. But as a combination of high-noon sheriff and proselytizing missionary, the United States expects gratitude and affection. It was bound to be disappointed; gratitude is not an emotion that one associates with the behavior of states.

THE NEW WORLD DISORDER

This is an old story. Two sets of factors make the current twist a new one. First, the so-called Westphalian world has collapsed. The world of sovereign states, the universe of Hans Morgenthau's and Henry Kissinger's Realism, is no longer. The unpopularity of the hegemonic power has been heightened to incandescence by two aspects of this collapse. One is the irruption of the public, the masses, in international affairs. Foreign policy is no longer, as Raymond Aron had written in *Peace and War*, the closed domain of the soldier and the diplomat. Domestic publics—along with their interest groups, religious organizations, and ideological chapels—either dictate or constrain the imperatives and preferences that the governments fight for. This puts the hegemon in a difficult position: It often must work with governments that represent but a small percentage of a country's people—but if it fishes for public support abroad, it risks alienating leaders whose cooperation it needs. The United States paid heavily for not having had enough contacts with the opposition to the shah of Iran in the 1970s. It discovers today that there is an abyss in Pakistan, Saudi Arabia, Egypt, and Indonesia between our official allies and the populace in these countries. Diplomacy in a world where the masses, so to speak, stayed indoors, was a much easier game.

The collapse of the barrier between domestic and foreign affairs in the state system is now accompanied by a disease that attacks the state system itself. Many of the "states" that are members of the United Nations are pseudo-states with shaky or shabby institutions, no basic consensus on values or on procedures among their heterogeneous components, and no sense of national identity. Thus the hegemon—in addition to suffering the hostility of the government in certain countries (like Cuba, Iraq, and North Korea) and of the public in others (like, in varying degrees, Pakistan, Egypt, and even France)—can now easily become both the target of factions fighting one another in disintegrating countries and the pawn in their quarrels (which range over such increasingly borderless issues as drug trafficking, arms trading, money laundering, and other criminal enterprises). In addition, today's hegemon suffers from the volatility and turbulence of a global system in which ethnic, religious, and ideological sympathies have become transnational and in which groups and individuals uncontrolled by states can act on their own. The world of the nineteenth century, when hegemons could impose their order, their institutions, has been supplanted by the world of the twenty-first century: Where once there was order, there is now often a vacuum.

What makes the American Empire especially vulnerable is its historically unique combination of assets and liabilities. One has to go back to the Roman Empire to find a comparable set of resources. Britain, France, and Spain had to operate in multipolar systems; the United States is the only superpower.

But if America's means are vast, the limits of its power are also considerable. The United States, unlike Rome, cannot simply impose its will by force or through satellite states. Small "rogue" states can defy the hegemon (remember Vietnam?). And chaos can easily result from the large new role of nonstate actors. Meanwhile, the reluctance of Americans to take on the Herculean tasks of policing, "nation building," democratizing autocracies, and providing environmental protection and economic growth for billions of human beings stokes both resentment and hostility, especially among those who discover that one can count on American presence and leadership only when America's material interests are gravely threatened. (It is not surprising that the "defense of the national interest" approach of Realism was developed for a multipolar world. In an empire, as well as in a bipolar system, almost anything can be described as a vital interest, since even peripheral disorder can unravel the superpower's eminence.) Moreover, the complexities of America's process for making foreign-policy decisions can produce disappointments abroad when policies that the international community counted on—such as the Kyoto Protocol and the International Criminal Court—are thwarted. Also, the fickleness of U.S. foreign-policy making in arenas like the Balkans has convinced many American enemies that this country is basically incapable of pursuing long-term policies consistently.

NONE OF THIS MEANS, OF COURSE, THAT THE UNITED STATES has no friends in the world. Europeans have not forgotten the liberating role played by Americans in the war against Hitler and in the Cold War. Israel remembers how President Harry Truman sided with the founders of the Zionist state; nor has it forgotten all the help the United States has given it since then. The democratizations of postwar Germany and Japan were huge successes. The Marshall Plan and the Point Four Program were revolutionary initiatives. The decisions to resist aggression in Korea and in Kuwait demonstrated a commendable farsightedness.

But Americans have a tendency to overlook the dark sides of their course (except on the protesting left, which is thus constantly accused of being un-American), perhaps because they perceive international affairs in terms of crusades between good and evil, endeavors that entail formidable pressures for unanimity. It is not surprising that the decade following the Gulf War was marked both by nostalgia for the clear days of the Cold War and by a lot of floundering and hesitating in a world without an overwhelming foe.

STRAINS OF ANTI-AMERICANISM

The main criticisms of American behavior have mostly been around for a long time. When we look at anti-Americanism today, we must first distinguish between those who attack the United States for what it does, or fails to do, and those who attack it for what it is. (Some, like the Islamic fundamentalists and terrorists, attack it for both reasons.) Perhaps the principal criticism is of the contrast between our ideology of universal liberalism and policies that have all too often consisted of supporting and sometimes installing singularly authoritarian and repressive regimes. (One reason why these policies often elicited more reproaches than Soviet control over satellites was that, as time went by, Stalinism became more and more cynical and thus the gap between words and deeds became far less wide than in the United States. One no longer expected much from Moscow.) The list of places where America failed at times to live up to its proclaimed ideals is long: Guatemala, Panama, El Salvador, Chile, Santo Domingo in 1965, the Greece of the colonels, Pakistan, the Philippines of Ferdinand Marcos, Indonesia after 1965, the shah's Iran, Saudi Arabia, Zaire, and, of course, South Vietnam. Enemies of these regimes were shocked by U.S. support for them—and even those whom we supported were disappointed, or worse, when America's cost-benefit analysis changed and we dropped our erstwhile allies. This Machiavellian scheming behind a Wilsonian facade has alienated many clients, as well as potential friends, and bred strains of anti-Americanism around the world.

A second grievance concerns America's frequent unilateralism and the difficult relationship between the United States and the United Nations. For many countries, the United Nations is, for all its flaws, the essential agency of cooperation and the protector of its members' sovereignty. The way U.S. diplomacy has "insulted" the UN system—sometimes by ignoring it and sometimes by rudely imposing its views and policies on it—has been costly in terms of foreign support.

Third, the United States' sorry record in international development has recently become a source of dissatisfaction abroad. Not only have America's financial contributions for narrowing the gap between the rich and the poor declined since the end of the Cold War, but American-dominated institutions such as the International Monetary Fund and the World Bank have often dictated financial policies that turned out to be disastrous for developing countries—most notably, before and during the Asian economic crisis of the mid-1990s.

Finally, there is the issue of American support of Israel. Much of the world—and not only the Arab world—considers America's Israel policy to be biased. Despite occasional American attempts at evenhandedness, the world sees that the Palestinians remain under occupation, Israeli settlements continue to expand, and individual acts of Arab terrorism—acts that Yasir Arafat can't completely control—are condemned more harshly than the killings of Palestinians by the Israeli army or by Israeli-sanctioned assassination squads. It is interesting to note that Israel, the smaller and dependent power, has been more successful in circumscribing the United States' freedom to maneuver diplomatically in the region than the United States has been at getting Israel to enforce the UN resolutions adopted after the 1967 war (which called for the withdrawal of Israeli forces from then-occupied territories, solving the refugee crisis, and establishing inviolate territorial zones for all states in the region). Many in the Arab world, and some outside, use this state of affairs to stoke paranoia of the "Jewish lobby" in the United States.

ANTIGLOBALISM AND ANTI-AMERICANISM

Those who attack specific American policies are often more ambivalent than hostile. They often envy the qualities and institutions that have helped the United States grow rich, powerful, and influential.

The real United States haters are those whose anti-Americanism is provoked by dislike of America's values, institutions, and society—and their enormous impact abroad. Many who despise America see us as representing the vanguard of globalization—even as they themselves use globalization to promote their hatred. The Islamic fundamentalists of al-Qaeda—like Iran's Ayatollah Khomeini 20 years ago—make excellent use of the communication technologies that are so essential to the spread of global trade and economic influence.

We must be careful here, for there are distinctions among the antiglobalist strains that fuel anti-Americanism. To some of our detractors, the most eloquent spokesman is bin Laden, for whom America and the globalization it promotes relentlessly through free trade and institutions under its control represent evil. To them, American-fueled globalism symbolizes the domination of the Christian-Jewish infidels or the triumph of pure secularism: They look at the United States and see a society of materialism, moral laxity, corruption in all its forms, fierce selfishness, and so on. (The charges are familiar to us because we know them as an exacerbated form of right-wing anti-Americanism in nineteenth- and twentieth-century Europe.) But there are also those who, while accepting the inevitability of globalization and seem eager to benefit from it, are incensed by the contrast between America's promises and the realities of American life. Looking at the United States and the countries we support, they see insufficient social protection, vast pockets of poverty amidst plenty, racial discrimination, the large role of money in politics, the domination of the elites—and they call us hypocrites. (And these charges, too, are familiar, because they are an exacerbated version of the left-wing anti-Americanism still powerful in Western Europe.)

On the one hand, those who see themselves as underdogs of the world condemn the United States for being an evil force because its dynamism makes it naturally and endlessly imperialistic—a behemoth that imposes its culture (often seen as debased), its democracy (often seen as flawed), and its conception of individual human rights (often seen as a threat to more communitarian and more socially concerned approaches) on other societies. The United States is perceived as a bully ready to use all means, including overwhelming force, against those who resist it: Hence, Hiroshima, the horrors of Vietnam, the rage against Iraq, the war on Afghanistan.

On the other hand, the underdogs draw hope from their conviction that the giant has a heel like Achilles'. They view America as a society that cannot tolerate high casualties and prolonged sacrifices and discomforts, one whose impatience with protracted and undecisive conflicts should encourage its victims to be patient and relentless in their challenges and assaults. They look at American foreign policy as one that is often incapable of overcoming obstacles and of sticking to a course that is fraught with high risks—as with the conflict with Iraq's Saddam Hussein at the end of the Gulf War; as in the flight from Lebanon after the terrorist attacks of 1982; as in Somalia in 1993; as in the attempts to strike back at bin Laden in the Clinton years.

Thus America stands condemned not because our enemies necessarily hate our freedoms but because they resent what they fear are our Darwinian aspects, and often because they deplore what they see as the softness at our core. Those who, on our side, note and celebrate America's power of attraction, its openness to immigrants and refugees, the uniqueness of a society based on common principles rather than on ethnicity or on an old culture, are not wrong. But many of the foreign students, for instance, who fall in love with the gifts of American education return home, where the attraction often fades. Those who stay sometimes feel that the price they have to pay in order to assimilate and be accepted is too high.

WHAT BRED BIN LADEN

This long catalog of grievances obviously needs to be picked apart. The complaints vary in intensity; different cultures, countries, and parties emphasize different flaws, and the criticism is often wildly excessive and unfair. But we are not dealing here with purely rational arguments; we are dealing with emotional responses to the omnipresence of a hegemon, to the sense that many people outside this country have that the United States dominates their lives.

Complaints are often contradictory: Consider "America has neglected us, or dropped us" versus "America's attentions corrupt our culture." The result can be a gestalt of resentment that strikes Americans as absurd: We are damned, for instance, both for failing to intervene to protect Muslims in the Balkans and for using force to do so.

But the extraordinary array of roles that America plays in the world—along with its boastful attitude and, especially recently, its cavalier unilateralism—ensures that many wrongs caused by local regimes and societies will be blamed on the United States. We even end up being seen as responsible not only for anything bad that our "protectorates" do—it is no coincidence that many of the September 11 terrorists came from America's protégés, Saudi Arabia and Egypt—but for what our allies do, as when Arabs incensed by racism and joblessness in France take up bin Laden's cause, or when Muslims talk about American violence against the Palestinians. Bin Laden's extraordinary appeal and prestige in the Muslim world do not mean that his apocalyptic nihilism (to use Michael Ignatieff's term) is fully endorsed by all those who chant his name. Yet to many, he plays the role of a bloody Robin Hood, inflicting pain and humiliation on the superpower that they believe torments them.

Bin Laden fills the need for people who, rightly or not, feel collectively humiliated and individually in despair to attach themselves to a savior. They may in fact avert their eyes from the most unsavory of his deeds. This need on the part of the poor and dispossessed to connect their own feeble lot to a charismatic and single-minded leader was at the core of fascism and of communism. After the failure of pan-Arabism, the fiasco of nationalism, the dashed hopes of democratization, and the fall of Soviet communism, many young people in the Muslim world who might have once turned to these visions for succor turned instead to Islamic fundamentalism and terrorism.

One almost always finds the same psychological dynamics at work in such behavior: the search for simple explanations—and what is simpler and more inflammatory than the machinations of the Jews and the evils of America—and a highly selective approach to history. Islamic fundamentalists remember the promises made by the British to the Arabs in World War I and the imposition of British and French imperialism after 1918 rather than the support the United States gave to anticolonialists in French North Africa in the late 1940s and in the 1950s. They remember British opposition to and American reluctance toward intervention in Bosnia before Srebrenica, but they forget about NATO's actions to save Bosnian Muslims in 1995, to help Albanians in Kosovo in 1999, and to preserve and improve Albanians' rights in Macedonia in 2001. Such distortions are manufactured and maintained by the controlled media and schools of totalitarian regimes, and through the religious schools, conspiracy mills, and propaganda of fundamentalism.

WHAT CAN BE DONE?

Americans can do very little about the most extreme and violent forms of anti-American hatred—but they can try to limit its spread by addressing grievances that are justified. There are a number of ways to do this:

- First—and most difficult—drastically reorient U.S. policy in the Palestinian-Israeli conflict.
- Second, replace the ideologically market-based trickle-down economics that permeate American-led development institutions today with a kind of social safety net. (Even *New York*

Times columnist Thomas Friedman, that ur-celebrator of the global market, believes that such a safety net is indispensable.)
- Third, prod our allies and protégés to democratize their regimes, and stop condoning violations of essential rights (an approach that can only, in the long run, breed more terrorists and anti-Americans).
- Fourth, return to internationalist policies, pay greater attention to the representatives of the developing world, and make fairness prevail over arrogance.
- Finally, focus more sharply on the needs and frustrations of the people suffering in undemocratic societies than on the authoritarian regimes that govern them.

America's self-image today is derived more from what Reinhold Niebuhr would have called pride than from reality, and this exacerbates the clash between how we see ourselves and foreign perceptions and misperceptions of the United States. If we want to affect those external perceptions (and that will be very difficult to do in extreme cases), we need to readjust our self-image. This means reinvigorating our curiosity about the outside world, even though our media have tended to downgrade foreign coverage since the Cold War. And it means listening carefully to views that we may find outrageous, both for the kernel of truth that may be present in them and for the stark realities (of fear, poverty, hunger, and social hopelessness) that may account for the excesses of these views.

Terrorism aimed at the innocent is, of course, intolerable. Safety precautions and the difficult task of eradicating the threat are not enough. If we want to limit terrorism's appeal, we must keep our eyes and ears open to conditions abroad, revise our perceptions of ourselves, and alter our world image through our actions. There is nothing un-American about this. We should not meet the Manichaeanism of our foes with a Manichaeanism of self-righteousness. Indeed, self-examination and self-criticism have been the not-so-secret weapons of America's historical success. Those who demand that we close ranks not only against murderers but also against shocking opinions and emotions, against dissenters at home and critics abroad, do a disservice to America.

STANLEY HOFFMANN *is the Paul and Catherine Buttenwieser University Professor at Harvard University.*

Reprinted with permission from *The American Prospect,* November 19, 2001, Vol. 12, No. 20, pp. 18-21. © 2001 by The American Prospect, 5 Broad Street, Boston, MA 02109. All rights reserved.

Which America Will We Be Now?

BILL MOYERS

For the past several years I've been taking every possible opportunity to talk about the soul of democracy. "Something is deeply wrong with politics today," I told anyone who would listen. And I wasn't referring to the partisan mudslinging, the negative TV ads, the excessive polling or the empty campaigns. I was talking about something fundamental, something troubling at the core of politics. The soul of democracy—the essence of the word itself—is government of, by and for the people. And the soul of democracy has been dying, drowning in a rising tide of big money contributed by a narrow, unrepresentative elite that has betrayed the faith of citizens in self-government.

But what's happened since the September 11 attacks would seem to put the lie to my fears. Americans have rallied together in a way that I cannot remember since World War II. This catastrophe has reminded us of a basic truth at the heart of our democracy: No matter our wealth or status or faith, we are all equal before the law, in the voting booth and when death rains down from the sky.

We have also been reminded that despite years of scandals and political corruption, despite the stream of stories of personal greed and pirates in Gucci scamming the Treasury, despite the retreat from the public sphere and the turn toward private privilege, despite squalor for the poor and gated communities for the rich, the great mass of Americans have not yet given up on the idea of "We, the People." And they have refused to accept the notion, promoted so diligently by our friends at the Heritage Foundation, that government should be shrunk to a size where, as Grover Norquist has put it, they can drown it in a bathtub.

These ideologues at Heritage and elsewhere, by the way, earlier this year teamed up with deep-pocket bankers—many from Texas, with ties to the Bush White House—to stop America from cracking down on terrorist money havens. How about that for patriotism? Better that terrorists get their dirty money than tax cheaters be prevented from hiding theirs. And these people wrap themselves in the flag and sing "The Star-Spangled Banner" with gusto.

Contrary to right-wing denigration of government, however, today's heroes are public servants. The 20-year-old dot-com in-stant millionaires and the preening, pugnacious pundits of tabloid television and the crafty celebrity stock-pickers on the cable channels have all been exposed for what they are—barnacles on the hull of the great ship of state. In their stead we have those brave firefighters and policemen and Port Authority workers and emergency rescue personnel—public employees all, most of them drawing a modest middle-class income for extremely dangerous work. They have caught our imaginations not only for their heroic deeds but because we know so many people like them, people we took for granted. For once, our TV screens have been filled with the modest declarations of average Americans coming to each other's aid. I find this good and thrilling and sobering. It could offer a new beginning, a renewal of civic values that could leave our society stronger and more together than ever, working on common goals for the public good.

Already, in the wake of September 11, there's been a heartening change in how Americans view their government. For the first time in more than thirty years a majority of people say they trust the federal government to do the right thing at least "most of the time." It's as if the clock has been rolled back to the early 1960s, before Vietnam and Watergate took such a toll on the gross national psychology. This newfound respect for public service—this faith in public collaboration—is based in part on how people view what the government has done in response to the attacks. To most Americans, government right now doesn't mean a faceless bureaucrat or a politician auctioning access to the highest bidder. It means a courageous rescuer or brave soldier. Instead of our representatives spending their evenings clinking glasses with fat cats, they are out walking among the wounded.

There are, alas, less heartening signs to report. It didn't take long for the wartime opportunists—the mercenaries of Washington, the lobbyists, lawyers and political fundraisers—to crawl out of their offices on K Street determined to grab what they can for their clients. While in New York we are still attending memorial services for firemen and police, while everywhere Americans' cheeks are still stained with tears, while the President calls for patriotism, prayers and piety, the predators of Washington are up to their old tricks in the pursuit of private plunder at public expense. In the wake of this awful tragedy wrought by terrorism, they are cashing in. Would you like to know the memorial they would offer the thousands of people who died in the attacks? Or the legacy they would leave the children who lost a parent in the horror? How do they propose to fight the long and costly war on terrorism America must now undertake? Why, restore the three-martini lunch—that will surely strike fear in the heart of Osama bin Laden. You think I'm kidding, but bringing back the deductible lunch is one of the proposals on the table in Washington right now. And cut capital gains for the wealthy, naturally—that's America's patriotic duty, too. And while we're at it, don't forget to eliminate the corporate alternative minimum tax, enacted fifteen years ago to prevent corporations from taking so many credits and deductions that they owed little if any taxes. But don't just repeal their minimum tax; refund to those corporations all the minimum tax they have ever been assessed.

What else can America do to strike at the terrorists? Why, slip in a special tax break for poor General Electric, and slip inside the EPA while everyone's distracted and torpedo the recent order to clean the Hudson River of PCBs. Don't worry about NBC, CNBC or MSNBC reporting it; they're all in the GE family. It's time for Churchillian courage, we're told. So how would this crowd assure that future generations will look back and say "This was their finest hour"? That's easy. Give those coal producers freedom to pollute. And shovel generous tax breaks to those giant energy companies. And open the Alaska wilderness to drilling—that's something to remember the 11th of September for. And while the red, white and blue waves at half-mast over the land of the free and the home of the brave—why, give the President the power to discard democratic debate and the rule of law concerning controversial trade agreements, and set up secret tribunals to run roughshod over local communities trying to protect their environment and their health. If I sound a little bitter about this, I am; the President rightly appeals every day for sacrifice. But to these mercenaries sacrifice is for suckers. So I am bitter, yes, and sad. Our business and political class owes us better than this. After all, it was they who declared class war twenty years ago, and it was they who won. They're on top. If ever they were going to put patriotism over profits, if ever they were going to practice the magnanimity of winners, this was the moment. To hide now behind the flag while ripping off a country in crisis fatally separates them from the common course of American life.

Once again the Republican Party has lived down to Harry Truman's description of the GOP as Guardians of Privilege.

Some things just don't change. When I read that Dick Armey, the Republican majority leader in the House, said "it wouldn't be commensurate with the American spirit" to provide unemployment and other benefits to laid-off airline workers, I

thought that once again the Republican Party has lived down to Harry Truman's description of the GOP as Guardians of Privilege. And as for Truman's Democratic Party—the party of the New Deal and the Fair Deal—well, it breaks my heart to report that the Democratic National Committee has used the terrorist attacks to call for widening the soft-money loophole in our election laws. How about that for a patriotic response to terrorism? Mencken got it right when he said, "Whenever you hear a man speak of his love for his country, it is a sign that he expects to be paid for it."

Yes, there's a fight going on against terrorists. But there's also a fight going on to decide the kind of country this will be.

Let's face it: These realities present citizens with no options but to climb back in the ring. We are in what educators call "a teachable moment." And we'll lose it if we roll over and shut up. What's at stake is democracy. Democracy wasn't canceled on September 11, but democracy won't survive if citizens turn into lemmings. Yes, the President is our Commander in Chief, but we are not the President's minions. While firemen and police were racing into the fires of hell in downtown New York, and now, while our soldiers and airmen and Marines are putting their lives on the line in Afghanistan, the Administration and its Congressional allies are allowing multinational companies to make their most concerted effort in twenty years to roll back clean-air measures, exploit public lands and stuff the pockets of their executives and shareholders with undeserved cash. Against such crass exploitation, unequaled since the Teapot Dome scandal, it is every patriot's duty to join the loyal opposition. Even in war, politics is about who gets what and who doesn't. If the mercenaries and the politicians-for-rent in Washington try to exploit the emergency and America's good faith to grab what they wouldn't get through open debate in peacetime, the disloyalty will not be in our dissent but in our subservience. The greatest sedition would be our silence. Yes, there's a fight going on—against terrorists around the globe, but just as certainly there's a fight going on here at home, to decide the kind of country this will be during and after the war on terrorism.

What should our strategy be? Here are a couple of suggestions, beginning with how we elect our officials. As Congress debates new security measures, military spending, energy policies, economic stimulus packages and various bailout requests, wouldn't it be better if we knew that elected officials had to answer to the people who vote instead of the wealthy individual and corporate donors whose profit or failure may depend on how those new initiatives are carried out?

That's not a utopian notion. Thanks to the efforts of many hardworking pro-democracy activists who have been organizing at the grassroots for the past ten years, we already have four states—Maine, Arizona, Vermont and Massachusetts—where state representatives from governor on down have the option of rejecting all private campaign contributions and qualifying for full public financing of their campaigns. About a third of Maine's legislature and a quarter of Arizona's got elected last year running clean—that is, under their states' pioneering Clean Elections systems, they collected a set number of $5 contributions and then pledged to raise no other money and to abide by strict spending limits.

These unsung heroes of democracy, the first class of elected officials to owe their elections solely to their voters and not to any deep-pocketed backers, report a greater sense of independence from special interests and more freedom to speak their minds. "The business lobbyists left me alone," says State Representative Glenn Cummings, a freshman from Maine who was the first candidate in the country to qualify for Clean Elections funding. "I think they assumed I was unapproachable. It sure made it easier to get through the hallways on the way to a vote!" His colleague in the Statehouse, Senator Ed Youngblood, recalls that running clean changed the whole process of campaigning. "When people would say that it didn't matter how they voted, because legislators would just vote the way the money wants," he tells us, "it was great to be able to say, 'I don't have to vote the way some lobbyist wants just to insure that I'll get funded by him in two years for re-election.'"

It's too soon to say that money no longer talks in either state capital, but it clearly doesn't swagger as much. In Maine, the legislature passed a bill creating a Health Security Board tasked with devising a detailed plan to implement a single-payer healthcare system for the state. The bill wasn't everything its sponsor, Representative Paul Volenik, wanted, but he saw real progress toward a universal healthcare system in its passage. Two years ago, he noted, only fifty-five members of the House of Representatives (out of 151) voted for the bill. This time eighty-seven did, including almost all the Democrats and a few Republicans. The bill moved dramatically further, and a portion of that is because of the Clean Elections system they have there, Volenik said.

But the problem is larger than that of money in politics. Democracy needs a broader housecleaning. Consider, for example, what a different country we would be if we had a Citizens Channel with a mandate to cover real social problems, not shark at-tacks or Gary Condit's love life, while covering up Rupert Murdoch's manipulations of the FCC and CBS's ploy to filch tax breaks for its post-terrorist losses. Such a channel could have spurred serious attention to the weakness of airport security, for starters, pointing out long ago how the industry, through its contributions, had wrung from government the right to contract that security to the lowest bidder. It might have pushed the issue of offshore-banking havens to page one, or turned up the astonishing deceit of the NAFTA provision that enables secret tribunals to protect the interests of investors while subverting the well-being of workers and the health of communities. Such a channel—committed to news for the sake of democracy—might also have told how corporations and their alumni in the Bush Administration have thwarted the development of clean, home-grown energy that would slow global warming and the degradation of our soil, air and water, while reducing our dependence on oligarchs, dictators and theocrats abroad.

Even now the media elite, with occasional exceptions, remain indifferent to the hypocrisy of Washington's mercenary class as it goes about the dirty work of its paymasters. What a contrast to those citizens who during these weeks of loss and mourning have reminded us that the kingdom of the human heart is large, containing not only hatred but courage. Much has been made of the comparison to December 7, 1941. I find it apt. In response to the sneak attack on Pearl Harbor, Americans waged and won a great war, then came home to make this country more prosperous and just. It is not beyond this generation to live up to that example. To do so, we must define ourselves not by the lives we led until September 11 but by the lives we will lead from now on. If we seize the opportunity to build a stronger country, we too will ultimately prevail in the challenges ahead, at home and abroad. But we cannot win this new struggle by military might alone. We will prevail only if we lead by example, as a democracy committed to the rule of law and the spirit of fairness, whose corporate and political elites recognize that it isn't only firefighters, police and families grieving their missing kin who are called upon to sacrifice.

Bill Moyers is editor in chief of Public Affairs Television, the independent production company he founded in 1986. This article, prepared with the help of Micah L. Sifry, is adapted from a speech Moyers gave to the Environmental Grantmakers Association.

"We"—Not "Me"

Public opinion and the return of government

BY STANLEY B. GREENBERG

Distrust of government is down and the public is clearly looking for an expanded governmental role in a vast range of areas related to the September 11 attacks. How else can we explain the big debate on airline safety? The U.S. Senate wants to federalize security workers and the U.S. House wants to subject them to intense regulation independent of the airlines. Federalize or regulate? This is a Democratic dream.

But the opportunity for Democrats goes well beyond the public's support for a more expansive government. During the two months following the attacks, my associates and I listened to people in 23 focus groups all across the country. The emerging mood and values in this new period—with a strong emphasis on unity, coming together, community, seriousness of purpose, freedom of choice, and tolerance—reflect the instinctive impulses of Democrats surely more than they do Republicans'. Indeed, the short-term and consumerist perspective inherent in the Republicans' aggressive tax-cut initiative seems oddly out of sync with the emerging mood.

THE POST-SEPTEMBER 11 MOOD AND VALUES

The first pattern in the emerging mood is the pride taken in the country's unity. People think the United States is headed in the right direction because Americans have come together as one in the face of adversity: As people affirmed repeatedly in the group discussions, "United we stand." After sadness or heroism, this pride in unity is almost the first thing participants talked about: "To me, it has brought people in our country together"; "United States of America, again behind the government"; "the country seems to have banded together for the first time since World War II or Korea."

Participants explicitly noted that this is no Vietnam—a time when the country was divided and thereby weak-

ened itself. In fact, people were reluctant to get into the blame game. As one participant said, there is "a lot of blame to go around." That would divide the country, they believe, and we cannot afford that.

This unity has consequences that affect the current political terrain. First, the unity is all-encompassing; politicians of all stripes are seen as part of the unified national response. In some respects, then, the "security issue" has been neutralized by popular request. When we asked whether Democrats are as patriotic as Republicans, respondents said yes without qualification.

The second pattern of thinking—a newly evident consciousness of community—is closely related to unity. People were proud that in the aftermath of the tragedies Americans are working together, thinking about one another, and helping others. They noted: "Everybody [is] bonding together"; "I just feel we have more in common with people, knowing they feel bad too"; "[It's been] a long time since we pulled together to help each other.... We're going to help each other whether it's our neighbor or a stranger across the country."

This emerging sense of community contains within it the notion that, at this moment, individual desires should give way to the needs of community and country. Some see young people as the barometers of this new climate. Young people are "into themselves," said one respondent. "They're going to have a chance to see what it means to be an American."

The third pattern is a new sense of seriousness, in both private and public purpose. Even two months after the attacks, the events of September 11 led many to say that they "need to figure out what is really important," as one person put it. "I think it's darn time that finally this country got back to caring about what's important, which is, you know, your family and home and self, and you know, stop being quite so materialistic."

The perceived need to refocus our priorities as individuals extends to the public level: We are at "a point in our history [where] we have some very important things to do," one of the participants asserted. While people talked about dealing with many issues—"animal rights," for example—they suggested we have "bigger things to think about right now." One person summed up with the simple instruction: "Prioritize. We need healing and we need each other.... Turn your attention to helping our nation."

The final pattern of thinking that has emerged centers on the freedom to choose. We asked people in the focus groups what it means to be an American and why America is under attack. The great bulk of the responses raised the concept of "freedom." In the face of the attacks by Islamic fundamentalists, people are defining freedom as "the freedom to choose." In America, we have "options." "We're free here. We all make our choice."

Many people think that this freedom of choice is central to our way of life—and that it is now under attack. They consider this concept of choice to be missing from those societies that would impose traditional patterns on the individual, the family, and women. The focus group participants were ready to elaborate:

> You know… you choose who you're going to marry, and you choose if you're going to have children, and you choose if you're going to go to school, and you choose to move out of state to get a better job, and you choose whether you get on a plane. And that's why a lot of people want to come here… because there's a lot of choices.
>
> You could choose your religion; you don't have to be one thing or another. If you're a woman, you can walk down the street; you don't have to hide under a veil.

But also under attack are freedom of religion and the concept of religious pluralism: the ability of many religions to co-exist in the same society without dividing it. "We tolerate others' religion"; "we have a mix and nobody seems to care what you are or what your faith is." In fact, someone said, "that is what drives them nuts… the fact we can show respect. You're a Buddhist, fine. As long as you don't harm me or force your religion onto me, let me make my choices—they can't stand it over there."

The central importance that Americans accord to freedom of choice, particularly concerning life choices and religion, was reflected in the fairly tolerant attitude toward Muslims in America expressed in all of the focus groups. Respondents clearly favored tighter border controls and limiting the number of immigrants, views that are also reflected in the polls. But it is striking that during the many weeks of focus-group discussions, hostile comments from participants toward foreigners and Muslims were few and isolated. The events of September 11 did not unleash expressions of pent-up prejudice.

In fact, freedom of choice is at the heart of what Americans are defending, and that is apparently elevating the value of tolerance in our country. The concept of freedom that Americans are fighting to preserve, moreover, poses problems for the fundamentalist religious forces in the United States that have sought to bring religion more forcefully into politics. Writing in the November 5 *Weekly Standard*, David Brooks gingerly raised the idea that this may not be the best moment for "faith-based initiatives and religion in the public square." No wonder Pat Robertson, Jerry Falwell, and Franklin Graham seem so off balance in the current environment.

Unity and togetherness; bonding and community; family and country over materialism and selfishness; freedom to choose in life and religion—these are the elements that form the public consciousness during this period. Small wonder that voters are having trouble understanding the Republicans' tax-cut approach at a time when the country faces so many challenges.

Compared to the GOP, the Democrats seem more aligned with this emerging consciousness—above all, because of the centrality of community. British Prime Minister Tony Blair understood this when he gave his speech on the "power of community" to a Labour Party conference. The attacks, he said, left us with a renewed respect for the public services because they represent our capacity to act together. After September 11, we dare not think that each individual and each country can go it alone. The power of community, said Blair, infuses our "modern social democracy."

The public's renewed interest in government is a symptom of the powerful impulse to act together and protect our freedoms.

TAX CUTS AND THE NEW POLITICS

The Republican House and President Bush have made tax cuts their central proposition for addressing the economy and meeting the country's domestic needs. But this position is at odds with the emerging national mood after the September catastrophe. While voters clearly want tax cuts as part of an overall approach, they oppose an aggressive program of tax cuts because the country faces other financial needs, because such cuts endanger the budget and economy, and because they are at odds with the emerging commitment to community and nation.

Given a choice, voters have other priorities. They would delay the large tax cuts passed last year and use the money to fund Social Security, rebuild after the terrorist attacks, help the unemployed, and increase support for education. In a poll of 1,000 likely voters commissioned by Democracy Corps and conducted by Greenberg Quinlan Rosner Research from October 30 through November 1, voters greatly preferred this choice (54 percent to 39 percent) to the Republican one that offers expanding tax cuts to get the economy moving, help businesses invest, and create jobs.

At a moment when the country is looking for seriousness of purpose, Americans see Republicans' big tax cuts as irresponsible. The aggressive cuts President Bush supports clash with Americans' worries about federal budget deficits and the economy; many fear that the cuts may plunge the country into red ink again—and into long-term financial uncertainty. For some participants, the connection and the risks are very clear.

> [The] biggest thing for me is the economy. As far as the tax cuts and things, I thought he [Bush] is going overboard on that. My biggest concern is the deficit.... We are paying so much interest on the deficit itself.... We were on a great path to get this knocked down to a reasonable level, if not eliminate the damn thing altogether.

While there is some understanding that a broad economic program might include tax cuts, we found particular public discomfort with tax cuts that are individualistic and indulgent. The tax rebate for those who did not receive tax cuts in the first round has a progressive purpose and has been championed by both Democrats and Republicans. Yet Americans wonder whether even this rebate proposal comports with their new sense of seriousness.

In fact, voters do not currently bring a strong partisan filter to the various economic proposals being considered by Congress. Nonetheless, when given a list of individual Democratic proposals, a large majority of respondents support each one. Two-thirds favor every Democratic proposal but one (the tax rebate). The strongest support is for providing unemployment benefits to the newly unemployed; delaying tax cuts for the wealthiest 1 percent in order to fund post-September 11 rebuilding and Social Security; funding infrastructure projects such as airport improvements and school construction to create jobs; accelerating the broad, middle-class tax cuts that are already scheduled; including the newly unemployed under COBRA health insurance ; and offering tax incentives to businesses—if clearly linked to new investment. The backing for construction of public projects—which wins the support of 85 percent of likely voters (more than for any other proposal except extending unemployment benefits, which also garners 85 percent support)—is a particularly notable expression of the current public mood.

Overall, the Democrats' proposals poll better than the Republicans'—particularly those Republican brainstorms that have already become part of the public debate, like retroactively eliminating the "alternative minimum tax" on corporations. One person in a focus group observed, to the agreement of many: "We've got the deficit, we've got increased spending, we've got military action going on, and don't really need to keep handing out money right now." That $600 may not add up to much for the individual, another elaborated, "but all our $600s would" add up to a lot of public funds—

> and right now we need a lot of money. We're spending tons of money right now. And as far as I'm concerned, if it's there, if the government's expensive and it's not breaking us, leave it alone. It don't make any sense to keep sending it back and we go further in the hole. Because we're going to be the ones that's going to pay the taxes to make it up.

Voters talk about a tax rebate as "nice" but see it as an option that conflicts with their thinking about the emergent challenges for the country. The tax cut, they say, offers small immediate benefits at the expense of the future: "It's nice to get your little rebate back. Enjoy it now. I do have concerns about the future." Another called it "a dumb thing" and continued: "I can't understand why they did that. It was in my benefit, it was in anybody's benefit. But in the future, it's not."

The argument that tax cuts spur spending and therefore help the economy also clashes with what some voters think should be the proper emphasis—community and country. What the president is calling for, one suggested, is for people "to go on a shopping spree," but if "he would have said education, that's important." We are missing the opportunity to invest in the country:

> What did we do with the money after I got my little check? I didn't run down and buy stock or reinvest it in the country. I just absorbed it.... Did it go back into the country... or did... [we] just go out and buy something like a TV or something?

Another participant, reflecting on past wars, recalled that people bought bonds and were asked "to do something for the entire country. So, [by contrast,] Bush has asked us to lead our lives."

All across the country, what people told us is that the tax cut seems short-term, diminished, individualistic, and consumerist at a time when citizens are looking for something more for the nation. People are thinking about community needs, government, and the future.

A season for Democrats.

STANLEY B. GREENBERG *is chairman and CEO of Greenberg Quinlan Rosner Research and co-founder of Democracy Corps, which was the primary sponsor of this research.*

America's Ignorant Voters

This year's election is sure to bring more lamentations about voter apathy.
No less striking is the appalling political ignorance of the American electorate.

by Michael Schudson

Every week, the *Tonight Show's* Jay Leno takes to the streets of Los Angeles to quiz innocent passersby with some simple questions: On what bay is San Francisco located? Who was president of the United States during World War II? The audience roars as Leno's hapless victims fumble for answers. Was it Lincoln? Carter?

No pollster, let alone a college or high school history teacher, would be surprised by the poor showing of Leno's sample citizens. In a national assessment test in the late 1980s, only a third of American 17-year-olds could correctly locate the Civil War in the period 1850–1900; more than a quarter placed it in the 18th century. Two-thirds knew that Abraham Lincoln wrote the Emancipation Proclamation, which seems a respectable showing, but what about the 14 percent who said that Lincoln wrote the Bill of Rights, the 10 percent who checked the Missouri Compromise, and the nine percent who awarded Lincoln royalties for *Uncle Tom's Cabin?*

Asking questions about contemporary affairs doesn't yield any more encouraging results. In a 1996 national public opinion poll, only 10 percent of American adults could identify William Rehnquist as the chief justice of the Supreme Court. In the same survey, conducted at the height of Newt Gingrich's celebrity as Speaker of the House, only 59 percent could identify the job he held. Americans sometimes demonstrate deeper knowledge about a major issue before the nation, such as the Vietnam War, but most could not describe the thrust of the Clinton health care plan or tell whether the Reagan administration supported the Sandinistas or the contras during the conflict in Nicaragua (and only a third could place that country in Central America).

It can be misleading to make direct comparisons with other countries, but the general level of political awareness in leading liberal democracies overseas does seem to be much higher. While 58 percent of the Germans surveyed, 32 percent of the French, and 22 percent of the British were able to identify Boutros Boutros-Ghali as secretary general of the United Nations in 1994, only 13 percent of Americans could do so. Nearly all Germans polled could name Boris Yeltsin as Russia's leader, as could 63 percent of the British, 61 percent of the French, but only 50 percent of the Americans.

How can the United States claim to be a model democracy if its citizens know so little about political life? That question has aroused political reformers and preoccupied many political scientists since the early 20th century. It can't be answered without some historical perspective.

Today's mantra that the "informed citizen" is the foundation of effective democracy was not a central part of the nation's founding vision. It is largely the creation of late-19th-century Mugwump and Progressive reformers, who recoiled from the spectacle of powerful political parties using government as a job bank for their friends and a cornucopia of contracts for their relatives. (In those days before the National Endowment for the Arts, Nathaniel Hawthorne, Herman Melville, and Walt Whitman all subsidized their writing by holding down federal patronage appointments.) Voter turnout in the late 19th century was extraordinarily high by today's standards, routinely over 70 percent in presidential elections, and there is no doubt that parades, free whiskey, free-floating money, patronage jobs, and the pleasures of fraternity all played a big part in the political enthusiasm of ordinary Americans.

The reformers saw this kind of politics as a betrayal of democratic ideals. A democratic public, they believed, must reason together. That ideal was threatened by mindless enthusiasm, the wily maneuvers of political machines, and the vulnerability of the new immigrant masses in the nation's big cities, woefully ignorant of Anglo-Saxon traditions, to manipulation by party hacks. E.

A tradition of ignorance? Making sober political choices wasn't the top priority of these Kansas Territory voters in 1857.

L. Godkin, founding editor of the *Nation* and a leading reformer, argued that "there is no corner of our system in which the hastily made and ignorant foreign voter may not be found eating away the political structure, like a white ant, with a group of natives standing over him and encouraging him."

This was in 1893, by which point a whole set of reforms had been put in place. Civil service reform reduced patronage. Ballot reform irrevocably altered the act of voting itself. For most of the 19th century, parties distributed at the polls their own "tickets," listing only their own candidates for office. A voter simply took a ticket from a party worker and deposited it in the ballot box, without needing to read it or mark it in any way. Voting was thus a public act of party affiliation. Beginning in 1888, however, and spreading across the country by 1896, this system was replaced with government-printed ballots that listed all the candidates from each eligible party. The voter marked the ballot in secret, as we do today, in an act that affirmed voting as an individual choice rather than a social act of party loyalty. Political parades and other public spectacles increasingly gave way to pamphlets in what reformers dubbed "educational" political campaigns. Leading newspapers, once little more than organs of the political parties, began to declare their independence and to portray themselves as nonpartisan commercial institutions of public enlightenment and public-minded criticism. Public secondary education began to spread.

These and other reforms enshrined the informed citizen as the foundation of democracy, but at a tremendous cost: Voter turnout plummeted. In the presidential election of 1920, it dropped to 49 percent, its lowest point in the 20th century—until it was matched in 1996. Ever since, political scientists and others have been plumbing the mystery created by the new model of an informed citizenry: How can so many, knowing so little, and voting in such small numbers, build a democracy that appears to be (relatively) successful?

There are several responses to that question. The first is that a certain amount of political ignorance is an inevitable byproduct of America's unique political environment. One reason Americans have so much difficulty grasping the political facts of life is that their political system is the world's most complex. Ask the next political science Ph.D. you meet to explain what government agencies at what level—federal, state, county, or city—take responsibility for the homeless. Or whom he or she voted for in the last election for municipal judge. The answers might make Jay Leno's victims seem less ridiculous. No European country has as many elections, as many elected offices, as complex a maze of overlapping governmental jurisdictions, as the American system. It is simply harder to "read" U.S. politics than the politics of most nations.

The hurdle of political comprehension is raised a notch higher by the ideological inconsistencies of American political parties. In Britain, a voter can confidently cast a vote without knowing a great deal about the particular candidates on the ballot. The Labor candidate generally can be counted on to follow the Labor line, the Conservative to follow the Tory line. An American voter casting a ballot for a Democrat or Republican has no such assurance. Citizens in other countries need only dog paddle to be in the political swim; in the United States they need the skills of a scuba diver.

If the complexity of U.S. political institutions helps explain American ignorance of domestic politics, geopolitical factors help explain American backwardness in foreign affairs. There is a kind of ecology of political ignorance at work. The United States is far from Europe and borders only two other countries. With a vast domestic market, most of its producers have relatively few dealings with customers in other countries, globalization notwithstanding. Americans, lacking the parliamentary form of government that prevails in most other democracies, are also likely to find much of what they read or hear about the wider world politically opaque. And the simple fact of America's political and cultural superpower status naturally limits citizens' political awareness. Just as employees gossip more about the boss than the boss gossips about them, so Italians and Brazilians know more about the United States than Americans know about their countries.

Consider a thought experiment. Imagine what would happen if you transported those relatively well-informed Germans or Britons to the United States with their cultural heritage, schools, and news media intact. If you checked on them again about a generation later, after long exposure to the distinctive American political environment—its geographic isolation, superpower status, complex political system, and weak parties—would they have the political knowledge levels of Europeans or Americans? Most likely, I think, they would have developed typically American levels of political ignorance.

Lending support to this notion of an ecology of political knowledge is the stability of American political ignorance over time. Since the 1940s, when social scientists began measuring it, political ignorance has remained virtually unchanged. It is hard to gauge the extent of political knowledge before that time, but there is little to suggest that there is some lost golden age in U.S. history. The storied 1858 debates between Senator Stephen Douglas and Abraham Lincoln, for example, though undoubtedly a high point in the nation's public discourse, were also an anomaly. Public debates were rare in 19th-century political campaigns, and campaign rhetoric was generally overblown and aggressively partisan.

Modern measurements of Americans' historical and political knowledge go back at least to 1943, when the *New York Times* surveyed college freshmen and found "a striking ignorance of even the most elementary aspects of United States history." Reviewing nearly a half-century of data (1945–89) in *What Americans Know about Politics and Why It Matters* (1996), political scientists Michael Delli Carpini and Scott Keeter conclude that, on balance, there has been a slight gain in Americans' political knowledge, but one so modest that it makes more sense to speak of a remarkable stability. In 1945, for example, 43 percent of a national sample could name neither of their U.S. senators; in 1989, the figure was essentially unchanged at 45 percent. In 1952, 67 percent could name the vice president; in 1989, 74 percent could do so. In 1945, 92 percent of Gallup poll respondents knew that the term of the president is four years, compared with 96 percent in 1989. Whatever the explanations for dwindling voter turnout since 1960 may be, rising ignorance is not one of them.*

As Delli Carpini and Keeter suggest, there are two ways to view their findings. The optimist's view is that political ignorance has grown no worse despite the spread of television and video games, the decline of political parties, and a variety of other negative developments. The pessimist asks why so little has improved despite the vast increase in formal education during those years. But the main conclusion remains: no notable change over as long a period as data are available.

Low as American levels of political knowledge may be, a generally tolerable, sometimes admirable, political democracy survives. How? One explanation is provided by a school of political science that goes under the banner of "political heuristics." Public opinion polls and paper-and-pencil tests of political knowledge, argue researchers such as Arthur Lupia, Samuel Popkin, Paul Sniderman,

and Philip Tetlock, presume that citizens require more knowledge than they actually need in order to cast votes that accurately reflect their preferences. People can and do get by with relatively little political information. What Popkin calls "low-information rationality" is sufficient for citizens to vote intelligently.

TUNING OUT THE NEWS?

In 1998 a Gallup poll asked respondents where they got their news and information. The results paint a portrait of a less-than-enlightened electorate. Other indicators are discouraging: daily newspaper circulation slid from 62 million in 1970 to 56 million in 1999.

	Every day	Several times/week	Occasionally	Never
Local newspapers	53%	15%	22%	10%
National newspapers	4	11	26	59
Nightly network news	55	19	19	7
CNN	21	16	33	29
C-SPAN	3	4	25	65
National Public Radio	15	12	25	47
Radio talk shows	12	9	21	58
Discussions with family or friends	27	26	41	6
On-line news	7	6	17	70
Weekly news magazines	15	6	27	52

Source: The Gallup Organization. (Not shown: those answering "no opinion.")

This works in two ways. First, people can use cognitive cues, or "heuristics." Instead of learning each of a candidate's issue positions, the voter may simply rely on the candidate's party affiliation as a cue. This works better in Europe than in America, but it still works reasonably well. Endorsements are another useful shortcut. A thumbs-up for a candidate from the Christian Coalition or Ralph Nader or the National Association for the Advancement of Colored People or the American Association of Retired Persons frequently provides enough information to enable one to cast a reasonable vote.

Second, as political scientist Milton Lodge points out, people often process information on the fly, without retaining details in memory. If you watch a debate on TV—and 46 million did watch the first presidential debate between President Bill Clinton and Robert Dole in 1996—you may learn enough about the candidates' ideas and personal styles to come to a judgment about each one. A month later, on election day, you may not be able to answer a pollster's detailed questions about where they stood on the issues, but you will remember which one you liked best—and that is enough information to let you vote intelligently.

The realism of the political heuristics school is an indispensable corrective to unwarranted bashing of the general public. Americans are not the political dolts they sometimes seem to be. Still, the political heuristics approach has a potentially fatal flaw: It subtly substitutes *voting* for *citizenship*. Cognitive shortcuts have their place, but what if a citizen wants to persuade someone else to vote for his or her chosen candidate? What may be sufficient in the voting booth is inadequate in the wider world of the democratic process: discussion, deliberation, and persuasion. It is possible to vote and still be disenfranchised.

Yet another response to the riddle of voter ignorance takes its cue from the Founders and other 18th-century political thinkers who emphasized the importance of a morally virtuous citizenry. Effective democracy, in this view, depends more on the "democratic character" of citizens than on their aptitude for quiz show knowledge of political facts. Character, in this sense, is demonstrated all the time in everyday life, not in the voting booth every two years. From Amitai Etzioni, William Galston, and Michael Sandel on the liberal side of the political spectrum to William J. Bennett and James Q. Wilson on the conservative side, these writers emphasize the importance of what Alexis de Tocqueville called "habits of the heart." These theorists, along with politicians of every stripe, point to the importance of civil society as a foundation of democracy. They emphasize instilling moral virtue through families and civic participation through churches and other voluntary associations; they stress the necessity for civility and democratic behavior in daily life. They would not deny that it is important for citizens to be informed, but neither would they put information at the center of their vision of what makes democracy tick.

Brown University's Nancy Rosenblum, for example, lists two essential traits of democratic character. "Easy spontaneity" is the disposition to treat others identically, without deference, and with an easy grace. This capacity to act as if many social differences are of no account in public settings is one of the things that make democracy happen on the streets. This is the disposition that foreign visitors have regularly labeled "American" for 200 years, at least since 1818, when the British reformer and journalist William Cobbett remarked upon Americans' "universal civility." Tocqueville observed in 1840 that strangers in America who meet "find neither danger nor advantage in telling each other freely what they think. Meeting by chance, they neither seek nor avoid each other. Their manner is therefore natural, frank, and open."

Rosenblum's second trait is "speaking up," which she describes as "a willingness to respond at least minimally to ordinary injustice." This does not involve anything so impressive as organizing a demonstration, but something more like objecting when an adult cuts ahead of a kid in a line at a movie theater, or politely rebuking a coworker who slurs a racial or religious group. It is hard to define "speaking up" precisely, but we all recognize it, without necessarily giving it the honor it deserves as an element of self-government.

We need not necessarily accept Rosenblum's chosen pair of moral virtues. Indeed a Japanese or Swedish democrat might object that they look suspiciously like distinctively American traits rather than distinctively democratic ones. They almost evoke Huckleberry Finn. But turning our attention to democratic character reminds us that being well informed is just one of the requirements of democratic citizenship.

The Founding Fathers were certainly more concerned about instilling moral virtues than disseminating information about candidates and issues. Although they valued civic engagement more than their contemporaries in Europe did, and cared enough about promoting the wide circulation of ideas to establish a post office and adopt the First Amendment, they were ambivalent about, even suspicious of, a politically savvy populace. They did not urge voters to "know the issues"; at most they hoped that voters would choose wise and prudent legislators to consider issues on their behalf. On the one hand, they agreed that "the diffusion of knowledge is productive of virtue, and the best security for our civil rights," as a North Carolina congressman put it in 1792. On the other hand, as George Washington cautioned, "however necessary it may be to keep a watchful eye over public servants and public measures, yet there ought to be limits to it, for suspicions unfounded and jealousies too lively are irritating to honest feelings, and oftentimes are productive of more evil than good."

If men were angels, well and good—but they were not, and few of the Founders were as extravagant as Benjamin Rush in his rather scary vision of an education that would "convert men into republican machines." In theory, many shared Rush's emphasis on education; in practice, the states made little provision for public schooling in the early years of the Republic. Where schools did develop, they were defended more as tutors of obedience and organs of national unity than as means to create a watchful citizenry. The Founders placed trust less in education than in a political system designed to insulate decision making in the legislatures from the direct influence of the emotional, fractious, and too easily swayed electorate.

All of these arguments—about America's political environment, the value of political heuristics, and civil society—do not add up to a prescription for resignation or complacency about civic education. Nothing I have said suggests that the League of Women Voters should shut its doors or that newspaper editors should stop puffing politics on page one. People may be able to vote intelligently with very little information—even well-educated people do exactly that on most of the ballot issues they face—but democratic citizenship means more than voting. It means discussing and debating the questions before the political community—and sometimes raising new questions. Without a framework of information in which to place them, it is hard to understand even the simple slogans and catchwords of the day. People with scant political knowledge, as research by political scientists Samuel Popkin and Michael Dimock suggests, have more difficulty than others in perceiving differences between candidates and parties. Ignorance also tends to breed more ignorance; it inhibits people from venturing into situations that make them feel uncomfortable or inadequate, from the voting booth to the community forum to the town hall.

What is to be done? First, it is important to put the problem in perspective. American political ignorance is not growing worse. There is even an "up" side to Americans' relative indifference to political and historical facts: their characteristic openness to experiment, their pragmatic willingness to judge ideas and practices by their results rather than their pedigree.

Second, it pays to examine more closely the ways in which people do get measurably more knowledgeable. One of the greatest changes Delli Carpini and Keeter found in their study, for example, was in the percentage of Americans who could identify the first 10 amendments to the Constitution as the Bill of Rights. In 1954, the year the U.S. Supreme Court declared school segregation unconstitutional in *Brown v. Board of Education*, only 31 percent of Americans could do so. In 1989, the number had moved up to 46 percent.

Why the change? I think the answer is clear: The civil rights movement, along with the rights-oriented Warren Court, helped bring rights to the forefront of the American political agenda and thus to public consciousness. Because they dominated the political agenda, rights became a familiar topic in the press and on TV dramas, sitcoms, and talk shows, also finding their way into school curricula and textbooks. Political change, this experience shows, can influence public knowledge.

This is not to say that only a social revolution can bring about such an improvement. A lot of revolutions are small, one person at a time, one classroom at a time. But it does mean that there is no magic bullet. Indeed, imparting political knowledge has only become more difficult as the dimensions of what is considered political have expanded into what were once nonpolitical domains (such as gender relations and tobacco use), as one historical narrative has become many, each of them contentious, and as the relatively simple framework of world politics (the Cold War) has disappeared.

In this world, the ability to name the three branches of government or describe the New Deal does not make a citizen, but it is at least a token of membership in a society dedicated to the ideal of self-government. Civic education is an imperative we must pursue with the full recognition that a high level of ignorance is likely to prevail—even if that fact does not flatter our faith in rationalism, our pleasure in moralizing, or our confidence in reform.

---

*There is no happy explanation for low voter turnout. "Voter fatigue" is not as silly an explanation as it may seem: Americans have more frequent elections for more offices than any other democracy. It is also true that the more-or-less steady drop in turnout starting in about 1960 coincided with the beginning of a broad expansion of nonelectoral politics that may have drained political energies away from the polling places: the civil rights movement, the antiwar demonstrations of the Vietnam years, the women's movement, and the emergence of the religious Right. The decline in turnout may signify in part that Americans are disengaged from public life, but it may also suggest that they judge electoral politics to be disengaged from public issues that deeply concern them.

MICHAEL SCHUDSON, *a professor of communication and adjunct professor of sociology at the University of California, San Diego, is the author of several books on the media and, most recently,* The Good Citizen: A History of American Civic Life *(1998).*

From *The Wilson Quarterly*, Spring 2000, pp. 16-22. © 2000 by Michael Schudson. Reprinted by permission.

The Black-White Wealth Gap

NET WORTH, MORE THAN ANY OTHER STATISTIC, SHOWS THE DEPTH OF RACIAL INEQUALITY

DALTON CONLEY

In all the discussions about the Bush tax cut, it seems no one has mentioned the issue of race. This is too bad, since more than any "diverse" Cabinet appointment, more than executive changes in affirmative action regulations, indeed more than any explicitly race-based policy, the $1.6 trillion tax reduction currently on the table will affect prospects for racial equality—for the worse. While African-Americans will be disproportionately left out of the income tax bonanza, the most troubling aspect of Bush's proposal, from the point of view of racial equity, lies in the repeal of the estate tax.

The federal estate tax, which has been in place since 1916, affects only the richest 1.4 percent of the deceased. As the law currently stands, the first $675,000 of net estate value is exempt from tax for individuals ($1.35 million for couples). Because of a 1997 change in the law, this exemption amount will rise steadily until it reaches $1 million for individuals ($2 million for couples) in 2006. Exemptions are even higher for businesses and farms. Since the number of African-Americans who would benefit is infinitesimally small, Bush's goal of eliminating the tax altogether would exacerbate the already growing wealth gap between blacks and whites.

In fact, if there is one statistic that captures the persistence of racial inequality in the United States, it is net worth. (If you want to know your net worth, all you have to do is add up everything you own and subtract from this figure your total amount of outstanding debt.) When we do this for white and minority households across America, incredible differences emerge: Overall, the typical white family enjoys a net worth that is more than seven times that of its black counterpart. (Latinos—a very diverse group—overall fare slightly better than African-Americans but still fall far short of whites.)

This "equity inequity," which has grown in the decades since the civil rights triumphs of the sixties, cannot be explained by income differences alone. That is, while African-Americans do earn less than whites, asset gaps remain large even when we compare black and white families at the same income levels. For instance, at the lower end of the economic spectrum (incomes less than $15,000 per year), the median African-American family has a net worth of zero, while the equivalent white family's net worth is $10,000. Likewise, among the often-heralded new black middle class, the typical white family earning $40,000 per year enjoys a nest egg of around $80,000; its African-American counterpart has less than half that amount. Among the wealthiest Americans, the story is much the same: Oprah Winfrey and Robert L. Johnson (founder of Black Entertainment Television) are the only African-Americans on the Forbes annual list of the 400 richest people in the United States, and they are both on the lower end of the list.

This racial wealth gap accounts for many of the racial differences in socioeconomic achievement that have persisted in the post-civil rights era. When we compare black and white families who have the same income and net worth, we find that African-American kids are more likely to graduate from high school than whites and are just as likely to complete college. And when we compare individuals who grew up in families with the same economic resources—income and wealth—we find that the wage gap between blacks and whites disappears and that African-Americans are just as likely as Anglos to be working full time. But among the poor, a lack of assets makes blacks more likely to rely on welfare.

Stacey Jones, an African-American woman with a graduate degree and a solidly middle-class job, describes a common bind for minority parents: "I am, in effect, priced out of homebuying in good school districts," she says. "This, in turn, makes it difficult for me to pay more for housing, since I am spending a good deal of my income on education for my children." For much of the growing black middle class, a lack of assets means living from paycheck to paycheck, being trapped in a job or a neighborhood that is less beneficial in the long run, or not being able to send one's kids to top colleges. Income provides for day-to-day, week-to-week expenses; wealth is the stuff that upward mobility is made of. Equality of opportunity cannot be achieved under unequal conditions (such as differential access to wealth). Indeed, whether the parents enjoy the American dream of the house, the car and the 401(k) is one of the best predictors of whether a child will have a chance to achieve the same.

For the minority poor, the situation is even more precarious. The $10,000 in equity that impoverished white families enjoy certainly comes in handy when the inevitable economic downturn puts a family member out of work or when a medical crisis strikes. With no asset cushion to speak of, minorities are much more quickly devastated by such a blow.

Equity inequity is, in part, the result of the head start that whites have enjoyed in accumulating and passing on assets. Whites not only earn more now, they have always earned more than African-Americans—a lot more. Wealth differences, in turn, feed off these long-term income differences. Some researchers estimate that up to 80 percent of lifetime wealth accumulation results from gifts in one form or another from past generations of relatives. These gifts can range from the down payment on a first home, to a free college education, to a bequest upon the death of a parent. Over the long run, small initial differences in wealth holdings multiply.

There have also been institutional restraints on black property accumulation. After emancipation, blacks were promised "forty acres and a mule" by the Freedmen's Bureau. Yet the lion's share of confiscated plantations went to white Northerners, who hired the former slaves to cultivate them, inaugurating the system of sharecropping that would keep blacks asset-poor for many decades. For blacks who tried to escape sharecropping, there were formidable obstacles as well. In many Southern states, African-Americans who tried to set up their own businesses were stopped by "black codes" that required African-Americans (but not whites) to pay exorbitant licensing fees. Similarly, if former slaves tried to go west with the promise of free land by virtue of the Homestead Act, they were likely to find that their claim to title was not legally enforceable in some areas.

In the twentieth century, barriers to black property accumulation remained formidable. The Home Owners' Loan Corporation helped many white homeowners avoid default during the Depression, but not black homeowners—in fact, it was this agency that instituted the technique of redlining, in which those neighborhoods deemed high-risk would be assigned a red—no loan—rating. Black neighborhoods invariably received this designation, a practice that private banks adopted, too. Meanwhile, Social Security (originally Old Age Insurance) excluded most black workers, since it exempted the agricultural and service sectors. The result was that a greater proportion of black assets had to be spent on sup-

porting elderly family members, and less could be passed on to the next generation.

Such discrimination persisted after the Depression. The Federal Housing Authority, established in 1937, in combination with the Veterans Administration's home-lending program, which was part of the Servicemen's Readjustment Act of 1944, made homeownership possible for millions of Americans after World War II by underwriting low-interest, long-term loans for first-time homebuyers. But African-Americans were systematically shut out of participation in these programs because loans were channeled to suburbs and away from central cities, where blacks largely resided.

> *Occasional efforts have been made to promote minority asset accumulation, but they have not amounted to much.*

Since the sixties, occasional efforts have been made to promote minority asset accumulation, but they have not amounted to much. In the wake of the urban unrest of the late sixties, there was much talk of fostering black capitalism, mainly through educational programs that aimed to bolster business skills and entrepreneurial spirit. This approach was eclipsed in the seventies by community development corporations (CDCs), which have sought to attract capital to economically depressed minority neighborhoods. Today, CDCs and community development banks, some of which are part of the "enterprise" or "empowerment" zones championed by Jack Kemp and implemented under former President Bill Clinton, continue to promote asset accumulation through inner-city investment.

A more radical policy alternative has called for reparations to black Americans. Espoused by black separatist organizations in the sixties, the argument for reparations was refined during the seventies. One researcher applied compound interest on 1790-1860 slave prices, calculated since the slavery era. The figure he came up with matched what the Republic of New Africa (RNA), a prominent separatist group, was asking for: between a half-trillion and a trillion dollars back in the early 1970s. Today Randall Robinson, co-founder and president of TransAfrica, and others are arguing for reparations through comprehensive social programs [see Randall Robinson, "America's Debt to Blacks," March 13, 2000].

Redlining was outlawed by the 1977 Community Reinvestment Act, although this law was weakened by Congress in 1999. In any case, simply providing African-Americans with the opportunity—or even the means—to become homeowners will not be enough. The problem is that homes in black neighborhoods don't accrue value at the same rate as those in mostly white areas. Property has the particular attribute of quantifying the social value of ideas or objects. A diamond or a misprinted stamp or a Van Gogh has no inherent productive value. Its price reflects only the value accorded to it in the marketplace. In this vein, when a neighborhood's housing values precipitately decline as the proportion of black residents rises, the price changes provide a record of the social value of "blackness."

The devaluation of black neighborhoods is partially a result of white fears of a decline in property values and the "white flight" that ensues. It is in the economic interest of white homeowners to sell off when they anticipate that the neighborhood has reached a racial "tipping point," for fear that others will make the same calculation and sell off first, causing their property to lose value. In other words, there is a causal loop: As long as black neighborhoods are devalued, and whites are a majority and have the ability to decide where they will live, they will have an economic incentive to flee integrated neighborhoods, thus perpetuating the vicious circle.

In this way, blacks and whites are both trapped into reproducing current residential patterns. Even if African-Americans were allowed equal access to the homebuying market and if interest rates were prescribed by law to be the same for blacks and whites, African-Americans would still be at a disadvantage in terms of housing equity, since whites could flee, depressing values for those who remain. Remedies for this situation are difficult to come by. Politically, any policy limiting the market (restricting the ability of white homeowners to sell, for instance) would likely face fierce resistance, since it would fly in the face of the notion of individual choice central to American ideology.

One solution would be to provide "integration insurance." This form of insurance would protect property owners from any rundown in prices that results from a rash in selling as a neighborhood tips from white to black.

With this policy in place, the economic incentive to pull out when a neighborhood starts to integrate would be eliminated. The difficulty lies in the details, of course, especially the task of factoring out changes in prices that may result from other forces.

Other policy options to promote wealth equity include a national wealth tax: At the end of each calendar or fiscal year, each individual would use a checklist to assess his assets and liabilities and would be required to pay the government a certain percentage of that net worth if it exceeded a certain deduction. These funds would be redistributed to the asset-poor through dollar-for-dollar government matching funds, as has been proposed in the Savings for Working Families Act of 2001. Removing the asset restrictions currently built into the welfare system is another good idea: If welfare recipients were able to save without being penalized for their asset accumulation, they would be less dependent on public assistance. Finally, the creation of Individual Development Accounts could foster savings among the asset-poor through matching funds provided by the government through a progressive, refundable tax credit. The Bush tax plan, by contrast, helps (predominantly white) millionaires. If tax credits and other asset-encouraging programs were instead to target individuals and communities that are both income- and asset-deprived, they would inevitably favor minorities while being ostensibly color-blind. Sixty-four years ago, W.E.B. Du Bois claimed that if freed slaves had been provided with the forty acres and a mule they had been promised, it would have made for the basis of a real democracy. He is still right today.

Dalton Conley, director of the Center for Advanced Social Science Research, is associate professor of sociology at New York University and the author of Honky *and* Being Black, Living in the Red: Race, Wealth and Social Policy in America *(California).*

DON'T TREAT INNOCENT PEOPLE LIKE CRIMINALS

Stuart Taylor Jr.

The Bush Justice Department's focus on preventing terrorist acts rather than solving past crimes is justified by the magnitude of the threat. It's unfortunate but understandable that by throwing a broad net to catch people who *might possibly* be terrorists, the government has arrested and detained hundreds of Middle Eastern men on the basis of unconfirmed suspicions that—in the vast majority of cases—have been or seem likely to be dispelled. What's unfortunate and unforgivable is the mounting evidence that many of these men have been treated badly or abusively while detained, even after being cleared of involvement in terrorism. Such mistreatment will not win the hearts and minds of potential informers, and it will ultimately prove unhelpful to the war on terrorism.

Anglo-American jurisprudence has for centuries aimed at finding and prosecuting those responsible for completed crimes, and has largely shunned "preventive detention," or locking up unconvicted suspects who might be dangerous. "Imprisonment to protect society from predicted but unconsummated offenses," Justice Robert Jackson wrote in 1950 in *Williamson v. United States* "is... unprecedented in this country and... fraught with danger of excesses and injustice." But since September 11, Attorney General John D. Ashcroft has explicitly embraced a preventive-detention approach to counterterrorism. His goal is to disrupt terrorist cells by locking up hundreds of men of Middle Eastern descent, based on unconfirmed scraps of information suggesting their possible links to terrorism.

In most cases, this scanty evidence falls far short of the "probable cause" traditionally required to charge a suspect with a crime and to lock him up if he can't meet bail. So the Administration has invoked alleged immigration law violations and minor criminal charges as technical grounds for locking up people who could not be detained based on mere suspicions of terrorist links and would not be detained but for those suspicions. "Let the terrorists among us be warned," Ashcroft declared on October 25, "If you overstay your visas even by one day, we will arrest you. If you violate a local law, we will... work to

make sure that you are put in jail and... kept in custody as long as possible."

In effect, Ashcroft has supplemented the traditional presumption that suspects are innocent until proven guilty with a new presumption that possible terrorists should be detained until proven harmless—until, in the words of INS spokesman Russ Bergeron, "it has been absolutely ascertained with as much certainty as humanly possible that the individual is not linked... to terrorism."

OFFICIALS SHOULD TREAT DETENTIONS AS A REGRETTABLE BUT NECESSARY EVIL. INSTEAD, THEY'RE TREATING DETAINEES LIKE TERRORISTS.

So far, so good. While many civil-libertarian critics see this detain-until-proven-harmless approach as a dangerous betrayal of the presumption of innocence, I see it as a dangerous but necessary expedient to deal with unprecedented threats. As Harvard Law Professor Laurence Tribe has written, "The old adage that it is better to free 100 guilty men than to imprison one innocent describes a calculus that our Constitution—which is no suicide pact—does not impose on government when the 100 who are freed belong to terrorist cells that slaughter innocent civilians, and may well have access to chemical, biological, or nuclear weapons."

The problem is that—far from treating detentions as a regrettable but necessary evil—officials from Ashcroft on down appear to be gratuitously treating the detainees like terrorists. Although little is publicly known about most of the them, the media have carried horror stories told by more than a dozen people who plausibly claim that officials arrested them unceremoniously, interrogated them rudely and even abusively, limited their access to families and lawyers severely, threw them into jails where guards and other prisoners taunted and (in at least one case) badly beat them, kept them behind bars long after abandoning any claim that they were terrorists, and offered those released little explanation, no apologies, and no compensation.

Consider the case of Ali al-Maqtari, a teacher of French from Yemen who was jailed for almost eight weeks based on a groundless suspicion of terrorist links and immigration charges such as overstaying his visa while seeking resident status, for which he apparently qualified based on his June 1 marriage to his wife Tiffinay, a U.S. citizen. In Senate Judiciary Committee testimony on December 4, al-Maqtari described an ordeal that started on September 15, when he and his wife drove up to the gate of the Army base at Fort Campbell, Ky., so that she could report for duty as a new recruit. Federal agents descended upon them, separated them, and interrogated them—"wild and full of anger," al-Maqtari recalled—for more than 12 hours. The agents accused him falsely of abusing his wife and conspiring with terrorists from Russia, claimed to have evidence that turned out to be nonexistent, and threatened him with beatings. Three days later, the agents, after giving him and his wife polygraph tests, told al-Maqtari that they now believed him and that he would probably be released the next day, al-Maqtari testified. Instead, he was locked up for another seven weeks in two jails in Tennessee, housed with hardened criminals, taunted by a guard, and limited to one phone call a week. Meanwhile, his wife, concerned that the Army might send her overseas while her husband was still in jail and that people seemed to mistrust her, gave up her hoped-for Army career and took a voluntary discharge. (A senior Justice Department official declined to comment when asked whether al-Maqtari's story was true.)

The government may be justified in subjecting people such as al-Maqtari to the burden of detention for a few days, pending investigation. But shouldn't it limit the damage by treating them with courtesy and housing them in comfortable surroundings away from hardened criminals? Or at least apologize to them after determining that they are not terrorists? "No," Ashcroft told *Newsweek* in an interview. "The United States of America does not apologize to law violators." Not even, it appears to those charged with no more than overstaying their visas by a day.

What we have here is a refusal to face the new preventive-detention policy's logical corollary: Most of these detainees have done nothing wrong enough to justify treating them like criminals. It is bad enough (if all too common) to mistreat suspects who have been arrested on the traditional basis of "probable cause" to believe that they have committed serious crimes. It is outrageous to treat as criminals and terrorists people who have been locked up based on mere suspicions that, as officials have reason to know, will in most cases turn out to be mistaken.

The pretense of shunning all politically incorrect forms of profiling—even while Ashcroft seeks to interview all of the 5,000 men between the ages of 18 and 33 who entered this country after January 1, 2000 with passports from certain Middle Eastern and other Muslim countries—makes matters worse. The Justice Department's claim that these men "were not selected in order to single out a particular ethnic or religious group" may be true in a literal sense: The profile appears to be based on national origin, not ethnicity or religion as such. (It does not appear to include native-born Arab-American Muslims, for example.) But most people do not distinguish between these forms of profiling. And Ashcroft has avoided acknowledging the national-origin profiling at the heart of his enforcement policy. This obfuscation of the real (and legitimate, if politically awkward) reason for locking up Middle Eastern "law violators" who would be neither detained nor suspected of terrorism were they European, or Mexican, or Chinese increases the temptation for Ashcroft's subordinates to come up with something to pin on the detainees and to exaggerate the seriousness of their alleged violations.

And even the smallest of immigration or criminal charges, once filed and invoked to justify detention, tend to take on a life of their own. "A large number of those still in detention," reports *The New York Times*, "are simply fighting the garden-variety criminal and immigration charges that the government used to arrest them in the first place. The FBI has lost interest in them as possible terrorists, but local authorities and immigration officials feel obliged to continue their pursuit of the original charges, which often resulted from tips or traffic stops."

Old habits die hard. It would take a forceful and sustained push by the Attorney General to mitigate his new preventive-detention policy's dangers by breaking rank-and-file prosecutors, agents, and jail guards of their habit of assuming that "if a person is innocent of a crime, then he is not a suspect," in the memorable phrase of former Attorney General Edwin Meese III. So far, Ashcroft doesn't even seem to be trying.

Speech Isn't Cheap

WENDY KAMINER

Despite the materialism that defines American culture and our reverence for financial success, a suspicion that money really is the root of all evil retains its appeal, especially among progressives. The association of wealth with corruption is particularly clear in debates about campaign finance reform. Reformers are self-proclaimed proponents of "clean elections"; their opponents are presumed to favor dirty politics. Even centrist politicians eager to occupy the moral high ground (along with the occasional conservative like John McCain) fulminate against "big money" and "special interests."

Bribery is an especially sturdy political tradition.

Of course, the view that political contributions exert undue influence on policy is not exactly unfounded. Bribery, or what one Tammany Hall figure called "illegal graft" (as opposed to "honest graft"), is an especially sturdy political tradition. Voters, as well as politicians, are subject to being bought (however unwittingly) by the political ads and image-making machines that contributions finance. But fear and loathing of concentrated wealth does sometimes blind "clean election" advocates to the complexities of campaign regulations and the role of money in politics.

Nothing seems to irritate reformers more than the assertion that limits on money—whether campaign contributions or expenditures—are the equivalent of limits on speech. Money isn't speech; it's property, Supreme Court Justice Stevens declared in a recent case upholding a Missouri law limiting campaign contributions. His insistence that money isn't speech has visceral appeal; it seems so egalitarian, so democratic. But it's also wishful thinking.

It's an American fact of life that money facilitates the exercise of rights.

Money isn't speech? Try telling that to the folks at National Public Radio the next time they beg you for donations to keep their programming on the air. Money makes speech possible. *The American Prospect* now publishes biweekly, thanks to the generous support of wealthy benefactors. If Congress passed a law limiting the amount of money we could spend annually on books or newspapers, we would probably not say, "Never mind. Money isn't speech."

In our society, money facilitates the exercise of rights. Children who attend schools in poor districts don't receive equal educations unless schools throughout the state are equitably funded. Poor women don't exercise abortion rights if they can't afford abortions, unless Medicaid provides funding. Often, people need public subsidies to achieve some measure of equality, which is why progressives advocate expanding our notions of individual rights so that they protect basic economic needs, like housing or health care.

Like it or not, this relationship between money and the enjoyment of rights is an American fact of life, and as a practical matter (absent a revolution), it is essentially immutable. It is an argument for public financing of campaigns designed to subsidize candidates who do not have personal fortunes or major party support, and an argument against limits on contributions and expenditures.

When the government restricts our ability to spend money, it restricts our ability to speak. That fact doesn't end debates about campaign finance reform, but it does complicate them. They become debates about balancing individual rights (free speech) with other social goods that some presume will follow from reform—expanded access to the electoral process and increased public faith in it.

On balance, the damage done to First Amendment rights seems much greater than the promised benefits of reform proposals to limit the flow of money in and out of campaigns. Expanded access can be facilitated by public financing systems that establish a financial floor, but not a ceiling, for candidates. (Public subsidies generally provide minimum support for poor people without dictating maximum expenditures for the rich.) The promise of increased faith in the system is quite speculative. Advocates of reform claim that campaign finance abuses cause voter apathy; the claim is plausible, but I've never seen much evidence to support it. The counterclaim that these abuses have little effect on voter participation seems equally plausible. Politics has long been regarded as a scoundrel's game. Regardless of campaign finance laws, people seem to expect a certain amount of thievery from elected officials. At the same time, they manage to put their faith in quite a few.

The harms of reform to free speech (and political discourse), however, are clear. Existing restrictions on campaign contributions have already created more problems than they have solved. As almost everyone knows, federal reforms passed in 1974 limited both campaign contributions and expenditures. The Supreme Court struck down the limits on expenditures but upheld the limits on contributions. This ruling greatly advantaged incumbents, who don't need to buy as much speech as insurgents. In the 1996 congressional election, for example, all incumbents who spent less than half a million dollars were re-elected, while only 3 percent of all challengers who spent less than half a million dollars succeeded in knocking off an incumbent.

Still, the Supreme Court remains somewhat blindly sympathetic to reform efforts. It recently upheld limits on contributions, in a case that clearly demonstrated their dangers. *Nixon v. Shrink Missouri Government PAC*, which was decided in January, involved a challenge to Missouri's campaign limits by a third-party candidate who was substantially disadvantaged by the cap on individual contributions. Major party candidates had much greater visibility and access to soft money—money contributed to the parties ostensibly for party-building purposes. The law provides that soft money can be used for issue advocacy, not in support of particular candidates, but in this respect, the law is practically unenforceable. In political campaigns, it's not always possible to distinguish between advocating for issues and advocating for candidates.

Reformers propose solving access problems for insurgents by restricting soft money (the market for which was created by the 1974 reforms). But we know what new problems will follow from soft-money restrictions. Dissatisfied with the disclosure requirements that accompany contributions to political parties, wealthy contributors are already forming their own not-for-profit issue advocacy groups, which are not required to disclose their donors. These are stealth groups whose political interests or agendas aren't clear, which operate under vague names like Americans United for Good Things, and groups like Republicans for Clean Air (organized by a wealthy Bush ally, it ran anti-McCain ads in New York prior to the Republican primary).

As Supreme Court Justice Kennedy observed in his dissent in *Nixon v. Shrink*, limits on campaign contributions have greatly increased incentives for a new kind of "covert" political speech. Campaign finance reform "forced a substantial amount of speech underground."

Of course, covert speech can be made overt with effective disclosure requirements. Prohibiting anonymous contributions to political parties or advocacy groups does raise First Amendment concerns: Anonymity is an important element of free speech. On balance, however, the danger of a secret campaign finance system outweighs the danger of restricting the right to speak anonymously through large political contributions.

But reformers are not necessarily content with stringent disclosure requirements. Many want to limit independent expenditures and to prohibit issue advocacy groups from advertising within 30 or 60 days of an election. A provision limiting independent expenditures was originally included in the McCain-Feingold bill and in the Massachusetts Clean Elections law. It was dropped from the final proposals, partly because it cut the heart out of individual rights to political speech. Imagine being prohibited by the government from buying television time or taking out an ad in your local newspaper arguing for or against particular public policies or criticizing particular candidates a month or two before an election, when people are actually paying attention.

This is the dilemma for reformers: If they limit independent expenditures, they deprive private citizens of First Amendment rights during political campaigns; if they don't, they cannot hope to limit effectively the influence of "big money" on elections.

Now imagine that we have accepted restrictions on independent expenditures as necessary evils of campaign reform. Who would be left to speak? Mort Zuckerman could write an editorial in the *New York Daily News* the week before the New York Senate election, endorsing Rick Lazio. But the government would prohibit you and the public interest groups you support from buying an ad in his paper criticizing Lazio and the policies of the Republican Congress. It's not surprising that *The New York Times* supports restrictions on fundraising by independent groups. Taken to its logical extreme, campaign finance reform will give media moguls, pundits, and elected officials exclusive rights to effective political speech in the crucial month or two before an election. I doubt that will open up our democracy in ways that reformers have in mind.

Reprinted with permission from *The American Prospect*, Vol. 11, Issue 17, July 31, 2000, pp. 38-39.

INSURANCE AGAINST THE ONCE UNTHINKABLE

BY WILLIAM SCHNEIDER

Insurance agents are pros at getting people to contemplate the unthinkable. Now, in the aftermath of September 11, one member of Congress has assumed the role of insurance agent for the Republic. "These are questions that were once unthinkable," Rep. Brian Baird, D-Wash., said in an interview last week. "They certainly could not have been contemplated by the Founders of our great country."

Remember that one of the four airplanes hijacked on the morning of September 11 crashed in Pennsylvania before it could hit its target, which may have been the U.S. Capitol. What if the Capitol had been destroyed and, with it, much of the membership of Congress? Nine of the 10 top leaders of the House and Senate were in the Capitol that morning.

"What could happen? How could we prepare for it?" Baird asks. "And how do we clarify exactly what would be done so that, if the American people were to turn on CNN and see that the Capitol had been hit and many members of the House and Senate had been killed, we would have a clear-cut answer for them that says, 'Your constitutional democratic Republic will persevere. These are the steps that will be taken to replace the members and rebuild the government.' "

It sounds like the stuff of fiction. In fact, in two of his novels, Tom Clancy imagined a hijacked airliner crashing into the Capitol during a presidential State of the Union address.

There is a line of succession to the presidency. But what about Congress's line of succession? That's not a problem in the Senate. The Constitution allows governors to "make temporary appointments until the people fill the vacancies by election." In every state except Oregon, governors have the power to appoint new Senators immediately.

However, the Constitution requires that House vacancies be filled by special elections. No House member has ever served without being elected by the people. "We're very proud of that," Baird says. But special elections usually take three to six months to organize—with each state determining the timing and procedure for those elections.

REP. BRIAN BAIRD WANTS NATION PREPARED IF DISASTER CLAIMS ONE-QUARTER OF THE U.S. HOUSE.

Could the President simply govern without Congress? The Constitution is clear: No. As Baird points out, "There is no provision that authorizes the President to appropriate funds, unilaterally declare war, or choose a vice presidential [replacement] without [congressional] confirmation. The Framers wanted it that way."

Most rank-and-file House members were not in the Capitol building on the morning of September 11. Suppose they had been. Suppose an attack occurred during a joint session of Congress, such as the one President Bush addressed on September 20. How many House members would have to survive an attack to constitute a quorum?

The House rules say a quorum consists of "a majority of those members chosen, sworn, and living." So a handful of surviving House members, totally unrepresentative of the country, could take power and potentially create a good deal of mischief with the full authority of the Constitution, pending elections to replenish their ranks.

Baird's insurance policy aims to prevent that from happening. "What I've proposed is this," the Congressman says. "If a quarter or more of the membership of the House is killed or disabled and can't function, then the governors of those states would be authorized to appoint replacement members who would serve during a 90-day period, which would give us time for direct elections to take place."

In order to do that, Congress would have to pass and the states would have to ratify a 28th amendment to the Constitution. Amending the Constitution is no small matter. An amendment must be approved by two-thirds of both houses of Congress and then ratified by three-quarters of the state legislatures.

Baird decided not to complicate the issue by defining what would constitute "incapacitation" of a House member. "Believe it or not," he points out, "there are no provisions in the House rules or in the Constitution for removing a member of the House due to disability. Indeed, members have served in the House who were comatose for extended periods of time." Baird's amendment leaves the definition of "incapacitation" to be resolved by enforcement legislation and by the courts.

His amendment also does not mention political parties. That is in deference to the Constitution itself, which has never included any reference to parties. His proposed amendment has more than 40 co-sponsors, who include both Democrats and Republicans. Why doesn't it have more? Debating such a measure carries the risk of further frightening voters and making Congress appear panicky.

Inaction carries a different kind of risk: The unthinkable could happen—again. "If fate is unkind to us," Baird says, "history will judge us on how well we... prepared our nation to deal with the worst-case scenario." It's a scenario that Congress and the Republic may have only narrowly escaped—this time.

Baird recommends caution. He is urging Congress to pass his amendment now, but he notes that the states may choose to delay adoption in order to give the matter careful deliberation. But if the measure has passed Congress, the states would have an amendment in place that they could ratify quickly, if it is ever needed.

Overruling the Court

The Supreme Court has been interpreting civil rights
laws narrowly. It's time for Congress to intervene.

BY LEON FRIEDMAN

ONE OF THE MYTHS OF OUR POLITICAL
system is that the Supreme Court has the
last word on the scope and meaning of federal law. But time and time again, Congress has shown its dissatisfaction with Supreme Court interpretations of laws it
passes—by amending or re-enacting the
legislation to clarify its original intent and
overrule a contrary Court construction.

The Supreme Court often insists that
Congress cannot really "overrule" its decisions on what a law means: The justices'
interpretation has to be correct since the
Constitution gives final say to the highest
court in the land. But Congress certainly
has the power to pass a new or revised law
that "changes" or "reverses" the meaning
or scope of the law as interpreted by the
Court, and the legislative history of the
new law usually states that it was intended
to "overrule" a specific Court decision

Often the reversal is in highly technical
areas, such as the statute of limitations in
securities-fraud cases, the jurisdiction of
tribal courts on Indian reservations, or the
power of state courts to order denaturaliza-
tion of citizens. But in the last 20 years, a
main target of congressional "overruling"
has been the Supreme Court's decisions in
the area of civil rights

In 1982, for example, Congress
amended the Voting Rights Act of 1965 to
overrule a narrow Supreme Court holding
in *Mobile v. Bolden*, a 1980 decision that
addressed whether intentional discrimination must be shown before the act could be
invoked. In 1988, Congress overruled another Supreme Court decision (in the 1984
case *Grove City College v. Bell*) by passing
the Civil Rights Restoration Act, which
broadened the coverage of Title VI of the

Civil Rights Act of 1964. The legislative
history of that law specifically recited that
"certain aspects of recent decisions and
opinions of the Supreme Court have unduly narrowed or cast doubt upon" a number of federal civil rights statutes and that
"legislative action is necessary to restore
the prior consistent and long-standing executive branch interpretations" of those
laws.

And in 1991, Congress passed a broad,
new Civil Rights Act that specifically reversed no fewer than five Supreme Court
cases decided in 1989—decisions that severely restricted and limited workers'
rights under federal antidiscrimination
laws. Led by Massachusetts Democrat Edward Kennedy in the Senate and New York
Republican Hamilton Fish, Jr., in the
House, Congress acted to undo those rulings, as well as make other changes to federal law that strengthened the weapons
available to workers against discrimination. Despite partisan contention over the
language of certain provisions (which led
to last-minute-compromise language),
President George Bush the elder supported
the changes. The new law recited in its pre-
amble that its purpose was "to respond to
recent decisions of the Supreme Court by
expanding the scope of relevant civil rights
statutes in order to provide adequate protection to victims of discrimination."

GIVEN THE CURRENT SUPREME
Court's track record in civil rights cases,
there can be no doubt that congressional
remediation is again necessary. In a series
of cases over the past two years, the Court
has been giving narrow readings to various

federal civil rights laws. And once again,
an attentive Congress can and should overrule the Court's decisions if the legislators
care about fairness in the operation of government and in the workplace. The recent
cases were decided by identical 5–4 votes:
Three conservative justices (William
Rehnquist, Antonin Scalia, and Clarence
Thomas) were joined by two centrists (Sandra Day O'Connor and Anthony Kennedy)
to narrow the reach of the laws at issue.
Four liberal justices (John Paul Stevens,
David Souter, Ruth Bader Ginsburg, and
Stephen Breyer) dissented in all of the
cases, four of which are described below.

- Last year, on the grounds of federalism, the Supreme Court held in *Kimel
  v. Florida Board of Regents* that persons working for state governments
  cannot sue in federal court under the
  Age Discrimination in Employment
  Act, which Congress adopted in 1967.
  Such suits, the high court said, were
  constitutionally barred by the 11th
  Amendment's prohibition of suits
  against states in federal court. This ruling removed 3.4 percent of the nation's total workforce from the federal
  law's protections against age bias—
  some 5 million state employees across
  the country.
- On the same basis as the age-discrimi-
  nation case, the Court held in February
  of this year that state employees cannot
  sue in federal court under the Americans with Disabilities Act. In this ruling, *Board of Trustees of the University
  of Alabama v. Garrett*, state workers
  who alleged disabilities discrimination

were relegated to seeking recourse through state courts, where the available remedies are often much weaker than those provided under federal law.

- In April of this year, the Supreme Court narrowed the reach of Title VI, the 1964 provision that prohibits recipients of federal financial assistance from discriminating on the basis of race, color, or national origin. In *Alexander v. Sandoval*, the Court held that Title VI is violated only if a plaintiff proves that the funded party *intentionally* discriminated on the basis of race—an interpretation that runs contrary to the rule for other civil rights laws (such as Title VII), which require only a showing of a discriminatory impact to trigger enforcement. At the same time, the justices held that neither public nor private recipients of federal financial aid who violate the nation's antidiscrimination regulations can be sued in federal court. Thus the state of Alabama was not vulnerable to suit when it established an "English only" requirement for taking a driver's license exam, even though federal regulations prohibit such restrictions. The only remedy, the Court held, was termination of federal funding to the state entity that violated the regulations (a sanction that entails a complicated administrative process).

- On May 29, the Court decided that civil rights litigants who bring suit against the government or an employer cannot collect attorney fees if the defendant voluntarily ceases the practice complained of or settles the claim before going to trial (the case was *Buckhannon Board and Care Home, Inc., v. West Virginia Department of Health and Human Services*). In 1976, Congress passed the Civil Rights Attorneys Fees Award Act to encourage lawyers to take civil rights cases as "private attorney generals." Such cases "vindicate public policies of the highest order," Congress explained when it passed the law. The act specified that the legal fees of "prevailing parties" would be paid by the losing party— generally a government that violated

the plaintiffs' constitutional rights. As Justice Ginsburg pointed out in her dissent in the *Buckhannon* case, Congress enacted the law to "ensure that nonaffluent plaintiffs would have effective access to the Nation's courts to enforce… civil rights laws." The effect of the *Buckhannon* decision is that a government body can tenaciously litigate a case until the last minute, then throw in the towel and evade the requirement of paying attorney fees. Since lawyers can no longer be sure that they'll be paid if they file civil rights suits, this ruling will certainly discourage them from taking on such cases, even those that clearly have merit.

Two of these cases are quite easy to correct. Congress can reverse the Supreme Court's decision about attorney fees by simply amending the civil rights law to provide that a litigant is considered a prevailing party entitled to fees if the lawsuit "was a substantial factor" in remedial action taken by the government and the suit brought by the plaintiff had a "substantial basis in fact and law." That was the rule generally applied by the lower courts before the Supreme Court decision.

The *Sandoval* rule can also be corrected by legislation. Congress could amend Title VI to provide that "any person aggrieved by the violation of any regulation issued pursuant to this act may bring a civil action in an appropriate federal court. Such actions may include suits challenging any discriminatory practice or policy that would be deemed unlawful if it has a disparate impact upon persons protected by this title."

The *Kimel* and *Garrett* decisions are more difficult to attack. The Supreme Court held that the 11th Amendment to the Constitution protects states against suits in federal court for age or disabilities discrimination by their employees. Although Congress cannot overrule a constitutional determination made by the Court, it can condition federal financial assistance on state adherence to federal requirements. In 1987 the Supreme Court held in *South Dakota v. Dole* (a 7–2 decision written by Chief Justice Rehnquist, in which Justice Scalia joined) that Congress could insist that South Dakota increase the minimum

drinking age to 21 as a condition of obtaining federal highway funds. In other words, while Congress cannot force states to do its bidding, it in effect may bribe them to follow federal requirements

Thus Congress could condition federal grants under Medicaid, Medicare, or the Social Security Act on the states' surrendering their 11th Amendment immunity under the federal acts banning discrimination based on age and disability. If a state wished to obtain federal funds under various social-welfare provisions, it would have to accede to the U.S. antidiscrimination laws and waive its immunity from being sued by its employees in federal court. Indeed, the 1986 Civil Rights Remedies Equalization Amendment specifically declared that Congress intended for states to waive their 11th Amendment immunity in order to receive federal financial assistance.

Congress could use the same device to overrule another recent Supreme Court decision: last year's 5–4 holding in *United States v. Morrison* that the civil-remedy provisions of the Violence Against Women Act of 1994 are unconstitutional. The majority held that the law exceeded congressional power under the Constitution's commerce clause—the first time a federal law had been invalidated on that basis since 1936. But Congress can counter the Court's action by ensuring that such civil remedies are available to victims of gender-motivated acts of violence through state courts. How? By making the federal funds that are available through Medicare or Social Security programs contingent on a state's provision of such remedies

In 1991, Congress and the first President Bush acted courageously to overrule manifestly narrow decisions of the Supreme Court that violated a national consensus against discrimination by government or by employers. Now that the Democrats have control of the Senate, they should make similar corrective legislation one of their first objectives. And who knows? This President Bush might even follow the lead of his father and endorse the changes.

LEON FRIEDMAN *is a professor of constitutional law at the Hofstra University School of Law.*

The 28th Amendment

It is time to protect marriage, and democracy, in America

ROBERT P. GEORGE

MARRIAGE is so central to the well-being of children—and society as a whole—that it was, until recently, difficult to imagine that it might be necessary to mount a national political campaign to protect the institution from radical redefinition. Yet today it can scarcely be denied that such a campaign is needed.

Everybody knows that marriage is in trouble. The rise of divorce, illegitimacy, and cohabitation have all taken a toll. If the institution of marriage in our society is to be restored to good health, a reversal of trends and tendencies in all of these areas is required. Still, there is something unique in the threat posed by the movement for "same-sex marriage."

At the core of the traditional understanding of marriage in our society is a *principled* commitment to monogamy and fidelity. Marriage, as embodied in our customs, laws, and public policies, is intelligible and defensible as a one-flesh union whose character and value give a man and a woman *moral reasons* (going beyond mere subjective preferences or sentimental motivations) to pledge sexual exclusivity, fidelity, and permanence of commitment. Yet any argument for revising our law to treat homosexual relations as marital will implicitly do what clearheaded and honest proponents of "same-sex marriage" explicitly acknowledge: It will deny that there are such moral reasons. Any such argument would have to treat marriage as a purely private matter designed solely to satisfy the desires of the "married" parties. If that is the case, there is no principled reason marriage need imply

Thoughtful people *on both sides of the debate* recognize this. It is evident, then, that legal recognition of same-sex marriages, far from making marriage more widely available (as well-intentioned but misguided conservative advocates of same-sex marriage say they want to do), would in effect abolish the institution, by collapsing the moral principles at its foundation.

So while it is true, as Bill Bennett among others has acknowledged, that marriage in the past 35 years or so has been damaged more severely by heterosexual immorality and irresponsibility than by homosexual activism, it is also true that same-sex marriage, were it to be instituted, would strike a blow against the institution more fundamental and definitive even than the disastrous policy of "no-fault" divorce.

What can be done?

It is noteworthy that proponents of same-sex marriage have sought to change public policy through judicial decree. Where they have won, they have won through the courts. Where the issue has been settled in the court of public opinion, they have lost. The lesson is clear: If the institution of marriage is to be preserved, a campaign to settle the issue democratically at the national level must be mounted—and quickly.

At the time the U.S. Constitution was adopted, it was taken for granted that marriage is the union of a man and a woman ordered to the rearing of children in circumstances conducive to moral uprightness. Its legal incidents and civil effects were part of the common law and regulated by the states. There was no need at the time for marriage to be expressly defined or protected by federal law or the Constitution. Consequently, the word "marriage" does not appear in the Constitution (nor, for that matter, does the word "family"). Our forefathers shared the consensus of humanity, which viewed marriage as a union between sexually complementary persons—that is, persons of opposite sexes. The common law that we inherited from England was clear about marriage as the union of man and woman: "Marriage... includes the reciprocal duties of husband and wife."

Only in the last decade has our country's time-honored recognition that marriage is, in its very essence, the union of male and female come under attack in the courts. In the earliest phase of this campaign, activists tried to establish a right of marriage for same-sex partners through lawsuits in state courts premised on state constitutional guarantees. The strategy was to get some state supreme court to recognize same-sex marriage. Other states would then be compelled to recognize these "marriages," because of the constitutional requirement that states extend

"Full Faith and Credit" to one another's "public Acts, Records, and judicial Proceedings."

The supreme court of Hawaii, purporting to interpret the state constitution, went so far as to hold in 1993 that the state's marriage law "discriminated on the basis of sex." A lower court acting on its instructions then found the marriage law unconstitutional—but stayed its order pending appeal. In the end, though, the courts did not get the final say. In 1998, the people of Hawaii, by a very substantial majority (69 to 31 percent), enacted a state constitutional amendment affirming the heterosexual character of marriage. Hawaii's same-sex marriage case had to be dismissed.

Undaunted, attorneys for homosexual activist groups continued to press the issue in other venues. In Alaska, a trial judge read that state's constitution to include a fundamental right to "choose a life partner." Again, the voters responded by backing a constitutional amendment defining marriage as the union of a man and a woman—by 68 to 32 percent. Other states, such as California, passed similar amendments by wide margins without even facing an immediate legal threat.

Having been stopped by the democratic process in Hawaii and Alaska, homosexual activists decided to press their legal case in a state where it is very difficult for voters to amend the state constitution: Vermont. On December 20, 1999, the Vermont supreme court decided that the Vermont constitution requires the state either to grant marriage licenses to same-sex couples or to give them all of the benefits of marriage. The Vermont legislature chose the latter response to this judicial dictate: It passed, and the governor signed, a "civil unions" law that amounts to same-sex marriage in all but name.

The Vermont law, which took effect on July 1, 2000, contained no residency requirements for entering into a civil union. In the first six months, over 1,500 couples entered into civil unions. Only 338 involved at least one Vermont resident. The vast majority of Vermont civil unions, then, have been entered into by non-Vermont couples. Some of them will surely file suit in their home states to demand legal recognition of their Vermont status.

There is still an obstacle in the activists' path. The U.S. Constitution explicitly gives Congress the authority to make exceptions to the Full Faith and Credit Clause. So in 1996, Congress passed (and President Clinton signed, albeit reluctantly and without fanfare) the Defense of Marriage Act. That legislation defines marriage for purposes of federal law as the union of a man and a woman, and says that no state is required to recognize another state's same-sex marriages (though it does not forbid states to create same-sex marriages or recognize out-of-state same-sex marriages or civil unions). Subsequently, 34 states have enacted laws that deny recognition to same-sex marriages granted out of state.

But activists are putting forward a number of theories to persuade judges to declare the Defense of Marriage Act, and the state acts, unconstitutional. They may well succeed. The same year the Defense of Marriage Act was passed, the U.S. Supreme Court handed down *Romer v. Evans*. The case concerned a Colorado constitutional amendment forbidding the state government or localities to pass "gay rights" laws. The Court concluded that the amendment could be explained only on the basis of irrational "animus" toward homosexuals. The Defense of Marriage Act could surely be characterized the same way by socially liberal federal judges.

■

The only sure safeguard against this assault is to use the ultimate democratic tool available to the American people...

■

There is also the prospect of same-sex marriage migrating from abroad. On April 1, 2001, the Netherlands became the first country in the world to recognize same-sex marriage as such. The law requires only one of the parties to be a resident of the Netherlands. Ordinarily, a marriage validly entered into anywhere is valid everywhere. Our country has a public-policy exception to this rule, which allows states with a policy against same-sex marriage to decline to recognize it; but this exception may not cover states that—like Massachusetts—haven't enacted explicit bans on the importation of same-sex marriage. In addition, given the current culture of the American legal profession, there is good reason to expect that many American judges will eventually reason their way around the public-policy exception in favor of the legal arguments crafted for them by activist attorneys and other supporters of same-sex marriage.

The momentum of the movement to redefine and, in effect, abolish marriage has brought America to a crossroads. Evan Wolfson, former head of the marriage project at the Lambda Legal Defense and Education Fund, says he will file more lawsuits: "We have it within our reach to marry within five years." The judicial assault on marriage is accelerating and encompassing every dimension of our legal system-state, federal, and international law.

TIME TO AMEND

The only sure safeguard against this assault is to use the ultimate democratic tool available to the American people: a constitutional amendment. Pro-marriage activists are inclined to back an amendment that would read: "Marriage in the United States shall consist only of the union of a man and a woman. Neither this constitution or the constitution of any state, nor state or federal law, shall be construed to require that marital status or the legal incidents thereof be conferred upon unmarried couples or groups."

The first sentence simply states that marriage anywhere in the United States consists only of male-female couples. This would prevent any state from introducing same-sex marriage by, for example, recognizing a Dutch same-sex marriage. The name and substance of "marriage" is reserved to husband and wife alone.

The second sentence seeks to prevent the judicial abuse of statutory or constitutional law to force the extension of marriage to include non-marital relationships. The word "construed" indicates that the intention is to preclude a judge or executive-branch official from inferring a requirement of same-sex marriage, or something similar, from a state or federal law.

The expression "legal incidents" is intended to convey the consequences "either usually or naturally and inseparably" dependent upon marriage. The Supreme Court has called "incidents of marriage" those "government benefits (e.g., Social Security benefits), property rights (e.g., tenancy by the entirety, inheritance rights), and other, less tangible benefits (e.g., legitimization of children born out of wedlock)" that follow upon marital status. Another example would be the marital privilege against being forced to testify against one's spouse.

The amendment would not prevent private corporations from treating same-sex couples as married couples for purposes of health-care benefits, nor the extension of hospital visitation privileges to same-sex partners. If a benefit is not made to depend on marriage, it can be applied more generally. What the amendment prevents is the automatic, across-the-board qualification of same-sex partners for whatever marital benefits happen to exist.

The Federal Marriage Amendment has a very narrow purpose. It seeks to prevent one very specific abuse of power by the courts, to make sure that on an issue of this importance, they don't confer a victory on the Left that it has not won in a fair contest in the forum of democratic deliberation. The amendment is intended to return the debate over the legal status of marriage to the American people—where it belongs. This amendment would have prevented the Vermont supreme court from ordering the legislature to grant the benefits of marriage to same-sex couples, but would not prevent a fair democratic struggle to decide the question of civil unions one way or the other in Vermont or any other state.

Why, some will ask, should we not go further, and use constitutional amendment to settle the issue of civil unions once and for all at the national level? While the legal recognition of non-marital sexual acts and relationships undermines the institution of marriage and should be opposed, the actual threat of the imposition of same-sex marriage and civil unions comes from the courts, not the legislatures. The amendment is thus tailored to the threat at hand. Moreover, it does not depart from principles of federalism, under which family law is, for the most part, a state matter. State autonomy on family-law matters is preserved.

As a practical matter, the chances of passing a more comprehensive amendment are small. Moreover, some potential allies would perceive an amendment as offending democratic principles if it were to reach beyond the abuse of judicial power in this area. We should not fear the democratic resolution of the question of marriage. If we lose the people on this question, constitutional law will not save us.

If state and federal judges remain free to manufacture marriage law as they please, the prestige of liberal sexual ideology in the law schools and other elite sectors of our society will eventually overwhelm conventional democratic defenses. The only sure means of preserving the institution of marriage for future generations of Americans is a federal constitutional amendment protecting marriage as the union of a man and a woman.

Mr. George is a professor of jurisprudence and the director of the James Madison Program in American Ideals and Institutions at Princeton University.

From the *National Review*, July 23, 2001, pp. 32-34. © 2001 by the National Review, Inc., 215 Lexington Avenue, New York, NY 10016. Reprinted by permission.

THE CONSTITUTION

Immigrants for President

Why the foreign-born should be allowed to compete for the big job

JOHN J. MILLER

WHEN President Bush spoke at Ellis Island on July 10, his speech was full of patriotic boilerplate: "America at its best is a welcoming society." It was a ho-hum address that just about any president might have given. Praising America's immigrant tradition in the shadow of the Statue of Liberty is like making nice with farmers at the county fair: a job requirement for public officials.

Buried in Bush's remarks, however, was a comment that deserved notice. A group of immigrants were taking the oath of citizenship that day, the final step in their naturalization. "This is one of the things that makes our country so unique," said Bush. "With a single oath, all at once you become as fully American as the most direct descendant of a Founding Father."

That's almost true. Right beside Bush were two members of his own cabinet who wouldn't be allowed to succeed him as president, even though they're both citizens: labor secretary Elaine Chao, who was born in Taiwan, and housing secretary Mel Martinez, who is from Cuba. The Constitution is pretty clear on this point: "No Person except a natural born Citizen, or a Citizen of the United States, at the time of the Adoption of this Constitution, shall be eligible to the Office of President."

In other words, an immigrant won't ever call the shots from behind the big desk in the Oval Office—unless the Constitution is amended. This is not done easily, but it is something the Bush administration ought to consider seriously. One senior official calls the idea "intriguing" and says it has been tossed around at least informally. Pursued wisely, such an amendment has the potential to force millions of voters to take a fresh look at their president.

Alerting the Constitution is a grave act, and the first step in even considering it is to know why the document says what it does. The prohibition against immigrant presidents, however, was not the subject of much debate by the Founders, partly because it was a late addition. Yet it is not hard to guess at their reasoning. They probably recognized that many European kings weren't born in the lands they ruled, and wanted to take America in another direction. They also may have believed that the country's chief elected official must possess an inborn sense of American culture. At a time when a newly independent United States was struggling to find its place in the world, this was understandable—though it's also worth noting that the drafters included a loophole permitting foreign-born people living at that time to become president. (The eminent constitutional scholar Edward S. Corwin wryly observed that founder James Wilson "seems to have felt the need of such a clause in his own behalf especially keenly.") So the concept of a foreign-born president was not off-limits to the Founders, and they understood that historical circumstances might warrant different rules.

Today, it is hard to imagine voters electing a foreign-born candidate who wasn't in essence an American. An immigrant president most likely would embrace the United States with the fervor of a convert—a flag-waving nationalist whose public displays of love for country would match Joe Lieberman talking about his faith. People would start rolling their eyes by the third Pledge of Allegiance in every stump speech. This candidate, too, probably would have been raised in the U.S. since early childhood, making him a product of American culture. At the very least, the president would not be fresh off the boat: The Constitution already requires any president, even a native, to have lived in the U.S. for 14 years.

One of the wonders of American culture, of course, is the spectacle of people *becoming* American. We call this assimilation or, less clinically, Americanization. It is a rough process that affects people in different ways. On an individual level, it includes successes, failures, and much in between. It also holds a special place in the public imagination—most Americans can name an immigrant forebear, and a great many know immigrant ancestors as more than names. Their stories of arriving here, learning English, and gaining citizenship are central not just to millions of family histories, but to the whole country's sense of itself. As Harvard's Oscar Handlin remarked 50 years ago, "Once I thought to write a history of the immigrants in America. Then I discovered that immigrants *were* American history." By proposing to remove the single legal distinction the United States makes between citizens by birth and citizens by choice (their own or their parents'), Bush would fit himself inside a grand tradition of assimilation and acceptance.

The political case for the amendment is obvious: America's 27 million immigrants—roughly a third of them citizens—would look up to Bush with a new appreciation. Bush and the GOP have committed enormous resources to courting immigrant-heavy Hispanic and Asian-American communities. Their efforts are often harmless (the Philadelphia convention), and at least once they have been terribly misguided (the capitulation on Vieques). It's not clear that these moves have been at all effective on the level of partisan politics. By offering this amendment—a completely unexpected proposal—Bush would force people to sit up and pay attention. Suppose he turned its passage into a pet cause he mentioned at every opportunity; suddenly it becomes the Bush Amendment, and it operates with awesome symbolic power. Because he's already gone to Ellis Island, Bush could announce his intentions at what is arguably a better place anyway: the immigration station at Angel Island in San Francisco Bay, where thousands of Asians once entered the U.S.

Sometimes the smallest initiatives have the biggest impact. Americans are sure to remember Bill Clinton's presidency in many ways, but focus groups suggest there's a single policy accomplishment they are more likely to recall than all the others: school uniforms. By proposing them in 1996, Clinton sent a reassuring signal to parents worried about social order in public schools and inoculated himself against charges of ACLU-style liberalism. For Bush, offering to amend Article II, Section 1, of the Constitution would generate similar levels of positive feeling in voter blocs he has targeted. Even if his efforts fail—as most amendments do—he gets credit: The GOP has found the flag-burning amendment politically useful without actually passing it.

There is, however, a potential danger in this plan. The opponents of immigration currently operate in a state of suspended animation; they have nothing to organize around because the public isn't crying out for new restrictions and there's no significant bill in Congress addressing their concerns (despite rumblings of a plan to amnesty millions of illegal aliens). The Bush Amendment could change the tone. As state legislatures move to consider it, nativist voices would emerge. Many of these would belong to Republicans and pit Bush against his base in the type of internecine fight the media love to publicize. In this environment, the plan to win immigrant votes might backfire.

But that's a worst-case scenario, and there is seldom a risk-free political idea. There's a best-case scenario, too: It has Americans of all stripes backing up the words they enjoy hearing from their president with an actual deed to make those words a reality. It also encourages voters to think about Bush in a new light and find areas of agreement in places where they may not have looked before. One of our country's great notions about itself is the belief that every boy (or girl) can grow up to be president. The Bush Amendment is just another way of leaving no child behind.

From the *National Review*, August 6, 2001, pp. 22-24. © 2001 by the National Review, Inc., 215 Lexington Avenue, New York, NY 10016. Reprinted by permission.

GUNS AND TOBACCO: GOVERNMENT BY LITIGATION

Stuart Taylor Jr.

"The legal fees alone are enough to bankrupt the industry."

—John Coale, one of the private lawyers suing gunmakers on behalf of municipalities, as quoted in *The Washington Post* after the March 17 settlement in which Smith & Wesson agreed to adopt various safety measures that have stalled in Congress.

In its March 21 ruling that the Clinton Administration lacked authority to regulate the tobacco industry, no matter how great the need for regulation, the Supreme Court reaffirmed the broad principle that the power to set national policy on such hotly contested issues belongs to Congress. But the Justices have taken little note of other bold efforts to bypass Congress—and short-circuit the judicial process to boot—by using the threat of ruinous litigation to impose de facto regulation and taxation on targeted industries, including guns and tobacco. As *The Wall Street Journal* observed, the gun lawsuits could bring about "a more sweeping round of gun regulation than any single piece of legislation in 30 years."

And the far larger tobacco companies, which seem to have been sued by almost everyone alive, could be bankrupted by litigation, including a pending class action by smokers in Florida and a Clinton Administration lawsuit that invokes far-

fetched legal theories to seek many billions of dollars to compensate the government for the cost of treating smokers covered by Medicare. Also in the dock are HMOs, companies that sold lead paint more than 40 years ago, and makers of latex gloves. Later may come purveyors of liquor, beer, fatty foods, and, someday, maybe even fast cars and violent videos.

THE FOUNDERS CREATED CONGRESS TO SET NATIONAL POLICY. THEY DIDN'T INTEND FOR POLICY TO BE FASHIONED BY LAWSUITS.

(For a fuller taste of these and other peculiar workings of our legal system, with copious links to news reports, check out an amusingly depressing Web site called *Overlawyered.com,* created and edited by Walter K. Olson of the conservative-libertarian Manhattan Institute.)

The alliance of would-be lawmakers behind many of these broad legal assaults includes the Clinton Administration, state attorneys general, and municipalities, working closely with public interest activists and wealthy pri-

vate lawyers who started it all. Their incentives to sue variously include hopes of raising vast new revenues, bringing unpopular industries to heel, protecting public health and safety, and reaping billions of dollars in fees for the lawyers, who also tend to be big campaign contributors.

This public-private alliance's most recent triumph illustrates the combination of policy-making ambitions and financial incentives that drives such litigation. The triumph was the March 17 decision by British-owned Smith & Wesson, the nation's largest maker of handguns, to abide by a long list of restrictions on gun sales demanded by the Clinton Administration. Smith & Wesson entered the agreement to extricate itself from some or all of the lawsuits against the industry by 29 cities, counties, and other plaintiffs.

The gun lawsuits were bankrolled by contingent-fee lawyers who are also prominent in the more-lucrative tobacco wars and have lots of money to invest in multifront attacks on other industries. They recruited municipalities as clients by dangling the prospect of imposing previously unimagined liability on gunmakers for selling unnecessarily dangerous guns, and selling them to the wrong people, thus allegedly contributing to governmental costs associated with murders, accidental shootings, and other gun violence. Every shooting by a spouse, a child, an armed robber, or a drug dealer is at least theoretically a potential source of liability to the gunmakers. Seizing on the fact that many such shootings occur in federally subsidized housing projects, President Clinton and Housing and Urban Development Secretary Andrew Cuomo jumped in by pressing the gun companies to accept new restrictions or face "death by a thousand cuts," as Cuomo put it.

The plaintiffs have never had to prove their flimsy theories of liability in court. Indeed, judges have dismissed some of the lawsuits. But in this era of astronomical jury awards, a few losses could bankrupt the gun companies even if they win most of their cases. And the legal fees alone are potentially crushing, given the plaintiffs' strategy of deploying massive firepower on multiple fronts, the better to force the companies to settle.

This strategy forced Smith & Wesson to raise the white flag. The restrictions drafted by Administration officials and agreed to by the company require it to develop "smart gun" technology within three years, so that only authorized users can fire new handguns; to limit bulk purchases; to bar dealers from selling at gun shows unless the buyers have passed background checks; to include trigger locks with all new handguns (which Smith & Wesson was already doing); and more. Others may be driven to make similar concessions.

If the plaintiffs' divide-and-conquer strategy forces the rest of the industry to fall into line, the effect would be the de facto imposition of new, nationwide gun-control rules much like those that President Clinton has urged but that Congress has refused to pass. This is reminiscent of the far richer tobacco industry's $246 billion in settlements with state attorneys general in 1998: The intent, and effect, was to finance the payments (and the billions in legal fees) by sharply raising cigarette prices, in what

was the functional equivalent of a new nationwide tax on smokers—a tax that neither Congress nor state legislatures had voted to impose.

Will restrictions like those in the Smith & Wesson settlement reduce the number of shooting deaths? There's great dispute about that. Even some advocates of more-radical controls such as banning all handguns worry that "smart gun" technology might increase total gun deaths by stimulating the sale of tens of millions more guns to people who mistakenly think them safe. The National Rifle Association and other, more scholarly opponents of the new gun controls sought by the Administration argue that they would not have prevented the rash of highly publicized shootings since the Littleton, Colo., massacre last year, and that "smart guns" might fail when most needed for legitimate self-defense.

I suspect that restrictions such as those agreed to by Smith & Wesson would save some lives, and so I would like to see Congress pass most, or all, of the Administration's proposals. But with scholarly experts, detailed empirical studies, and millions of people on all sides of the issue, I can't be sure.

One thing I am sure of is that the Framers of the Constitution created Congress—and assigned to it "all legislative powers herein granted"—to set policy for the nation on such complex questions of social engineering. They also made it hard to enact legislation unless backed by a fairly broad national consensus. That's a far cry from what's going on now, with the Clinton Administration and its allies boasting of using lawsuits to bypass partisan gridlock in Congress.

Do the ends justify the means? After all, these lawsuits represent just the latest in a succession of mushrooming theories

of liability, expansive constitutional doctrines, and other trends that have led to deep intrusions by the judicial and executive branches into what was once the province of Congress. Why stop now, when so much needs to be done, and Congress is so unhelpful?

But the gun litigation represents a deeply disturbing way of making public policy. It was started by private lawyers and municipalities with big financial interests at stake. The courts have largely been bystanders as the Clinton Administration and its allies have sought to bludgeon gunmakers into settling before trial. And in the words of Robert B. Reich, Clinton's former Labor Secretary, in *The American Prospect:* "If I had my way, there'd be laws restricting cigarettes and handguns. [But] the White House is launching lawsuits to succeed where legislation failed. The strategy may work, but at the cost of making our frail democracy even weaker.... You might approve the outcomes in these two cases, but they establish a precedent for other cases you might find wildly unjust."

After the Supreme Court's 5–4 ruling that the federal Food and Drug Administration lacks the power to regulate tobacco without new legislation, President Clinton appropriately stressed that the Justices had been unanimous in asserting that "tobacco use... poses perhaps the single most significant threat to public health in the United States." He also called on Congress to pass a new law incorporating the now-voided FDA rule. Senate Majority Leader Trent Lott, R-Miss., immediately announced his opposition. It will be a bitter election-year struggle, with all players attending closely to how the voters will react to whatever they do.

That's called democracy. It's not always the quickest or easiest way to get things done. But it's the best way.

UNIT 2
Structures of American Politics

Unit Selections

Key Points to Consider

- How might the presidency and Congress change in the next 100 years?

- Which position in American government would you most like to hold? Why?

 **Links: www.dushkin.com/online/**
These sites are annotated in the World Wide Web pages.

Department of State
   http://www.state.gov

Federal Reserve System
   http://woodrow.mpls.frb.fed.us/info/sys/index.html

National Archives and Records Administration (NARA)
   http://www.nara.gov/nara/welcome.html

National Center for Policy Analysis
   http://www.ncpa.org

Supreme Court/Legal Information Institute
   http://supct.law.cornell.edu/supct/index.html

United States House of Representatives
   http://www.house.gov

United States Senate
   http://www.senate.gov

James Madison, one of the primary architects of the American system of government, observed that the three-branch structure of government created at the Constitutional Convention of 1787 pitted the ambitions of some individuals against the ambitions of others. Nearly two centuries later, contemporary political scientist Richard Neustadt wrote that the structure of American national government is one of "separated" institutions sharing powers. These two eminent students of American politics suggest an important proposition: the very design of American national government contributes to the struggles that occur among government officials who have different institutional loyalties and potentially competing goals.

This unit is divided into four sections. The first three treat the three traditional branches of American government and the last one treats the bureaucracy. One point to remember when studying these institutions is that the Constitution provides only a bare skeleton of the workings of the American political system. The flesh and blood of the presidency, Congress, judiciary, and bureaucracy are derived from decades of experience and the shared expectations of today's political actors. A second point to keep in mind is that the way a particular institution functions is partly determined by those who occupy relevant offices. The presidency operates differently with George W. Bush in the White House than it did when Bill Clinton was president. Similarly, Congress and the Supreme Court also operate differently according to who serve as members and who hold leadership positions within the institutions. There were significant changes in the House of Representatives after Republican Newt Gingrich succeeded Democrat Tom Foley as Speaker of the House in 1995. With Speaker Dennis Hastert succeeding Gingrich in January 1999, additional changes occurred in the way the House of Representatives functioned.

The first section contains articles on the presidency. After 12 straight years of Republican presidents (Ronald Reagan and the elder George Bush), Democrat Bill Clinton assumed the presidency in 1993. For the first two years of his presidency, Democrats also held a majority of seats in the House of Representatives and the Senate. But in the 1994 and 1996 congressional elections, Republicans won control of the House and Senate, a development that inevitably led to changes in the way that Clinton functioned as president. When George W. Bush became president in 2001, Republicans held a narrow majority in the House of Representatives and the Senate was split 50-50 between Republicans and Democrats. In May 2001, Senate Democrats gained a 50-49 working majority when Senator Jim Jeffords abandoned the Republican party and became an independent. On September 11, 2001, terrorist attacks on the World Trade Center and the Pentagon suddenly transformed the context in which American government institutions were operating. An important point to remember is that neither the presidency nor any other institution operates in isolation from the other institutions of American national government or from the wider political environment.

The second section addresses Congress. The legislative branch underwent substantial changes in recent decades under mostly Democratic control. Reforms in the seniority system and the budgetary process in the 1970s brought an unprecedented

degree of decentralization and, some would say, chaos to Capitol Hill. In addition, during the 1970s and 1980s, both the number of staff and special-interest caucuses in Congress increased. The unexpected Republican takeover of the House of Representatives as a result of the November 1994 elections brought even more changes to that body. The new Republican speaker, Newt Gingrich, reduced the power of committees, imposed term limits on committee chairs, consolidated power in the Speaker's office, and became a prominent figure on the national scene. But 1998 brought the downfall of Gingrich as a result of the November congressional elections and, for the second time in history, the impeachment of a president. And the 2000 congressional elections narrowed the Republican majority in the House to a handful of seats and resulted in a historic 50-50 split of Democrats and Republicans in the Senate. These events will likely affect the functioning of Congress (and the presidency) for some time to come.

The Supreme Court sits at the top of the U.S. legal system and is the main topic of the third section in this unit. The Court is not merely a legal institution; it is a policymaker whose decisions can affect the lives of millions of citizens. The Court's decisive role in determining the outcome of the 2000 presidential election showed its powerful role in the American political system. Like all people in high government offices, Supreme Court justices have policy views of their own, and observers of the Court pay careful attention to the way the nine justices interact with one another in shaping decisions of the Court.

The bureaucracy of the national government, the subject of the fourth and last section in this unit, is responsible for carrying out policies determined by top-ranking officials. The bureaucracy is not merely a neutral administrative instrument, and bureaucratic waste and inefficiency often seem excessive. On the other hand, government bureaucracies also share credit for many of the accomplishments of American government. Most presidents claim that they want to make the bureaucracy perform more efficiently, and it remains to be seen how effective President Bush will be in this regard.

For many readers, the selections in this unit will rank among the most enjoyable in the book. Not surprisingly, most of us are more comfortable on familiar territory, and the separate branches of government are likely to be familiar from earlier study in school or from media coverage of politics. Nevertheless, the selections in this unit should provide additional and more sophisticated insights into how the institutions of American national government actually work.

Gone Are the Giants

TODAY IN THE WHITE HOUSE, CONGRESS, AND THE SUPREME COURT, THE NATION SEEMS TO LACK THE LARGER-THAN-LIFE FIGURES WHO RULED THE CAPITAL IN EARLIER ERAS. WHY?

By Burt Solomon

Listen to the somber reflections of an eminent historian and statesman: "The ordinary American voter does not object to mediocrity.... The best men do not go into politics.... Great men have not often been chosen Presidents, first because great men are rare in politics; secondly, because the method of choice may not bring them to the top; thirdly, because they are not, in quiet times, absolutely needed."

How could James Bryce, a professor of law at Oxford University and later a British ambassador to the United States, have possibly known of the presumptive American presidential nominees in 2000 when he penned *The American Commonwealth* in 1888? He knew that the Presidents between Andrew Jackson and Abraham Lincoln, and again during the decades following the Civil War, had been—as he spelled it—"intellectual pigmies." Was he imagining Texas Gov. George W. Bush, a Republican who smirks while discussing his decision to send a murderer to her death, and Vice President Al Gore, a Democrat whose pandering meanderings on Elián González suggest that he has no political core? "They are underwhelming, aren't they?" says presidential scholar Fred I. Greenstein of Princeton University.

Yet either of them could turn out to be a very capable 43rd President, says historian Alonzo L. Hamby of Ohio University, a biographer of Harry S. Truman. This era of peace and prosperity, he points out, "is probably the easiest time to be President, ever." And it's dangerous to predict how history will ultimately judge. As Truman's case shows, politicians scorned in their own time may rise in reputation later.

Still, it seems as if pygmies have come to dominate American political life. In all three branches of the federal government, the giants—officials with vast influence, foreseeable historic importance, or merely a larger-than-life presence—have practically vanished from the scene. In the past quarter-century, the White House has arguably had only one, a simple-thinking ex-actor. The sort of

giants who prevailed in the Senate (and occasionally in the House) during the 1950s and 1960s are, with one or two exceptions, history. Even the Supreme Court has, at most, a single Justice, Antonin F. Scalia, who may be remembered by educated citizens a century hence. Around the statehouses, ex-wrestler (and Minnesota Gov.) Jesse Ventura may be literally larger-than-life, but the Al Smiths and Huey Longs and Nelson A. Rockefellers are gone. The only truly powerful American public official with a worldwide sweep may be Alan Greenspan, the taciturn Federal Reserve Board chairman who has never been elected to anything.

What's going on? Why have we entered the land of the pygmies—or, at least, of the absence of giants? It isn't just coincidence, venerable Washington-watchers say. A lot of it is the times we're in. It's almost a cliché that it takes a great crisis to make a great President; in this lovely era of peace and prosperity, we're out of true crises—and we should thank our stars for it.

Also, the political system has changed. The near death of the political parties as power brokers has left every politician to his or her own devices, shorn of the natural stature that comes from being bolstered by—and identified with—a mighty institution. At the same time, the capital's unrelenting partisanship has produced a dearth of officeholders willing to work across party lines, the sort of for-the-greater-good behavior that magnifies a politician's enduring reputation. And if the opposition won't tear a politician down, the news media will. Anyone running for political office must expect to "have every human flaw, pimple, and boil lanced," says former Sen. Alan Simpson, R-Wyo., now the director of Harvard University's Institute of Politics. Such scathing treatment not only cuts officeholders down to size but also discourages many potential candidates from trying. Not only are the giants gone, laments the 6-foot-7-inch Simpson, but they're never coming back.

Of course, as Bryce suggested more than a century ago, the lack of giants is nothing new. Harry McPherson, an aide to President Lyndon B. Johnson who became a prominent Washington lawyer, says he first noticed this in the early 1970s, amid the Watergate scandal, when he was riding downtown on the bus past a labor union headquarters and realized that labor bosses were a dying breed. So, too, were the giants of politics, literature, civil rights, and education. He blamed Americans' characteristic suspicion of leadership—"a paucity of followers," as he wrote at the time—and media overexposure. Sound familiar?

Maybe the only thing that has changed is that the nation's political leadership matters even less to Americans now than it did in 1974. After all, it is Silicon Valley and Wall Street—not Washington—that are driving American life. "The society is about making money right now," says Leon E. Panetta, who served eight terms in Congress and two and a half years as President Clinton's chief of staff before going home to California. "The public has basically written off Washington. They don't think that it impacts on their lives."

It may not be the political figures who have shrunk so much as the political times. The great issues are gone, at least for the moment. The Cold War is kaput. So, it seems, is any longing to use the government to do ambitious things. Grand crusades are a shadow of what they were; the most passionate race-related issue right now is a symbolic dispute in South Carolina over flying the Confederate flag.

"It's the politics of small issues—isn't it?" says Richard Fenno, an expert on Congress at the University of Rochester. The biggest issue that Washington now faces is the rescue of federal entitlement programs, notes Michael J. Boskin, a Stanford University economist who chaired President Bush's Council of Economic Advisers. It's "a vital issue," he adds, "[but] it's not Pearl Harbor."

There may be some nostalgia involved in judging the older generations of notables as grander than the current incumbents. But truly, the mega-issues of World War II and its aftermath—the Marshall Plan, nuclear weaponry, the Cold War between capitalism and socialism—brought outsized actors to the fore. Small issues, though, make decision-makers look, well, small. Had Franklin D. Roosevelt become President in 1993, history might come to consider him as something other than great. Or had Bill Clinton taken the oath of office in 1933, he might have become a top-rank President.

Political giants may rise again when giant issues return, as surely they must. This suggests, in turn, that some of the apparent pygmies who stand before us may harbor a latent greatness that has yet to be glimpsed.

Perhaps. But there's also some evidence that the quality of the individuals who run the country has suffered. "Certainly, in my judgment," says Robert S. Strauss, who has counseled Presidents of both political parties, "the demise of civility, combined with the press mentality, has made it exceedingly difficult to attract top people,

whether it's to elective or appointive office." Trent Lott is no Everett M. Dirksen, as Senate Republican leaders go. Among the chamber's Democratic leaders, Thomas A. Daschle isn't a Lyndon B. Johnson or even a Mike Mansfield. And House Speaker J. Dennis Hastert, R-Ill., isn't Newt Gingrich. Quiet times seem to bring leaders to power who don't need to lead, and quite possibly can't.

PRESIDENTS OF HUMAN SCALE

When it came to the quality of its political leaders, a young nation was spoiled early on. Historians speak of the *golden* and *silver* generations of American statesmen—respectively, the Founding Fathers and the pre-Civil War giants of Congress such as Henry Clay, John C. Calhoun, and Daniel Webster.

But too soon, the nation learned that its luck wouldn't last. From Lincoln's death to around 1900, the national government was run by what Keith W. Olson, a historian at the University of Maryland, describes as "a bunch of second-raters." The reasons weren't very different when Bryce wrote than they are now. Inventors and titans of commerce—the likes of Thomas A. Edison and John D. Rockefeller, the Bill Gateses of their day—dominated the nation's course. By comparison, Presidents and politicians didn't matter much. This proved true again during the 1920s, as peace and prosperity prevailed, and the voters elected a succession of forgettable Presidents.

Great Presidents "tend to come very sporadically, under very particular conditions," explains Stephen Skowronek, a presidential scholar at Yale University. And now, he adds, "we're in kind of a lull period."

Becoming a giant in the presidency takes a strong will and the fortune to hold office in politically momentous times. Theodore Roosevelt's vivid personality, in part, earned him a place on Mount Rushmore. Princeton's Greenstein describes TR as "Giuliani on acid," comparing the current New York City mayor, Rudolph W. Giuliani, with the city's one-time police commissioner who conducted splashy midnight raids, later served as assistant Navy Secretary, quit to ride up San Juan Hill, then (in 1901) became a President who invited in reporters to watch him shave. While in the White House, the first Roosevelt never had to fight a war or an economic depression. But his trust-busting progressivism was meant to tame the Industrial Revolution so that capitalism might survive, and his big-stick internationalism projected the United States as a world power.

Leading the nation through imminent peril is a more reliable route to becoming a giant. Woodrow Wilson led America in a war intended to end all wars; Franklin D. Roosevelt commanded the next war, which ended the Great Depression. FDR's greatness was a stroke of timing, in more ways than one. Suppose James Cox, the Democratic candidate in 1920, had won the presidency and then— like the man who defeated him, Warren G. Harding—died. His successor, Hamby wrote in the latest issue of *The Key Reporter*, a quarterly newsletter of Phi Beta Kappa, would have been "his charming lightweight of a Vice President, Franklin D. Roosevelt." Even in 1932, after polio had deepened FDR's character, pundit Walter Lippmann portrayed him as a pleasant, indecisive man—a smart judgment at the time, political historians say today.

The next five Presidents, from Truman through Richard M. Nixon, also led the nation through war, whether it was hot or cold. Some of them led in domestic policy, too. LBJ pushed through the landmark civil rights law of 1964 and sought to abolish poverty. Nixon opened the way to China and made the environment a federal concern. "He had a concept" of how to govern with a Democratic-run Congress, says Charles O. Jones, a retired political scientist at the University of Wisconsin. "Nixon was impressive."

It may have been Nixon's overreaching for power, however, that broke the string. The next two Presidents, Gerald R. Ford and Jimmy Carter, acted as pygmies, and purposely so, in reaction to the disgraced Nixon's imperial ways. Ever since, the White House has been home to "a pretty unmemorable lot," says John Milton Cooper, a historian at the University of Wisconsin. "The only memorable President since Nixon," he adds, "is, maybe, Ronald Reagan." Reagan's tough-minded, effective approach toward the Soviet Union and his success in changing many of the premises of domestic politics have moved him onto some historians' list of near-great Presidents.

His successor's tenure, however, inspired a book-length recounting called *Marching in Place: The Status Quo Presidency of George Bush*. And then there's Clinton, a President of large talents but middling accomplishments. Cass Sunstein, a law professor at the University of Chicago, argues that Clinton will rank as a historically important President because of his "Third Way," the use of government as a catalyst instead of a bludgeon in dealing with social ills. But Sunstein's view is in the minority. John R. Hibbing, a political scientist at the University of Nebraska, says he "can't see any tremendously lasting legacy" in either Clinton's foreign policy or his "nickel-and-dime approach" to domestic policy. Even Panetta has his doubts. Clinton helped to balance the federal budget and bring on prosperity, the former aide says, but he "probably" won't be compared to FDR or Wilson a century hence. Impeachment will be "always a shadow," he explains, and Clinton has fallen short in another way: "Reagan took risks. Clinton hasn't, very much."

But it isn't as if giants would have occupied the White House if Bush and Clinton had lost the elections they won. President Dukakis? President Dole? Tomorrow's political historians would probably have yawned.

TIMIDITY IN BLACK ROBES

Judicial biographers, too, may be in for a rough time. Who among the current nine Justices on the Supreme Court might be remembered a century hence? "No one," says John Hart Ely, a constitutional scholar at the University of Miami. The Court is crowded with smart, capable Justices, Court-watchers say. But it includes nobody like Oliver Wendell Holmes, Louis Brandeis, Felix Frankfurter, Earl Warren, or—most recently—William J. Brennan Jr.

The only serious prospect, Ely and others say, seems to be Antonin Scalia, an eloquent judicial minimalist with a libertarian streak. Sunstein describes him as the sole sitting Justice "with a large concept of where the law should be taken." He is so out of step, though, with most of the Court—and probably most of the public—that a lot would have to change for Scalia's closely reasoned dissents to ultimately prevail.

It isn't because of trivial issues that the Court lacks giants. To the contrary. In their current session, the Justices have taken up a range of consequential matters, including assisted suicide, affirmative action, prayer in schools, and the rights of criminal suspects. "They do have great questions," says Sunstein, "but they give small answers to them."

This isn't, of course, an accident of history. It dates to 1987, when an angrily divided Senate rejected the nomination of Robert Bork precisely because they feared that he would become a giant by undoing some of the Warren Court's crucial holdings. Ever since, Presidents have usually aimed low in their Supreme Court choices. President Bush nominated the self-effacing David H. Souter, in part because his judicial career had left no paper trail of controversial opinions. Clinton named a pair of sober moderates, Ruth Bader Ginsburg and Stephen G. Breyer.

"The process filters out the kind of Justices who would tend to think in grand terms," says A.E. Dick Howard, a law professor at the University of Virginia. The current Justices, he suggests, show the incrementalist temperament of former appellate court judges, which all but one of them were, instead of the broader vision of the politicians who dominated the Warren Court (including an ex-governor as Chief Justice, an ex-Senator, a former Securities and Exchange Commission chairman, and an FDR brain-truster). "We may never see [such giants] again," Howard says, "at least for the foreseeable future."

THE MORTALS ON CAPITOL HILL

Soon after he published the Pulitzer Prize-winning *Profiles in Courage* in 1957, Sen. John F. Kennedy chaired an elaborate process to pick five legendary Senators and to have their portraits painted in alcoves just off the Senate floor. The 19th century was represented by Clay, Calhoun, and Webster; the 20th by Wisconsin progressive Robert M. La Follette Sr. and Ohio conservative Robert A. Taft, who had died a few years earlier.

Now the search for immortals is beginning again. Last November, the Senate approved a proposal by Lott to choose two more deceased Senators for portraits by the time Congress finishes its work this year. Excluded are any Senators who had a Senate office building named for them, became Vice President, or served during the past 21 years. This leaves out LBJ, Hubert H. Humphrey, Dirksen, Richard Russell, and Philip Hart.

That still leaves plenty to choose from. The 1950s and 1960s alone saw a multitude of other Senate giants, including—just among Democrats—Paul Douglas of Illinois, J. William Fulbright of Arkansas, Henry "Scoop" Jackson of Washington state, Lister Hill of Alabama, Estes Kefauver of Tennessee, Robert Kerr of Oklahoma, Mansfield, and Wayne Morse of Oregon. The Republicans of the period include John Sherman Cooper of Kentucky, Barry Goldwater of Arizona, Jacob Javits of New York, and—depending upon one's criteria—Joseph R. McCarthy of Wisconsin. Even the House of Representatives, which offers less of a stage for its egos, boasted the likes of Speaker Sam Rayburn of Texas, Emanuel Celler of New York, and Wilbur Mills of Arkansas, all Democrats.

Today, you don't even need the fingers on one hand to count up the giants; flashing a peace symbol will probably do. How does Jesse Helms stack up as a chairman of the Senate Foreign Relations Committee against Arthur Vandenburg, who helped a President of the opposite party enact the Marshall Plan, or against Fulbright, who fought a President of his own party over a war? The list of giants has shriveled to almost nothing. The House doesn't have an obvious one right now, since Newt Gingrich quit as Speaker after the 1998 elections. In bringing the Republicans to power in 1994 after decades of Democratic control, Gingrich changed the nation's political landscape. The longer the Republicans keep control of the House, the likelier that history will judge Gingrich a giant. But he also made it harder for anyone else to qualify. He shifted power from the committee chairmen into the Speaker's hands and also left House Republicans longing for someone weaker at the helm. Hastert was chosen as Gingrich's successor largely because he was Gingrich's antithesis and would leave much of the Speaker's authority unasserted. Only Henry J. Hyde, R-Ill., the white-maned Judiciary Committee chairman, is oft cited as a congressional lion—though his handling of Clinton's impeachment "didn't do him any favors," says Burdett A. Loomis, a political scientist at the University of Kansas. Rep. John D. Dingell of Michigan, long the dominant Democrat on the Commerce Committee, could refurbish his own claim if his party regains control of the House.

A couple of prospective giants quit the arena—Democratic Sens. George J. Mitchell of Maine and Sam Nunn of Georgia—apparently because so little was getting done. Close observers of the current Congress can only come to a consensus on one remaining giant—Sen. Edward Kennedy, D-Mass. Once Kennedy became convinced that his transgressions at Chappaquiddick would prevent him from ever winning the White House, he became what Loomis describes as "a serious Senator of the first order," one who has "affected the tides of the Senate [as] a strong polar force" and embodied the liberal viewpoint on a wide range of domestic policies. On any issue except maybe agriculture or the environment, says Fenno, the Senate "can't have debate" without taking Kennedy into account. His joint legislative ventures with Republicans to enact bills on health insurance, job training, immigration, and judicial issues have added to his reputation as a legislative heavyweight.

Sen. Daniel Patrick Moynihan, D-N.Y., is considered by some to be a giant, though to a lesser extent than Kennedy. Legislative craftsmanship isn't Moynihan's forte, despite his years as the Finance Committee chairman and his pivotal role in brokering a compromise to rescue Social Security in 1983. Instead, he's thought of as an intellectual giant, a one-time Harvard University urban studies professor who (while an adviser to President Nixon) famously suggested treating the race problem with "benign neglect." As a Senator, people want to know what he thinks—colleagues, journalists, and policy wonks. "Any debate he entered, he became part of it," Fenno says. Once he retires in January, after four terms, he'll probably stand a better chance of ultimately being judged a giant if an economic recession finds children asleep on heating grates, as he forewarned during the 1996 debate over welfare reform.

Many other members of Congress are considered competent and, on occasion, courageous. (Ask ex-Rep. Marjorie Margolies-Mezvinsky, D-Pa., who lost her seat for backing Clinton's 1993 economic package.) Congress-watchers say that, given the right circumstances, others may qualify someday. They offer scattered votes for Republican Sens. Pete V. Domenici of New Mexico, Phil Gramm of Texas, Orrin G. Hatch of Utah, and—"on some days," says Loomis—Fred D. Thompson of Tennessee, and for Democratic Sens. Robert C. Byrd of West Virginia and Joseph I. Lieberman of Connecticut.

But the circumstances, quite clearly, aren't right. The Senate, notably, isn't the autocracy it used to be—rife with powerful fiefdoms and run by Senators-for-life. Instead, the world's supposedly greatest deliberative body has become a chaotic and even occasionally childish democracy. Richard A. Baker, the Senate's in-house historian, traces what he calls "the fragmentation of power" to the looser style that Mansfield used after he took over as Senate Majority Leader in 1961 from the intimidatingly powerful LBJ. Filibusters are more frequent, and committee chairmen are weaker. What McPherson described years ago as a Senate of "whales and minnows" has now become "a lot of speckled trout," says Bruce Oppenheimer, a Vanderbilt University scholar of the Senate.

There are other reasons, too, for the Senators' shrinking stature. In the Senate's midcentury heyday, they weren't "campaigning or running for President as the end-all and be-all in politics," says McPherson. Nor were they always running so scared for re-election. Many seats used to be safe, so Senators could act like statesmen—ignoring the will of the people, if need be, to do the right thing—at least during the first three or four years of a six-year term. But now "it's harder to drive colleagues into dangerous terrain," says Ross K. Baker, a political scientist at Rutgers University. The daunting cost of campaigns and Senators' vulnerability to well-financed challengers have increased the political risks of thoughtful independence. "Nobody can be idiosyncratic anymore," sighs Stephen Hess, a senior fellow at the Brookings Institution and the author of *The Little Book of Campaign Etiquette*.

Surely something has been lost. Charles D. Ferris, who spent 14 years as Mansfield's top legislative aide, remembers the "genuine agonizing" that lawmakers endured in judging Nixon's fate after the Watergate scandal, compared with the rote, party-line debate over Clinton's fate, which changed few minds. Are shallower people in charge now? Not necessarily, in Ferris' mind. "The environment has changed so drastically," he says, "that it is much more difficult for them to act" as they once did—from time to time—for the greater good.

PERSONAL GLORY

Ah, yes, the greater good—remember that? The giants of old, "when the national interest was involved, they found a compromise," says Panetta. He and others say they can't imagine Trent Lott signing on to the 1964 civil rights bill after opposing it for years, as Dirksen did, or conversely, Dirksen telling the public not to answer questions they found offensive in the federal census forms, as Lott recently did. "Dirksen took a risk," Panetta recounts. "Ultimately, leadership is about taking risks."

Part of the problem may be generational. The people in power in the '50s and '60s, shaped by privation and war, "were institutionalists—the institution really meant something," Ferris recalls. "It wasn't personal glory [they] sought." But ironically, acting on behalf of the greater good increased, not diminished, their stature.

Structural reasons also help explain why giants in Washington are rare. Weaker political parties have made officeholders, more than ever, into independent entrepreneurs. A politician tied to the vagaries of public opinion polls isn't likely to look larger-than-life. Also, the trust in government that bolsters giants has sagged under a constant media glare. Often, mediagenic politicians are happy to oblige, down to revealing (as Clinton did) their preferred style of underwear. Suppose Dirksen showed up regularly on CNN's *Crossfire* or CNBC's *Hardball*, says Jones of Wisconsin. "Familiarity breeds smallness."

Of course, if Washington mattered more than it seems to, politics might draw more giants. "Colin Powell would have been [a giant]," says Hess, "and still might be." Possibly his wife would consent to letting the popular ex-chairman of the Joint Chiefs of Staff run for President (or Vice President) were the stakes higher. But, Nebraska's Hibbing suggests, "once he started taking positions, and people started probing, he wouldn't look like a giant."

Still, there's evidence that Americans yearn for giants, or think that they do. Much of the appeal of Sen. John McCain, R-Ariz., in his recent presidential surge, came from his larger-than-life story and the perception that he needed no one to tell him what he thought. If we faced a foreign crisis, or if the political times seemed more dramatic, Republican primary voters might have chosen McCain over Bush. In both parties, the quality of candidates seems to be declining. George W. Bush apparently lacks the depth of his father, who had lost a child and several political races before winning the presidency. Gore has nothing of Clinton's political verve.

Maybe we should be grateful, though, that political giants will not be running our lives. They usually show up, after all, in the presence of crisis. In happier times, amid peace and prosperity, pygmies will do.

From the *National Journal*, May 27, 2000, pp. 1668-1673. © 2000 by National Journal Group, Inc. All rights reserved. Reprinted by permission.

Hooked on Polls

THEY'RE BEING USED LIKE NEVER BEFORE. WHATEVER HAPPENED TO REPRESENTATIVE GOVERNMENT?

BY CARL M. CANNON

In 1992, Ross Perot brought a radical idea to American presidential politics: the real-time plebiscite. In Perot's world, decisions on the great issues of the day, from federal budget policies to war-making, could be reached instantaneously by the American people through the use of high-tech referendums conducted by telephone or the Internet. This voting would follow televised presentations on the issues in which various policy options would be explained to the public.

Perot called his concept the "electronic town meeting," but what he really was describing was elevating the public opinion polls to the status of a kind of super-Congress and president-in-chief that would trump the desires and machinations of Washington's elected leaders.

"With interactive television every other week, we could take one major issue, go to the American people, cover it in great detail, have them respond, and show by congressional district what the people want," Perot explained. "If we ever put the people back in charge of this country and make sure they understand the issues, you'll see the White House and Congress, like a ballet, pirouetting around the stage getting it done in unison."

Perot placed a lot of faith in "experts" to explain to the public what needed to be done, but most experts in politics and government tended to view his electronic town hall idea as simplistic and unworkable, if not an affront to the Constitution.

"It just gives me the shudders, the potential for manipulation, the one-sidedness, that a thing like this could do," said Norman Bradburn, director of the polling center at the University of Chicago.

Vice President Dan Quayle asserted that Perot's plan entailed nothing less than "nullifying representative democracy with a bizarre scheme of government by polls." And President Bush said Perot "was out of touch with re-

ality" when he suggested Bush could have used the electronic town hall to build a mandate for liberating Kuwait. Perhaps most scathing was liberal journalist Sidney Blumenthal, who now works in the Clinton White House. "Thus the Madisonian system would be replaced by the Geraldo system; checks and balances by applause meter," Blumenthal wrote.

In hindsight, however, the most instructive response to Perot's idea was the one offered by the Democratic presidential nominee in 1992. Asked about Perot's electronic town hall ideas—on CNN's *Larry King Live*, fittingly—Bill Clinton replied, "Oh, I think it's a good idea." Clinton went on to make the obligatory comments about how polls don't absolve elected officials from their responsibilities, but the most animated part of his answer was this: He took credit for holding electronic town hall meetings before Perot did.

Today, barely six years after the putative rise and demise of Ross Perot, polls are being used more aggressively than ever before by the president and his loyalists, he and they, both, endless consumers and endless peddlers of polls. "They become addictive," said a former White House official. "They work once, and then they become a crutch; you don't do anything without them."

As president, Clinton has commissioned polls on issues ranging in gravity from whether he ought to stop genocide in Bosnia (the public gave a qualified thumbs-up) to whether it was better public relations to vacation in Wyoming or Martha's Vineyard (voters preferred he go out West). It is now common for polling results to be offered as validation in themselves, an argument—sometimes the primary argument—for such disparate positions as whether tax cuts are warranted, what an independent counsel should properly investigate, what the president's legal strategy should be, whether he should apologize for having sex with an intern, how much coverage the media should devote to the topic, and, of course, the dominant political question of the day: whether Bill Clinton should be impeached.

"On [impeachment], polls are our religion," said a Clinton loyalist. "We cite them, we flog them, we beat people over the head with them." Some Democrats, in fact, say polling numbers are more definitive than election returns. This postulate was advanced by the president and his press secretary as recently as Oct. 7. That day, the president said on the question of his own impeachment that "ultimately, it's going to be up to the American people to make a clear statement there."

Hours later, at the regular White House briefing, Clinton spokesman Joe Lockhart reiterated this point. Lockhart was asked if he and the president had the upcoming November elections in mind. Oh no, Lockhart said, adding that congressional elections are usually decided on local considerations. So then, Lockhart was asked, was he talking about the public opinion polls? "Yes," he replied. "People in Congress, people in elective office do, properly, stay in touch with their constituents."

One member who seems to have taken this doctrine literally is Rep. Ted Strickland of Ohio, one of the 31 Democrats who voted for the sweeping GOP impeachment inquiry. "It was not a particularly courageous vote," he told The Washington Post. "I think I did what my constituents wanted me to do."

How did he know what they wanted him to do? He commissioned a poll.

It's almost impossible to resist comparing this approach with the stance taken by Sen. Edmund G. Ross of Kansas in 1866 as pressure mounted on him back home to vote for conviction in the impeachment proceedings against President Andrew Johnson. No scientific public opinion surveys existed back then, but public opinion certainly did, and on the eve of Ross' fateful vote, he received this telegram from well-connected Republicans back home:

Kansas has heard the evidence and demands the conviction of the President. [signed] D.R. Anthony and 1,000 Others.

The morning of the vote, May 16, 1866, Ross sent a telegram back:

To D.R. Anthony and 1,000 Others: I do not recognize your right to demand that I vote either for or against conviction. I have taken an oath to do impartial justice according to the Constitution and laws, and trust that I shall have the courage to vote according to the dictates of my judgment and for the highest good of the country. [signed] E.G. Ross.

To David W. Moore, a Gallup Organization vice president and political scientist by training, the dichotomy of their two approaches has echoes in the venerable civics debate over how much pure democracy a representative form of government ought to have. Are the voters back home supposed to choose representatives whose judgments they trust, and who are then free—indeed, obligated—to exercise their wisdom as they see fit? Or are

officeholders bound to vote the prejudices, viewpoints and passions of the majority in their districts?

"In political science, we call these two approaches the 'trustee model' and the 'delegate model,'" notes Moore. "I would be perfectly willing to debate either side of the question."

But there are several possible problems with the 'delegate model.' One is that despite the mythic faith pollsters and political consultants put in polls, they aren't infallible. They are also often misinterpreted and misused. And, finally, there are times when leadership is needed, not polls.

HOW ACCURATE?

Today polls are taken on subjects ranging from the profound to the profoundly silly. Is O.J. Simpson guilty or innocent? Whom do you want to break Roger Maris' home run record? Would a woman rather be married to a man who looked like Danny DeVito and did the dishes or a man who looked like Robert Redford and did no dishes? Do you approve of Monica Lewinsky?

But polling's origins, and its bread and butter, have always been the business of predicting elections. The question traditionally asked is basic: "If the election were held today, would you vote for x or for y?" The tricky part is ensuring that question is asked of a representative sample. Since the Truman-Dewey debacle of 1948, polling firms, led by the Gallup Organization, have refined their techniques for gathering this information to a fine art and have compiled an impressive record for accuracy. In the early 1990s, however, venerated California pollster Mervin Field began to notice a troubling trend: the plummeting response rates in his polls.

This phenomenon seems to be caused by a variety of factors, including the availability of call-screening devices, the fact that polling is not a novelty anymore and, probably more than anything else, the vast increase in telemarketing that has left the public surlier and less cooperative. With response rates dipping below 40 percent—half what he sought when he started out—Field said he feared that eventually the industry was going to be simply wrong about an election.

That election happened, in 1996, though nobody seemed to notice. As late as Oct. 23 of that year, the major polling organizations said Clinton had a huge lead over Bob Dole that ranged from the mid-teens to nearly 20 percentage points. The final numbers were 49 percent for Clinton, 41 percent for Dole and 8 percent for Perot. The only pollster who was right was an unknown named John Zogby, who polled for Reuters. For his efforts, Zogby found his methods harshly attacked—he is still attacked to this day—by the pollsters he'd embarrassed.

The 1996 results were hardly in the league of 1948—at least the pollsters picked the right winner—but they sent alarm bells ringing at Gallup, which concluded that it had waited far too long to start polling only "likely voters" instead of registered voters.

But was this lesson really learned?

In recent months, the airwaves have been inundated with polls showing a significant majority of the American people do not want Bill Clinton impeached over lies he told about Monica Lewinsky. From that fact, all kinds of other theories emanate: that the Republicans are overplaying their hand, that Clinton is out of the woods, that this issue will actually work in Democrats' favor in the upcoming elections.

But a closer examination of the numbers, what pollsters call the "internals," raise doubts. For starters, who is being polled? Well, it turns out that it is not likely voters or even registered voters, but the general public. This is quite relevant. Zogby, who polls only likely voters year-round, consistently finds an approval rating for Clinton that's 10 points lower than the other major polls find. "The demographics of all adults is very different from the demographics of likely voters," Zogby says.

MARK PENN:
At a Tuesday morning staff meeting, he assured everyone that Clinton's Lewinsky speech had struck just the right tone.

Underscoring this point is a new Gallup poll in which the impeachment question is broken down by likely voters. The results are interesting: Whereas the general population opposes impeachment 62 percent to 34 percent, the likeliest voters are against it only 54 to 42. If you add party affiliation to the mix (registered Republicans *favor* impeachment by more than 2-to-1) one can see how unlikely it is that a Republican candidate in a solidly Republican district could be hurt by making Clinton's life difficult.

Take another frequently bandied-about poll number—Clinton's approval rating. Gallup and others have this figure in the mid-60s. Assume for a moment that number is accurate. What does it really tell us? Well, it's 10 points higher than Clinton's normal number, even when things are going well. Not to put too fine a point on it, but even White House officials concede privately that nothing Clinton has done in the policy arena in his second term can really explain the upward spike in support that came after the Lewinsky story broke.

So here's a postulate: It's no coincidence that the approval rating and the anti-impeachment numbers are virtually the same; voters are substituting one question for the other because they know how polls are used today to try to win debates.

USE AND ABUSE

The day after Clinton's disastrous pseudo-apology on the Monica Lewinsky matter, Clinton Pollster Mark Penn assured everyone at the Tuesday morning staff meeting that the president had struck just the right tone—because 58 percent of those polled in Penn's surveys told him this, according to one participant in the session.

But those polls didn't take into account—and couldn't, really—a host of other factors, including that Clinton's new story meant he had personally lied to the very Democrats who could give him cover, including Cabinet members and Capitol Hill leaders. In other words, as every reputable pollster readily admits, there are limits to what polling can tell us. "There are just things you can't poll," said one White House aide, with a laugh. "But we try."

They aren't alone. The last president who didn't employ polling was Herbert Hoover. Jimmy Carter actually began the tradition of having an in-house pollster, and Ronald Reagan's extensive polling operation was the model for the Clinton White House.

The first president to study polls, to commission his own private polls and, ultimately to ignore the polls, was Franklin D. Roosevelt. In 1940, FDR desperately wanted to help Britain stave off Nazi aggression, but Americans were in an isolationist mind-set. According to Robert Eisinger, assistant professor of political science at Lewis & Clark College, Roosevelt began quietly obtaining poll data from Gallup and another Princeton pollster with ties to Gallup named Hadley Cantril.

Roosevelt consulted polls on everything from support for Lend-Lease to whether Catholic voters would be offended if strategic bombing by the Allies harmed religious sites in Italy. In the end, however, Roosevelt scholars say that FDR set his own course. "I don't think there's any evidence that he relied on polls," said Eisinger. "They are feeding into his policy decisions, but they are not driving them."

Two, more recent, examples of presidents and polls are also instructive. In 1990, after Iraqi tanks overran Kuwait, polls showed Americans overwhelmingly opposed to the idea of American ground troops being deployed to the Arabian peninsula. But President Bush, asserting that national security was at stake, decided to send troops anyway. The following winter, 10 days before the ground war began, only 11 percent of Americans were in favor of launching one. A month later, this figure was closer to 90 percent—and so was Bush's approval rating.

A third example is Clinton's 1995 decision to send troops to the Balkans to halt ethnic genocide. After agonizing over this issue for a year, Clinton finally decided to act. Deeply concerned about public opinion polls that were running 2-to-1 against committing American ground troops, the White House pollsters delved deeply into exactly what the public would accept. Clinton pollster Dick Morris insists that the purpose of these polls was to know how to explain the Bosnian commitment to the public, but it also seems that the American public helped set the parameters of the military mission. The public told Clinton's pollsters it didn't want American troops scouring mountainsides looking for war criminals or disarming the Bosnian militias, and that it wanted a firm timetable for withdrawal. All these elements ultimately became conditions of the deployment.

DICK MORRIS:
"You don't use a poll to reshape a program, but to reshape your argumentation for the program so the public supports it."

"Clinton does polls to decide what to do," says Republican pollster Frank Luntz, who tested the GOP "Contract With America" in surveys. "That's not what they should be used for. When we did the contract, we used polls to decide what to say, not what to do."

Morris insists that this is what Clinton does as well.

"A misuse of polls is when a politician switches positions because of a poll," Morris said. "You don't use a poll to reshape a program, but to reshape your argumentation for the program so that the public supports it and it works." Morris points out that Bosnia was not the first time Clinton bucked the polls, and he rattles off a litany of issues, ranging from the International Monetary Fund bailout and the rescue of the Mexican peso to support for late-term abortion and affirmative action.

Clinton also uses polls to tell people what they want to hear about a policy—sometimes even when the language doesn't actually describe the policy. In the case of affirmative action, for instance, Clinton's polling told him what to say—"mend it, don't end it"—and he said it, but he made no real changes in policy.

Lawrence Jacobs, a political scientist at the University of Minnesota, says this example highlights the real abuse of polling. Jacobs argues that since 1980, presidents and members of Congress have charted their courses mostly on the basis of special-interest pressure, campaign contributions and ideology, while using polls to help them put a (sometimes false) face on their policies. "They use polls to learn how to manipulate the language and to employ buzzwords and symbols," he says. Thus voters get the worst of both worlds. They don't believe their elected officials are listening to them, and when the politicians pretend to listen, it's merely to learn how to fool them.

So where does this leave us on impeachment?

One possible answer is that on this issue, the public knows it has a right to be consulted and is taking back some of the power of politicians, pollsters and the media to spin.

Republican House members keep stressing "the rule of law," and holding out hopes that they can bring public opinion along with them. But this issue is not as remote as understanding the menace of the Third Reich—or even of Saddam Hussein. Infidelity (and lying about it) is domestic policy, literally, and the public seems to believe it knows as much about it as do members of Congress, the media and these lawyers who keep popping up on television. "I'm not saying we should have a national referendum on it, clearly that's not what the Constitution and the Founders had in mind," White House Press Secretary Joe Lockhart said in an interview. "But the public ought to be heard on this, on what constitutes an impeachable offense. They have a right to be heard."

Certainly the facts are in the public domain—Independent Counsel Kenneth W. Starr and the Republicans made sure of that—and on this issue, at least, the polls are probably accurate. "If there's one clear message in all this data," said Gallup's David Moore, "it's that they don't want him impeached."

Sydney J. Freedberg Jr. contributed to this report.

OBSERVATIONS

When Presidents Speak

Michael J. Lewis

Not very long ago it seemed that George W. Bush—he of the mangled syntax, chronic malapropisms, and conspicuously laissez-faire attitude toward the relationship between nouns and verbs—was simply too inarticulate to be President. Eight months before the election, the columnist Michael Kelly, an otherwise sympathetic observer, was speaking authoritatively of the "pinhead factor," as if Bush's tongue-tied manner constituted plain evidence of a fatally incapacitated brain. On the same basis, it was confidently predicted that in televised debate Bush would be a ready victim for the allegedly nimble and tenacious Al Gore. For a time it seemed that the election itself pivoted not on great questions of public policy, where differences between the candidates were often muted, but on the ability to speak an intelligent sentence without stumbling.[1]

Of course it was really Bill Clinton, rather than the hectoring Al Gore, against whom Bush was being measured. For almost a decade, Clinton's fluid and assured speech had been regarded as the modern standard for effective communication. This was not due to Clinton's famous volubility, first glimpsed during his interminable nominating speech for Michael Dukakis at the Democratic convention in 1988. Rather, it lay in his much-vaunted knack for "connecting" with an audience, that mysterious process by which an intangible exchange of impulses and responses leads to a communion of feeling. Every stage actor or performing musician knows, and yearns for, this communion. Most impressively of all, Clinton was able to achieve it effectively on television, tailoring his delivery to the scale of the living room in much the same way that the young Frank Sinatra calibrated his voice for the microphone, singing into it as if whispering into someone's ear.

Still, for all the high premium now placed on "communication skills"—formerly known as public speaking—few would call this a Periclean age of oratory. It is a commonplace that modern television campaigning has promoted a slick and cloying style of delivery, organized around the regular and mechanical ejection of focus-group-tested sound bites. Anyone who has not mastered this style has little chance of entering American public life.

In presidential politics, the avatar of this style is usually said to be Ronald Reagan. As it happens, Clinton's technique was avowedly modeled on Reagan's, whose speeches he carefully studied even as he also sought consciously to emulate his true hero, John F. Kennedy. But two recent books cast a revealing light on Reagan's and Clinton's rather different relationship to the words they used.

THE LEGEND of Reagan as the Great Communicator was a creation at least as much of the Left as of the Right. In liberal usage this was, at best, a backhanded compliment, meant to expose his success as an achievement of public relations rather than of ideas. According to this view, Reagan, another "pinhead," brought to the presidency the same limited bundle of skills he had brought to Hollywood: a facility for projecting trustworthiness and sincerity, and a certain folksy charm in reading the words of other men. (That this was also a fairly accurate description of many of the TV journalists covering Reagan probably did not occur to them.) Reagan's eloquence, such as it was, was dismissed as a secondhand product devised by a stable of writers like Peggy Noonan, who joined him in 1986.

Abundant anecdotes reinforced this view. Reagan's habit of cupping his ear in feigned deafness at a shouted question occasioned much ridicule as a ploy to conceal an inability to think on his feet. His most celebrated ad-libs—such as "There you go again," his display of mock-exasperation during his 1980 debate with Jimmy Carter—were derided as rehearsed. An unscripted Reagan—so the legend went—had nothing to say or, even worse, was liable to say anything, as when he once joked, in the presence of an open microphone, that he was going to launch a nuclear strike on the Soviet Union in ten minutes.

With the publication of *Reagan, In His Own Hand*, this legend requires substantial revision.[2] This is not a collection of important public utterances, and it includes virtually none of Reagan's presidential addresses. Instead, it is limited to only those texts for which a handwritten manuscript survives. Many of these come from the periphery of Reagan's career, ranging from high-school juvenilia to a weekly column on Hollywood for the *Des Moines Sunday Register* to the tragic letter in which he bade farewell to public life. They have been carefully transcribed to show Reagan's own deletions and insertions, and in some cases they are accompanied by photographs of the texts themselves. In all this there is a clear tone of defensiveness. As the book jacket rather flatly claims, "Here is definite proof that Ronald Reagan was very much the author of his own ideas."

The defensive note is unfortunate, for what the book proves is actually more important—namely, that Reagan's talent for communicating was as much the talent of a writer as of an actor. If this aspect of his career has gone unremarked, it is because he did not write the books that are our measure of literary achievement. His two autobiographies were ghostwritten and, unlike Nixon or Carter, he was not interested in publishing for its own sake. Reagan's literary persona was essentially that of a journalist.

This is amply demonstrated in the most substantial portion of the book, Reagan's scripts for *Viewpoint,* the five-minute daily radio broadcast he delivered from 1975 to 1979, between his term as governor of California and his successful run for the presidency. Consisting of pointed commentaries on topical issues, they have the dated feel of old editorials; but as political history they are high drama. In them we see him formulating the comprehensive platform with which he would soundly drub Carter. If, during that campaign, Reagan seemed so effortlessly and maddeningly glib, it was because he had already thought through and epitomized for himself virtually every issue of public and foreign policy—from arms control to energy policy to public education. Here is the secret of what many assumed to be careful coaching.

A FIVE-MINUTE talk runs to about 600 words, that is, about two double-spaced pages, and to make a point thoughtfully and persuasively it requires an extraordinary economy of means. (Where the issue at hand could not be treated in a single commentary, Reagan extended the discussion over several programs.) In essence, these are the radio equivalent of op-ed pieces. Reagan had been a radio announcer in his formative years, well before he went to Hollywood, and had thus acquired the lifetime habits of a profession in which success depends on sustaining interest through the compelling use of words. But it is nevertheless striking how he crafted these pieces for the spoken voice.

Every program began with a "teaser," an opening hook that was immediately followed by a commercial. Generally these are the parts of a script that are written last, as an afterthought; but when Reagan sat down to write, he invariably began with them, establishing at the outset the dramatic momentum that would pull both him and his listeners through until the end. From the very first he showed a talent for capturing the kernel of a controversy in an arresting or unexpected formulation. For example: "Will Alaska wind up as our biggest state or will it be our smallest state surrounded by our biggest national park? I'll be right back."

In his foreword to *Reagan, In His Own Hand,* former Secretary of State George P. Shultz recalls how, as President, Reagan once approved a foreign-policy speech Shultz was about to deliver but then added,

"Of course, if I were giving that speech, it would be different." The text, he opined to an abashed Shultz, had been written to be read in the *New York Times*, not to be spoken aloud. Flipping through the manuscript, he penciled in a few changes and marked out the section that contained, or should contain, the "story." Nothing of substance was altered, but, writes Shultz, "I saw that he had changed the tone of my speech completely."

Reagan's interest in maintaining a continuous arc of interest explains the lengths to which he went to avoid seeming to read his speeches. This, he felt, disturbed the sense of spontaneous thought that was essential to gaining a listener's attention. The editors provide a vivid vignette of his technique on the campaign trail, where Teleprompters were not in use. Reagan painstakingly transferred his texts onto 4"-by-6" index cards, abbreviating in large block letters. The cards were then placed in the side pocket of his suit, out of sight as he strode to the podium, his arms swinging jauntily. Only as he waved at the audience with one hand did he slide the cards onto the podium with the other.

Reading itself was a challenge. Reagan's contact lenses were for distance, and he learned to remove one of them just before he arrived at a speaking engagement. The right eye read the cards while the left eye read the audience. As the editors suggest, "Reagan's speech system gave the appearance of being casual and spontaneous, while in reality his speeches had the cold precision of any carefully researched and typed speech manuscript."

THAT BILL Clinton attached a similar importance to direct and spontaneous engagement with an audience is clear from *POTUS Speaks: Finding the Words that Defined the Clinton Presidency*, a memoir by Michael Waldman.[3] Like Reagan's editors, Waldman, who was hired to help write Clinton's first inaugural address and served as director of speechwriting from 1995 to 1999, also brings a somewhat defensive tone to his subject, conceding that Clinton lacked the gift of "soaring rhetoric":

Clinton does not leave a long trail of chiseled phrases... Frequently his speeches read like what they are: transcripts of a highly persuasive man trying to win a listener's agreement. The prose of policy, not the prose of rhetoric, was what mattered.

This is a retrospective judgment.

The truth is that Clinton clearly yearned to make sweeping, plangent pronouncements, and he incessantly demanded vivid and memorable phrases on the order of John F. Kennedy's "Ask not what your country can do for you, ask what you can do for your country." For a time the search for a counterpart to this phrase threatened to paralyze the writers of his first inaugural address, until Waldman posted the rule, "No Reversible-Raincoat Sentences" (Calvin Trillin's term for those neat inversions, what rhetoricians call chiasmus, that Theodore Sorensen had devised for Kennedy).

As might be expected, the writing of Clinton's first inaugural was an extraordinarily loose affair. Apart from the ceremonial theme of renewal, Clinton gave no specific program to his speechwriters. Instead, as Waldman found, he liked "to act by reacting," developing his own ideas by talking to as many people as possible. The inaugural shows the strengths and weakness of this approach. It contained its share of striking phrases, including the unusual horticultural metaphor that introduced it: "This ceremony is held in the depth of winter. But, by the words we speak and the faces we show the world, we force the spring." There was also a certain measure of sentimental bathos ("Anyone who has ever watched a child's eyes wander into sleep knows what posterity is") and even a reversible raincoat: "There is nothing wrong with America that cannot be fixed by what is right with America." The speech was widely praised; William Safire compared it favorably to the Gettysburg Address.

Even as his speechwriters continued to labor over their stately lyrical prose, however, Clinton was also drawn to a rhetoric of emotional sincerity and authenticity. In this he showed his roots in the 60's, and in a generation instructed to "tell it like it is." But, as his first State of the Union address in February 1993 would attest, he also showed his roots in another and much older American tradition. During that speech, his writers were stunned to watch him drift from the text. Waldman reports their reaction: " 'He's ad-libbing! He's ad-libbing the State of the Union!' we shouted, and gave each other a high five." (It is hard to believe they actually felt quite so joyous at the time.) Waldman attributes the improvisation to the President's ability "to surmount an inadequate draft," but this hardly accounts for what was, in Clinton, a nearly irresistible urge, one that shows up again and again in this account and that occasionally got him into hot water (as with his rambling speech nominating Dukakis

It is reasonable to speculate that what ultimately lay behind this tendency to ad-lib was a variant of the old low-church tradition of bursting forth in unpremeditated public declarations of faith. Introduced during the Great Awakening of the 1740's, this was the "enthusiasm" that so alarmed high-church clerics of the late 18th century. It has since developed deep roots in the American South, where "testifying" plays a major role in black evangelical worship (and where the tradition of powerful public oratory still survives). For all Clinton's envy of Kennedy's formal poetry, this was one natural background of his own oratory, and one that, for better or worse, proved all but irrepressible.

BUT WHAT was being expressed in this oratory? To return to the inaugural that so impressed Safire and others, it consisted almost entirely of generalities. As was often the case with subsequent Clinton speeches, listeners were enthusiastic but unable to summarize precisely what its content was. Everything remained on a high plane of abstraction, without any of the startlingly concrete statements—"It is my intention to curb the size and influence of the federal establishment"—that had made Reagan's first inaugural so bracing.

The fact that Clinton's own "intention" was to do the opposite of what Reagan had promised was not the real problem. The real problem was that, politically, he could not say so, and did not want to say so; the rhetoric was thus designed to dissemble rather than truly to communicate. Not until the Republican congressional victories in the midterm election of 1994 did Clinton feel compelled to concentrate his mind. Waldman provides an engrossing account of the sudden appearance at that time of Dick Morris and his role in disciplining Clinton's response to the loss of Democratic control of Congress. During the weeks of the government shutdown, Morris coordinated the public-relations offensive, playing the part of *consigliere* to the chagrin of the discredited George Stephanopoulos and Harold Ickes.

Morris was not one to back into a speech through free association; each speech prepared under his direction followed a disciplined program. A lean and forceful writer himself, he was responsible for much of the 1995 State of the Union address, Clinton's response to the congressional Republicans' Contract with America. The most important speech of the Clinton presidency (not involving personal matters), it marked the public unveiling of Morris's celebrated strategy of triangulation, by which Republican ideas would either be appropriated or else branded as extreme and therefore un-American.

This was accomplished with a piece of stagecraft that was singularly repugnant, but also effective. Clinton called attention to a man in the audience, a hero of the Oklahoma City bombing who at great personal risk had repeatedly entered the destroyed federal building to carry out injured victims. After Republicans rose in a thundering ovation, Clinton abruptly revealed that the same man was a victim of the recent government shutdown, and had been working without pay to counsel Social Security recipients. While Republicans looked on confused, he delivered the *coup de grâce*: "I challenge all of you in this chamber: never, ever shut the federal government down again."

Ironically enough, the speech might have been even more effective but for the tireless commissars of political correctness at the White House. Morris himself wrote the central line: "The era of big government is over. But the era of every man for himself must never begin." This was a succinct formulation of triangulation, expressed in crisp Anglo-Saxon cadences. Although Waldman expected the first part of the statement to unleash an internal furor among Clinton's more liberal advisers, to his surprise Ann Lewis, a campaign spokesman, objected to the second, calling it sexist.

The phrase was rewritten in appallingly turgid fashion: "The era of big government is over," the President eventually declared, "but we cannot go back to the time when our citizens were left to fend for themselves." The phrase backfired spectacularly. The vigorous first line resonated while the second one was ignored, taking away the impact of the parallel construction. And thus Clinton's second term came

inadvertently, if fittingly, to be characterized by a phrase that was a straw man, rather than by the withering rebuttal that was meant to knock it down.

THE FACT that Clinton's message could so easily be read, or heard, in more than one way is also a clue to why, for all his celebrated charisma as a public speaker, his oratory has not stayed with us. It was, in the end, all rhetoric. By contrast, the spoken formulations of the man who allegedly owed the most to the techniques of modern mass communication and the sound bite were palpably in harmony, at least at crucial moments, with his deepest personal conviction.

"Mr. Gorbachev, open this gate! Mr. Gorbachev, tear down this wall." Such elegant alignment of word and feeling came naturally to Ronald Reagan. It did not come naturally to Bill Clinton, whose most memorable lines, delivered with the greatest of passion and evident sincerity—"I did not have sexual relations with that woman," "It depends on what the meaning of the word 'is' is"—concerned precisely those things he did not mean and knew to be false. In this regard, and despite his verbal clumsiness, George W. Bush would so far seem the truer heir of the Great Communicator.

Notes

1. For an unflattering collection of quotations from the President and President-to-be, see *George W. Bushisms: The Slate Book of the Accidental Wit and Wisdom of Our 43rd President*, edited by Jacob Weisberg. Simon & Schuster (paperback), 96 pp., $9.95.

2. Edited by Kiron K. Skinner, Annelise Anderson, and Martin Anderson. Free Press, 549 pp., $30.00.

3. Simon & Schuster, 224 pp., $25.00.

MICHAEL J. LEWIS *teaches American art at Williams College and is the author of* Frank Furness: Architecture and the Violent Mind (Norton). *Among his recent contributions to* COMMENTARY *are "Mumbling Monuments" (February) and "Of Kitsch and Coins" (October 1999).*

The imperial presidency

Power is returning to the White House. But George Bush's room for manoeuvre is still circumscribed

AUTUMN has hardly begun, and yet Washington is already enveloped in an impenetrable fog. Most people do not have a clue where they are going, and the few who do are not telling. But at least one thing is clear amid the general confusion: the United States is witnessing the most dramatic expansion in presidential power for a generation.

In the 28 years since Arthur Schlesinger attacked Richard Nixon's "imperial presidency", the prevailing feature of the office has been its weakness. The Watergate scandal enormously increased Congress's power to monitor the White House, introducing an obsession with process that even "strong" presidents, such as Ronald Reagan, had to endure. The growing impertinence of the media, the movement for states' rights, even the political apathy of a prosperous country, all gradually chipped away at the imperial stucco. The end of the cold war seemed another body-blow. Bill Clinton's hyperactivity did not save him from earning headlines about "the incredible shrinking presidency", and his habit of using his official powers to conceal his personal failings only undermined the structure further.

George Bush's presidential campaign last year was designed for this era of diminished expectations. His mantra was localism at home and modesty abroad. Compassionate conservatism was all about little local acts of charity. As president, Mr Bush has seemed happiest away from Washington: hence his decision to spend all of August on holiday. At his desk he often seemed half-hearted, an aristocratic scion doing something slightly tedious to please his family. The morning of September 11th found the leader of the free world reading to school-children, trying to push through relatively minor education reforms.

The collapse of the twin towers jolted both Mr Bush and his office back into life. Washington immediately reorganised itself around the executive branch. And Mr Bush equally immediately reorganised his presidency around the struggle against terrorism. The distracted dilettante became a purposeful monarch. Almost at once, the administration persuaded Congress to approve a $40-billion recovery package that also strengthened intelligence and security. An anti-terrorism bill that hugely increases the executive's power was also passed quickly.

But it is not just a case of specific powers forged anew. For years, America's political culture has been strongly anti-authoritarian. Republicans have called for power to be returned to the states and to individuals. Democrats have peddled conspiracy theories about the army and the intelligence agencies. Now the opinion polls show a greater appreciation not just of big government but also of the work of once-demonised institutions such as the FBI and the CIA. About 1,000 people have been detained without much more than a whisper of dissent. Mr Bush's revived presidency comes equipped with a powerful armoury.

Which is exactly as it should be. In "The Federalist Papers" Alexander Hamilton pointed out that war naturally increases the executive at the expense of the legislative authority. He also explained why this should be so: "The direction of war most peculiarly demands those qualities which distinguish the exercise of power by a single hand." The commander-in-chief is the single uniting voice in a political system that institutionalises babble, with 100 senators and 435 representatives.

How will all this change Washington? Most importantly by shifting attention from means to ends. In the 1990s Washington was obsessed with due process. Now the only thing that matters is results. The president has almost unprecedented powers to shape the political agenda and direct the flow of information. The leak-happy city of Mr Clinton's days has been silenced. In October the president told the members of Congress that he would cease sharing information with them if they continued to hand it to the press. They have meekly complied.

There is probably more of the same to come. The White House has actually been fairly restrained, so far, in its recapture of power. For instance, the failed move to give Tom Ridge, the new homeland security tsar, a full-blown department came from Congress rather than Mr

Bush. And wars have a way of putting muscle into the president's hands. Abraham Lincoln happily imprisoned troublesome congressmen during the Civil War. Woodrow Wilson crushed any opinion that he considered "disloyal, profane, scurrilous or abusive". Franklin Roosevelt interned 120,000 Japanese-Americans without consulting anyone. Should another terrorist attack happen, both Congress and the public will be begging the president to seize even more power.

In terms of partisan politics, the increase in presidential power is not producing the dividend Republicans would like. In 1943, FDR disappointed hard-line progressives by telling them that "Dr New Deal" would have to transform himself into "Dr Win the War". Mr Bush is having to do much the same with his conservative base. Indeed, the importance of appearing to be above the fray is severely limiting Mr Bush's ability to raise funds or campaign for embattled Republicans. Sitting presidents should be vacuum-cleaners for party funds. But Mr Bush recently failed to turn up to a $1m "evening with the president", leaving Dick Cheney to take his place. His absence from the campaign trail is likely to hurt Republican candidates running in tough gubernatorial races in Virginia and New Jersey.

If the need to stay bipartisan is one constraint on Mr Bush's re-imperialised presidency, the other is the necessity of winning the war. The memory of Vietnam still hangs heavily over Washington. Another quagmire would surely lead Congress to make an attempt to rein in presidential power. But the comparison should not be pushed too far. America always had the option of withdrawing from Vietnam. No such option exists in the war on terrorism. Autumn fog notwithstanding, Americans know that they have to pursue this war to the end; and that the only way to do that effectively is to rally around Caesar.

THE ART OF COMPROMISE

BY JAMES A. BARNES

Before George W. Bush decided to allow limited federal funding for stem-cell research, who knew he had a touch of the canny Irish pol in him?

In the classic political novel *The Last Hurrah*, Mayor Frank Skeffington faced a seemingly no-win decision over whom to honor with a statue in a vacant plaza in an Italian ward critical to his re-election prospects in a fictional city modeled after Boston. The Knights of Columbus wanted a tribute to their namesake, the great discoverer, but the Sons of Italy were pushing for a statue of their longtime leader, Charlie di Mascolo.

"That's where compromise comes in," Skeffington told his nephew, Adam, who was making the rounds with the mayor as he was stumping near the contentious site.

"Who will it be?" asked Adam.

"Mother Cabrini," Skeffington replied with a chuckle. "Italian-born, and the first American saint. Let's see them get out of that."

Of course, it was Bush who needed maneuvering room—to wiggle out of a campaign promise not to allow federal funding of research involving the destruction of "living human embryos." His compromise—allowing federal funding of stem-cell research using cells only from embryos that had already been destroyed before his speech—appears to have placated many on the right without antagonizing middle-of-the-road voters. While his compromise got him out of a political jam, the decision's lasting impact on his image is debatable.

Bush's compromise didn't give potential critics much room to maneuver, either. As one veteran Democratic strategist noted: "I think Democrats are going to be hard-pressed to push this [issue] much further. Are we going to fight for... more than

he gave? There's no edge to that, and it's too complicated."

Perhaps the best a President can hope for when deciding a delicate political issue is that he doesn't alienate those in his own camp who are upset by his compromise. "A lot of it is how you couch the final decision, because that tells a lot about where your basic instincts are," said former White House Chief of Staff Leon E. Panetta, who watched President Clinton struggle over such decisions.

"In the end, you are not going to please everybody, and someone will be angered. What you have to hope for is that those people [who're disappointed], at the very least, believe that you listened to their viewpoints, and they will carry the hope that in the next battle, they have a chance to win," Panetta added.

Leon Panetta: "What you have to hope for is that those people [who're disappointed], at the very least, believe that you listened to their viewpoints."

Bush apparently did at least that well with his conservative base. A number of leading abortion opponents, including televangelist Pat Robertson, the founder of the Christian Coalition, and James C. Dobson, the president of Focus on the Family, saluted the President's decision. Laura Echevarria, spokeswoman for the National Right to Life Committee, the nation's largest anti-abortion group, declared: "We are delighted

that President Bush's decision prevents the federal government from becoming a party to any further killing of human embryos for medical experimentation."

Even some conservatives who opposed Bush's decision seem to fall in Panetta's category of upset but not estranged. At a news conference held the day after Bush announced his decision, a number of opponents sounded ready to continue fighting but unwilling to switch their basic allegiance away from the President. The way Bush couched his decision—he stressed the need to "protect life"—seemed to have made it more palatable to many who equate killing comma-sized embryos with abortion.

Commenting on the timing of Bush's speech, Ken Connor, the president of the Family Research Council, said: "I think in no small part, that reflects the fact that the President—and I take him at his word—was doubtless struggling with this decision.... So we don't fault him for that process at all." Connor even saw a silver lining in Bush's comment about the need for a national debate on the role of science in American life. "This is not a discussion we've really had before, and I applaud the President for ratcheting this up to the level of importance that it deserved," Connor said.

Nigel Cameron, the founding editor of *Ethics & Medicine* and dean of the Wilberforce Forum, Chuck Colson's prison ministry, said that one could view Bush's stem-cell decision as a glass that is half full. Cameron said that because of Bush's selection of conservative University of Chicago ethicist Leon Kass to head an advisory council on stem-cell research, "we will have a fundamentally moral framework for the development of public policy."

In briefing reporters on the President's deliberations leading up to his nationally televised address on August 9, White House Counselor Karen P. Hughes stressed that many people had "told him, 'This may be the most important decision of your presidency.'"

Rep. Jim Ramstad, R-Minn., recalled that White House senior adviser Karl Rove told a group of moderate GOP lawmakers that Bush equated the "gravity and magnitude" of his stem-cell decision "to an issue of war and peace and whether to commit American troops."

To some observers, that sounds like a White House spin machine working a little too hard. "Look, all Presidents are contrived, but some are less obvious than others," said presidential historian Robert Dallek of Boston University. "They hold the speech when he's down in Texas, because he's getting flak for being on vacation, so now they are going to show us that he's working hard and a deep thinker. I don't think people are fooled by this kind of public relations."

Indeed, if Bush really did think this was one of the most important decisions of his presidency, perhaps equaled only by the question of whether to send America's sons and daughters into battle, it's hard to understand why he chose to announce it from his home in Crawford, Texas.

In 1957, when President Eisenhower had to make a high-profile choice on how to deal with the growing violence in Little Rock, Ark., over school integration, he was taking a little time off from the job. But when the time came to inform the nation of his decision to send federal troops to enforce the court-ordered desegregation plan for Central High School, Eisenhower not only flew back to Washington to deliver his remarks from the Oval Office, he highlighted that fact at the beginning of his televised address.

"I could have spoken from Rhode Island, where I have been staying recently, but I felt that, in speaking from the house of Lincoln,

of Jackson, and of Wilson, my words would better convey both the sadness I feel in the action I was compelled today to take and the firmness with which I intend to pursue this course," Eisenhower said.

In the view of Princeton University presidential scholar Fred Greenstein, Bush ought to have taken a cue from Eisenhower: "My thought is that it would have been a good move for Bush to go to the Oval Office. If he had invested a little more effort and gotten himself up to speed on this, I think it would have been more natural for him to give this presidential address [from the White House]. He's been so anti-Clinton [that] he's been sub-Carter and sub-Ford as a public communicator."

Bush has struggled as a communicator. And his advisers have disagreed over how effective he is when he delivers remarks in a formal setting. One GOP communications strategist consulted by the White House staff remarked, "He does not convey a commanding presence. If they said, 'Where are you more comfortable doing this—Crawford or the Oval Office,' he would have said, 'Crawford.'"

But another outside Bush adviser, GOP pollster Fred Steeper, thinks that the White House venue was not needed. "There are passions about saving embryos, but we don't have a stem-cell-embryo crisis. For a crisis message, you would fly back to the Oval Office. This was a decision about a profound issue, as opposed to one stirring anger or fear, when the nation needs to be calmed by an Oval Office address."

Even though Bush wasn't responding to a national emergency, the White House staff was eager to portray his deliberations as a model of presidential decision-making. The day after his address, counselor Hughes provided an unusual amount of detail about the number of meetings that Bush had held on the issue, the range of people he had consulted, the briefing materials he had read, and even the notes he took.

"They are very sensitive to the knock that he's a disengaged President. And this was an opportunity to show him in a way that has not been seen, struggling with the difficult questions of science and life," said one Republican strategist. "Frankly, I think they were putting a little bit more into this [decision] than you could reasonably expect to get out of it."

Although the polls show that support for Bush's action on stem cells is fairly solid, it's unclear whether his long-awaited decision will turn out to be a defining moment for him. "I'm not convinced that this is a decision, or the event, on which his image in the early stage of his presidency will turn," said pollster Andrew Kohut, director of the Pew Research Center for the People and the Press. "Things that decide a presidency have to do more with what a President says than the process that he used."

In her briefing, White House counselor Hughes said a critical moment in Bush's decision-making process came on July 9, when he met with bioethicist Kass and Daniel Callahan of the Hastings Center, a bioethical think tank. It was during that session, Hughes said, that an ethical distinction was clearly drawn between using existing stem cells from embryos that had already been destroyed and using stem cells that could be derived by destroying "living" embryos.

That distinction also allowed Bush to remain true, at least on some level, to his campaign pledge not to finance research involving the destruction of embryos. Of course, Mayor Skeffington didn't need a philosophical discussion to figure out how to fulfill a campaign pledge. As he told his nephew: "There's a considerable difference between what they say they want, and what they'll really settle for. You can promise them the first, but you only have to deliver the second."

From the *National Journal*, August 18, 2001, pp. 2632-2633. © 2001 by the National Journal Group, Inc. All rights reserved. Reprinted by permission.

THE WHITE HOUSE

Leakproof?

At the Bush White House, mum's the word

BYRON YORK

ON August 26, the *Washington Post* ran a front-page story headlined "Bush Plan Could Cut Federal Workers; President Proposes Buyouts, Merit Pay, More Competition." In his weekly radio address the day before, George W. Bush unveiled what might be called his own version of reinventing government, a far-reaching proposal to reduce the number of federal employees and streamline dozens of programs, from food stamps to student loans to federal housing to Medicare. Details of the plan were contained in a 71-page report that the White House released at the time of Bush's speech.

That the story ended up on Page One was no surprise; the *Post* counts a huge number of government employees among its readers. But there was one surprising—almost amazing—thing about Bush's new management agenda: It didn't leak ahead of time. The report had been finished and printed well in advance of the presidential rollout—in fact had sat around in boxes for weeks—but word never got out. The president's team kept it a secret.

That's a huge change from recent administrations, when leaking sometimes reached epic proportions. "I've had it up to my keister with these leaks," an angry Ronald Reagan said in 1983 after his White House had become a virtual sieve of information about the budget, about squabbles inside the cabinet, about foreign-policy initiatives—about almost

everything. Last year, Reagan biographer Edmund Morris told the *New York Times* that he once sat in on a meeting in which White House chief of staff Donald Regan had a fit over leaks. Morris was astonished to see Regan's words reproduced verbatim in the next day's *Times*. "Someone had to have had a pocket tape recorder to get it so exactly," Morris told the paper.

Things were little better in the first Bush administration, as Richard Darman and James Baker burnished their reputations as masters of the leak. And there were times when the Clinton White House was so consumed with scandal management that it could not keep anything else a secret. But now there seems to be little if any unauthorized information coming out of the White House. What's going on?

Perhaps the most important reason is one of the least noticed: George W. Bush is the first president ever to have seen the workings of the White House from a staff-level perspective. While he had no official post in his father's administration, he often served as a de facto deputy chief of staff. As such, he saw the leaks that continually bugged the White House. And he learned how to read the newspapers—not for the news, but to divine the identities and agendas behind quotes attributed to "presidential advisers" or "senior officials." Now members

of Bush's own White House staff know he has a knack for decoding leaks.

Another reason is what several officials describe as Bush's ability to project a sense of loyalty to his staff. Almost all presidents benefit from the strong allegiance that comes upward from the staff—God knows Bill Clinton's people took bullet after bullet for him—but fewer can give their staff a sense that the loyalty is returned from the top. Reagan, often aloof, couldn't do it. The first George Bush wasn't that good at it, either. And Clinton was legendary for hanging his aides out to dry. But W. seems to have the ability—critical in controlling leaks—of keeping most of the staff happy. "At some point, every senior and mid-level staffer is faced with the opportunity to make himself look better by doing something that is damaging to the president," says one aide. "And the question they ask themselves is, Do I take advantage of this opportunity? One of the big restraints is, I don't want to hurt the president, and one of the reasons you don't want to hurt him is that he's been nice to you."

On top of that, there's also the remarkable cohesiveness—so far—of Bush's senior staff. Top political adviser Karl Rove and communications director Karen Hughes have been working with each other and with Bush for years now and have done an effective job at marking off their own territory. Andrew Card, the chief of staff, goes even father back; he first worked for a Bush candidacy when the elder Bush ran for president in 1980. The inner circle's tight control of information has impressed some veterans of White House leak wars. "The Bush loyalists have done an amazing job," says Donald Regan, watching from retirement. "They don't need personal flattery, and they don't need to have their egos stroked, and therefore they don't have to leak to show how important they are."

That said, there have been a few breakdowns. The most notable was a *Time* magazine story in July that concerned an internal White House debate over the patients' bill of rights. "Karen Hughes didn't like what she was hearing," the story began. The story described Hughes in a staff meeting, as she listened "with pursed lips" to White House legislative chief Nicholas Calio urging Bush to veto the bill then under consideration in Congress. "To Hughes…promising to veto a popular bill was sure to be a PR disaster," *Time* continued. "Bush had to

be for the people, not the HMOs. 'This will hurt us,' she warned."

It had all the signs of a classic hit-leak: a one-sided perspective, with a hero looking very smart, trying to warn the other side against stumbling into disaster. (As it turned out, Bush's veto threat played a critical role in helping him reach a deal with Congress.) Card was said to be mightily miffed, delivering stern lectures, but not embarking on the kind of Ahab-and-the-whale search for leakers that has characterized earlier administrations. Even though there have been a few other leaks—White House officials weren't happy when news got out about the planned "Communities of Character" initiative—there has been nothing of magnitude before or since the patients'-bill episode.

Instead, there has been day after day of "message discipline"—and a few deliberate leaks designed to make the president look good. While Bush hasn't engaged in that practice as much as Clinton did—after all, he has fewer friends in the press—he has pulled off one masterful strategic leaking initiative. In the

weeks leading up to the decision on stem-cell research, the White House put out story after story about how much the president was agonizing over the decision, about how he brought up the issue with virtually everyone who came into the Oval Office, about members of his staff with particularly deep feelings on the issue. Coupled with Bush's carefully crafted, split-the-difference decision, the leaks were a great success. They portrayed the president as serious, studious, and fair-minded.

Now come the fall battles over spending and the surplus. It's easy to imagine a scenario in which Bush, trying to hold the line on spending, is hurt by leaked reports that his staff is bitterly divided over strategy and substance. While that might happen—the smooth-running White House message machine can't run smoothly forever—don't look for a major breakdown. "I don't think they'll ever reach the point of the 'keister' comment," says David Gergen, the aide who announced Reagan's (unsuccessful) anti-leaking crusade back in 1983. "They run a button-up place."

Fixing
the Appointment Process

What the Reform Commissions Saw

by Alvin S. Felzenberg

After the British electorate turned his party out of office in 1945, Winston Churchill's wife Clementine advised him to look upon the results as a "blessing in disguise." He replied that if she was correct, the blessing was "very much disguised."

Churchill had reason for remorse. When Britain struggled, alone, to resist the advance of Hitler's forces in 1940, Churchill had summoned his nation to its "finest hour." Together with Franklin Roosevelt, who later provided assistance—first through lend-lease and after Pearl Harbor with manpower—Churchill devised the strategy that saved Western civilization as he knew it. He could hardly be blamed for indulging in a brief bout of self-pity after what he regarded as a personal repudiation on the part of an ungrateful citizenry.

But Mrs. Churchill had it right. Defeat spared Churchill blame for the industrial strife that followed the war. It also assured that Clement Atlee, rather than he, would "preside over the dissolution of the British Empire," something Churchill vowed never to do. It also gave him time to produce a literary classic: his six-volume history of World War II. Churchill was returned to power in 1951, beginning a dozen-year span of uninterrupted Conservative party rule. When he died in 1965, he was

hailed as the savior of his nation. His magisterial funeral set a record for a non-royal, equaled only by that afforded the Duke of Wellington almost a century earlier.

Recount 2000: Another Disguised Blessing?

It is hard to envision how George W. Bush or Al Gore, or their supporters, can ever regard the five weeks of court battles that followed the 2000 election and the truncated transition it produced as a blessing in disguise. But like that earlier instance, it too presents an opportunity for reflection, recharging, and repair.

Two institutions the 2000 election revealed as ripe for reform were the rickety and discordant election practices common in so many American counties, with no uniform standards to resolve disputes, and the lengthy, convoluted, and unwieldy procedures by which appointees of a new administration assume positions of responsibility.

Electoral practices and devices are attracting ample attention, and the legislative hopper is filling with reform proposals. But little has been done to streamline a presidential appointment process almost universally regarded as broken. Vice President Richard Cheney, who spear-

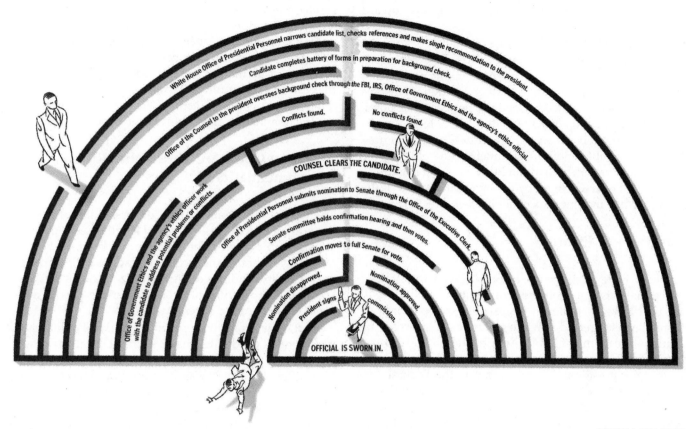

White House Office of Presidential Personnel narrows candidate list, checks references and makes single recommendation to the president.

Candidate completes battery of forms in preparation for background check.

Office of the Counsel to the president oversees background check through the FBI, IRS, Office of Government Ethics and the agency's ethics official.

Conflicts found.

No conflicts found.

COUNSEL CLEARS THE CANDIDATE.

Office of Government Ethics and the agency's ethics officer work with the candidate to address potential problems or conflicts.

Office of Presidential Personnel submits nomination to Senate through the Office of the Executive Clerk.

Senate committee holds confirmation hearing and then votes.

Confirmation moves to full Senate for vote.

Nomination disapproved.

Nomination approved.

President signs commission.

OFFICIAL IS SWORN IN.

STEVE McCRACKEN

headed George W. Bush's transition effort, stated that the greatest obstacle that post-electoral events in Florida posed to a smooth and orderly transfer of power were delays in obtaining the necessary "clearances." Most observers of recent transitions heartily agree.

What's So Hard about a Clearance?

Background checks may seem to lay-people a simple undertaking, one that corporations, universities, credit companies, and state and local governments routinely do with great speed. But in Washington these clearances have become a torturous and lengthy trial by ordeal. The typical appointee must complete a minimum of three forms: SF-278, a financial disclosure statement; SF-86, a form that begins an FBI background investigation; and the White House Personal Data Statement Questionnaire. Although the White House and FBI are free to modify their forms, information on the financial disclosure form is required by statute.

Nominees needing Senate confirmation must also complete forms required by the appropriate committee. Nominees who will be engaged in national security matters must complete still others. Each form comes with appropriate "waivers" granting permission for investigators to obtain medical and academic records, tax returns, and credit histories.

Unless improvements are made soon, more will be lost than the speed with which a new administration begins discharging its full obligations to the American people. Delays in placing people in their posts impede the president's ability to direct the workings of the government.

All the forms have lengthened over the years in response to accumulating scandals that embarrassed past nominees and administrations. In 1990, to dramatize the mushrooming of questions on the White House personal data form, the staff of the President's Commission on the Federal Appointments Process took to naming questions after past controversies that plagued past nominees and candidates. They named a mental health question (long since expunged), for example, after a discovery that led presidential candidate George McGovern to drop his first running mate, Missouri Senator Thomas Eagleton, from his ticket. The "drug use in college" question took the name of a federal judge whom Ronald Reagan had wanted to name to the Supreme Court. Proving the President's Commission's point, the Clinton administration added a question about hiring foreign nationals as domestics after withdrawing the nominations of two prospective attorneys general who had failed to pay Social

Security taxes for such employees. With an eye toward protecting new administrations against similar blowups, the FBI has also extended its fields of inquiry.

The rush of paper that sweeps through Washington during each transition has all but brought the process to a standstill. Scholars estimate that in Lyndon Johnson's day, it took about six weeks for an appointee, once nominated, to assume his or her job. By Bill Clinton's time, it was averaging more than eight months. The system now in place resembles nothing so much as the old "I Love Lucy" show in which Lucy and Ethel, working in a candy factory, are overwhelmed by the increasing speed of the conveyor belt moving chocolates in their direction.

Past Reform Efforts

All who have participated in or observed the process agree that this is a problem crying out for a solution. In the past 15 years, no fewer than six blue-ribbon commissions have suggested ways to improve the process: the National Academy of Public Administration (in 1983 and 1985), the National Commission on the Public Service (1989), the President's Commission on the Federal Appointments Process (1990), the National Academies of Sciences and Engineering and the Institute of Medicine (1992), and the Twentieth Century Fund (1996). Most of their recommendations have gone unheeded, largely through the force of inertia. Although parties to the appointment process have been sensitive to growing backlogs, duplication of effort, and wasted energies, few saw it in their immediate interest or capacity to make the needed reforms.

That may change. What post-election controversies may have done to improve election equipment and methods, the Clinton-Bush transition may do for the presidential appointment process. Americans have always been adept at applying Jonathan Swift's adage about "necessity" being the "mother of invention."

Indeed, unless improvements are made soon, more will be lost than the speed with which a new administration begins discharging its full obligations to the American people. Delays in placing people in their posts impede the president's ability to direct the workings of the government. "Holdovers" from the past administration may be unsympathetic to his goals, and civil servants may be unable to anticipate his policy preferences and unwilling to take bold action in the absence of political leadership.

An excessively slow appointment process also prevents the public from holding public officials to account through duly elected representatives. That is best achieved by having top-level, presidentially selected officials in place early to testify before Congress and present the administration's case through the media.

Extensive background checks and confusing and contradictory forms that are more obstacle than invitation to service may discourage the most able people from joining an administration. Even under the best of circumstances, potential candidates for high-level policy positions may find their salaries cut, their careers interrupted, and their privacy lost. To that list might be added "exit restrictions" that can limit their future earnings, as well as the potential harm of politically inspired "leaks" and rumors during the nomination and confirmation processes.

Just How Good Are Those Blue-Ribbon Recommendations?

The new administration and Congress will not need to name another commission or hold lengthy hearings to decide how to proceed. The problem has been studied extensively. Although the recommendations vary as to their practicability, findings of the half-dozen bodies that have studied the appointment process over the past two decades cluster around seven major ideas.

First, start transition planning early. Traditionally, presidential candidates have eschewed talking about plans for a possible transition, lest they appear presumptuous. Ronald Reagan was an exception, and scholars attribute much of his success to his early planning. In 2000, candidates George W. Bush and Al Gore, following in the Reagan mold, placed trusted advisers in charge of planning their transition. The impact of those efforts was clouded, of course, by the unprecedented delay in determining the winner of the election.

Second, assist new nominees. All the studies speak to the "isolation" nominees endure while awaiting appointment or confirmation. They recommend that a new White House Office of Presidential Personnel or inter-agency committee guide candidates through the process and advise them periodically where they stand. Another common suggestion is that either the Office of Management and Budget or the executive clerk to the president maintain job descriptions for every position the president is free to fill. These suggestions are sound and can easily be implemented.

Third, decide which positions merit a "full-field" FBI investigation. The Twentieth Century Fund panel found the full-field investigation, standard practice since 1953, "too blunt and intrusive an instrument for the purposes for which it is currently used." Its study and several others questioned whether certain appointed positions required an FBI investigation. Mindful of its professional role, the agency prefers to "treat all comers the same." But it is not the FBI's responsibility to decide which nominees to investigate or exempt. Present coverage can be streamlined either statutorily or by executive order.

Reports issued by the President's Commission on the Federal Appointments Process and the scientific communities recommended limiting investigations of nominees to the time since they last departed government service. The President's Commission suggested leaving the matter to the discretion of the agency where the appointee would serve.

Recent "leaks" of raw data from FBI files and misuse of files by either White House or congressional personnel underscore the need to enforce existing statutes and to enact others to protect the privacy of citizens. Information available to those who review a nominee's suitability should also be made available to the nominee before his or her fate is decided.

Fourth, clarify conflict-of-interest restrictions. This may be another area crying out for statutory change. Commonsense practices, subject to peer review, should replace "straitjacketing" restrictions that now determine conflicts of interest and set exit requirements. Requirements that nominees divest themselves of holdings in industries over which they have jurisdiction should be modified to allow them to spread capital gains taxes over several years or otherwise avoid forced "losses." Rules regarding blind trusts could be clarified.

Fifth, allow cabinet officers to do the hiring in their departments. Although several commissions urged this measure both to enhance the efficiency of government and to relieve the president and his staff of the need to pass upon people with whom their interaction will be slight, the recommendation flies in the face of recent history. Presidents who delegated this task exclusively to the cabinet (Nixon and Carter) found that appointees were more likely to pursue interests other than and often contrary to the president's. Those who exerted a firm hand over hiring decisions (Reagan and Clinton) put together administrations that worked better as a team.

Sixth, make fewer political appointments. This has become all but gospel in most of the foundation-supported, "good government" commissions on the appointment process. Noting the burden on the president of filling numerous positions, they see having fewer political appointees as a way to increase efficiency, especially during transitions.

Overlooking the practical obstacles to these proposals—why would any president want to give up this hefty instrument for asserting control over the executive branch?—such recommendations do not consider the costs such "reforms" would entail. Surely fewer than 6,000 people in a government workforce of 1.7 million is hardly a sign of the "politicization" of the government. That relative handful of appointees is one primary means presidents have of assuring that their directives are carried out. The more committed they are to the president's goals, the more energy they are likely to invest in furthering them.

It is through political appointees, who set policy, rather than through career civil servants, who execute it,

that Congress, the media, and the public hold administrations accountable. Success in this arena may require skills more readily acquired in the political arena or outside government entirely. Appointees who are not effective can be easily dismissed.

Seventh, establish limits on senatorial "holds" and make fewer positions subject to Senate approval. Senators value their prerogatives highly. Often they use holds to extract concessions from the administration or influence the direction an agency is to take. This is a scepter they are unlikely to give up. And, given its committee structure, the Senate can hardly be expected to agree on which posts to exempt from the reach of its advise and consent authority.

A more promising route would be for the new president to request the Senate's leaders to supply the White House with its forms so that all required paperwork can go to nominees at the same time. This simple measure can save nominees days, if not months, of paperwork and fees spent on lawyers and accountants. The president may be able to persuade the Senate to adopt a common form, with each committee free to request additional information as an attachment. Perhaps the Senate can even be persuaded to follow the White House form.

An Undisguised Blessing

Anything the new president and Congress do to assist new nominees, clarify conflict-of-interest rulings, reduce the tax liabilities and exit requirements placed on new nominees, establish order, logic, and priorities to FBI and other "clearance" processes, and bring the Senate's demands and requirements into closer conformity with the White House's will go a long way to streamline what has become an excessively burdensome and antiquated process. All can be achieved without intruding upon the prerogatives of either the president or the Senate to discharge their constitutional obligations.

Practical measures such as these will improve both the functioning of American democracy and the quality of public service not only for the Bush administration, but for all administrations to come. That would constitute an important part of President Bush's legacy—and that of the 107th Congress. If such remedies are successfully undertaken, historians of the future may proclaim them the "blessing in disguise" that flowed from the aftermath of the 2000 election.

Alvin S. Felzenberg is director of the "Mandate for Leadership 2000" project at the Heritage Foundation. He is editor of Keys to a Successful Presidency.

From the *Brookings Review*, Spring 2001, pp. 17-21. © 2001 by the Brookings Institution Press, Washington, DC. Reprinted by permission.

Crackup of the Committees

A MAJOR REASON FOR THE CHAOS PERVADING CAPITOL HILL IS THAT COMMITTEE POWER HAS ERODED TO THE POINT OF COLLAPSE

BY RICHARD E. COHEN

From the scant handful of major bills passed by the House and the Senate this year, one unmistakable fact emerges: The congressional committees have lost their long-standing pre-eminence as the center of legislative ideas and debates. A major reason for the chaos pervading Capitol Hill is that committee power has eroded to the point of collapse.

During May and June, for example, both the House and the Senate considered major gun control proposals that were not written or reviewed by either chamber's Judiciary Committee. Earlier this month, Senate Majority Leader Trent Lott, R-Miss., after bowing to Democratic demands for action on patients' rights, took the unusual step of selecting as the focus of the floor debate a bill crafted by key Democrats. Republicans offered an alternative measure that was initially prepared by a Senate GOP task force and was modified only slightly by the committee with jurisdiction. Meanwhile, key House committees are so splintered over their managed care legislation that Speaker J. Dennis Hastert, R-Ill., this week devised a plan to bypass them altogether.

Also in recent days, both chambers have taken up major tax cuts that were cleared by the tax-writing committees, but were not really the handiwork of a majority of their members. The chairmen of the House Ways and Means and Senate Finance committees wrote their tax legislation in consultation chiefly with a handful of senior aides. The committees then spent only a few hours on token review of the major budgetary and tax-policy consequences and made modest changes before the full House and Senate advanced the bills with little debate and amid grumbling, even from some Republicans.

Publicly and privately, "there was virtually no discussion of the [tax] bill with members," complained moderate Rep. Michael N. Castle, R-Del., who forced last-minute changes in the House proposal. "Everything has been fed to everybody."

This ad hoc legislating flouts the textbook model for how Congress makes laws. As generations of high school students have learned in civics courses, legislation is sup-posed to result when thorough hearings are followed by a committee review of alternatives in an attempt to build consensus, and then by a second and third round of those same debates on the House and Senate floors. Such a framework was described more than a century ago by a respected political scientist who initially framed his ideas as a Princeton University undergraduate and later became President.

WOODROW WILSON:

"Whatever is to be done must be done by, or through, the committee."

"Congress in session is Congress on public exhibition, whilst Congress in its committee rooms is Congress at work," wrote Woodrow Wilson in his classic 1885 study, *Congressional Government*. "Whatever is to be done must be done by, or through, the committee."

For most of the 20th century, Wilson's doctrine remained the rule on Capitol Hill. Small groups of members working in committees typically won deference for their expertise on particular policy matters. Generally, committee chairmen were recognized as first among equals. Their legislation was carefully crafted after extensive debate and deal-making and was rarely challenged on the House or Senate floor.

MY WAY OR THE HIGHWAY:

Newt Gingrich circumvented committees by demanding that GOP task forces write bills for him.

Over the past 30 years, however, committee power has eroded to the point where it now has largely collapsed. In many respects, this process has been both gradual and purposeful. It began during the era of Democratic control and has been greatly accelerated by both parties during the past decade. The death warrant for the old system came in 1995, when Newt Gingrich, R-Ga., assumed power as House Speaker. As part of his top-down management style, Gingrich circumvented and intentionally undermined the committee process by creating Republican task forces and demanding that they write legislation reflecting his own views.

With Gingrich gone, this legislative year began with promises that a more mature and steady Republican majority would pay greater homage to committee perquisites. Upon taking over as House Speaker in January, Hastert embraced a return to the "regular order." More comfortable than Gingrich with the committee system, Hastert promised to give the panels free, or at least freer, rein to achieve his general goals.

To be sure, some of the same chairmen who meekly ducked decisions under Gingrich have sought to impose their own marks on legislation in Hastert's House. "There is a stronger sense that our members are charting their own course," said a veteran House GOP aide. But Hastert often has found that implementing his lofty goal of a return to legislating-as-usual hasn't worked out smoothly.

In the Senate, Lott, now in his fourth year as Majority Leader, seems more settled in his post and less inclined to create party task forces to guide the work of committee chairmen. Nevertheless, Senate committees, like their counterparts in the House, routinely find that they, too, suffer because of their own ineffectiveness or lack of deliberation—or simply are ignored by party leaders. In both chambers, this has been the case in recent months with the gun control, tax cut, and patients' rights legislation. A similar scenario is likely to develop this fall on campaign finance reform.

Democrats, for their part, have been eager to criticize the Republicans for their continued efforts to detour around the conventional committee process. "It's an everyday occurrence now for committees to lose control," said Rep. Martin Frost of Texas, the chairman of the House Democratic Caucus.

Even GOP allies see little prospect for resolving the problem. Committees "will become increasingly irrelevant from the standpoint of legislation," veteran conservative activist Gordon S. Jones wrote last September in *The World & I*, a magazine published by *The Washington Times*.

That judgment may sound radical, but it is really only what has been obvious for some time. Despite occasional bursts of nostalgia from chairmen seeking to reclaim what they view as their due prerogatives, the arrangements that Woodrow Wilson described are as dated as quill pens and snuffboxes. And as the century ends, the breakdown of the committee system has become a major factor in the chaos that pervades Capitol Hill. Congres-

sional leaders repeatedly have encountered difficulties with party-driven legislation that was hastily brought to the House or Senate floor without a thorough vetting—or any attempts at bipartisan compromise—among the experts at the committee level.

Republican leaders, said Frost, "have danced on the edge several times and are flirting with disaster. You can't always cram for the final exam and get A's. Plus, their incompetence emboldens our side to go after them."

The increasing use of the filibuster in the Senate is one indicator that objectionable legislation is being scheduled more frequently for floor consideration, thus boosting combativeness. In a paper presented this month to a Capitol Hill conference on civility in the Senate, congressional scholar Barbara Sinclair, a political science professor at the University of California (Los Angeles), wrote that in the Senate during 1997–98, "half of all major measures ran into filibuster problems." During June, the Senate was hamstrung by simultaneous gridlock on managed care reform, appropriations, and steel-import legislation.

Moreover, the disruptive nature of the current legislative process has left the Republican majority struggling to effectively enunciate a party message. Consultant Steven Hofman, a House Republican leadership aide during the 1980s who became a senior Labor Department official in the Bush Administration, noted that in contrast to the congressional GOP, President Clinton often "produces a proposal and then goes to the country to talk about it." Hofman contended: "With divided government, narrow majorities, and a cynical public, moving policy forward requires public support. If I were a strategist for Hastert, I'd bring in our committee and subcommittee chairmen to see how we can engage issues with the country and have a dialogue."

Although there has been little serious discussion of institutional alternatives, the coming years may dictate a search for new models of legislative order—no matter who is elected President and who controls Congress.

BARONIES UNDER SIEGE

Democrats these days are well-positioned to criticize Republican operations, but they had plenty of their own problems in running the House and Senate committees while they held the majority. And the Democrats were responsible for major changes in the committee system that have had a lingering impact on the GOP-controlled Congress.

For most of the 20th century—following the Republicans' 1911 revolt against their domineering Speaker Joseph G. Cannon, who was called "czar"—the majority party in the House under both Democratic and GOP control gave the committees broad authority to dictate the agenda. The seeds for the destruction of that system were planted in the 1960s, when the mostly Southern and conservative Democratic committee chairmen in both the

House and the Senate resisted large parts of President Kennedy's "New Frontier" program.

The views of most of these conservative Democratic chairmen ran counter to those of most of their party colleagues, who wanted to increase the role of the federal government on economic and social issues. But during the early 1960s, Democratic congressional leaders lacked the muscle to break the deadlocks that resulted.

The old-style Democratic committee barons changed course and went along with President Lyndon B. Johnson's "Great Society" initiative only when LBJ's huge election victory in 1964 allowed him to define the terms of debate the following year. Perhaps the best example occurred in 1965, when Wilbur D. Mills, D-Ark., the masterful consensus builder who chaired the Ways and Means Committee, abandoned his longtime opposition to government-sponsored medical care for the elderly and took the lead in painstakingly building a bipartisan coalition to enact what became the Medicare program. "Generally, the committee system accommodated change," Hofman said. "Committees knew where the wind was blowing."

Even in those days, however, the committee system hardly functioned perfectly. Segregationist Chairman James O. Eastland, D-Miss., and other Southern Democrats who controlled the Senate Judiciary Committee opposed civil rights legislation so ferociously that Democratic leaders were forced to take those bills directly to the Senate floor.

Eventually, President Johnson's popularity waned, and the coalition of Southerners and cautious Northern Democrats who took their cues from the big-city political machines regained control of the House and its committees. They engaged in a titanic struggle with liberal Democratic reformers who demanded a more activist federal government. The struggle continued until after the 1974 election, when the "Watergate babies" eliminated the final vestiges of the old system—including the iron-clad seniority rules, closed-door deal-making, and Southern dominance among congressional Democrats. Another key step in 1974 was passage of the Congressional Budget Act, which created an annual budgeting process that supersedes the committees' role.

What followed was the democratization of the Democratic Caucus and of House committees: Subcommittee chairmen gained vast new influence; junior members won seats on the most powerful committees; party leaders—notably Speaker Thomas P. "Tip" O'Neill Jr., D-Mass.—became national figures.

With the introduction of C-SPAN coverage of the House in 1978, Hofman said, "members viewed themselves as much more independent, through the use of modern communications techniques." A prime early example was the move in 1982 by two young lawmakers—then-Sen. Bill Bradley, D-N.J., and Rep. Richard A. Gephardt, D-Mo.—to craft a massive tax reform plan and sell it to the nation. Slowly, reluctantly, the old-style committee chairmen accommodated themselves to the changes.

FILIBUSTER-HAPPY

As Senate committees and leaders increasingly send party-driven legislation to the floor, opposition forces have mounted a growing number of filibusters. Many of these filibusters have succeeded in killing the bills, since Senate rules require 60 votes to invoke cloture and limit further debate. By the 1990s, according to Barbara Sinclair, a political science professor at the University of California (Los Angeles), "The Senate's big workload and limited floor time made threats to filibuster a potent weapon, and Senators increasingly employed such threats." The data below, compiled by Sinclair, showed the increased numbers of filibusters and cloture votes during the past half-century.

YEARS	FILIBUSTERS PER CONGRESS	CLOTURE VOTES PER CONGRESS
1951-60	1.0	0.4
1961-70	4.6	5.2
1971-80	11.2	22.4
1981-86	16.7	23.0
1987-92	26.7	39.0
1993-94	30.0	42.0
1995-96	25.0	50.0
1997-98	29.0	53.0

During the Reagan years of politically divided government, important legislation was written largely in informal settings outside of the committee process. This was the case with the crafting of Social Security reform in 1983 and the so-called Gramm-Rudman-Hollings deficit reduction scheme in 1985.

In 1994, the final year of the Democratic majority, the committee system collapsed under the combined weight of its own decrepitude and the Clinton Administration's legislative naivete. The Administration's insistent demand for action on a costly, indigestible plan for national health care coverage triggered the final, whimpering end: Neither House nor Senate committees were able to produce credible legislative proposals.

TRANSFORMING THE WAY CONGRESS WORKS

When the Republicans took control of Congress in January 1995, armed with their ready-made legislative agenda, the Contract With America, the committees became all but superfluous. The document, signed by nearly all Republican House candidates in 1994, committed a Republican-controlled House to voting on 10 main planks and a variety of sub-topics, ranging from balancing the budget to congressional term limits.

What the committee chairmen may have thought about those goals simply did not matter. Gingrich was viewed by colleagues, and saw himself, as the political revolution's paramount leader. Members of the large and feisty GOP freshman class in each chamber emphasized that they would oppose a return of domineering committee chairmen of the type that had flourished during the era of Democratic control.

Especially in the House, Republicans "rightly sensed that their enemies were not just the Democrats' policies, but also their prevailing policy-making structures," wrote University of Maryland political scientist Roger H. Davidson in a recently published book, *New Majority or Old Minority?* The book, an assessment of the GOP-controlled Congress, was edited by Nicol C. Rae and Colton C. Campbell.

In keeping with the Contract With America's promise to "transform the way Congress works," House Republicans during early 1995 approved significant procedural reforms to weaken the grip of committee chairmen, including a six-year term limit for full-committee and subcommittee chairmen. (In the Senate, a similar six-year rule for committee chairmen, which has received less public attention, took effect in 1997.)

Other significant changes that weakened the power of House chairmen include the elimination of proxy voting in committees and the enhancement of the Speaker's authority to refer legislation to committees. In addition, Republicans cut committee staff positions by one-third in the House and by one-sixth in the Senate. They also eliminated three minor House committees and merged or eliminated several dozen House and Senate subcommittees.

"The corporate party leadership, and the Speaker in particular, gained substantial power at the expense of committees and committee chairs," wrote Christopher Deering, a George Washington University professor, in the Rae-Campbell anthology.

During the Gingrich years, Republicans also moved away from the Democratic majority's practice of calling in federal agency officials for oversight hearings to pinpoint bureaucratic failures. Rather than focus on programmatic oversight, Republicans trained their committee guns on investigative oversight to uncover scandal, especially among Clinton Administration officials.

Rep. Barney Frank of Massachusetts, a senior Democrat on both the Banking and Financial Services and the Judiciary committees who has been a Clinton loyalist during GOP investigations, said that Republicans have spent less time in committees on programmatic oversight because they oppose many of those programs in the first place. "To blame an Administration for a program not working, you have to believe the program *should* work," Frank said.

According to official records, the Democratic-controlled House committees issued reports on 55 federal programs and related matters in 1991–92, while the comparable total from the GOP majority in 1997–98 was a mere 14. Republicans concede that their cutback in committee staffing has left them with few aides experienced

in conducting oversight. Indeed, the House Rules Committee recently has been working with the Congressional Research Service to assist Capitol Hill staffers in learning how to conduct program oversight.

The committees' supervisory role also has been diminished by the Clinton Administration's unusually aggressive efforts to deny or at least limit oversight. At a recent hearing of a House Rules subcommittee chaired by Rep. John Linder, R-Ga., five House GOP chairmen recounted their difficulties in securing information from the Clinton Administration.

"Trying to get the facts out of this Administration is some trick," said Judiciary Committee Chairman Henry J. Hyde, R-Ill., who voiced frustration with White House responses to his impeachment inquiry last fall. Linder said that the panel may seek a House rules change to improve compliance with committee inquiries.

THE BUMPY ROAD TO REGULAR ORDER

The regimen of the early Gingrich years gradually broke down following the unpopular federal government shutdowns during the winter of 1995–96, the House reprimand of the Speaker for ethics violations in early 1997, and an aborted coup attempt against him in mid-1997. These incidents crippled Gingrich, weakened his command of his leadership team, and gave committees an opportunity to regain legislative primacy.

Yet members still complain of an absence of true debate and thoughtfulness in most committee actions. "The deliberative process does not happen very often," said GOP Rep. Castle.

In recent years, a growing number of members seeking to learn about issues have often found committee hearings so stage-managed as to be useless, and these members have stopped relying on the committees as a source for education and deliberation. In one alternative approach, small groups of members get together and call experts to their offices for private discussions. Likewise, the failure of many committees to promote serious debates on issues has created pressure—especially in the clubbier Senate—for bipartisan closed-door meetings in party leaders' offices.

Moreover, the past two years have seen recurring examples of committee chairmen on both sides of Capitol Hill who have been unprepared for the task and have documented their irrelevance by failing to act. For instance, House Commerce Committee Chairman Tom Bliley, R-Va., has become a prime target of criticism from his own party because his committee, despite its broad jurisdiction, has had a very limited output during the past four years.

Bliley has repeatedly failed to move managed care reforms because of disagreements among committee Republicans on the scope of the legislation. With Bliley's panel deadlocked, the action shifted several months ago to the House Education and the Workforce Committee, which had been largely dormant on health care issues. Hastert this week said that he would follow through on his private warning that if Republicans can't settle their differences soon, he will bypass the committees altogether and bring one or more "patient protection" bills directly to the House floor. Critics also point to embarrassing setbacks that Bliley suffered in June, when his panel took up the banking reform bill, on privacy and thrift-regulation issues. "Bliley is out of his element," said one House GOP leadership source. "John Dingell [the Michigan Democrat who is the panel's ex-chairman] runs circles around him." The source, like other detractors, would not speak for attribution about the chairman, whom they regard as thin-skinned.

At other times, committee chairmen have had problems when their views have run counter to a majority of their party. For instance, House Armed Services Committee Chairman Floyd Spence, R-S.C., sparked an uproar on July 1, when he made what is usually a routine motion on the House floor to send the defense authorization bill to a House-Senate conference committee. In doing so, Spence backed what appeared to be an innocuous effort by committee Democrats to "recognize the achievement of goals" by U.S. forces and the Clinton Administration in the Kosovo conflict.

GOP hard-liners seized the opportunity to launch another rhetorical attack on Clinton's handling of the war, which had ended weeks earlier. Rep. Randy "Duke" Cunningham, R-Calif., termed the legislative commendations of the Administration "sickening." Although the House—including Hastert and Spence—voted for the language, 261–162, most Republicans were opposed.

This incident underscores a larger point: Congress's entire debate on Kosovo this spring occurred largely outside of the committee process, again because of divisions among Republicans on the key panels and weak leadership by their chairmen, who couldn't settle differences. Debate resulted chiefly when GOP leaders called measures directly to the House or Senate floor. Rep. Tom Campbell, R-Calif., took the unusual route of filing proposals under the 1973 War Powers Resolution in what became a futile effort to force the House to take a position.

On gun control, which gained great urgency this spring following the high school massacre in Littleton, Colo., the key House committee of jurisdiction was also circumvented because of its inability to resolve splits among Republicans. In May—after Democrats forced the GOP to move the issue directly to the Senate floor, where Vice President Gore cast the tie-breaking vote to give his party a ringing victory—Hastert voiced support for some gun control steps.

Hyde favored action akin to the Senate-passed measure, but most of the predominantly Southern and Western Republicans on his panel strongly opposed new gun restrictions. The Judiciary Committee lost control of the issue, and House Majority Whip Tom DeLay, R-Texas, worked with Dingell to produce a weak alternative; then the Rules Committee structured the House debate to permit votes on various alternatives. In the end, the House rejected the Dingell amendment and other gun control provisions, and instead approved several steps designed to address moral decay and to expand juvenile justice programs. Since then, procedural objections have delayed efforts to craft a limited House-Senate compromise.

After the House vote, DeLay proclaimed, "I think the process moved very well." Likewise, Rules Committee Chairman David Dreier, R-Calif., praised the GOP's handling of the issue and blamed the failure on Democratic partisanship. "It was a brilliant process," Dreier said in an interview. "It allowed the House to work its will.... I would have preferred a different outcome. But we still may get something in a conference committee."

The most successful House chairman under Republican rule has been Bud Shuster, R-Pa., the head of the Transportation and Infrastructure Committee, who has frequently defied party leaders by pressing for public works spending that far exceeds their budget plans. Shuster generally has prevailed because—unlike other House chairmen—he works assiduously to develop bipartisan consensus on his 75-member committee, and he is willing to challenge current GOP dogma. "He embarrasses the leadership, but I admire the ways he gets things done," said a victim of Shuster's exploits.

Even when House and Senate committees manage to handle their legislation in a relatively routine fashion, they often face setbacks later in the process at the hands of Republican leaders. For instance, in resolving differences between two competing bank reform proposals before House floor debate began, committee chairmen and other senior Republicans dropped controversial amendments—one, from the Banking and Financial Services Committee, to restrict redlining (refusal to do business in poor neighborhoods) by insurance companies; the other, from the Commerce Committee, to strengthen privacy of banking records.

Neither proposal was debated on the House floor, even though each was supported by committee majorities that included Democrats and some Republicans. "In each case, the Rules Committee dictated the winner," charged a Rules Committee Democratic aide.

TAXING MATTERS

The House Ways and Means and Senate Finance committees, though long regarded as two of the most powerful panels on Capitol Hill, recently have been something less than models of legislative effectiveness.

This spring, the two committees behaved haphazardly when a bipartisan congressional coalition of steel-industry allies demanded action on steps to limit steel imports. Most Ways and Means and Finance members tend to oppose protectionist measures, so Republican leaders, having made commitments for floor votes, circumvented the committees. Ways and Means reported a steel import quota bill to the floor "adversely," but the House approved it anyway. Then the proposal was placed directly on the Senate calendar to avoid the prospect of committee delay; an attempt to force Senate action was stymied on a cloture vote in June.

The two committees' handling of tax cut legislation this summer has been haphazard as well. Ways and Means Chairman Bill Archer, R-Texas, unveiled his bill to both committee Republicans and Democrats on July 12—the day that Congress returned from its Fourth of July recess and less than 24 hours before the panel began its debate.

"Tax legislation is so complex that one word can change the entire meaning," said Rep. Robert T. Matsui of California, a Ways and Means Democrat. With so little time for review, "you don't have the opportunity to find unintended, or intended, consequences," Matsui said. "This wasn't a fair process." Rep. Sander M. Levin, D-Mich., added that Archer's lack of interaction with committee members conveyed the attitude that "he was telling us what was written on the tablets."

Although Ways and Means Republicans conceded that they, too, had little time to examine the bill, many said that Archer had kept them informed of his general direction and that the result included no real surprises. "Most of us had a pretty good idea of what was in it," said Rep. Rob Portman, R-Ohio. "You need to approach a tax bill with a lot of discretion for the chairman to make tough choices. Otherwise, it leaks out by dribs and drabs." In addition, members—especially those who do not sit on the committee—usually don't focus on the details until the final days before the vote, Portman said. "A lot of things around here don't get done until crunch time."

But after Ways and Means approved the tax package on a party-line vote, clusters of GOP moderates and conservatives met and identified an armful of problems with Archer's proposal. The issues ranged from the proposal's failure to completely eliminate the "marriage penalty" on certain middle-income couples to excessive benefits for the wealthy by means of a reduction in the capital gains tax rate and the phase-out of the estate tax. Other Republicans complained that the tax cuts did not leave enough money to restore the fiscal soundness of Social Security and Medicare. "People don't understand this bill," Rep. Ray LaHood, R-Ill., complained two days before the House floor debate.

Republican leaders were forced to postpone the floor vote by a day as they worked in a last-minute frenzy to round up their dissidents. To appease GOP moderates, the leaders agreed to condition the 10 percent, across-the-board income tax cut in Archer's bill on a commitment to reduce interest payments on the public debt. In addition, the Rules Committee wrapped highly technical—and perhaps ineffectual—tax-policy changes to Archer's proposal into the separate resolution setting the terms of debate on the overall bill. In the end, on July 22 the House passed the tax bill, 223–208, with all but four Republicans on board.

"The Republicans are operating by the seat of their pants," complained Frost, a Rules Committee Democrat. "Either they can't count, or they are not competent." Even a senior House GOP aide complained that the tax bill was "not deftly handled" and that Archer had placed party leaders in an awkward position because "he didn't reach out to many Republicans."

Like Archer, Senate Finance Committee Chairman William V. Roth Jr., R-Del., unveiled his tax cut proposal after only limited exchanges of views with other panel members—mostly by letter or through staff discussions. "He didn't have many discussions with Senators," said Virginia K. Flynn, Roth's spokeswoman. "But he's been signaling for months what are his plans."

Unlike Archer, Roth included provisions that were designed to reach out to Democrats, two of whom voted for the measure in committee on July 21. However, some Finance Committee Republicans complained about Roth's details, even though they voted for his bill. Four of the panel's most conservative Republicans, including Lott, offered an alternative modeled after Archer's proposal, but it was defeated, 13–7. GOP leaders hope to resolve House-Senate differences before the August recess.

The effort to finalize the tax legislation is sure to be a major headache during the remainder of the session. But also still looming is a related conflict that will probably prove the most difficult to resolve—how to pass the 13 appropriations bills to finance federal operations in fiscal 2000. Both problems stem directly from policy assumptions laid out by the House and Senate Budget committees in their budget resolutions earlier this year and approved on the floors in April in nearly party-line votes.

Although House Budget Committee Chairman John R. Kasich, R-Ohio, held listening sessions to seek the views of other Republicans on his budget resolution, it has become apparent that many members did not fully understand or embrace the consequences of the plan they approved—which included the large tax cut, tight spending caps in keeping with the 1997 balanced-budget agreement, and a "lockbox" that Republicans said will direct $1.8 trillion of the budget surplus to the Social Security trust funds during the next 10 years.

"The numbers don't work out in the long run," Rep. Fred Upton, R-Mich., complained on the eve of the House vote on the tax bill. When Hastert privately reminded the tax measure's GOP critics that they had supported the budget, Upton—who voted for the final version of the budget plan with all but three House Republicans—said he responded that other budget details, including more money for education, had not been fulfilled.

Now Republican members of the House and Senate Appropriations committees are desperate to avoid a repeat of last year's budget endgame, in which Gingrich took control of decisions. Complaining that their pool of money is inadequate, they say that they will be forced to engage in fiscal sleight of hand to meet the political prerequisites for enacting their budget. Other Republicans, however, bitterly respond that the free-spending Appropriations committees have gone off the party reservation.

In recent weeks, House and Senate Republicans have deferred committee and floor action on various appropriations measures because they feared that they lacked a majority to approve them. "We're suffering from inadequate internal communications," said a House Republican aide who has been actively engaged in the budget debate. "When no one has a standard understanding [of the spending legislation details], it's hard to grow the vote."

FLOUNDERING TO EXERT CONTROL

Despite the setbacks that House and Senate committees have encountered this year, congressional Republican leaders contend that, with some exceptions, they have restored legislative power to the committees. The leaders also emphasize their continuing desire for a less active federal government and make clear that they would not sanction a return to the old system of omnipotent chairmen.

Republicans, to be sure, have been handicapped by the nearly hopeless dynamics of the 106th Congress. They currently have only five-seat control in both the House and the Senate, and they must contend with a wounded Democratic President bent on reasserting his political primacy and leaving a legacy of peace and prosperity. Their dual challenge is keeping their diverse forces unified while confronting Democrats—especially in the House—who have become increasingly confident that they will regain control in next year's election. It is easy to see why Republican leaders, when confronted with difficult legislation, might surmise that the only way to exert control in the current climate is to move decisively, without waiting for often-wayward committees to work their will.

For their part, Gephardt and other Democrats have said that they will promote closer party coordination with the committees if they regain the majority. At the start, at least, the Democrats' desire to effectively manipulate the levers of power most likely would override some of their past excesses. But the prospect that most of the Democrats' House chairmen would be strong liberals could soon pose the same kinds of problems that Republicans have had since 1995.

Few in the House or Senate—or, for that matter, in the news media or academia—give much thought to the committee system's problems. With most lawmakers spending only three or four days a week in Washington and focusing mainly on the crisis of the week, they find little reward in thinking about seemingly intractable dilemmas. In the meantime, the problem deepens.

Can It Be Done?

**CONGRESS SEEMS RELUCTANT TO TRY TO ABOLISH THE ELECTORAL COLLEGE,
AND SMALL STATES PROBABLY WOULDN'T GO ALONG ANYWAY.
STILL, SOME HOLD OUT HOPE FOR A PUBLIC GROUNDSWELL.**

BY RICHARD E. COHEN
AND LOUIS JACOBSON

For Congress, junking the Electoral College appears to be an idea whose time has passed or hasn't yet arrived. At this stage, only a handful of lawmakers or top aides are even remotely interested in or familiar with the proposal's lengthy history and far-reaching consequences. And even those few are pretty dubious about overcoming the steep challenges of changing the Constitution.

To be sure, the controversy over the Electoral College's role in this year's presidential election has already resonated across the country and in Congress, and public officials may well undertake a serious debate over the issue in the months and years to come. A Nov. 11–12 Gallup survey for *USA Today* and CNN found that 61 percent of those surveyed favor a popular-vote system that directly elects the President. Moreover, interest groups are launching petition drives and Internet campaigns to try to stir up significant interest at the grass-roots level for abolishing the Electoral College.

Several lawmakers, in turn, have stepped forward since the election with calls for action. Some, such as Sen.-elect Hillary Rodham Clinton, D-N.Y., Sen. Richard J. Durbin, D-Ill., and Rep. Ray LaHood, R-Ill., want to eliminate the Electoral College altogether. Others have taken a more measured approach by calling for commissions to study the Electoral College, or for modernizing and standardizing the way that the nation votes.

It's also true that in 1969, the House—at the urging of President Nixon—voted overwhelmingly to replace the Electoral College with a popular-vote system, only to see the proposal subsequently die in the Senate. But even among the current lawmakers and aides who are interested in the issue, few remember what happened three decades ago. "I'm not aware that it passed the House" in 1969, said a senior House Republican legislative aide who has worked on Electoral College reform. "That's ancient history."

---

30 YEARS AGO:

In 1969, the House voted to eliminate the Electoral College, but in the Senate, foes of the proposal, led by Sen. Sam Ervin prevailed over proponents, such as Sen. Birch Bayh.

Why do the prospects for congressional action appear so slim? The short answer is that would-be proponents recognize that it might be impossible to persuade states with small populations to relinquish the disproportionate power that they believe they hold in the Electoral College. By constitutional design, those states also have disproportionate influence in the Senate, and that body has stifled past attempts at reform.

Ratifying an amendment to the Constitution requires two-thirds approval in the House and in the Senate, followed by a majority vote by legislatures in three-fourths

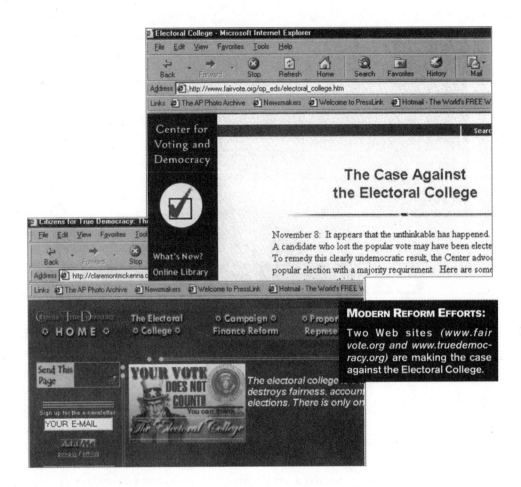

of the states. Only 17 amendments have been ratified since the basic framework, including the Bill of Rights, was completed in 1791. "Some of the states would be in favor of it, but it would be an uphill battle to get to three-quarters of the legislatures," said Tim Storey, an elections specialist with the National Conference of State Legislatures, which is neutral on Electoral College reform.

Under the current system, small-state proponents contend, each state's votes are important. That has become apparent in recent days as the world has breathlessly monitored the tally of a few hundred stray votes in, for instance, New Mexico, which has five electoral votes. (New Mexico's 1 percent of the total Electoral College vote is nearly twice its share of the nation's population.) Were the presidential election to hinge on a single nationwide popular vote, these small-state advocates contend, presidential candidates would focus their attention where the most votes are available—chiefly, in large metropolitan areas and on television.

"If this country elected a President on the basis of a popular vote, New Hampshire's sentiments would be entirely irrelevant," the state's Manchester *Union-Leader* editorialized this week. "An American President should be beholden to all 50 states, not just two," said the newspaper, referring to the "teeming metropolises of Los Angeles and New York." During this year's presidential campaign, Al Gore and George W. Bush fought actively

over New Hampshire's four electoral votes, and Bush eked out a narrow victory.

Direct-election proponents counter that the mathematics of the Electoral College give a lot of influence to the big-population states anyway. They cite the fact that Bush and Gore spent most of the campaign's final weeks battling for several large "swing" states, such as Florida and Michigan, and ignored most other states. (The two candidates, however, waged only limited campaigns in California and New York, because of Gore's big advantage in those states.)

Regardless of the fine points of the dichotomy between large and small states, Electoral College reform "won't happen, because the small states won't agree to it," said Rep. Jerrold Nadler, D-N.Y., a Judiciary Committee member who this week proposed a commission to examine how the nation conducts elections, with the goal of modernizing voting procedures. Nadler, an outspoken liberal, says he has "qualms" about holding a single national count because, as the current "mess in Florida" shows, "if we had to count 100 million votes and we had a close contest, we'd have a real problem."

Rep. Tom Davis of Virginia, the chairman of the National Republican Congressional Committee, voiced a similar fear. "A recount in 50 states wouldn't simplify the election," he said. Like other lawmakers, Davis added that he hasn't thought much about Electoral College reform. At least not yet.

PAST AS PROLOGUE

Not that long ago, the drive to abolish the Electoral College was on America's front burner. Throughout the 1960s, the proposal generated extensive public support, partly because of John F. Kennedy's razor-thin victory in the 1960 election, which runner-up Richard Nixon decided not to challenge.

SPLIT SENATORS

Dick Durbin wants to repeal the Electoral College, while Arlen Specter now just wants to study voting procedures.

Support grew further following the 1968 election, in which then-Gov. George C. Wallace of Alabama won six states, giving him 46 electoral votes. That was potentially enough to swing that year's contest between Nixon and Vice President Hubert Humphrey, the Democratic nominee, each of whom had won 43 percent of the total vote. The immediate problem was avoided when Nixon won 301 electoral votes, but leaders of both parties envisioned the nightmare scenario in which Wallace or another fringe candidate could have won enough support to throw a presidential election into the House.

In September 1969, the House voted 338-70 for a proposed constitutional amendment to do away with the Electoral College and substitute direct election of the President. Following the House vote, Nixon said the need for reform was "urgent and should be our controlling consideration."

But the constitutional amendment died a year later, the victim of a Senate filibuster by a coalition of Southern Democrats and conservative Republicans, many from small states. Their leader was Sen. Sam J. Ervin Jr., D-N.C., who would gain renown in 1973 for chairing the investigation of the Watergate break-in. That inquiry led to Nixon's resignation a year later, and Ervin became a liberal icon. But Ervin's opposition to Electoral College reform left him with a negative legacy as a retrograde states' righter.

Proponents continued to press the issue following the 1970 setback, but public interest gradually faded, and the political battlefield has since changed radically. During a Senate debate in 1979, the measure was rejected 51–48, 15 votes short of the required two-thirds majority.

As years passed, and several presidential elections were decided by wide margins, calls for reform of the Electoral College became outdated. In 1992, when Ross Perot received 19 percent of the vote as a third-party candidate, his vote was spread relatively evenly across the nation, and he was no threat to the Electoral College count. And Bill Clinton that year defeated President Bush 43 percent to 38 percent in the popular vote.

"Because recent elections have not been close in their popular-vote margin, there has been no hue and cry," said former Sen. Birch Bayh, D-Ind., who devoted much of his 18-year Senate career to advocacy of constitutional amendments, including one for direct election of the President, and was a key player during the chamber's Electoral College debates of the 1970s. "The feeling has been that we looked the tiger in the face."

Meanwhile, many interest groups turned to other government-reform causes or decided to trim their budgets. The American Bar Association, for example, had played a leading role in what Bayh called his "consortium" of supporters for abolishing the Electoral College. But that position was "archived"—or set aside—several years ago, according to an ABA spokesman, because the issue had lain fallow for too long without discussion.

The League of Women Voters, which has actively advocated campaign finance reform in recent years, has remained a consistent if relatively quiet voice for Electoral College reform. "We're hearing from our grass roots, and they seem pretty keyed up," Paul Boertlein, the group's senior director of communications, said this week.

Newer groups have also entered the debate. Since 1992, the Center for Voting and Democracy has urged the abolition of the Electoral College. The Takoma Park, Md.-based group, whose president is former third-party presidential candidate John Anderson, boasts a staff of roughly a half-dozen and a membership spanning the ideological spectrum.

In addition, a two-year-old group called Citizens for True Democracy has also seized the day with its call to abolish the Electoral College. The Los Angeles-based group is the brainchild of David Enrich, a Claremont-McKenna College graduate who's in his "early 20s" and dabbled early on in Ralph Nader's third-party campaign. He said he hopes to expand his mailing list of "probably a couple thousand supporters" by reaching out to voters over the Internet.

The main voices defending the Electoral College have historically been scholars, who are usually not really media-savvy. But philosophical conservatives might also rally, especially over talk radio, to retain the Electoral College, said John Samples, a supporter of the current system who directs the Center for Representative Government at the libertarian Cato Institute.

"I've appeared on 15 talk shows in the last three days," Samples said. "I've been struck by the level of phone calls and the intelligence of the comments by the callers and hosts" who oppose abolishing the Electoral College.

In a national debate over eliminating the Electoral College, another voice supporting the current system would be the American Legislative Exchange Council, an association of conservative state legislators. "State legislatures would more than likely oppose such [a constitutional] amendment, the reason being that it would be an erosion of state power," said spokesman Bob Adams.

ORRIN VS. HILLARY

On Capitol Hill, defenders of the Electoral College have a powerful ally in Senate Judiciary Committee Chairman Orrin G. Hatch, R-Utah, who vigorously opposes eliminating the institution. Hatch plans extensive hearings next year on proposals to abolish the Electoral College, and said he is confident that "reason will prevail" once the topic is fully debated. The fact that Hillary Clinton, in particular, already has announced her support for such proposals has grabbed his attention. "She needs to study this," Hatch admonished.

Nevertheless, the problems with this year's election clearly have registered with many members of Congress. In interviews this week, a broad cross section of lawmakers voiced support for exploring the states' disparate voting procedures and unreliable ballot-counting mechanisms, and said that a strong possibility exists for congressional action in these areas in the next two years.

Hatch himself said he would support steps to assist local governments in upgrading their voting machinery, as Nadler has proposed. "We can provide the financial wherewithal to purchase machines so that we have uniform action," Hatch said. "I can imagine that happening, even though it would be expensive." He also said he is open to reviewing proposals for a uniform poll-closing time across the nation, partly to deal with problems in the West resulting from televised coverage of early election returns.

Even before the current brouhaha, a handful of members of Congress already were pushing—with persistence but little impact—for eliminating the Electoral College. According to Thomas, which is the Library of Congress database, lawmakers in the past two years filed three proposed constitutional amendments calling for abolishing the Electoral College. By contrast, 265 such constitutional amendments were proposed between 1947 and 1968, according to a Congressional Research Service study.

The most active recent proponents of abolishing the Electoral College have been Durbin and LaHood. When they held a pre-election press conference at the Capitol, coverage was greater than they expected, probably because of the prospect for a close presidential election. Since then, interest has grown exponentially, both said this week. "When it comes to issues, you have to take advantage of the moment," said Durbin, who has sponsored similar legislation since 1993, when he was serving in the House.

Durbin plans to press for Senate action next year, starting in Hatch's Judiciary Committee, although he would not predict the outcome. LaHood, meanwhile, said that he will urge House Speaker J. Dennis Hastert, R-Ill., a home-state colleague, to commit to scheduling a House vote on the issue during the 107th Congress. "I've been interested in the issue since I was a junior high school teacher," LaHood said. "I've always said that there needs to be a controversy to stir up the American people."

JERROLD NADLER:

Electoral College reform "won't happen because the small states won't agree to it."

Back in 1997, LaHood got a hearing on his proposal in the House Judiciary Constitution Subcommittee. Rep. Charles J. Canady, R-Fla., the panel's chairman, opened the hearing by stating, "There are indeed potential problems with the current manner in which we elect our President," and he added that the public "would not understand the election of a President who had not received the most votes in the election." But Canady concluded that the system "seems to have served the nation fairly well," and his panel took no further action.

During that 1997 hearing, House Judiciary Committee Chairman Henry J. Hyde, R-Ill., strongly opposed La-Hood's direct-election plan. "I like the system that recognizes competing interests, differing interests, and that synthesizes them into *E pluribus unum*," Hyde said. "By having to win this state and this state and this state, I think that consensus is better served" in electing a President.

CRUSADE OR PASSING FAD?

For the Electoral College reform issue to regain real currency, proponents would need to mount a new national crusade. That prospect depends, in part, on the extent of public unhappiness with the outcome of this year's presidential election. In addition, both parties will have to weigh the partisan implications of abolishing the current system.

For now, most Republicans have apparently become reluctant to discuss Electoral College reform, because such a step might be seen as undermining the legitimacy of a Bush victory, especially if he does not win a plurality of the popular vote.

This GOP skittishness has been evident in the recent maneuvers of Sen. Arlen Specter, R-Pa. On Nov. 8, the day after the election, Specter told reporters in Philadelphia that he would return to Washington the following week and file legislation to repeal the Electoral College, which he called "an anachronism… which doesn't make sense now" and is contrary to democratic principles.

But within a week's time, Specter retreated to the position of simply calling for a commission to study voting procedures. He told the Senate on Nov. 14 that the popular election of the President "appears to be unrealistic because there are so many smaller states."

Meanwhile, Rep. Christopher Shays, R-Conn., a leading GOP advocate of campaign finance reform, said that abolishing the Electoral College would be "a big mistake" because it would lead presidential candidates to focus on selected regions of the nation. If they could win "with a simple majority of the popular vote, they can play to a single area," Shays said. He also voiced fear that a tight race producing a national recount could create the "potential for civil unrest."

Democrats also are split on the issue. Durbin noted that he received a phone call after he held his pre-election press conference on his Electoral College reform plan from "a friend in the Gore campaign who asked why I was doing this."

During the Senate's debate in 1979, current Sens. Joseph R. Biden Jr., D-Del., and Daniel Patrick Moynihan, D-N.Y., opposed abolishing the Electoral College. And at a press conference in recent days, Sen. Robert G. Torricelli, D-N.J., said he, too, supports the institution, even though his home state presumably would benefit from reform. He depicted himself as an advocate of federalism and embraced the argument of the small-staters in calling the current voting system "an important element" for the nation. "Our sense of union and everyone's inclusion has now been based on this Electoral College," Torricelli said.

But Sen. Edward Kennedy, D-Mass., is a strong advocate of closing down the Electoral College. And although House Democratic Caucus Chairman Martin Frost of Texas has not taken a position on one side or the other on the Electoral College, he said "we ought to seriously look at the issue, with hearings," and noted that the public is clearly interested.

A congressional Democratic leadership aide speculated that Electoral College reform is merely the "flavor of the day" in political debate. Likewise, freshman Sen. Evan Bayh, D-Ind.—son of Birch Bayh—cautioned, "The prospects for change probably are not that good, once current passions cool."

It's impossible to predict whether these naysayers are right. And even if a significant movement develops to abolish the Electoral College, the prospects for ultimate success seem dim. But it is clear that the consequences of a close presidential election have once again registered on the American psyche.

CONGRESS

Feingold's Crusade

IN HIS DRIVE TO ROOT OUT CORRUPTION FROM GOVERNMENT, IS RUSS FEINGOLD DRIVING AWAY HIS SENATE COLLEAGUES?

BY KIRK VICTOR

NEW ORLEANS—Not many U.S. Senators would dare to stroll down bawdy Bourbon Street accompanied by a reporter. But Wisconsin Democrat Russell Feingold, who's not exactly known for boisterousness, did just that on one recent March night. Seemingly oblivious to the risqué bars offering topless—and bottomless—entertainment within, Feingold regaled the reporter with stories of his last re-election campaign as if he were walking along Main Street in Madison, Wis.

Can you imagine Senate Minority Leader Thomas A. Daschle, D-S.D.—or any other member of the World's Greatest Deliberative Body, for that matter—taking such a walk with a member of the press? Political calculations would never permit it. Senators' flacks would advise them that published accounts of a jaunt past such outlandish establishments might give voters the wrong impression—to put it mildly.

But Feingold is different from most, maybe even all, of his colleagues. Sure, he's a politician, but he is about as close to being guileless as anyone in the Senate. In his relentless crusade for a slew of good-government reforms, he comes off as more of a Boy Scout than the typical let's-cut-a-deal lawmaker on Capitol Hill.

Yet there Feingold was, on a crisp March evening, maneuvering his way through a throng a drunken revelers. His willingness to ask a reporter to tag along as he walked with his chief of staff, who had never seen Bourbon Street, reflected the sense that this 48-year-old former practicing attorney is absolutely comfortable in his own skin, knows who he is, and is unconcerned that somehow this outing will not "look senatorial."

Feingold, who had traveled to the Big Easy for one of the half-dozen town hall meetings that he and Sen. John McCain, R-Ariz., have held across the country to drum up support for their campaign finance reform legislation, also got a taste of humility. Despite the national promi-

nence that comes with teaming up with McCain, Feingold obviously was not a familiar figure in downtown New Orleans. When he asked a young woman for directions, she pointed and said, "Straight up that way, dude."

The youthful-looking Senator seemed to get a kick out of being called "dude.' The nickname is not what would pop into the minds of those who know him on Capitol Hill, or back home in Wisconsin. It's comical to think of the conscientious, studious, an sober Feingold as a "dude." Though he laughed easily and showed a sense of humor on this walk, those are traits that he seldom displays.

"He's very intense, very serious," said David Newby, who is the president of the Wisconsin AFL-CIO and has known Feingold since he was first elected to a state Senate seat in 1982. "Some would say too serious."

Serious, yes. But there's no pretentiousness about Feingold. Although he is a Rhodes scholar and a Harvard-trained lawyer, he is of modest means. He tends to overdo his "I can relate to ordinary Americans" bit, but it has the virtue of being true. Feingold's net worth was just under $80,000 as of his last financial disclosure filing—making him something of an anomaly in a chamber nearly filled with millionaires.

Feingold also sticks out in the Senate because he is no steadfast, to-the-line partisan. Since his first election to the Senate in 1992, after a decade in the Wisconsin Senate, Feingold has zealously pursued a sort of populist agenda and has also displayed a willingness to depart from Democratic orthodoxy, often to the dismay of his colleagues.

Most recently, he was the sole Democrat on the Senate Judiciary Committee to vote to confirm John Ashcroft for Attorney General. And he was the only Senate Democrat to vote against a motion to dismiss during the impeachment trial of President Clinton in 1999. Feingold is also the only Senator ever to tell his party to stop using unlimited, unregulated campaign contributions, called "soft money," on behalf of his election—a stance that some of his colleagues found puzzling, foolish, and potentially politically suicidal.

"There are occasions," Feingold explained in an interview, "when I simply cannot accept the premise of party loyalty, when [an issue] involves a more fundamental principle."

In unwaveringly adhering to his reform agenda, even at some political risk, Feingold seems to have taken a page from Wisconsin's long history of clean-government advocates that began in the early 20th century with Republican Sen. Robert La Follette, a leader of the progressive movement. More recently, Democrat William Proxmire, who retired from the Senate in 1988 after more than 30 years, became enormously popular in the state for his seeming delight in sticking it to his colleagues by attacking their favorite programs when he viewed them as too costly.

Nor has Feingold ever been one to bite his lip. He has increasingly taken on the mantle of the Democrats' "Mr. Clean," as he has aggressively pushed to overhaul what he sees as an out-of-control campaign fund-raising system—a system he frequently disparages as little more than "legalized bribery and influence-peddling." It is, of course, a hard sell to ask lawmakers to jettison the system that helped them get elected. And Feingold's relentless crusading style may come back to haunt him at this critical time in his political career, when the Senate is finally conducting a full-blown debate of the McCain-Feingold legislation to ban soft money.

Although Feingold is urging Democrats to stay the course and continue to support the McCain-Feingold bill, some are voicing concern that the measure's passage might put their party at a disadvantage. After all, the Democratic Party has just caught up with the GOP in raising soft money. Feingold's own past independence from the party hardly puts him in the best position to argue for Democrats to stick together during the fierce debate over his bill.

"If you're by yourself a lot, it's always hard to organize a team when you need a team," Sen. John B. Breaux of Louisiana said in an interview, after he recently became the first Senate Democrat to publicly announce that he will oppose the McCain-Feingold bill.

Feingold downplayed the significance of Breaux's move, saying that Breaux was never really committed to reform. But it was still a blow. It came just as Feingold and McCain continued to express confidence that they have sufficient Senate support—60 votes—to block a filibuster. They can ill afford to lose supporters, even though Senate Republican leaders have pledged not to use a filibuster or other procedural maneuvers to try to kill the McCain-Feingold bill, as they have repeatedly done with campaign finance measures in the past.

At bottom, Feingold's success—or failure—in getting Democrats to stay on board may demonstrate whether a tough-minded crusader for reform whose style is a throwback to an earlier era can be effective in today's legislative trenches. The debate might even provide some indication of whether Feingold will be a go-to player as he gains seniority in the Senate, or whether, like Proxmire, he comes to be seen as more of a very principled—but somewhat moralistic—maverick.

TSK, TSK, TSK

Time and again, Feingold has taken to the Senate floor to chronicle the boatloads of political action committee money and soft money that lobbyists pony up to try to influence legislation. A frequent target of Feingold's has been the bankruptcy reform legislation that Congress has debated over the past several years. He has pointed out that the National Consumer Bankruptcy Coalition, a lobbying group backed by major credit card companies and big banks, gave nearly $4.5 million in contributions to parties and candidates during the 1999–2000 election cycle. Feingold's conclusion? The legislation is nothing less than a "credit card industry bailout."

Russ Feingold: "He wants to win," one Senator said of Feingold, "but there is a part of him that would rather be right."

This "Calling of the Bankroll," as Feingold has dubbed it, has infuriated some colleagues, who have privately fumed that Feingold's approach is sanctimonious. But Feingold insists that he does not "personalize" these recitations—he names the donors, not the recipients. "I chose not to call it a bankroll of any particular Senators, because of my respect for the fact that that could cause real problems," he said in the interview.

Maybe so, but sometimes good intentions are not enough. Even Sen. Susan Collins, R-Maine, a big fan of Feingold's who has worked with him on everything from impeachment strategy to public health issues, acknowledged in an interview: "I don't endorse the approach he takes in implying direct links between contributions and various Senators' positions on bills, I don't think that that is the best approach to gain support for a bill. But because I know him so well, I know that what others may view as sanctimony is really a reflection of what he believes."

Collins added: "He's just very straightforward and gutsy, and is going to go out there and call it as he sees it, as opposed to someone who calculates, 'How can I put together the winning coalition?' He wants to win, but there is a part of him that would rather be right."

Still, Feingold, who first signed on to sponsor the campaign finance reform bill with McCain in 1995, gives every indication that he is playing hardball these days. Although he insisted that he is "certainly not in panic mode" about what he termed Breaux's "flip-flop," Feingold has turned up the heat on his fellow Democratic Senators in a bid to prevent any more defections.

Feingold said that, while Breaux has never been much of a fan of campaign finance reform, "it's going to be a real different story for Senators who have made it central to their campaigns. That's true of almost every Democratic Senator. About every Democratic Senator has emphasized heavily their support and co-sponsorship of McCain-Feingold. For those people, it won't be free" to turn against the McCain-Feingold bill.

Some observers doubt that Feingold has the sway with his colleagues to ultimately make the difference in keeping them together on the campaign reform legislation. "Give Feingold credit for hanging in there over a long period, but it's not obvious that he is the person to keep the Democrats on board," said Thomas E. Mann, a senior fellow at the Brookings Institution. "If it is to be done, it will be done by Daschle—not by Feingold.... Ironically, neither of the co-sponsors has much of a base in his own party."

Even McCain has joked that he and Feingold would not win "Miss Congeniality" awards in the Senate. In fact, partly in recognition of their maverick status, the two Senators have assembled a team of about a dozen of their colleagues who have taken a visible role in backing the McCain-Feingold bill during the Senate floor debate over campaign finance reform.

Still, when pressed about his dealings with other members of Congress, Feingold insists: "I think I have a good relationship with my colleagues. If I don't, I don't. But it feels good. People know that I am honest. I don't ever attack people on the floor personally in terms of record or background. I just try to talk about the issue."

But his perception is not always shared. Take an episode about a year and a half ago, when Feingold decried some oil companies' efforts to limit certain royalty payments. He went to the Senate floor and listed the mammoth campaign contributions behind the legislative proposal. Several other Senators tried, unsuccessfully, to get his statement ruled out of order.

"They tried to shut me up... and of course, it totally backfired," Feingold recalled in the interview. "I said, 'Oh yeah, you're damn right I can talk about it. I'm sick and tired of the American people not knowing the truth about what's going on with their democracy, which—I've said it too many times, but it's true—has been almost entirely corrupted in the last few years by soft money.'"

The scene on the Senate floor at the time was a variation on the theme in the classic Frank Capra film *Mr. Smith Goes to Washington*, about a do-gooder at war with the political Establishment. In this case, Feingold, playing the Jimmy Stewart role, tries to root out Big Money in politics, but as he does so, his colleagues are outraged by the implication that they are doing the lobbyists' bidding.

In response to the browbeatings from Feingold over the oil royalties issue, Sen. Kay Bailey Hutchison, R-Texas, scolded him on the Senate floor: "It borders on a personal attack on Senators who I think are doing something they think is in the best interest of this nation." Added Sen. Mary L. Landrieu, D-La.: "I just feel compelled to say how disappointed I am in my colleague from Wisconsin."

Landrieu in her floor statement went on to blast Feingold's insistence that soft-money contributions were "at the heart" of the debate over oil royalties. She called his statement "offensive to the members of the Senate on both sides of the aisle," and added: "It is particularly offensive to those of us who actually weren't supported by the oil and gas industry when we ran to get elected to the Senate, but... [who] find ourselves having to speak on this issue... because of the facts involved, and because this is a very important principle at stake on this vote."

When asked recently whether Feingold could be sanctimonious at times, Landrieu, who supports the McCain-Feingold measure, replied in her soft Louisiana accent: "We all have our moments. I'm not going to pick on him." Then she proceeded to join the two sponsors of the reform legislation onstage at their March 9 town hall meeting at Loyola University (New Orleans), where she reiterated her support for their bill.

Russ Feingold is definitely a principled person," said Ken Goldstein, a political science professor at the University of Wisconsin (Madison). "He passionately, passionately, and sincerely believes in what he believes. On the other hand, I think he sometimes does not recognize that other people who disagree with him are just as sincere and just as passionate."

THE ODD COUPLE

Although their names will always be joined because of their high-profile effort to overhaul the campaign fundraising system, McCain and Feingold are an odd couple. They could not be more different in ideology, temperament, or background. Yet, as they made their pitch before an enthusiastic crowd of several hundred Loyola students earlier this month, it was obvious that they have a comfortable, easy rapport and plenty of respect for one another.

McCain, a former fighter pilot who courageously withstood more than five years of torture in a North Vietnamese prison camp, took the microphone, to a standing ovation, after Feingold effusively praised him. McCain didn't miss a beat. "I appreciate the confidence of my friend Russ Feingold, who is a Commie-pinko liberal," he said, at which the hall erupted in laughter.

Then McCain said that "deeds are important," and he recalled Feingold's actions during his 1998 re-election campaign, when he was in danger of losing his Senate seat after being pummeled with "independent" attack ads. "His own party said, 'Don't worry, Russ, we'll [spend] millions of dollars... with our own negative ads,' and Russ Feingold said, 'Stay out.' Russ Feingold, for principle, was willing to sacrifice his own political career," McCain said. "My friends, some day, another book called *Profiles in Courage* will be written, and Russ Feingold will have a place in that book." The hall again erupted in applause.

It is unusual for a U.S. Senator to play a supporting role, but Feingold seems perfectly at ease playing second fiddle to McCain, even on an issue he cares so deeply about. "This is 'McCain-Feingold.' You don't see him bitching and moaning that it ought to be 'Feingold-McCain,'" observed Norman J. Ornstein, a resident scholar at the American Enterprise Institute for Public Policy Research. "He is effective because he is smart as can be, he cares about issues, does his homework, and… he has also been willing in some cases to subordinate his own ego for the good of the issues."

Back in Washington, McCain, the 64-year-old chairman of the Commerce, Science, and Transportation Committee, is a force to be reckoned with. The silver-haired firebrand with a combustible temper has been known to upbraid his colleagues during Senate debates. He has compiled a generally conservative voting record and has emerged as perhaps the Senate's most pre-eminent national figure, following his failed bid for the Republican presidential nomination last year.

Feingold, by contrast, is one of the chamber's more liberal members and, stylistically, is more studied and lawyerly in his approach to issues than McCain. He has no military experience and shows a strong disinclination to support the deployment of U.S. troops abroad—an issue on which he is at odds with McCain. Feingold has made it a practice to be easily available to reporters, but even on that score, McCain is in a different league: His accessibility is legendary, and his charisma and self-deprecating humor play extraordinarily well with reporters.

Both men have a fiercely independent streak, both show a strong interest in driving out waste from the federal government, including the "pork" programs that their colleagues often push, and, of course, both are committed to changing the way the campaign finance system operates. Even so, Feingold said he was stunned when McCain first called him "out of the blue" in 1994 to ask about working as partners in pushing for reform legislation.

According to an oft-told anecdote, their only encounter before that was a testy Senate floor exchange in 1993, when McCain had blistered Feingold for his opposition to the funding of a nuclear-powered aircraft carrier that was later renamed for Ronald Reagan. "Have you ever been on a carrier?" McCain demanded, according to an account in *The New York Times* several years ago. When Feingold acknowledged that he had not, McCain responded, "Then learn more about it!"

Then, after having very little contact except to say hello a few times, Feingold got the unexpected call. He remembers that McCain said, " 'I have been looking at your voting record on reform issues, on cutting spending, on attacking pork. I'd like to work with you.' I said, 'What do

you have in mind?' He said [he wanted my support] on the revolving-door legislation. I said, 'Great, I have already voted for it.'" The revolving-door bill, which would have strengthened restrictions on lobbying by former lawmakers and senior congressional staff, passed the Senate in 1994 and 1995, only to be killed in conference committees. (Current law requires a one-year waiting period before former members of Congress and staff may lobby Congress.)

In return for his support for that bill, Feingold sought McCain's help in passing a gift ban for lawmakers, an idea that Wisconsin had adopted. Feingold clearly was impressed when McCain joined Democrats in early 1995 in threatening to refuse to pass the rules to organize the Senate until Republican leaders agreed to bring the gift-ban proposal up for a vote. Eventually, the Senate in 1996 approved limits on free meals and other gifts paid for by lobbyists; the House has its own such restrictions. But even before the gift ban passed, Feingold and McCain had agreed to work on campaign finance reform. "It was a true example of bipartisanship, at about the least-bipartisan time in American history," Feingold said.

"We're very different people," Feingold added of himself and McCain. "Sometimes he says, 'Come on, boy we're going to [a town hall meeting in] Little Rock.' He's my senior in terms of age and stature, military record, and so on. But we've become close friends. And we've worked together very, very well."

McCain, for his part, said of Feingold's willingness to operate in his shadow: "He is remarkably lacking in personal ambition. It seems like he is not very self-absorbed."

Feingold said he has seen McCain's temper erupt only once in the years that they have worked together. "He stormed out of the office because we couldn't come together on something," Feingold recalled. "Each of us sort of figured out a way to come together the next night, and I went in the [Senate] Republican Cloakroom and we worked it out, and he gave me a hug. He's not a big hugger."

PAST AND FUTURE CAMPAIGNS

The 2002 race for Wisconsin governor is wide open, following the recent appointment of former Gov. Tommy Thompson as Health and Human Services Secretary. But Feingold is emphatic that he will not leave the Senate to run for governor of his home state. "I like what I am doing in the Senate," he said in the interview. "I feel like the Senate is a good place for me."

Feingold also virtually rules out a run for the White House, declaring that he is "extremely unlikely to ever want to run for President." Still, Feingold said it is important that the Democrats field a candidate who represents the "progressive traditions" of the party, who would support further campaign finance reform, and who would oppose the death penalty.

Former Rep. Mark W. Neumann, the Wisconsin Republican who came within an eyelash of knocking Feingold off in 1998, seems like a good bet to mount another challenge when Feingold is up for re-election in 2004. In an interview, Neumann was coy about his plans, but argued that Feingold in 1998 did not wage the clean campaign that others credit him with. "He ran on his campaign finance reform platform until he got behind," Neumann said. "He then abandoned it, and in the last 21 days of that race, [independent groups] spent $800,000 backing Feingold—the very people he rails against."

In response to that charge, Feingold produced letters he sent to the AFL-CIO and the League of Conservation Voters telling them he didn't want them involved in his campaign. In the letters, sent on Oct. 23, 1998, Feingold noted that he had asked independent groups to stay out of the race throughout the year, and reiterated that their involvement must end. "How can my request be any more clear?" he said.

Despite Feingold's objections, the AFL-CIO spent $200,000 in soft money and the league poured in $440,000 in "hard," or regulated, money. The Democratic Senatorial Campaign Committee spent another $200,000 in hard money. The "bozos" at the DSCC, as Feingold called them in the interview, decided that a hard-money independent expenditure technically would not violate his pledge to avoid using soft money. "But I didn't want it," Feingold said. "They were horrible ads. They were negative ads, just attacking my opponent. [They were] out of character of everything I've done for my entire career."

Former Sen. Bob Kerrey, D-Neb., who was the DSCC chairman at the time, recalled that it took a while to pull the ads back, because "it's not like a light switch, [since it involves] all of those [television] stations." Kerrey continued: "It took us longer than Russ would have liked. I don't think it hurt him to be able to say that I was a dirtbag and all that sort of thing, that he could take on the fat cats in Washington, D.C. I wouldn't say he did it inten-tionally, but he ended up getting the benefit of the ads—*and* of being able to kick around the people who paid for the ads."

When pressed a bit, Kerrey added: "I don't think he is being a hypocrite on this at all. I think he felt genuinely offended and wanted [the ads] off. But did he get the benefit of both? The answer is yes."

University of Wisconsin professor Goldstein has a different take. "Republican claims that he wanted it both ways are just preposterous," Goldstein said. "There are many things that one can say, positive or negative, about Russ Feingold... but to say that he tried to have it both ways in that election is wrong." Another Wisconsin professor of political science, David Canon, agrees: "Feingold knew there were costs attached to his position, and he was willing to lose the election on that issue. He didn't want to be a hypocrite."

A longtime Democratic strategist confirmed that national party officials (other than Kerrey) were not about to stand by and watch one of their Senate candidates roll over for the other side—and that's what some Democrats thought Feingold was doing in 1998. "They are not going to let individual members of their team disarm," said this strategist. "Campaign committees have the wherewithal and the independence... to have a separate [strategy]. It's a real basic bottom-line decision."

That sentiment would clearly infuriate Feingold, who has repeatedly made his message clear: "Stay the hell out of my state." And it will surely inspire both Feingold and McCain to keep battling for reform, regardless of the outcome on their legislation in the current Senate debate.

Asked whether he will continue the fight, Feingold didn't hesitate. "I know that I will," he said, because there is so much more to be done. "This is only plugging a loophole."

McCain agreed. "We have a whole big reform agenda," he said. "Unfortunately for some, we ain't going away. We ain't going quietly into the night."

Congress

JOHN DINGELL'S STAYING POWER

BY BRODY MULLINS

When Rep. John D. Dingell, D-Mich., arrived at the White House earlier this month to discuss energy legislation, President Bush greeted him with a friendly jab. "You're the biggest pain in the ass on Capitol Hill," joked the President. "Thank you for a high compliment," responded Dingell, who was first elected to Congress in 1955, right around the time that Bush began playing Little League. "I've worked 47 years for that reputation, and I'd hate to see it dissipate in one afternoon."

The exchange between the rookie President and the House's most senior member underscores the influence that Dingell still wields in his 24th term on Capitol Hill. During Bush's first six months in office, Dingell has schooled him in what nine Presidents, scores of agency heads, and hundreds of members of Congress learned before: He is a lawmaker who can thwart a President's priorities, muscle his own initiatives through Congress, and otherwise be a major-league pain to the White House, congressional Republicans, and even his fellow congressional Democrats.

> **JOHN DINGELL: "I just work like hell, and good things seem to happen."**

This month alone, Dingell has exploited his leverage as the ranking Democrat on the House Energy and Commerce Committee to wedge himself into a handful of key issues. He riled the While House by sparking a General Accounting Office investigation into the energy-policy task force that Vice President Dick Cheney put together earlier this year. He annoyed congressional Republicans by co-sponsoring popular bipartisan patients' rights leg-islation in the House that goes further than Bush prefers. He distressed senior Democrats by cutting a deal with Republicans that allows major elements of the President's energy plan to move forward. And he may anger members on both sides of the aisle by pushing broadband Internet legislation through the House before the August recess.

Of course, it's not unusual for Dingell to be in the middle of so many fights. He has long been known as one of Capitol Hill's most powerful and effective committee chairmen ever, thanks to his tenure at the helm of Energy and Commerce from 1981–95, and he has played a central role in many of the major laws enacted in the past half-century. Over the years, Dingell has also masterfully asserted Congress's right to oversee the executive branch. He once helped to throw a Reagan Administration official in jail for obstructing a committee investigation.

What is unusual is that after all his time in Congress, including the past six and a half years in the minority, the 75-year-old Dingell still has the fire and the wherewithal to continue to boldly make his mark. Dingell, after all, is in more than a few ways Capitol Hill's version of Cal Ripken—and Ripken is retiring this year. Elected in December 1955 to replace his father, Dingell has served more consecutive years than any other current member of Congress. He has even surpassed 98-year-old Sen. Strom Thurmond, R-S.C., who was elected in 1954 but took a few months off in 1956. Dingell is the only member of the House elected in the 1950s, and one of five elected before 1970. Nearly 20 percent of his current House colleagues were born after he first entered the chamber.

What's the secret to Dingell's longevity? Even in this era of poll-tested soundbites, he still counts on old-fashioned hard work and smarts to do the job. He takes the time to master the substance of legislation, with the help of one of the most experienced staffs in Congress, and he relies on his unmatched knowledge of the institution that he has honed since working as a congressional page in 1937. As Dingell himself said in a recent interview: "I just work like hell, and good things seem to happen."

Dingell's colleagues say that perhaps most important to his resilience, he has shrewd political instincts that allow him to build the coalitions needed to move legislation. "He understands which issues he absolutely has to solve to get the majority he is seeking," said Rep. Rich Boucher, D-Va., the ranking member of the committee's Energy and Air Quality Subcommittee. "That knowledge only comes with experience." Added Rep. W. J. "Billy" Tauzin, R-La., the current chairman of the Energy and Commerce Committee: "I've learned one thing in my years under Dingell—know what's do-able and what's not."

And Dingell isn't ready to quit yet. If anything, he seems more energized this year than in the recent past. Michigan's Republican-controlled Legislature has completed a redistricting plan that would put him in the same district as fellow Democratic Rep. Lynn Rivers, but Dingell has pledged to run for a 25th term next year, even though some senior members might take the opportunity to retire. "I expect," Dingell said without hesitation, "to be re-elected."

LEARNING FROM THE GROUND UP

The son of Polish Catholic immigrants, Dingell developed values and a work ethic that were ingrained during a dozen years of Jesuit education. The priests at Georgetown Prep and Georgetown University taught him to try to help others. But his true inspiration is his father, the late Rep. John Dingell Sr., a 12-term New Deal Democrat from Detroit who sponsored Social Security, the first interstate highway bill, and national health care legislation. "John still to this day loves his father," said Dingell's wife, Debbie, an executive at General Motors Corp., in an interview. "He is motivated by the kind of public servant his father was—that's what drives him."

In part because his father died of tuberculosis as a young man, Dingell each year faithfully reintroduces a bill to provide Americans with universal health care. Dingell said he remains "intensely proud" of his father. "I regard him as a giant," he said, although he adds: "I am not my father. I think for myself."

As Dingell made his way through Georgetown law school in the early 1950s, he worked as the Capitol's chief elevator operator—a job he got because of his dad's position in the House—and he literally learned from the ground up. When his father died in 1955, the 29-year-old Dingell was elected to replace him.

Two decades later, Dingell grabbed the reins of power for the first time when he and Rep. John Moss, D-Calif., organized a rebellion against the apathetic chairman of the Energy and Commerce Committee, Rep. Harley Staggers, D-W.Va. The pair launched the modern-day committee by boosting its budget and empowering subcommittee chairmen to pursue aggressive agendas. As his booty, Dingell claimed the gavel at the Energy and Power Subcommittee.

He took over at a perfect time. A few years later, a major energy crisis threatened the country, and Dingell soon proved he could produce. After a series of hearings, he drafted a far-reaching energy conservation bill and muscled it through his subcommittee in a legendary 1977 markup that lasted 17 straight days.

But Dingell also earned a reputation as a bully. With his broad new powers, he became fond of strong-arming opponents and burying their legislative priorities. After he was elected chairman of the full Energy and Commerce panel in 1981, he cemented his standing by preventing the committee's second-ranking Democrat, Rep. James Scheuer of New York, from chairing a subcommittee. "The day they passed out subcommittee chairs was known as 'Passover' in Scheuer's office," quipped a former committee aide.

Those close to Dingell say he never forgave Scheuer for breaking his word years earlier during some undisclosed dispute. But Dingell maintains he had nothing to do with his colleague's "misfortune." When asked why Scheuer never got a subcommittee chairmanship, Dingell replied: "The answer is simple: He never could get elected." He added smugly: "I never really worked hard to kill him. He did a fine job doing that himself."

Over the course of his 14-year reign as chairman, Dingell amassed quite a fiefdom. His committee managed to capture jurisdiction over nearly everything that moved. On a wall in the committee's cloakroom, Dingell hung a framed picture of the Earth. He said it represented the panel's jurisdiction.

During that time, Dingell developed another advantage often overlooked by his colleagues: a well-trained and experienced staff. Dingell paid his aides generously by congressional standards, gave them responsibility, and relied on their expertise. As a result, he was armed with some of the best talent on Capitol Hill. "That means that when he goes into battle, he has way more knowledge than anyone else," says John Arlington, a committee aide from 1987–91.

Dingell's staff recalls the peculiar occasions in the late 1980s when Bush Administration officials at the Environmental Protection Agency would enlist the help of Dingell aide Dick Frandsen to locate information about the agency that Dingell himself had requested. "Frandsen knew more about the EPA than they did," a former aide reminisced. Another aide, David Finnegan, worked for Dingell for so long that the two disagree on when they met. One thought 1958, the other 1960.

Downs and Ups

The mid-1990s brought setbacks for Dingell. First, the Republicans took control of the House in 1995 and pried the chairman's gavel from Dingell's clutch. Then, they stripped a chunk of the panel's jurisdiction. Soon after, rumors began spreading that Dingell would retire. Instead, he adjusted to his new role as ranking member under then-Chairman Tom Bliley, R-Va. Though Bliley pursued a less-active agenda than his tireless predecessor, Dingell contributed to approving major reforms of the telecommunications and financial services industries.

Though he no longer was chairman, Dingell's mastery of the procedural rules gave him strength. His favorite tactic: forcing the committee clerk to read aloud, line by line, 100-page bills that he objected to. If the clerk skipped a single word, he asked the reading to start all over again.

Then, in December 1999, Dingell fainted at a reception and an ambulance rushed him to the hospital. When a priest arrived at his bedside, Dingell was in good spirits. "Father, I hate to disappoint you, but I don't need you tonight," he reportedly said. The episode turned out to be a simple case of dehydration after a long day and a stiff martini, which Dingell says he enjoys shaken, not stirred.

But that was not the last of Dingell's health problems. Early last year, a stubborn ankle injury forced him to hobble around the House on crutches. When a metal screw in his ankle snapped, Dingell was consigned to the same kind of motorized scooter that ushers 79-year-old Sen. Jesse Helms, R-N.C., through his final years in Congress. The nagging injury seemed to lower Dingell's spirits. A distinguished career was thought to be on its last legs. If the Democrats won back control of the House in November 2000, a few aides whispered around election time, Dingell would face a Democratic challenge for the committee gavel.

In the Thick of It: Dingell's teaming with Republicans Greg Ganske and Charlie Norwood on patients' rights legislation has aggravated House GOP leaders.

Yet when Democrats failed to win control of the House, Senate, or White House, Dingell startled observers by returning to Capitol Hill in January fully energized. He junked the crutches, ditched his motor scooter, and took on an aggressive schedule. "A few years ago, the end was near," said one lobbyist. "I don't know what the hell he did, but he is being effective again."

Part of the credit goes to Tauzin, who took over as Energy and Commerce chairman in January. He's a former Democrat who learned how to run the panel during 14

years under Dingell, and he has revitalized the committee by modeling it after Dingell's reign. To do so, Tauzin has reached out to Dingell by giving him a larger budget, additional staff, and more sway over committee business.

Soon after Tauzin took over the committee, for example, he worked with Dingell on legislation to increase broadband Internet service. That measure—the ubiquitous "Tauzin-Dingell" bill—passed the committee earlier this year and could come to the House floor as early as next week.

More recently, when Tauzin needed to move Bush's energy policy through the committee, he sat down with Dingell over the Fourth of July recess and together they crafted a bill they both supported. As part of the deal, Dingell delivered Democratic votes for the Republican bill, and Tauzin headed off a large increase in automobile fuel-efficiency standards—a major concern to automakers in Dingell's Detroit-area district. The Energy and Commerce Committee approved the energy bill, 50-5, on July 19, and House Republicans plan to bring it to a floor vote next week.

But Dingell continues to cause trouble for Republicans on health care legislation. His latest effort on patients' rights legislation—which he is co-sponsoring with Republican Reps. Charlie Norwood of Georgia and Greg Ganske of Iowa—elicited a veto threat from Bush. Republican leaders hope to defeat the Dingell-Norwood-Ganske bill and pass a narrower alternative bill.

Meantime, the fact that the White House has gone Republican has invigorated Dingell's oversight activities. Although he has never been easy on Democratic Administrations (he once called President Clinton's Kyoto treaty "the most asinine treaty I've ever seen"), Dingell clearly enjoys pestering Republican Presidents. "Dingell understands that Congress is a separate branch of government, and he has fiercely asserted its prerogatives," said Rep. David R. Obey, D-Wis.

Earlier this year, Dingell launched a GAO investigation to find out which oil and gas company lobbyists helped the White House shape its energy policy. Dingell has also slammed the Administration for routinely responding to his requests for information with computer-generated form letters. In a biting speech on the House floor on June 7, Dingell sarcastically credited the White House's "remarkable, automated, and superbly efficient computer system" for "moving forward the science of communications to new and higher levels." He added: "Each time I have written to President Bush, I have received an identical response from this amazing computer... each faithfully signed by the President's aide, Nicholas Calio."

The 16th District of Dingell

Michigan Democrats are challenging the Republicans' redistricting map in court. But if Dingell is forced into a redistricting-induced election contest against fellow Democratic Rep. Rivers in November 2002, he is the heavy favorite to win. "Michigan is Dingell country," said one Democratic lawmaker. "He would cream her," Dingell has faced only token election opposition since the 1960s, and Rivers, according to Michigan insiders, is weighing a run for the Statehouse.

Even some Michigan Republicans want to see the generally liberal Dingell remain in the House, because of the considerable clout he has to help the state. "If a Democrat is going to be in that district, it might as well be John Dingell," said Paul Welday, an aide to Rep. Joseph Knollenberg, R-Mich.

Though the redistricting plan does not appear to pose a threat to Dingell, it may complicate plans to keep his House seat in his family. Insiders believe that Dingell would like to bestow the seat once held by his father on his son, Christopher, or on his wife, Debbie. But Christopher, a term-limited state senator, plans to run for a seat on the Wayne County circuit court. "Chris is not interested in running [for the House]," John Dingell said. Debbie, meanwhile, says she is focused on the corporate world. "I'm still climbing the ladder at GM," she said. "There is still a glass ceiling that needs to be broken here."

Dingell, for his part, disputed that he could hand his seat to a family member. "This is not something that can be passed around like a country club membership or a seat on the stock exchange. It has to be earned," he said. "The seat and the job all belong to the people. If you do a good job, they'll reward you with another two years."

Still, after nearly a half-century in the House, Dingell will not hold the seat forever. Asked how long he would serve in the House, Dingell responded: "Till I get tired of this—or the people get tired of me."

Brody Mullins is a reporter for National Journal's Congress-Daily.

Of Judges and Senators

How to think about judicial nominees

RAMESH PONNURU

It is a fact of American political life, predictable as the tides, that a party's view of the proper division of power among the branches of government depends on which branches it controls. During the New Deal, conservatives worried about the autocratic potential of a strong executive. By the 1980s, they were lustily cheering executive power and regarding Congress as a den of parochialism and obstruction. It was ever thus: The Jeffersonians who feared an American king stopped worrying when Andrew Jackson strengthened the presidency.

While a party's position may change, there is one constant: Whatever position is adopted will be defended in the most high-flown terms of principle. Congressmen will try to block a president from the other party, not to get their way, but to guard Congress's place in the constitutional order. The president's party will respond with a similar argument about executive prerogatives. Political choice becomes constitutional duty. As the late Meg Greenfield once remarked, in debates of this kind the politicians always seem to be saying, Don't blame me—Alexander Hamilton made me do it.

We're having one of those debates now, this time over judges. Senate Democrats have warned that they may refuse to confirm many of President Bush's nominees to the federal bench. This refusal, they say, is a proper exercise of their constitutional power to "advise and consent" on nominations. When Republicans object that the president's picks deserve deference, the Democrats retort

that the GOP showed no such deference to President Clinton.

Untrue: Republicans were not very tough on Clinton's judges. His Supreme Court nominees, Ruth Bader Ginsburg and Stephen Breyer, sailed through the Senate with 96 and 87 votes respectively. Clinton got 377 federal judges confirmed, about the same as Reagan. (Yes, the judiciary is slightly larger now than it was then, but Reagan also had a Senate controlled by his party longer than Clinton did.) Only one Clinton nominee, Ronnie White, was defeated on the Senate floor; another, Frederica Massiah-Jackson, had to withdraw her nomination. Both nominees were opposed mainly for their record in law-and-order cases. Almost half of all federal judges are Clinton appointees.

But a defense of the Republican position cannot rest with these points. For one thing, the Republicans did delay action on a lot of Clinton's nominations, especially toward the end of his second term (just as the Democrats balked at President Bush's nominations in 1992). They suggested that the federal judiciary was not severely understaffed and that therefore confirming judges was not an urgent matter.

Besides, and more important, the argument for senatorial deference isn't very compelling. It's certainly not the strongest argument for confirming Bush's nominees. Bush's nominees should be confirmed not because he's the president but because they would be good judges. And Clinton's nominees should have been op-

posed for the same reason. Inconsistency on procedure—opposing one president's nominees, deferring to another's—is dictated by consistency on a substantive commitment to a sound judiciary.

To put it another way, the question of whether a nominee should be confirmed cannot be answered without reference to judicial philosophy. President Clinton announced a litmus test for his judicial nominees in 1992: They would all favor *Roe v. Wade*. That was sufficient reason to oppose them. A judge who believes that judges are entitled to enforce a right to abortion not found in the text, history, structure, or logic of the Constitution is a judge with far too expansive a view of his own power. A senator who took seriously his oath of office, which pledges fidelity to the Constitution, should not have confirmed any of Clinton's judicial nominees. (After February 1999, Senate Republicans had an additional reason to say no: Almost all of those Republicans had taken the position that Clinton's law-breaking made him unfit for office, which presumably suggests that they didn't think he ought to be naming judges either.)

Bush, of course, has made no pro-*Roe* litmus test. That, indeed, is a basis for Democratic opposition: Some senators have suggested they will not vote for a judicial nominee unless he pledges to support *Roe*. A Republican, however, can consistently have opposed Clinton's nominees while supporting Bush's because of the anti-constitutional pledge of the former set. A consistently constitutionalist position would also render Republicans less vulnerable to the charge of hypocrisy on judicial vacancies. Whatever problems a vacancy creates cannot justify filling it with a bad judge.

By the way, isn't there a symmetrical hypocrisy on the Democratic side? Having said when Clinton was in office that there was a vacancy crisis on the federal bench that justified speeding up confirmations, how can they now block Bush's nominees?

Presumably the Democrats could make their own version of the argument sketched above. They could say, that is, that Clinton's nominees should have been confirmed because they were committed to protecting constitutional rights while Bush's should be rejected because they are not. And that is essentially the case Democrats are making. Because Republicans have made only procedural arguments, the Democrats have not had to spell out the implications of their position. They have not, for instance, had to defend the view that the Constitution requires that judges nullify almost any restriction on abortion.

The coming battles over the judiciary are not going to be won by the side playing defense.

But the Democrats are at least talking about the right thing. They are attacking the jurisprudence associated with Antonin Scalia and Clarence Thomas. So far, Republicans have not defended that jurisprudence. Nor have they criticized the alternatives at a level above the bumper sticker. There's no reason for Republicans to be scared to make their case: The prospect of conservative judges doesn't frighten most people, and the underlying principle of self-government should be popular and easy to explain. If the coming battles over the judiciary are going to be as fierce as advertised, they're not going to be won by the side playing defense.

Republicans should be willing to make the argument over judges into an argument over the Constitution. This time, they really can say that Alexander Hamilton made them do it.

From the *National Review,* June 11, 2001, pp. 29-30. © 2001 by the National Review, Inc., 215 Lexington Avenue, New York, NY 10016. Reprinted by permission.

Uninsured Americans Linger On Congress' Waiting List

Potential price of benefits unnerves lawmakers, but lack of coverage also has its costs

By Mary Agnes Carey

For the last three years, vast political and policy differences between Republicans and Democrats have stopped Congress from passing legislation to give millions of Americans more clout with their health insurers. Those same splits will likely block any action on broadening Medicare to include prescription drugs—even a scaled-down, $20 billion package introduced by Senate Finance Committee Chairman William V. Roth, Jr., R-Del., to help low-income beneficiaries.

With Congress in disarray over how to help people who already have insurance, it is no surprise that legislators have been unable to reach consensus on a far more sweeping problem—what to do about the nation's 44 million uninsured. Since President Clinton's plan for universal health care crashed in Congress in 1994, the number of Americans without health coverage has steadily increased. Experts predict as many as 55 million may be without medical insurance policies by 2008.

The staggering price tag for covering the uninsured—estimates range as high as $80 billion a year—frightens lawmakers, who would rather use the budget surplus for initiatives with more tangible election-year appeal, such as tax cuts or a hefty package of funding increases for Medicare providers. There is also dissent over how to approach the problem, with some lawmakers favoring tax-related solutions and others pushing to expand existing federal health programs.

The uninsured, many of whom are poor, do not have the same kind of political clout as senior citizens and consumer groups, who are well-financed and can afford to take their concerns to Congress every year, so their cause is easily forgotten. "Uninsured people don't vote," said Thomas A. Scully, president and chief executive officer of the Federation of American Hospitals, a trade group representing for-profit hospitals.

Congress' reluctance also stems in part from the lingering political damage of the Clinton health-care debacle. Confident that voters oppose a government-run health care system, House Republicans are reportedly planning an advertising campaign to link Democratic nominee Vice President Al Gore's prescription drug proposal to Clinton's failed Health Security Act.

"The Clinton plan scared the heck out of people," Dr. Michael T. Rapp, president of the American College of Emergency Physicians, said in a Sept. 1 interview. "It was too big, too much regulation." First Lady Hillary Rodham Clinton, who is seeking to replace retiring Democrat Sen. Daniel Patrick Moynihan of New York, has even joked about the disaster in her campaign. *(1994 CQ Almanac, p. 319)*

The GOP hunch might be on target. In Washington state, for example, supporters of a universal health-care initiative did not collect enough signatures to get the measure on the November ballot. "It's a lot harder than we expected it would be," psychiatrist Dr. Stuart Bramhall, president of the Health Care 2000 campaign, told the Seattle Times in May.

Yet a number of recent surveys suggest that many people view providing health insurance to all Americans as a priority for Congress:

- Respondents to a Pew Research Center for the People and the Press poll of 1,411 registered voters conducted last October ranked providing health insurance for those who cannot afford it a higher policy priority than efforts to bring more federal regulation to managed-care insurers.
- Half of the 1,020 people surveyed in October by The Washington Post said the rising number of

people without insurance bothered them "a great deal."

- A July poll of 1,183 registered voters by the Post, the Henry J. Kaiser Family Foundation and Harvard University found that increasing the number of Americans with health insurance was the second most important health care issue among those surveyed, just behind making Medicare "financially sound."

Though lawmakers and both major presidential candidates are steering clear of government-run universal health care, they are making feints at addressing at least part of the issue because they have seen how the price of providing care for the uninsured increases costs for consumers and the health care industry alike.

Republican nominee Gov. George W. Bush of Texas advocates a refundable tax credit and the lifting of federal regulations he deems onerous to insuring more Americans, such as the current cap on medical savings accounts, which allow people to pay for medical expenses with pre-tax dollars.

Gore would expand government programs to cover the uninsured. He advocates broadening of both the Children's Health Insurance Program (CHIP) and Medicaid to cover more children and would permit parents of CHIP-eligible children to purchase coverage through the program. Gore also would give tax credits to companies with fewer than 50 employees whose workers join "purchasing coalitions," which would allow businesses to form pools to receive more affordable rates for health insurance.

Democrats and Republicans alike have sponsored bills that would alter the tax code to help people afford insurance or broaden existing federal health programs to help cover the uninsured. Rep. John D. Dingell, D-Mich., has introduced a universal health care measure every year since 1956. (See chart: Bills to Help the Uninsured).

A package of so-called access provisions, which include tax deductions and insurance purchasing groups, is part of the House and Senate managed-care bill (HR 2990, S 1344) now stuck in a bicameral conference, (CQ Weekly, p. 1391)

"[Helping the uninsured] is the $64,000 question, isn't it?" Karen M. Ignagni, president and chief executive officer of the American Association of Health Plans, said in an Aug. 31 interview.

An Incremental Approach

With the Clinton failure in mind, lawmakers have focused on more incremental approaches, such as CHIP, which was created as part of the 1997 budget law (PL 105-33). While the law has made some progress in covering children, it has done nothing to solve the vexing problem of how to provide coverage to millions of other Americans. (Children's insurance, 1997 Almanac, p. 6–3)

Broader steps will not occur unless public demand for congressional action intensifies, said David Butler, a spokesman for the group Consumers Union. "It's unlikely that any lawmakers will tackle it.... It's the proverbial hot potato," he added.

Marcia Comstock, a health care policy and workplace issues fellow for the U.S. Chamber Foundation, an affiliate of the National Chamber of Commerce, said in an Aug. 30 interview that many Americans with coverage are unwilling to sacrifice their benefits to help provide coverage to those who do not have it.

Workers are spending more time, Comstock said, focusing on "what else can I get?" in health benefits rather than recognizing that some of those resources could be used to provide coverage to the uninsured.

Rapp said people mistakenly believe that if they have coverage, they are not affected by the growing number of uninsured. He noted, for example, that large numbers of uninsured patients slow an emergency room's speed and efficiency—the cases are often more medically

complex because medical treatment has been delayed.

The rising ranks of the uninsured also may reduce workers' paychecks as overall health care costs rise, according to a January report from the Employee Benefit Research Institute, a nonprofit organization based in Washington. If employers feel pressure to pass on those costs, that could mean higher health insurance premiums. Many employers are absorbing rising insurance costs in today's tight job market, but that is likely to change if the economy worsens.

Part of the problem in helping the uninsured is that they are a diverse and diffuse group. Some cannot afford coverage—even though their employers offer it—and others may work for small employers who do not provide it. Most people over 65 have Medicare, which provides health care to nearly 40 million disabled and elderly Americans.

Several reports combine to paint a telling picture of the uninsured. According to a May report from the Kaiser Family Foundation's Commission on Medicaid and the Uninsured, nearly three-quarters of the uninsured are in families where at least one person is working full time. Kaiser also found that:

- 10 percent of the uninsured are in families with at least one part-time worker and 16 percent of the uninsured are in families in which no one is employed.
- More than half of the uninsured population is low-income, which Kaiser defines as those who earn less than 200 percent of the federal poverty level, or $27,300 for a family of three in 1998.
- Nearly a third of workers earning under $20,000 a year are uninsured, while just 5 percent of workers earning over $50,000 a year do not have coverage.

Kaiser found that people with employer-sponsored insurance saw their average share of premiums rise

Bills to Help the Uninsured

Bill	Sponsor	Focus
HR 16	John D. Dingell, D-Mich.	Create a national health insurance program. Dingell has introduced this bill every session since 1956, continuing a tradition begun by his father in 1943.
HR 1819	Jim McDermott, D-Wash.	Allow individuals who are ineligible to participate in employer-subsidized health plans a refundable tax credit of up to 30 percent of their yearly health insurance costs, and limit the full credit to taxpayers whose income is less than $50,000 for a joint return.
HR 2185	Peter Stark, D-Calif.	Allow a refundable tax credit of $1,200 for an individual and up to $3,600 for a family for insurance costs and establish an Office of Health Insurance in the Department of Health and Human Services.
HR 2261	Nancy L. Johnson, R-Conn.	Create a tax credit for qualified health insurance coverage up to or equal to 60 percent of the premium paid and allow a deduction for the costs of health insurance premiums where a taxpayer pays 50 percent or more of the cost.
S 2337	Rick Santorum, R-Pa.	Create a refundable tax credit for the purchase of private health insurance (up to $1,000 for an individual and up to $3,000 for a family) and establish state health insurance safety-net programs for uninsurable individuals. Health insurers and HMOs would be required to participate in the safety net program.
S 2888	Paul Wellstone, D-Minn.	Provide federal matching funds to states that provide health care coverage to adults and children with incomes up to $50,000, require that all people receive health insurance benefits equal to the plan that covers members of Congress and provide that the same benefits for mental health and substance abuse treatment as for other medical conditions.

from 20 percent in 1988 to 27 percent in 1998.

Members of minority groups are more likely to be uninsured than whites, according to the federal Agency for Healthcare Research and Quality, a division of the Department of Health and Human Services.

In early 1998, almost one-third of all Hispanics and one-fifth of all blacks the agency surveyed had no health insurance, compared with 12.2 percent of whites.

Costly Care

The fallout from the uninsured is felt at every level of the health care system. For example, people without insurance often delay seeking medical care in the early stages of a problem, when cures are simpler and less expensive.

Kaiser found that uninsured children are 70 percent less likely than insured children to have not received medical care for such common conditions as ear infections, which, if left untreated, can lead to more serious health problems. Uninsured children are also 30 percent less likely to receive medical attention when they are injured.

When care is given, it is often done in the most expensive setting possible—the emergency room.

According to the American College of Emergency Physicians, three out of every four uninsured patients admitted to U.S. hospitals receive their care in emergency rooms—at a staggering cost. In 1996 alone, hospitals provided $10 billion of uncompensated care, according to a study by the emergency physicians group.

"The emergency department is the ultimate safety net for health care," said Rapp, who practices medicine in suburban Washington. On any given night, he said, 25 percent of the patients in his emergency room are uninsured. The number is probably higher in hospitals that serve poorer communities with larger numbers of uninsured.

Emergency room physicians, knowing that uninsured patients

may not have access to specialists, laboratory tests and other medical procedures, may also feel more pressure to admit them to the hospital.

"The problem is: How do we deal with them after they come to the emergency department? Although we have an open door, most of the health care system does not have an open door," Rapp said.

"We see the patient, then we send them out into the brave, new world, and then we don't know what happens to them."

Tax credits are popular with some Republicans and Democrats, but they would not go far enough in reducing the number of uninsured Americans, according to a study in the January-February 2000 issue of the journal Health Affairs. It found that the ability of tax subsidies to reduce the ranks of the uninsured was "uncertain and unproven."

Authors Jonathan Gruber, a professor of economics at the Massachusetts Institute of Technology, and Larry Levitt, director of the Changing Health Care Marketplace Project at the Henry J. Kaiser Family Foundation, found that a tax deduction for non-group health insurance premiums would cost the government under $1 billion annually but cover only about 250,000 people. A refundable tax credit of $1,000 for single adults and $2,000 for families would cost $13.3 billion annually and help 4 million people.

The most expensive option the authors studied, a refundable tax credit that could be used to purchase non-group and employer-provided insurance, would cover an estimated 12.4 million uninsured—less than a third of those without coverage—and cost a whopping $62 billion a year.

A White House analysis released Sept. 5 reached a similar conclusion. The report by the White House Council of Economic Advisers found that while tax credits would encourage some individuals to purchase group or individual coverage, they would not be a great incentive and would cost the government more than expanding existing federal health programs or combining any expansions with tax credits.

In the November-December issue of Health Affairs, Stuart Butler, a vice president for domestic and economic policy studies at the conservative Heritage Foundation, and David B. Kendall, senior fellow for health policy at the moderate Progressive Policy Institute, have urged Congress to give states maximum flexibility to use existing funding sources to supplement the value of a federal tax credit and help create stable insurance pools.

Baby Steps?

It is unclear whether Congress will ever make the broad, bold moves—major changes to the tax code, an expansion of existing public health programs or creation of new entitlements—that many experts argue could make health insurance available to the millions of Americans who now lack coverage.

"The steps we've taken have been small steps, not major steps," Diane Rowland, vice president of the Kaiser Family Foundation, said in a Sept. 1 interview. "The incremental strategies everyone knows are going to have a limited reach."

Sen. Paul Wellstone, D-Minn., in July unveiled a sweeping proposal (S 2888) to provide federal matching funds for states to help cover the uninsured.

"All the doctors and all the nurses and all the other health care providers in America cannot solve this problem nor right this injustice, but we in the Congress can," Wellstone said July 19 in floor remarks.

Some Republicans, such as House Ways and Means Health Subcommittee Chairman Bill Thomas, R-Calif., have advocated scrapping the current employer-based system of health care and replacing it with an individual tax credit. Such a dramatic change, however, would take years to evolve.

Piecemeal policy approaches such as CHIP will likely continue no matter which party controls Congress, said David Hebert, director of federal government affairs for the American Association of Nurse Anesthetists.

"I cannot see, in this political climate, the creation of a brand-new program," Hebert said in a Sept. 7 interview. "Those days have gone by."

Congress will likely want to make sure that existing programs have accomplished all they can before lawmakers create new approaches. Such concern is legitimate, because experts say that half of the nation's uninsured children could be covered by either the Medicaid or CHIP programs.

Many welfare recipients and their children still may qualify for Medicaid and CHIP once they have left welfare, but they often are not aware they can keep their benefits; sometimes state caseworkers misunderstand the law as well.

Rapp, the emergency room doctor, offers his own prescription for the dilemma: Start with infants.

Echoing the sentiments of former Democratic presidential hopeful and former Sen. Bill Bradley of New Jersey (1979–97) Rapp suggests that all children be given coverage at birth that cannot be canceled and stays with them their entire lives.

"Everybody likes new babies, right?" Rapp said. "Then in 65 years, we will have it nailed."

From *CQ Weekly*, September 9, 2000, pp. 2062-2065. © 2000 by Congressional Quarterly, Inc. Reprinted by permission.

'WE ALL (PARTICULARLY POLITICIANS AND THE MEDIA) NEED A CIVICS LESSON.'

A Judge Speaks Out

H. LEE SAROKIN

Democracy in America today faces many seemingly intractable problems—inequality, corruption, political disengagement—but is equally threatened by discrete official acts that eat away at its core institutions. Jesse Helms autocratically denies William Weld a hearing to be ambassador to Mexico. Janet Reno stubbornly drags her feet on appointing an independent counsel on campaign finance abuses. House majority whip Tom DeLay callously calls for impeachment of federal judges who heed a legal "technicality" called the Bill of Rights. These actions feed mistrust of government and must be loudly condemned, as they often are. But in the case of the assault on judicial independence by DeLay, Senator Orrin Hatch and others—which was ramped up during the 1996 elections and continues in an unprecedented stonewalling of President Clinton's nominees to the federal bench—the people who could fight back most eloquently, the judges themselves, are bound by a code of silence.

Judges should be loath to enter the fray, but there are extraordinary circumstances where their rebuttals are warranted, even necessary. When Bob Dole and Newt Gingrich threatened Judge Harold Baer with impeachment in March 1996 because of his decision to suppress evidence in a routine drug case (a decision that, under pressure, he later rescinded), it was inspiring to see four appellate judges publicly proclaim that the criticism had gone too far.

Now, we have the first riposte from one who was a target. Judge H. Lee Sarokin, a courageously independent federal trial and appellate judge for seventeen years in Newark, was for years a favorite scapegoat of those on the right. Last year, battered by increasingly malicious and distorted assault, Sarokin left the bench, saying he no longer wanted his rulings to be fodder for their twisted campaign. While we regretted his decision, we respected it and urged him to break the silence and explain just how corrosive these attacks have become [see "Gavel-to-Gavel Politics," July 1, 1996]. Here is his response.

—The Editors

I retired from the federal bench not because my opinions were being criticized but in protest over the politicization (what I characterized as the "Willie Hortonizing") of the federal judiciary. Politicians increasingly mischaracterize judicial opinions and then use them against those who nominated, appointed or voted to confirm the judges involved (like blaming a governor for crimes committed by a paroled prisoner). Not only do such tactics threaten the independence of the judiciary but, more important, they have a corrosive effect on the public's confidence in our judicial system and those who implement it. This is the toll when respected persons in high office constantly contend that judges are not following the law but rather are pursuing their own private agenda. I thought that by stepping down from the court and making my concerns public, I would convey the gravity of this dangerous course.

Now, a year later, I concede that my grand gesture was a complete fizzle, and indeed, rather than dissuade the practice, seems to have emboldened it, since it has been followed by demands, led by Representatives Tom DeLay and Bob Barr, to impeach judges for unpopular decisions. Although the election has ended, the political rhetoric attacking the judiciary has not.

The validity of a judicial opinion cannot rest on popularity. Resisting pressure to please the majority is judicial strength, not weakness.

Admittedly, from time to time there will be judicial decisions with which many will not agree. All too often that disagreement arises from the mischaracterization of the opinion and focuses on its result rather than its reasoning. But the validity of a judicial opinion cannot rest on its popularity. Resisting the pressure to please the majority is the strength of the judiciary, not its weakness. Judges who invoke the Constitution to protect the rights of people charged with crimes are not "soft on crime." Judges who declare that a statute or a public referendum violates the constitution are not "legislating" from the bench or "thwarting the will of the majority." They are carrying out their oath of office and following the rule of law.

The verdict in the Oklahoma City bombing trial may have restored some confidence in our judicial system. But a different scenario might illustrate the dangers of the current political vilification of judges and the resulting erosion of respect for our judicial system. Assume that prison guards, angered over the 168 deaths caused by the bombing of the Murrah Federal Building and frustrated by the lack of cooperation from those arrested, decided to beat one of those charged in order to obtain a confession.* As a result, they obtained a statement with sufficient detail so that there could be no doubt as to the knowledge and guilt of the confessor. Furthermore, these details led to the gathering of additional evidence regarding the source of the materials utilized in the making of the bomb, how they were transported, where they were stored, how the bomb was made and how it was ultimately delivered and detonated and by whom.

There are those who would argue, quite reasonably, that the guards should be punished, but that the evidence should be utilized. However, there are some protections that we view as so precious that nothing can be gained from their violation. Under existing law, the confession would not be admissible. In all probability, neither would any of the details, evidence and corroboration obtained as a result. Indeed, the taint of the illegally obtained confession and the fruits thereby gained might have led to an acquittal or dismissal of the charges. One can well imagine and understand the public outrage at such a result. Conservative politicians would be elbowing one another aside to reach microphones to lambaste the "liberal judge" who made such a ruling and decry the use of the "technicality" that made it possible—another example of a judicial system run amok, although there probably is not a judge in the country who would rule otherwise.

But suppose we were to change the above hypothetical scenario as follows: The guilty person beaten by law-enforcement officers was not the first but the tenth. Seven did not confess, because they were not guilty; two others did, even though they were not, just to bring the beatings to an end. One can imagine and hope for an equally vociferous outcry. If public confidence is essential to the maintenance of our judicial system—and it is—what lesson is to be drawn from these two hypothetical instances? What people really desire is two sets of rules and rights: one for the guilty and one for the innocent. People do not want criminals to gain advantage from the assertion of constitutional rights. On the other hand, they want those rights available to and enforced for the innocent. The problem with such an approach is that the determination of constitutional violations is frequently made by a judge before there is a determination of guilt or innocence. Furthermore, for the presumption of innocence to have any meaning, a determination of guilt must await a final verdict.

So if it is impossible or impractical to preserve the Bill of Rights for the innocent and deny it to the guilty, should the constitutional protections extended to those accused of crimes be repeated? Has crime become so prevalent and the need to combat it so great that we are willing to sacrifice some of our fundamental rights in order to win this battle? For both practical and principled reasons, the answer should be "no," even if the present atmosphere makes such amendments to the Constitution seem politically possible.

First, we all (and particularly the politicians and the media) need a civics lesson. Have we forgotten our history? The Fifth Amendment is not a "technicality." The right against self-incrimination was considered fundamental and essential to our freedom. Likewise, the restriction on searches and other government intrusions into our private lives was of sufficient importance that our forefathers were prepared to die for it.

Even if one is unmoved by the historical significance of these rights, their enforcement has virtually no impact on crime in this country. If the Bill of Rights were repealed tomorrow, insofar as its protections extend to those accused of crimes, it would not make the slightest ripple in the amount or nature of crime in this country. Law-enforcement officials themselves have repeatedly stated that enforcement of the Bill of Rights has not impeded them, and criminals hardly sit around a kitchen table and say: "If we are apprehended we can invoke our right against self-incrimination, and thus we shall go ahead and rob the corner candy store." They may be street-smart and "know their rights," but that knowledge is neither the catalyst nor cause of their unlawful activity. It probably never enters their thinking, assuming that there is much forethought given to the commission of most crimes.

Most significant, and contrary to the vision portrayed by conservative politicians and media, there is not a group of loony liberal judges out there leaping at the chance to set criminals free. The idea that any judge relishes ruling in favor of a person charged with a crime in the face of evidence of guilt, and particularly after a finding of guilt, is utter nonsense. Those rulings are made with great reluctance, but done because the law compels it. The suppression of the confession referred to earlier in this article would have to be made by any and every judge confronted with those facts. Furthermore, the number of such rulings is minuscule. Roughly, between 5 and 10 percent of all criminal cases are actually tried. In those that are tried, motions to suppress evidence are routinely denied every day, in every court in every state in this country. A dismissal of charges following the granting of a motion to suppress evidence is as rare an event as Senator Orrin Hatch recommending a liberal for a seat on the Supreme Court.

When motions to suppress are granted, those who wish to capitalize on such rulings invariably discuss the heinous nature of the crime or the long criminal history of the defendant, if one exists, neither of which is relevant to the question of whether the defendant's constitutional rights have been violated. Here again, we do not and cannot have two sets of rules—one for bad crimes and criminals and another for those less offensive. The exercise I posed above was chosen because there has been no more horrific crime in the history of this country than the Oklahoma City bombing; but the rights afforded by the Constitution cannot be reduced as the severity of the crime increases.

The law and those who administer it are not perfect. Mistakes are made. That is why we have courts of appeal. But it is essential that the public understand that in large measure the guilty are convicted (indeed, most plead guilty), the innocent are protected and the judicial system and its judges are devoted and dedicated to fairness and justice. Criticism has its place, but truth must have some role in the dialogue. (My nomination to the Court of Appeals was opposed on the basis that I "had a long history of freeing criminals in disregard of the rights of their victims." In fifteen years on the bench two people are free as a result of my rulings—Rubin "Hurricane" Carter, a decision affirmed by the Court of Appeals and left standing by the U.S. Supreme Court after review, and James Landano, who is still awaiting retrial while on bail—hardly a "long history of freeing criminals.") Indeed, granting a writ of habeas corpus orders a new trial and does not free the petitioner unless the state elects not to retry.

The Bill of Rights is meant to protect us all. If in the process a criminal benefits, we must decide whether that detriment outweighs the benefits and freedoms we all enjoy. It is ironic that the criticism leveled at the Bill of Rights and the frequent characterization of its parts as "technicalities" come from conservatives, since the rights enunciated are the embodiment of the conservative philosophy. They codify the fundamental conservative principle of excluding unwanted and unwarranted government intrusion in the private lives of citizens.

Although the critics of "judicial activism" insist that neither the result nor the identity of the judge is what motivates them, the evidence suggests otherwise. There are many former prosecutors who now sit on the judicial benches of this country who were strong advocates of the death penalty. When they rule in favor of capital punishment, none of these critics claim that the judges involved are "activists carrying out their own agendas"; but the personal motives or background of those who vote against the death penalty in a given case invariably becomes relevant. When the Chief Justice of the United States wrote an opinion declaring unconstitutional an act of Congress that prohibited guns within 1,000 feet of schools, there was no cry of "thwarting the will of the people"; if I had authored that opinion, *The Wall Street Journal* editorial world have read: "Sarokin Rules Schoolchildren Can Have Guns!"

The independence of the judiciary is essential to our democracy. Those who seek to tamper with it to gain a momentary political victory for themselves will cause a greater and more lasting loss to the public, and to the confidence in our judicial system, without which the rule of law cannot survive.

---

* There is no suggestion that any guard would engage in such conduct. The discussion is for illustrative purposes only.

H. Lee Sarokin is a retired judge of the United States Court of Appeals.

Reprinted with permission from *The Nation* magazine, October 13, 1997, pp. 15-16, 18-19. © 1997 by The Nation Company, L.P.

Reconsidering "Bush v. Gore"

Gary Rosen

INDIGNATION TOWARD the Supreme Court has been a defining feature of American conservatism since at least the early 1960's, when Chief Justice Earl Warren and his like-minded brethren launched the judicial "rights revolution" that has continued, more or less unabated, up to our own day. With each expansive new ruling over the years—on obscenity, school prayer, the death penalty, busing, abortion, and a host of equally inflammatory issues—conservatives have found fresh evidence of the Justices' disdain not only for the limits of their own office but, more gallingly, for the views of the American people and their elected representatives. In a controversial 1996 symposium, the religious journal *First Things* went so far as to wonder whether this "judicial usurpation of politics" should be seen as the "end" of American democracy.

Where this question stands now, in the wake of the extraordinary events that brought the 2000 presidential election to a close, is unclear Judging by the many books published in the past year—and especially in the past several months—on the legal aspects of the dispute over the Florida vote, the Right is hardly alone any longer in entertaining serious doubts about the role that the courts play in our democracy, nor is the Left alone in discounting such concerns.

To be sure, as matters unfolded in Florida after the vote on November 7, conservatives—or, to be more precise, the supporters of George W. Bush—saw their long-standing fears about the imperial judiciary confirmed yet again. In a series of remarkably freewheeling decisions, the Florida Supreme Court, invoking the "will of the people" to trump what it called "a hyper-technical reliance upon statutory provisions," allowed or ordered manual recounts that were seemingly designed to give Al Gore every opportunity to overtake the slim official lead of his Republican rival. James Baker, Bush's chief spokesman in Florida, called it "a sad day for America and the Constitution when a court decides the outcome of an election." For the conservative *Weekly Standard*, the Florida justices had become, as the magazine's cover declared, "Our Robed Masters."

But within a matter of days the entire situation had been turned on its head, both politically and ideologically. In short order, the five-Justice conservative majority of the U.S. Supreme Court—William Rehnquist, Anthony Kennedy, Sandra Day O'Connor, Antonin Scalia, and Clarence Thomas—intervened first to impose a stay on the recount and then to reverse the Florida high court, thus barring any further effort to discover

votes among the disputed ballots. The endless wrangling about hanging, dimpled, and pregnant chads was over, Bush was President-elect, and conservatives, who had spent weeks decrying the high-handed activism of judges, were elated.

Now it was the other side's turn to speak of a "stolen" election and to vent its fury at a purportedly out-of-control judiciary. Taking their cue from Justice Ruth Bader Ginsburg, who omitted from her opinion the "respectfully" that customarily softens the concluding phrase "I dissent," liberal commentators denounced *Bush* v. *Gore* as a "travesty" (Mary McGrory in the *Washington Post*), a "scandal" (Randall Kennedy in the *American Prospect*), and a ruling that lacked any "credible explanation" (Anthony Lewis in the *New York Times*). The "four vain men and one vain woman" of the Court's majority were accused of having simply indulged their "self-interested political preferences" (Jeffrey Rosen in the *New Republic*), rendering a decision that was at once "illegitimate, undemocratic, and unprincipled" (Cass R. Sunstein in the *Chronicle of Higher Education*).[1] In a full-page ad in the *New York Times*, 554 law professors—"teachers whose lives," in their own words, "have been dedicated to the rule of law"—declared that by acting as "political partisans, not judges," the Justices had "tarnished" the legitimacy of the Court.

There was, of course, an element of almost comic irony in these full-throated denunciations, coming as they did from intellectual quarters that have long rationalized or celebrated the overreaching of the American judiciary. Such self-righteous critics should themselves have cleaner hands. But it is not enough to answer a charge of hypocrisy with a charge of hypocrisy. The fundamental question, with all that it portends for our constitutional politics, remains: were the Justices of the Supreme Court right or wrong to play the role they did in the 2000 presidential election?

FROM THE moment reporters were handed *Bush* v. *Gore* in the waning hours of December 12, it was apparent that the case had deeply divided the Court. The decision consisted of an almost unprecedented six distinct opinions: an unsigned "per curiam" ruling by all five conservative Justices, a concurrence by the three most conservative of them, and separate but overlapping dissents by each of the four liberal Justices—Stephen Breyer, Ruth Bader Ginsburg, David Souter, and John Paul Stevens.

The concurrence written by Chief Justice Rehnquist and joined by Justices Scalia and Thomas hinged on the issue of just how activist the rulings of the Florida justices had been. Though "comity and respect for federalism" would normally compel the Justices to defer to a state court's interpretation of state law, Rehnquist wrote, the Constitution did impose certain limits when it came to the procedures for presidential contests. In particular, Article II provides that the electors of each state are to be selected "in such Manner as the *Legislature* thereof may direct" (emphasis added in the opinion). Thus it was that the election laws devised by the Florida legislature took on an "independent significance," demanding a degree of deference that the state's highest court, in its various reworkings of that law, had failed to show. By the light of Article II, the Court's most reliably conservative troika held, the Florida justices had "impermissibly distorted" the intention of the state's lawmakers.

The actual judgment of the Court—the ruling that carried the force of law—lay, however, in entirely different constitutional precincts, in concerns about the "equal protection" guaranteed by the Fourteenth Amendment. Here the conservative Justices, now including the more centrist Kennedy and O'Connor, formed a united front.

Where the Florida Supreme Court had run into constitutional trouble, the five Justices declared, was in ordering a recount whose lone instruction to election officials was to determine the "intent of the voter." In the absence of more specific standards, this open-ended rule had resulted in a range of abuses, with contested ballots treated differently not only "from county to county but indeed within a single county from one recount team to another." The mechanism set in motion by the Florida court failed, in short, to "satisfy the minimum [constitutional] requirement for non-arbitrary treatment of voters."[2]

Nor was there time, according to the Justices, to devise a new procedure, since the Florida legislature (at least in the estimation of the Florida court) had meant to protect the state's presidential vote from congressional challenge by taking advantage of the "safe harbor" provision of federal law, the deadline for which, as the decision was announced, was just minutes away. For the violations now before it, the Supreme Court concluded, the only available remedy was to bring the whole contentious process to a halt.

F OR THEIR part, the liberal Justices were unanimous in rejecting the idea that the Florida high court had somehow usurped the role of the state legislature. The rulings of the Florida justices may have been flawed—"other interpretations were of course possible," Justice Souter observed, "and some might have been better than those [that were] adopted"—but they certainly fell within the bounds of permissible interpretation. Furthermore, Justice Stevens maintained, Article II did not "create state legislatures out of whole cloth, but rather takes them as they come—as creatures born of, and constrained by, their state constitutions," a circumstance that, in this case, gave the Florida Supreme Court broad powers of review.

More complicated was the response from this side of the Court to the majority's equal-protection claim. On this question the liberal Justices split. Ginsburg saw no evidence that the recount "would yield a result any less fair or precise" than the official count that preceded it. Stevens pointed to the danger of "too literal" an interpretation of constitutional principles; after all, he wrote, if the recount was suspect on equal-protection grounds, so too was Florida's entire election system, which left "to each county the determination of what balloting system to employ—despite enormous differences in accuracy."

Justices Breyer and Souter, by contrast, agreed that the conduct of the recount raised serious questions about the unequal treatment of similarly situated voters. But their agreement with the majority only went that far, and still left them very much in dissent. As Breyer stipulated at the outset, and as Souter echoed in his own opinion, "The Court was wrong to take this case."

Moreover, having taken it and found a violation of equal protection, the Court was obliged to send it back to Florida for resolution. As both Breyer and Souter stressed, six days remained until the electoral votes absolutely had to be cast on December 18—meeting the imminent "safe harbor" deadline, all four liberal Justices insisted, was not in fact required by Florida law—and the state's high court deserved a chance, however fleeting, to devise the uniform standards now demanded of it.

T HE MOST curious feature of the reaction to *Bush* v. *Gore* among conservatives has been the widespread agreement on two seemingly contradictory propositions: first, that the majority's decision was a necessary vindication of the rule of law; second, that the equal-protection analysis upon which it relied was entirely unpersuasive. Thus, for Richard Lowry, the editor of *National Review*, the Supreme Court "had little choice but to overturn the Florida court," though the "reasoning in its hasty per-curiam decision was so shabby, one can only conclude that the Court did the right thing for the wrong reason." Robert H. Bork, writing in the *New Criterion*, also found "serious difficulties" with the Court's reliance on the equal-protection clause. As he (like Justice Stevens before him) pointed out, disparities like those in the Florida recount "have always existed within states under our semi-chaotic election processes." Nonetheless, Bork argued, the Justices could not permit "the stealing of a presidential election," even at the cost of an "inadequate majority opinion."

As a constitutional matter, what redeems *Bush* v. *Gore* in the eyes of Lowry, Bork, and most other conservative commentators is the concurring opinion of Justices Rehnquist, Scalia, and Thomas. Indeed, it is widely (and plausibly) assumed that the Court's three conservative stalwarts, having failed to persuade Justices Kennedy and O'Connor that the Florida court had violated Article II by rewriting the state's election laws, held their noses and accepted the egalitarian abstractions of what became the majority opinion. Either way, after all, the recount would be stopped.

That the concurrence had the better argument is hard to deny. As Richard A. Epstein of the University of Chicago and Michael W. McConnell of the University of Utah make clear in their separate contributions to *The Vote: Bush, Gore, and the Supreme Court*,[3] a useful collection of essays by legal academics on both sides of the controversy, the "interpretations" of the Florida Supreme Court went far beyond what was required to make sense of the sometimes ambiguous or conflicting provisions of the state's election code.

In the fateful first stage of the litigation, the Florida justices transformed a portion of the law concerned with rectifying "an error in the vote tabulation"—a transparent reference to problems with the counting *machinery*—into a mandate to correct errors committed by *voters* in the casting of their votes. For good measure, they also ignored a straightforward statutory deadline for certifying vote tallies and replaced it with a much later cut-off date entirely of their own making, thus throwing into disarray the whole process for mounting a challenge to the election results.

In the second stage of the litigation (and largely to compensate for their earlier errors), the Florida justices went still farther down the road of arrogation, ordering a statewide recount of all "undervoted" ballots under the direction of a single circuit judge—an action neither contemplated by state law nor requested by Gore or Bush. In all of these proceedings, the basic effect of the court's rulings was the same: to annul the far-reaching discretionary authority of the county and state officials to whom Florida law explicitly assigns the supervision of elections.

T HIS MUCH ground and considerably more are covered by Richard A. Posner in *Breaking the Deadlock: The 2000 Election, the Constitution, and the Courts*,[4] the only book-length defense of the ruling in *Bush* v. *Gore* yet to appear. For Posner—a federal appeals court judge, lecturer in law at the University of Chicago, and perhaps the country's widest-ranging and most prolific legal thinker—it is not enough to demonstrate that the Florida court went badly astray, "butchering" the state's election laws in violation of Article II. As he argues, with characteristic verve and intelligence, there are still deeper justifications for the Supreme Court's intervention.

Posner concedes that more Florida voters probably set out to support Al Gore than George W. Bush, and that the wider availability of user-friendly voting technology would very likely have sent the Democratic candidate to the White House. But this, he insists, is no defense for what the Florida Supreme Court did. In our representative democracy, with its concern for order and stability, an election is "a formal procedure, a statutory artifact," not "a public-opinion poll." What matters is not some inchoate "general will," à la Rousseau, but votes, and what constitutes a vote is determined by preestablished rules. By promulgating its own rules after the fact, Posner argues, the Florida court was not perfecting the democratic system, as many have claimed, but undermining one of its fundamental pillars: that succession take place according to procedures that are "fixed in advance, objective, administrable, and clear."

In a similar vein, Posner dismisses those who think that the Supreme Court should ultimately have remanded the case to Florida, allowing the state courts and legislature to resolve the election dispute. Florida *was* entitled to six more days, he acknowledges, but "a responsible recount could not have been concluded by then." In fact, the whole mess, with rival slates of

Florida electors, would soon have found its way to the divided halls of Congress, where it would have led to paralyzing chaos. With a new President still unnamed by inauguration day, Posner somewhat fancifully suggests, the office would have passed down the line of executive succession until coming to rest, for various reasons, on then-Secretary of the Treasury Lawrence Summers—thus making him our first Jewish President! "Eventually, with the nation's patience completely exhausted," he writes, either Bush or Gore would have prevailed in the House of Representatives, but his presidency "would have started behind the eight ball, with an irregular and disputed accession, an abbreviated term of office, and no transition."

For Posner, these "pragmatic" concerns are paramount in evaluating *Bush* v. *Gore*, and form what he considers its "hidden ground." As he concludes, the majority's decision may have "damaged the Court's prestige, at least in the short run; but it did not do so gratuitously—it averted a potential crisis."

T HERE IS much to be said for these exercises in apologetics. As its defenders have rightly stressed, *Bush* v. *Gore*, whatever the defects of the ruling, did bring an orderly conclusion to an unsettling chapter in our national politics, and it did so, at least in part, on the basis of a credible argument about the Constitution's Article II.

In these crucial respects, the Supreme Court's election-ending decision is not, as some of its critics have suggested, the ideological mirror image of *Roe* v. *Wade*, the 1973 abortion decision that has become synonymous with liberal judicial activism. As many liberals themselves are now willing to admit, the ruling in *Roe* was essentially a piece of judicial legislation, with no grounding in constitutional text or history. More important perhaps, the abortion decision, with its cavalier dismissal of how the states themselves wished to resolve the issue, continues to roil our politics even now, some 30 years after it was handed down—a marked contrast to the quiet that, outside the law schools, quickly descended over *Bush* v. *Gore*.

Still, in at least one key regard, the comparison to *Roe* is not favorable to the present Supreme Court. Say what one will about the authors of the abortion decision, their reasoning in the case, such as it was, was not a surprise; it followed their own activist precedents with respect to the so-called "right of privacy," and it reflected a judicial temperament that they had displayed many times before. In *Bush* v. *Gore*, by contrast, the five conservative Justices performed what can only be described as an ideological somersault, embracing an equal-protection claim that was not only unpersuasive on its own terms but irreconcilable with the basic tenets of their judicial philosophy.

T HIS IS the burden of Alan M. Dershowitz's instructive if at times intemperate and wrongheaded book, *Supreme Injustice: How the High Court Hijacked Election 2000*.[5] For Dershowitz—a professor at Harvard Law School who, when not himself taking part in the Florida litigation, was busily offering his opinions on it to any and all media takers—the clearest indication of the Justices' culpability is what he calls "the-shoe-on-the-other-foot test." As he sees it, "they would not have stopped a hand recount if George W. Bush had been seeking it." Acting as partisans, they sought a political end without regard to the ideological means.

In support of this claim, Dershowitz puts together a damning compilation of the conservative Justices' previous rulings and statements on the question of equal protection. All of these reveal, as anyone familiar with their views would expect, a profound reluctance to assign the idea anything like the sweeping effect they gave to it in the Florida case. Typical of the excerpts is this, from an opinion by Justice Rehnquist:

> In providing the Court with the duty of enforcing such generalities as the equal-protection clause, the framers of the Civil War amendments placed it in the position of Adam in the Garden of Eden. As members of a tripartite institution of government which is responsible to no constituency, and which is held back only by its own sense of self-restraint… we are constantly subjected to the human temptation to hold that any law containing a number of imperfections denies equal protection simply because those who drafted it could have made it a fairer or a better law.

And this, from Justice Thomas:

> The equal-protection clause shields only against purposeful discrimination: a disparate impact, even upon members of a racial minority,… does not violate equal protection.… [W]e have regularly required more of an equal-protection claimant than a showing that state action has a harsher effect on him or her than on others.

As Dershowitz writes, the "glaring and dramatic inconsistencies" between these earlier opinions and the Florida ruling strike at "the core of everything these Justices have stood for over many years."

Nor have the more clear-eyed members of the Left, despite their condemnation of the decision, failed to see the opportunity presented by the conservative Justices' epiphany on the meaning of equal protection. In the *Nation*, the historian Eric Foner found a "silver lining" in the Court's having "opened the door to challenging our highly inequitable system of voting." Harvard Law School's Lani Guinier, writing in the *New York Times*, invoked the decision to renew her call for dispensing with winner-take-all legislative districts and moving to a system of proportional representation, since the Court had been explicit in "valuing no person's vote over another."

Indeed, taken to its logical conclusion, the notion of equal protection affirmed by the Court in *Bush v. Gore* would draw into question virtually every aspect of the country's locally run, state-administered, and highly decentralized electoral system—a point that the conservative Justices themselves, confronted by a different set of litigants, could have been counted on to make. This may explain what is perhaps the most objectionable part of the majority's opinion. As if to confess their bad faith, the Justices announced toward the end of the decision that they were not, in fact, playing for keeps. Because "the problem of equal protection in election processes generally presents many com-

plexities," they wrote, "our consideration is limited to the present circumstances."

Alongside this extraordinary disavowal, Alan Dershowitz places the following passage from a 1996 opinion by Justice Scalia, in which the Court's most articulate conservative aptly described the institution's proper role:

> The Supreme Court of the United States does not sit to announce "unique" dispositions. Its principal function is to establish precedent—that is, to set forth principles of law that every court in America must follow. As we said only this term, we expect both ourselves and lower courts to adhere to the "rationale upon which the Court based the results of its earlier decisions".… That is the principal reason we publish our opinions.

N<small>O LESS</small> disturbing as a matter of judicial philosophy—and seeming partisan favoritism—was the Supreme Court's obvious unwillingness to let the election dispute work itself out in Florida or, if need be, in Congress. If judicial self-restraint means anything, it is that the Justices should respect the prerogatives of the other branches of the state and federal governments, especially with regard to those "political questions," as they are known in legal circles, that do not clearly fall within the Court's institutional competence and would needlessly involve it in partisan controversy. In such instances, the Justices should exercise what the legal scholar Alexander Bickel called, in his classic formulation, the "passive virtues."

In the Florida case, this would have required, at a minimum, letting the state's high court try to remedy the (supposed) violation of equal protection in its recount standards. Would this have resulted in the political chaos predicted with such flair by Richard Posner? Perhaps. But as he himself grants (and as other commentators on both sides of the political aisle have agreed), the "likeliest outcome of the remand that Justices Souter and Breyer wanted would have been abandonment of the recount when it became clear that it could not be completed, subject to appropriate judicial review, by December 18." Under this scenario, Bush would still have won—but his victory would not have been tainted by the peremptory action of the Court.

More fundamentally, there is the question of whether the Supreme Court should have taken any action at all in the Florida dispute. Even the better argument made by the conservative Justices, based on Article II, was, for all its force, without precedent. There can be no doubt that the intentions of the Florida legislature had been perverted, but this alone did not compel the Court to take the case or to find an infraction of the Constitution, and concerns about federalism might well have counseled restraint. Moreover, in light of the potential conflicts of interest involved—with candidate Bush having repeatedly declared his admiration for Scalia and Thomas and the Justices themselves having an obvious stake in who might be appointed to join them in the future the Court would perhaps have been well advised, in effect, to recuse itself.

Had this happened, we now know, Bush would almost certainly have retained his lead. As recounts conducted after the election at the behest of news organizations have shown, even the more open-ended counting standards advocated by Democrats and accepted by the Florida court would not have provided enough votes to put Gore ahead. Bush would have made it to the White House on his own.

Needless to say, the Justices of the Supreme Court had no way of knowing this as they considered whether to intervene (nor should it have mattered, if their concerns were exclusively of the constitutional variety). What they did know—and what should have furnished the strongest argument for holding back—was that, under both the Constitution and federal law, it was the duty of other, more democratically accountable institutions to safeguard the integrity of the presidential election. The Florida legislature was prepared to act, and so too was Congress, if disagreement among the branches of the state government had resulted in the naming of separate Republican and Democratic slates of electors.

Had it come to this, the scene on Capitol Hill would certainly have been partisan, and perhaps even ugly. But as we learned from the impeachment proceedings against President Clinton (and as we have had occasion to see again in the wake of the terrorist attack on September 11), our politicians are capable during times of crisis of conducting themselves with the necessary sobriety and seriousness of purpose. Though Posner is probably correct that "whatever Congress did would have been regarded as the product of raw politics," the same has been said, with some reason, about the *Court's* settling of the Florida case—and politics is not supposed to be the Court's business.

Why this should be so was well stated more than a century ago by the sponsor of the Electoral Count Act, the law under which Congress would have considered the Florida dispute. As Senator John Sherman noted in introducing the measure—a belated response to the fiasco surrounding the Hayes-Tilden presidential contest of 1876—some members of Congress had wished to involve the Supreme Court in the process.

> But there is a feeling in this country that we ought not to mingle our great judicial tribunal with political questions, and therefore this proposition has not met with much favor. It would be a very grave fault indeed and a very serious objection to refer a political question in which the people of the country were aroused, about which their feelings were excited, to this great tribunal, which after all has to sit upon the life and property of all the people of the United States. It would tend to bring that court into public odium of one or the other of the two great parties.

Naturally enough, much of the bitterness arising from the 2000 election has since evaporated, especially as the country has turned of late to decidedly more urgent matters. But American political life will gradually revert to something like its former state, and when it does, it is unlikely in the aftermath of *Bush* v. *Gore* that either of the "great parties" will see the Supreme Court in the same light.

The Democratic party, of course, has never been well disposed to the Court's current majority, and has fought energetically—often unfairly—to keep other conservative judges off the bench. But the critique of the conservative Justices has previously been ideological; their ideas were "extremist," their view of the Constitution unacceptably narrow. Now, as never before, liberals have at their disposal the argument that has long served as a rallying cry for conservative critics of the Warren and Burger Courts: that the Justices are not just mistaken but, in some sense, corrupt, having forgotten the limits of their office.

Perhaps more profound may be the effect on Republicans and conservatives, who, one suspects, will find it difficult to continue avowing their old judicial principles with a straight face. Phrases like "judicial restraint" and "strict construction" may not sound the same for some time. Conservatives will thus be hampered in resisting what may be, in due course, the Left's dominant reaction to *Bush* v. *Gore*: not second thoughts about its own history of judicial activism, but a renewed commitment to using the courts as an engine of social change. After all, if the judicial gloves are off, they are off for everyone.

The great shame in all this is that the 2000 election might have turned out very differently for the U.S. Supreme Court and our constitutional politics. Given the opportunity to decide who would be President, the conservative Justices, in the service of long-held principle, might have done what members of the high court have always found it difficult to do in the face of society's most pressing concerns and their own strongly held preferences: they might have passed.

Notes

1. For these and other opinion pieces written immediately after the key legal decisions in the Florida controversy (as well as for the decisions themselves), see *Bush* v. *Gore: The Court Cases and the Commentary*, edited by E.J. Dionne, Jr. and William Kristol (Brookings, 344 pp., $15.95, paper).
2. The majority found additional, if somewhat secondary, equal-protection problems in the Florida court's failure to include "overvotes" (ballots with more than one selection for President) in the statewide recount that it ordered, in its seeming indifference to whether those who would conduct the recount were adequately trained, and in its readiness to accept totals from incomplete county recounts.
3. Edited by Cass R. Sunstein and Richard A. Epstein. University of Chicago Press, 266 pp., $18.00 (paper).
4. Princeton University Press, 266 pp., $24.95.
5. Oxford University Press, 275 pp., $25.00.

GARY ROSEN *is the managing editor of* COMMENTARY *and the author of* American Compact: James Madison and the Problem of Founding.

Turkey Farm

*The government can't afford to keep ignoring the case
for reforming civil service tenure*

BY ROBERT MARANTO

JIM WORKED IN A DEFENSE DEPARTMENT office with an employee whose lack of productivity was matched only by his hostile attitude. Eventually, a good manager with the patience of Job, a mastery of detail to match, and the help of higher management took the time to record, day by day, the offender's record of non-work. After developing improvement plans for the employee and thoroughly documenting his failure to meet them for many months, the incompetent worker was actually fired. Then, the employee appealed before the Merit Systems Protection Board (MSPB). Two years into the appeal, when it looked as if the government would finally win, MSPB threw out the case when one of the team, moving to dismiss the employee, made an offhand remark that "even the people in his neighborhood association think he's unstable." The employee was reinstated with back pay. The agency went through the process all over again. By this time Jim had become boss. With the benefits of hindsight and existing records, the final try took only one more year of work!

Jim's predicament is faced by thousands of hardworking federal employees who must suffer a small number of lazy, incompetent, and, occasionally, dangerous co-workers. For the past three years, I taught high level federal managers at the Federal Executive Institute (FEI). Despite the stereotypes about bureaucrats, the vast majority of federal managers are capable people who take pride in their work. In dedication and smarts, the government bureaucrats I've worked with are more than a match for the college professors I taught alongside during 15 years in the academy. Unfortunately, these good people are thoroughly frustrated by a personnel system which forces them to work alongside (and get the same raises as) a small number of turkeys.

A Broken Personnel System

One of my games in the civil service was to ask a lunch table full of federal managers whether it was possible to fire low-performing employees. Save for the ever optimistic personnel specialists, the usual consensus was that it was possible, but hardly ever worth the effort. My informal focus groups mirrored public employee surveys.

While career civil servants and political appointees do not always see eye to eye, mail surveys I conducted in the mid-1990s found that each side did agree that the federal personnel system is broken, at least when it comes to separating non-performers. Eighty-eight percent of Clinton political appointees and 83 percent of career managers agreed that "personnel rules make it too difficult to fire personnel"—more than half of each group strongly agreed. This dovetails with the findings of University of Georgia political scientist Hal Rainey. Reviewing years of survey data, Rainey reports that "[r]oughly 90 percent of the public managers agreed that their organization's personnel rules make it hard to fire poor managers and hard to reward good managers with higher pay, while 90 percent of the business managers disagreed."

Since courts have ruled that federal employees have property rights in their jobs, they can only be terminated after lengthy due process and multiple venues of appeal. As a result, managers who decide to use official means to deal with turkeys may face the prospect of spending all their time managing that one person, to the detriment of the rest of the office. As one of my informants, a manager in a regional office, recalled of his one (eventually successful) effort to separate an employee who was both unproductive and breaking the law: "As the year went on, it took more and more of my time and became all consuming. I had to spend a lot of time explaining why I was doing this." Similarly, when asked if he had ever fired a non-performer, one manager told me that he had no intention of becoming like the one person in his agency who had fired several people and "wears that as a badge of honor, but he has no time to do his real work!"

Not only is firing a government employee time-consuming for managers, it is also dangerous. Managers who move against problem employees take serious risks. As Carolyn Ban details in *How Do Public Managers Manage?*, low performers facing personnel actions need not go gentle into that good night. They can make life difficult for months or years. They can take their case to the Merit Systems Protection Board (MSPB). They can file a grievance if they are covered by a union contract. Or if they belong to a protected class (by sex, race, age, or handicap), they can file an Equal Employment Opportunity complaint. Some bring their cases to the Office of the Special Counsel, claiming that they are being fired or otherwise harassed because they are whistle-blowers.

The problem of "low performing whistle-blowers" is particularly vexing for many federal managers, who, on the word of a single employee, can be subjected to prolonged investigations worthy of an independent counsel. Imagine having colleagues and subordinates questioned for months about whether you have ever used the long-distance line for personal calls or have padded the expense account. While the investigations go on, little work gets done and communication between co-workers stops, since everyone is afraid that a random remark could lead to a grand jury. Even when the boss is exonerated, a bad reputation can linger for years. And of course, if all else fails, the employee can simply sue his or her manager.

Not surprisingly, managers who have fired someone describe the process as traumatic. As one of the officials quoted above recalls, "here it is years later, the person has long since left the state, and I still don't want to talk about that sorry episode. It has an impact upon both the office and the family life of the individuals involved. It's something you only do once."

With the deck stacked against them, federal managers tend to avoid using official means of dealing with their turkeys. Phone surveys of managers by the U.S. Office of Personnel Management (OPM), reported in *Poor Performers in Government: A Quest for the True Story*, found that only 7.5 percent of the managers of low performing employees moved to reassign, demote, or remove them, and 77.8 percent of those managers reported that the efforts had no effect. While OPM gives a rough estimate of around 65,000 poor performers in government, from September 1997 to September 1998, only 159 federal employees were removed by performance based personnel actions, with another 1,693 removed for issues other than performance, such as breaking the law. Federal managers suffer low performers or act informally to improve their work and never use the federal personnel system, or only use it as a last resort.

Not infrequently, federal managers use two traditional means of shedding non-performers. By writing glowing letters of recommendation, a boss can get a turkey promoted to a different office. Fortunately, most civil servants are too ethical to use such tactics, and anyway, you can only do that once or twice before your credibility in the bureaucracy is shot. More typically, bosses place non-performers in "turkey farms," "dead pools," or (if it is a single person) "on the shelf." By quarantining non-performers, a good manager can save the rest of the organization from their influence.

The relative inability to act against a small number of poor performers has the effect of making that small number vexing to managers, who are people more used to solving problems than ignoring them. Managers don't like using turkey farms, but many feel they have no choice. At least, when downsizing comes, known turkeys make good candidates for reductions-in-force.

The Costs of Tenure

The sad part is that the vast majority of federal personnel do a good job. OPM's *Poor Performers in Government* report estimates that under 4 percent of federal civil servants are non-performers. One can quibble with OPM's methodology. I suspect that the real figure is a bit higher, but still, the poor performer problem is not nearly as bad as most Americans think. So why deal with it at all?

Aside from inefficiency, there are four huge costs of the federal government's inability to kick turkeys off the farm. First, non-performers themselves never get the message that they have to shape up or ship out and never get the chance for a new start. Instead, they often use the system to pursue old grudges for years. Second, good employees like Jim are forced to work alongside, do the work of, and often get the same raises as a small number of turkeys—a real morale killer.

Third, the low performance problem undermines the image and self-image of the bureaucracy. Business people have no tenure and look down on their government cousins who do. Military officers have an "up or out" promotion system—at key points in their careers officers either get promoted or get discharged. This makes the officer corps, at least at higher levels, a turkey-free zone, giving the brass a certain swagger in their dealings with their protected cousins in the civil service.

Most important, a tenured civil service undermines the legitimacy of the bureaucracy in the eyes of the public. After all, very few voters have tenure, so it is hard to tell citizens why their public servants cannot be fired. It is not surprising that college professors, public school teachers, and government bureaucrats have all come under attack in recent years. The very existence of tenure protects a small number of losers and leads the public to suspect the existence of a large number of low performers in government—a suspicion shared by many public managers.

Originally, the federal merit system was set up in 1884 to keep political parties from using government jobs to reward supporters. Patronage was seen as particularly onerous after President Garfield was assassinated by an insane "disappointed office seeker." Presumably, government would work better if run by technical experts than by political hacks. But on the federal level, at least, the spoils system got a bum rap. Even in the 19th century, a new president and Congress kept most of the incumbent civil servants in place, and only rarely replaced those with special expertise. Politicians have never relished the unpopular task of firing old employees to replace them with political supporters. As politicians have long lamented, each new political appointment provides 10 enemies who themselves wanted the job and one ingrate who got it. Besides, for perfectly sound electoral reasons, politicians cared (and still care) about the efficient management of government. As political scientist Michael Nelson has pointed out, even in the 19th century, more voters sent mail than delivered it. A party that replaces all the mail carriers disrupts service—not a good way to win re-election.

The temptation to "politicize" a bureaucracy in search of pork is even less apparent today. In the old days, political campaigns were won by precinct workers who might welcome a federal job. Today, politicians depend on big kickbacks from campaign contributors rather than small ones from government employees. More important, the greater size and expertise of modern government makes it less susceptible to political takeovers. In the old days, it may have made some sense for politicians to hire friends to deliver the mail, but imagine if a modern president hired precinct workers to run the Pentagon and NIH? To think that politicians would raid the civil service, you have to assume that they have an incredible capacity for both venality and stupidity, and the time to exercise both. In fact, modern presidents can hardly handle the 3,000 political appointments they have now. How could they place more? Sure, presidential political appointments have grown in number since 1960, but not nearly enough to match the growth in congressional staffs, interest groups, and reporters—the people appointees deal with on behalf of their agencies. Unless we downsize the rest of the Washington political class—something not likely to happen—we can't downsize political appointments.

Because of constant scrutiny by opponents, politicians in Washington do not have the sort of vast appointment powers they might have in some states and cities. Presidents are in fact very constrained in who they can appoint to government jobs and how many appointments they can make. *The Washington Post* test ("How will it look in *The Post*?") limits what they can do. Congressional scrutiny limits what they can do. Inter- and intra-party battles limit what they can do. Not surprisingly, the worst abuses under spoils were in states and localities with little political competition, not in a two-party, hyperpluralist Washington.

Rebuilding Public Service

To its credit, the Clinton administration has at least acknowledged the non-performer problem, and has begun to act on it. In accord with the *Poor Performer* study, OPM issued a CD-ROM guide to help managers, *Addressing and Resolving Poor Performance*. This is more than previous administrations dared try, but probably too little, too late. Not surprisingly, as the longtime guardian of the merit system, OPM's basic inclination is to save a system that should probably be buried. Real change in the merit system requires legislation to simplify procedures, followed by years of culture change inside government, along the lines of the National Performance Review's reforms of government procurement. The White House considered introduc-ing a bill to overhaul the civil service earlier this year but dropped it in deference to public employee unions, an important constituency in the 2000 presidential primaries.

Real change is occurring on an ad hoc basis, however, in the agencies. Currently, the Federal Aviation Administration and Internal Revenue Service are creating their own alternatives to the traditional merit system. The Pentagon and Department of Housing and Urban Development have floated trial balloons proposing to replace most tenured civil servants with contractors and fixed-term employees who can be separated with relative ease—something that is happening incrementally all over government. Further, the rise of Performance Based Organizations, called for by Vice President Gore's *Reinventing Government* reports, is likely to erode tenure by tying organization budgets and staffing levels to results. Indeed, on all levels of government, the reinventing movement is in part a way to use market mechanisms to get around civil service tenure. Declining demands for an organization's outputs force reductions in force, which in turn push marginal performers out the door.

Many of the most exciting changes are happening in the states. More than 30 states now have serious proposals to reform their civil service systems, but Georgia has gone the farthest. In 1996 Georgia removed tenure from new employees in state agencies. A detailed evaluation of the Georgia experiment does not yet exist, but early work by political scientist Steve Condrey suggests that removing tenure has increased the ability of public managers to manage for accountability. A single Georgia state agency reported terminating nearly 200 employees for cause in the first 20 months after the law came into effect—with no reported challenges or cases of impropriety. Notably, the Georgia civil service reform was developed and pushed through the legislature not by anti-government Republicans but by then Governor Zell Miller, a pro-government New Democrat who sees ending tenure as one way to restore the legitimacy of government.

In short, for the first time in decades, real civil service reform is beginning to happen. For historic context, it took 20 years from 1864 to 1883 to build political support for the original federal merit system, and another 40 years to put it in place. It may take another decade to reform the federal merit system, but tenure now lacks public legitimacy, and the first steps at reform have already been taken. This excites those of us who want to turn "civil service" from an epithet for cumbersome personnel rules into a public service ethic.

ROBERT MARANTO *is a visiting scholar at the Curry School of Education at the University of Virginia and co-editor most recently of* School Choice in the Real World: Lessons from Arizona Charter Schools.

Reprinted with permission from *The Washington Monthly*, November 1999, pp. 26-29. © 1999 by The Washington Monthly Company, 1611 Connecticut Avenue NW, Washington, DC 20009, (202) 462-0128.

REFORMING U.S. INTELLIGENCE
After the Terrorist Attack

"… The President and Congress must radically increase their surveillance of intelligence if America is to have a system that is both effective and reflective of democratic values."

BY CRAIG R. EISENDRATH AND MELVIN A. GOODMAN

THE COLD WAR ended 10 years ago with the demise of the Soviet Union and the Warsaw Pact, but the intelligence community of the U.S. is still pursuing old targets in Russia and China, despite the Third World political and economic status of these countries. U.S. intelligence seems unable to adjust to the political revolution that has taken place the world over. Its targets and priorities are still wedded to old threat perceptions, and the new and elusive spectre of international terrorism has not led to the out-of-the-box thinking that is required in the 21st century.

The successful targeting of the Pentagon and World Trade Center, unlike Pearl Harbor 60 years ago, has left America confused and disoriented because the enemy's hand was hidden from the intelligence community, and terrorists over the past 20 years have gone unpunished by the U.S. The FBI's quick response in establishing a list of suspects indicates that the perpetrators of these heinous acts in Washington and New York were known, but allowed to move freely around the nation. Equally,

the CIA was aware of the vulnerability of America to terrorist attacks, but has been ineffective in protecting the U.S., as evidenced by the damaging assault on the *U.S.S. Cole*. It is time to reassess the National Security Act of 1947, particularly the intelligence system it created.

With a budget of more than $30,000,000,000, the U.S. intelligence system dwarfs the intelligence budget of any other nation in the world and is larger than the full military budget of all but six countries. It includes not only the Central Intelligence Agency and Federal Bureau of Investigation, but a number of additional Federal agencies, including the National Security Agency (NSA), the National Reconnaissance Office (NRO), and the Defense Department's TIARA program, all of which are concerned with tactical intelligence.

A series of intelligence failures since the end of the Cold War gives strong indication that the system has failed to gear up for the new post-Cold War world. These have included the failure to predict India's

nuclear tests, assess accurately a North Korean missile launch, come up with a workable plan to undermine Iraqi leader Saddam Hussein and terrorist Osama bin Laden, and provide sharp analysis of global financial crises. FBI and CIA agents have been caught after handing over secrets to the Russians, resulting in a loss of vital intelligence. In 1999, during the continuing crisis in Kosovo, the system did not provide accurate information on the location of the Chinese embassy in Belgrade, resulting in its bombing—something which might have been avoided simply by consulting maps available to tourists on any home computer.

The destruction of the World Trade Center and the Pentagon has been rightly called a drastic intelligence failure and has given rise to numerous demands for reform. The attacks made clear that the U.S. is highly vulnerable to low-tech assaults, whether from planes, motor launches, or suitcase bombs. Nothing could have made this clearer than the fact that, for decades, America has been unable to stop the clandestine flow of drugs into the country by plane, boat, and suitcase. If drugs, why not bombs?

Several months prior to the tragic events of Sept. 11, Pres. Bush requested that CIA Director George Tenet handle a full-scale review of the intelligence community, similar to the review of the nation's defenses being conducted by Secretary of Defense Donald Rumsfeld. While Tenet nominally heads the intelligence community, he has little power over its budget and personnel, as the CIA uses up less than 10% of both. A political survivor of the Clinton Administration, Tenet is unable to think outside the box and make the recommendations that would fundamentally change the intelligence system and move beyond the priorities of the Cold War. He is totally wedded to the idea of covert action as the CIA's major role in the national security community.

We now know that our intelligence system served us badly even during the Cold War by providing unreliable data on the Soviet Union and other areas of Cold War conflict. It also frequently succumbed to political pressure to "cook the books." By radically overestimating Soviet military strength and capacity, U.S. intelligence goaded this country into vastly increasing its military budget, resulting in massive national debt and decreased standards of living for many Americans. The infamous "Team B" report of the CIA in the late 1970s, then under the direction of future president George H.W. Bush, incorrectly predicted massive Soviet increases in strategic expenditures, leading in the early Reagan years to the largest peacetime military buildup in our nation's history. When the figures proved totally inaccurate, this finding was suppressed as the buildup continued. In the end, the system failed to predict the fall of communism and the breakup of the Soviet empire, despite the fact that 70% of U.S. intelligence assets were targeted on the USSR.

Perhaps even worse, U.S. intelligence wreaked havoc around the world, supporting dictatorships, promoting international narcotics by trading support of drug dealers such as Panama dictator Manuel Noriega for support of American paramilitary operations, and repeatedly violating both foreign and domestic laws. For example, in 1954, the U.S. overthrew the democratically elected government in Guatemala through paramilitary action and maintained a series of dictatorships over a 40-year period, actions for which no justification, even within the logic of the Cold

War, could be produced. Equally unjustifiable were the overthrow of the government in Iran, the Bay of Pigs fiasco, and CIA drug operations in Laos, Iran, Afghanistan, Pakistan, and Central America, which flooded the world market with narcotics.

Still other covert actions over the last 40 years indicate just how deeply enmeshed in skullduggery U.S. intelligence became: assassination plots in Cuba, the Congo, and the Dominican Republic; the alliance between death squads and the CIA in Honduras; the training of terrorists in Afghanistan who eventually attacked not only Saudi Arabia, Egypt, and Pakistan, but U.S. targets at home and abroad; the support of dictator Joseph Mobutu in Zaire; the subversion of the Salvador Allende government in Chile; the support of the bloody contra war in Nicaragua; and the compromise of the United Nations inspection group, UNSCOM, in Iraq by CIA operatives. Finally, the U.S. has been caught red-handed attempting to gain commercial advantages unfairly for its corporations through economic espionage, operations conducted not just against neutral or potentially hostile states, but friendly nations such as France and Israel.

The composite effect of these operations has been not only a loss of U.S. security, but an erosion of American prestige and leadership around the world. For many of the globe's 6,000,000,000 people, the U.S. is identified as the CIA—immoral, undemocratic, and ineffective. Our continuing disregard for international and national laws has been documented by a House Intelligence Committee report which estimated that the U.S. violates the laws of other countries 100,000 times a year. It is particularly shocking that the terrorists who bombed the World Trade Center in 1993 had received their training by the CIA in its paramilitary operations against then-communist controlled Afghanistan.

Clearly, reform is in order, but there is little will to effect it. The domestic CIA abuses of the 1960s and 1970s, the illegal Iran-contra operations in the 1980s, and the Aldrich Ames espionage scandal in the 1980s and 1990s did not lead to reform. Massive government studies, concluded in 1996, failed to suggest even the mildest reforms. Indeed, one study, by the House Intelligence Committee, stated that the committee should be the "advocate" for the CIA, maintaining that "Intelligence, unlike other federal programs, has no natural constituency; therefore, Congress plays a vital role in building public support."

Congress has traditionally played a hands-off role and has given blanket authority to the intelligence community, rather than seek justification for proposed actions and demand accountability. It has, for the most part, accepted the intelligence budget and conveniently buried it in the budget of the Department of Defense so that it is not subject to public scrutiny. The total intelligence budget remains an educated guess, as specifically are the budgets of the individual agencies.

Congress has failed to monitor closely the intelligence agencies' use of funds, allowing sloppy accounting, inadequate reports, and conflicts of interest that would not have been tolerated in other operations. Thus, we find Congressional staffers passing on intelligence affairs who themselves have past positions with contacting agencies or the agencies themselves, as well as the ever-present possibility of future employment. Most of the top leadership positions of the CIA are filled by former staffers of the Senate Select Intelligence Committee, who are political operatives, not intelligence professionals.

The nature of reform

If the system is to be reformed, it must be clear what intelligence is for. Its primary role is to supply the president and Congress with information about possible strategic threats to the U.S. Intelligence is thus needed on potentially threatening states, terrorism, and the proliferation of nuclear, biological, and chemical weapons. This suggests a far-more-specialized role than the virtually limitless license of Cold War days. For instance, we no longer need to corrupt some young Latin American student about to enter a university on the hope that he may serve as a future source of intelligence on Latin American student movements. We no longer need to photostat the UN delegation plans of friendly or neutral nations. We no longer need to use our intelligence system to gain commercial information from such nations that is not already in the public domain.

Espionage and covert action. Today, espionage should only be exercised when reliable, open information cannot be secured on topics having direct bearing on American security. Covert action should only be resorted to when the security of the U.S. is directly threatened, when statecraft can be shown not to work, and when the possible ill effects of the action do not outweigh its possible benefits. We can no longer tolerate an open license to practice espionage or covert action without the most stringent review.

Curtailment of espionage and covert action also requires the proper administrative arrangements within the CIA itself. Current efforts to create a separate organization for espionage within the CIA should stop, else it be given a free hand; espionage and intelligence should be detached from analysis, else the one corrupt the other. The current interest in ending the ban on political assassinations is a serious retrograde move that would not be consistent with the values of this nation. Finally, it makes sense that we work out arrangements with friendly countries not to practice either espionage or covert action, that such practices be strictly limited to areas of the world where open diplomacy and free exchange of information do not exist. The job of our intelligence agents in such countries should emphasize intelligence collection and liaison with other intelligence agencies.

Intelligence and diplomacy. Intelligence should become the servant of policy, not its initiator. The State Department, not the CIA, should be the premier agent of American foreign policy. Today, as the budget of the State Department has fallen radically in relation to that of the CIA and other intelligence agencies, the U.S. finds itself in the embarrassing situation of having its diplomatic personnel being covert intelligence officers. Our counterparts in other countries know this, and assess our diplomatic personnel accordingly. Rather than closing dozens of embassies and consulates, the State Department should be given the funds to operate whenever American diplomatic and consular presence is required. Intelligence collection should rely predominantly and whenever possible on open sources.

Greater transparency. One of the reasons the intelligence community has escaped surveillance and public criticism is that it has shrouded itself in secrecy. To balance openness and the requirements of secrecy, there should be the presumption of openness, a public-interest balancing test for secrecy, and the capacity for outside review, with Congress setting specific limits on the intelligence community's ability to conceal information. Declassification should be an ongoing process, not an occasional activity. Specifically, Congress should establish a clear and expeditious process whereby documents of public concern can be reviewed for declassification, and adequate funds should be provided to the Freedom of Information Act offices so that they can do their work.

In addition, legislation and administrative procedures should be strengthened to protect American citizens from infringements of their privacy rights by U.S. intelligence organizations.

Narcotics and economic espionage. In the last years of his administration, Pres. Bill Clinton proposed that the CIA become a major player in international narcotics enforcement. Such a proposal flies in the face of a 40-year record of ignoring drug trafficking and working with drug dealers in support of covert operations. Too often, the CIA ignored drug smuggling (even into the U.S.) in order not to compromise its operational assets. The CIA should leave drug enforcement to the Drug Enforcement Administration (DEA). No temporary gain from association with dealers can justify the long-term effects of increasing the world supply of drugs, and particularly the supply of drugs available to American citizens. Equally, the intelligence community, whatever inducements it may receive from U.S. corporations, should refrain from economic espionage; this is simply an improper use of its resources.

Ending compromising relations. While the public is preoccupied by the CIA, the lion's share of the intelligence budget is taken up by agencies that are concerned with technical intelligence, like the NRO and the NSA. In 1997, the intelligence analysis of all satellite photography was given to the Defense Department, which uses such analysis to justify increases in the defense budget. The huge budgets of these agencies have been justified not on the basis of national security needs and cost benefits, but on the fact that they are controlled by the Department of Defense and that supervising committees in Congress are compromised by contractors who spread considerable funds to Congressmen in the areas of their operation. There has also been a revolving door arrangement among contractors, intelligence agencies, and Congressional committees. Compromising relations such as these should be prevented by legislation and administrative practice.

A need for control

We need a far tighter control of how these agencies operate. Today, they seriously compromise freedom of speech and privacy. Legal defenses are thwarted by arrangements, instituted over 30 years, that do not provide protection for U.S. citizens

and foreign nationals. We must determine exactly what we are listening for, and how our citizens particularly can protect themselves against abuses.

Terrorism. U.S. intelligence must devote additional resources to counter international threats of terrorism. Recent spectacular failures indicate this is a long-term project. In addition to setting up a more competent anti-terrorism capacity, we must not train people ourselves in operations like Afghanistan who later become terrorists working against us. We need to work harder to uncover the root causes of discontent through diplomatic and economic means. Terrorism is a last resort of desperate people. Cut the despair and you cut the terrorism. We have our work cut out for us.

Improving administration and the budgetary process. The present administrative situation is a nightmare. Although the Director of Central Intelligence (DCI) has statutory responsibility for foreign intelligence and the authority to participate fully in the preparation of the intelligence budget, he lacks the ability to impose his priorities on most of the agencies theoretically under him. The directors of the NRO, NSA, and the National Imagery and Mapping Agency should be hired in peacetime by the DCI, not the Secretary of Defense. The input of agencies that use intelligence, rather than bureaucratic leverage, should determine the allocation of intelligence resources and tasking.

In the U.S. government, the budget process is usually the focal point of policy. However, the budget process for intelligence has been overwhelmed by detail and unable to deal with the basic issues. For openers, a top-down review of requirements must replace the incremental budgeting approach used in past years. Our estimate is that, if such means are used, roughly $4–6,000,000,000 could be cut, or a reduction of 15–20% of the present intelligence budget.

Oversight. The present review by Tenet offers the best possible opportunity for reform, if the Bush Administration is willing to seize it. What we need is a president committed to reform and a courageous, independent DCI, not one whose primary loyalty is to the bureaucracies he heads.

Meanwhile, Congress must tighten its legal provisions about its right to know and about the timeliness of reports to Congress. It must take a close look at various laws and procedures, like the Classified Information Procedures Act, which presently enable the agencies to block legitimate inquiry into their activities. Finally, the President and Congress must radically increase their surveillance of intelligence if America is to have a system that is both effective and reflective of democratic values.

If such changes are made, the capacities developed by the intelligence community over the last 50 years need not be lost. While continuing to protect U.S. security, American intelligence resources can be pooled with those of other nations, as they will be in the new NATO arrangements, to fight international terrorism. They hold possibilities for the monitoring of international agreements through the UN as well, if such arrangements are not used to gain clandestine information for the U.S. American intelligence technology can be put at the disposal of United Nations specialized agencies such as the World Meteorological Organization, or international and national scientific organizations.

We do not know what kind of world we will have 10, much less 50 or 100 years from now. Still, as the leading military and economic power, the U.S. has the option of designing its institutions and setting standards which can indeed structure the future. By reforming the intelligence system, and by cutting down on its disruptive operations, the U.S. can work to enhance a world that differs materially from the violence-prone century from which we are just emerging.

Craig R. Eisendrath, a senior fellow at the Center for International Policy, Washington, D.C., is a former Foreign Service Officer, editor of National Insecurity: U.S. Intelligence After the Cold War, *and coauthor of* The Phantom Defense: America's Pursuit of the Star Wars Illusion. *Melvin A. Goodman, professor of international security studies and chair of the International Relations Department of the National War College, Washington, D.C., was division chief and senior analyst at the CIA's Office of Soviet Affairs from 1976 to 1986, is a senior fellow at the Center for International Policy, and is coauthor of* The Phantom Defense.

From *USA Today* magazine, November 2001, pp. 10-13. © 2001 by the Society for the Advancement of Education. Reprinted by permission.

What the FBI is doing wrong.

Police Blotter

By JASON ZENGERLE

OF ALL THE criticism John Ashcroft has received for his counterterrorism efforts, none has seemed so damning as the brickbats thrown his way on the front page of *The Washington Post* on November 28. There, under the banner headline "EX-FBI OFFICIALS CRITICIZE TACTICS ON TERRORISM," eight former bureau officials (including former Director William Webster) laid into Ashcroft—not for trampling civil liberties, but for devising a stupid plan. Ashcroft's counterterrorism strategy, former FBI assistant director Kenneth P. Walton acidly told the *Post,* was straight out of "the Perry Mason School of Law Enforcement, where you get them in there and they confess. Well it just doesn't work that way."

The *Post* article nicely framed the debate over how the FBI can best prevent terrorist attacks. On one side are the former officials quoted in the *Post*—whose views are shared by some agents still in the bureau—who favor what had been, until September 11, the FBI's counterterrorism strategy of nearly two decades. That strategy resembled the one the FBI uses to fight organized crime: Relying on electronic surveillance and human informants, the bureau conducted long-term investigations of suspected terrorist cells before making any arrests. That way the FBI could identify all the members of a terrorist cell and learn all the details of that cell's plot before they shut it down. "The idea is to let things get down to the last stage and then step in so you make sure you get everyone involved," explains one former agent. "You don't want anyone slipping away."

On the other side are Ashcroft and new FBI Director Robert Mueller who, in light of September 11, have dropped the old watch-and-wait strategy in favor of an aggressive dragnet approach, arresting and jailing "suspected terrorists" using any immigration or unrelated criminal charges they can find. The Justice Department is also trying to conduct informational interviews with 5,000 Middle Eastern men who have entered the United States over the past two years, and Ashcroft reportedly hopes to relax restrictions on the FBI's surveillance of religious and political organizations in the United States. "Our single ob-

jective," the attorney general has explained, "is to prevent terrorist attacks by taking suspected terrorists off the streets."

There's just one problem with this debate: Neither side has a good answer for how to defend the nation against Al Qaeda-style terrorism. For all the talk about the relative merits of long-term investigations versus short-term disruptions, none of the methods and techniques promoted by either side in the counterterrorism debate would have prevented the September 11 attacks. Indeed, the challenge the FBI now faces in battling Al Qaeda—with its decentralized structure of tightly knit, highly autonomous, virtually anonymous cells—likely can't be solved by traditional law enforcement tactics. If the FBI hopes to prevent future attacks by the Osama bin Laden network, it must expand its cooperation with foreign law enforcement agencies—which it has already begun to do—and commit itself to the kind of strategic intelligence that could help predict attacks—which it hasn't. Overnight, fighting Al Qaeda-style terrorism has become the FBI's number-one goal. But so far, it is a goal that neither the bureau nor its internal critics are ready to achieve.

The key to preventing terrorism is always knowledge. "You can't prevent anything unless you have some scintilla of information that it's going to happen," says Oliver "Buck" Revell, a former FBI executive assistant director who helped craft the bureau's old counterterrorism strategy. In the 1970s and early 1980s, the country suffered a rash of terrorist attacks: Puerto Rican separatists—like the Macheteros and the FALN—set off bombs around New York City and pulled off a string of armored-car robberies; New Left groups—like the May 19th Communist organization and the United Freedom Front—carried out bomb attacks against targets up and down the East Coast. And so in 1982 the FBI made counterterrorism one of its four national priorities (along with foreign counterintelligence, organized crime, and white-collar crime). One year later Attorney General William French Smith issued new guidelines—revising those issued by Attorney General Ed Levi in the wake of Watergate—that gave the FBI more leeway in conducting domestic intelligence investigations: Now, instead of probable cause, the bureau only needed to show a "reasonable indication" of a domestic security threat to open an investigation.

In its new counterterrorism campaign, the FBI was operating, from an information-gathering perspective, in a target-rich environment. In the '80s and '90s most terrorists planning attacks in the United States were tied to larger political or cultural movements (the New Left and Puerto Rican separatists), or to foreign governments such as Libya and Iraq. Consequently, the FBI had a good idea where to look for terrorist activity. And once the information came in—providing the "trip wire," as former FBI agent Robert Heibel, who did counterterrorism in the '80s, calls it—the bureau would spring into action. "It was like hounds going after the hare," says Heibel.

Sometimes the trip wire came from human informants. In 1983, for example, the FBI prevented a FALN terrorist cell in Chicago from committing a string of armed robberies and prison breakouts thanks to information from another FALN member the bureau had flipped a few years earlier. New Left groups were also relatively easy places from which to recruit informants—and since, in accord with Leninist principles, the groups were structured hierarchically with tight central control, when the bureau arrested the top guy, the rest of the organization often crumbled. What's more, many New Left terrorists were meticulous record keepers: "They all thought they were going to write the book about the Revolution," says Heibel; in sniffing out one plot, the bureau often found clues to several more.

In other instances electronic surveillance did the trick: In 1990, during the run-up to the Gulf war, the FBI monitored calls to the Iraqi Embassy, one of which came from a Jordanian immigrant living in New Jersey who offered to commit terrorist attacks on behalf of Saddam Hussein. No one at the embassy, which had recently suffered a severe staff reduction, was interested; but the FBI followed up, sending an agent posing as an Iraqi intelligence officer to meet with the man, who revealed his plans to blow up the Holland Tunnel and two military installations. After further surveillance to see if the man had any compatriots—he didn't—he was arrested. It was one of many successes: Between 1981 and 2000, the FBI prevented 131 terrorist attacks.

But September 11 changed everything—not least counterterrorism policy. Faced with an apparent threat of unprecedented danger and immediacy, Ashcroft abandoned the FBI's traditional practice of long-term investigations in favor of a new policy of disruption, relying on an aggressive dragnet. (Technically this was the FBI director's decision; but Mueller, who had been in his job only one week on September 11, works unusually closely with—and his critics inside the bureau say is unusually subservient to—the attorney general.) While Ashcroft compared his new counterterrorism strategy to Robert Kennedy's campaign against organized crime, the analogy is bogus. As one former Justice Department official quips, when the FBI was going after organized crime, "it wasn't rounding up everyone in Little Italy, putting them in jail, and then figuring out what to charge them with."

The problems with Ashcroft's strategy, as articulated by his many critics, are straightforward. Even leaving aside civil-liberties concerns, the dragnet approach wastes valuable man-hours on thousands of suspects who will ultimately prove innocent; engenders resentment in the very Arab and Muslim communities whose cooperation investigators need; and, most of all, alerts any terrorists not caught in the initial roundup to go underground. But given the danger of further attacks in the immediate aftermath of September 11, the dragnet approach—with its premium on getting suspected terrorists off the street and disrupting any ongoing terrorist plots—was probably the right one.

Moreover, Ashcroft's efforts represent a less clear break with past approaches to counterterrorism than his critics maintain. The interviews with recent Middle Eastern immigrants, and efforts to loosen guidelines on surveillance of religious buildings, suggest that the FBI has not lost sight of the value of information. According to one former Justice Department official familiar with counterterrorism efforts since September 11, the bureau is also desperately trying to build up contacts and recruit potential informants in Muslim communities throughout the country. "They're spending a lot of time sending agents out to the local mosque, saying, 'Hi, I'm Special Agent Fred Smith, let's talk,'" says the former official.

The real problem is that neither strategy is likely to work against Al Qaeda in the longer term. Ashcroft's dragnet is largely a holding strategy—eventually most of those in custody will have to be released; and terrorists who avoided capture in the days after September 11 will eventually resurface. But the old-school infiltration method is insufficient as well.

IT'S TRUE THAT after two successful operations by proto-Al Qaeda cells in New York-area mosques associated with the blind Egyptian cleric Sheik Omar Abdel Rahman (the 1990 assassination in New York of Meir Kahane and the first World Trade Center bombing in 1993), the FBI infiltrated Abdel Rahman's organization in 1993, ultimately preventing another plot to blow up landmarks in New York and sending Abdel Rahman and ten others to prison. But Al Qaeda seems to have learned several lessons from that FBI success. The first is to avoid mosques or other identifiably Islamic associations. A terrorist training manual found last year on the computer of a suspected Al Qaeda member in Manchester, England, advised: "[H]ave a general appearance that does not indicate Islamic orientation.... Be careful not to mention... common expressions... [such as], 'May Allah reward you,' [or] 'Peace be upon you,' while arriving and departing.... Avoid visiting famous Islamic places (mosques, libraries, Islamic fairs, etc.)." Indeed, of the 19 September 11 hijackers, it appears that only two attended a mosque in the United States; and they apparently did not reveal anything about their plans to their fellow worshipers.

Another lesson Al Qaeda apparently learned from the FBI's 1993 success is decentralization and compartmentalization. Most of the September 11 hijackers knew only a handful of their compatriots; the cells did not come together until the moment before the plot was executed. What's more, the full extent of the plot was known to only a handful of the hijackers—those who had taken flight training. This structure followed the training manual, which recommended an operation "composed of many cells whose members do not know one another, so that if a cell member is caught the other cells would not be affected, and work would proceed normally." In other words, the September 11 plot was virtually undetectable. "Even if they'd been aggressive in covering groups I know about, they might not have picked up these guys," says a former FBI official. "If we're talking about a small, tight-knit organization that doesn't go outside its own circle, that's tough."

Consider the extreme fortuitousness of the FBI's greatest counterterrorist success against Al Qaeda: thwarting the plan to blow up Los Angeles International Airport during the millennium celebrations. The trip wire that prevented that attack came only when, on December 14, 1999, an alert customs inspector in Port Angeles, Washington, stopped an Algerian national, Ahmed Ressam, with a trunk full of explosives as he crossed into the United States from Canada. Only after catching Ressam red-handed did authorities learn that he was part of an Al Qaeda cell in Montreal. The FBI's subsequent Operation Borderbom—a mad, two-week scramble to head off other millennium attacks—resulted in dozens of detentions and arrests. But the FBI still cannot say for certain whether any other planned attacks were in the works. And Ressam, now awaiting sentencing and cooperating with American authorities, has reportedly been of little help in identifying Al Qaeda cells besides his own.

So HOW CAN the FBI gather information that will prevent future Al Qaeda attacks? Or, as Kevin Giblin, chief of the FBI's Counterterrorism Threat Assessment and Warning Unit, puts it, "How do you find these very anonymous, capital-A anonymous, cells?"

One answer is for the bureau to work much more closely with foreign law enforcement and intelligence agencies. While Al Qaeda cells in the United States might not rely on support networks in this country, they may seek assistance abroad. Last week's indictment of Zacarias Moussaoui, for instance, states that the September 11 hijackers, once in the United States, received money transfers from Al Qaeda operatives in Germany and the United Arab Emirates. Intelligence officials estimate there are Al Qaeda cells in at least 60 countries, with the largest and most active located in Western Europe. The September 11 plot itself likely originated in Hamburg; and more than one dozen men suspected of playing direct or indirect roles in the attack have been detained in Europe.

Fortunately, over the past ten years, the FBI has dramatically expanded its global reach, doubling the number of FBI offices—known as legal attaches, or "legats"—in foreign countries. Those 44 legats have laid the groundwork for increased cooperation between the FBI and foreign law enforcement. "The legats have liaisons with foreign intelligence agencies, they know people on a first-name basis," explains former FBI agent Clint Van Zandt. "Instead of trying to broker these introductions in the heat of the battle, we're now past the mating dances in close to fifty different countries." And since September 11, this familiarity has paid off: The Moussaoui indictment probably wouldn't have been possible without the assistance of German authorities; and a number of the arrests of terror suspects in Europe since September 11 have resulted from joint investigations with the FBI. Last week Ashcroft and a handful of senior FBI officials went to Europe to meet with police officials in Britain, Spain, Germany, and Italy. Now if authorities in Milan discover that a suspected Al Qaeda member has wired money to someone in the United States, the FBI will likely know about it and can begin its own investigation here. "Since so much of this originates overseas," explains one former FBI official, "we're going to be extremely dependent on foreign agencies for information."

BUT THERE'S SOMETHING else the FBI has to do to gather good information on Al Qaeda, and here, unfortunately, the bureau still hasn't gotten the message. The FBI excels at what is called "tactical" intelligence. Focusing on the little picture, FBI intelligence analysts work closely with agents on the day-to-day necessities of law enforcement investigations—compiling evidence to support an agent's wiretap requests or, with the help of databases, helping an agent match a person to a particular address. For special events, like the Super Bowl or the Olympics, analysts will draw up "threat assessments" for local police. "What drives our analysts is the operational support we provide to the investigation," says Giblin.

In the 1990s some inside the FBI thought the bureau should begin doing more "strategic" intelligence—the big-picture work that is the forte of analysts at the CIA. "We needed to be like the CIA in certain areas," says one former FBI official. "We wanted to create a mechanism in the FBI that looked at long-term intelligence and made predictions about what was going to happen." But this effort never really got off the ground, in part because of a lack of funding, and in part because of an institutional unwillingness to enter the strategic area. "We're not the Federal Bureau of Analysis," says Giblin. Indeed, the FBI's investigative services division—created in the late '90s as part of the bureau's fledgling effort to produce strategic intelligence—was eliminated earlier this month when Mueller, as part of the post-September 11 shake-up, reorganized the bureau.

This is a shame, because if the FBI ever needed strategic intelligence, it's right now. (While the CIA may have analysts capable of producing good strategic intelligence, their focus is, understandably, on helping the agency accomplish its goals overseas, not assisting the FBI with its domestic security concerns.) To be sure, intelligence analysts are not infallible—and the FBI's fledgling investigative services division, before it was disbanded, did not exactly distinguish itself. But good analysts can sift through huge amounts of information—gathered from human assets, electronic surveillance, public sources, and previous investigations—and spot patterns that allow them to make predictions. And in the FBI's case, those predictions could help drive investigations, spotting new areas to target in a hunt for information—areas that, with a group like Al Qaeda, are often few and far between.

Consider the September 11 attacks—attacks that were seemingly impossible for the FBI to detect ahead of time. A smart intelligence analyst, looking at emerging trends in Islamist terrorism, might have predicted that terrorists would try to hijack airplanes and crash them into buildings. After all, September 11 may have been the first time terrorists carried out the strategy successfully, but it was not the first time they tried it. In 1994 hijackers from the Armed Islamic Group—which is affiliated with Al Qaeda—hijacked an Air France jet in Algiers and apparently planned to crash it into the Eiffel Tower, but failed when French commandos stormed the plane when it stopped for refueling. In 1995 Filipino authorities detected a Manila-based Al Qaeda cell's plan to blow up eleven American airliners in mid-flight and crash a twelfth into the CIA headquarters. (Unlike previous terrorists, who hijacked commercial airplanes because they wanted to take hostages and then use those hostages as bargaining chips in negotiations, Al Qaeda, with its fixation on inflicting heavy casualties, views airplanes as weapons of mass destruction.) With that terrorist m.o. in mind, and recognizing that the plot would only work if one of the terrorists involved could fly a jetliner, the analyst might have advised agents to keep an eye on flight schools that offered such training. At the very least, a good analyst—thinking along these lines—might have raised alarm bells at FBI headquarters in August when agents from the Minneapolis field office began investigating Moussaoui, whose suspicious behavior had led his instructors at a Minnesota flight school to contact the bureau. The Minneapolis agents had arrested Moussaoui on an immigration violation and—after getting a lead from French intelligence that he had ties to bin Laden—had asked headquarters in Washington for permission to seek a national security search warrant that would allow them go through Moussaoui's computer. But FBI lawyers denied the request for a search that might have tipped off the bureau to the September 11 plot.

THAT SCENARIO, OF COURSE, has all the benefit of hindsight. But there are other examples of how intelligence analysts can make educated guesses about where and how terrorists might attack next. One intelligence analyst who favors this one-step-ahead-of-the-terrorists approach (and who does not work for the FBI) notes two recent attacks by Kashmiri separatist groups believed to be affiliated with Al Qaeda. In October, Jaish-e-Mohammad terrorists set off a car bomb outside the Jammu and Kashmir state legislative assembly; last week terrorists from the same group, possibly joined by terrorists from the Lashkar-e-Toiba organization, stormed the Indian parliament building in New Delhi. The analyst thinks the FBI should start preparing for the possibility that terrorists might attack state capitols in the United States. "They should be ready for when a car pulls up, seven guys jump out with grenades and explosives, and they rush into the Nebraska legislature," says the analyst. "You need people who can think outside the box... who have imagination and aren't just paper pushers," the analyst adds. "A good analyst can't be a dullard."

Efforts to develop a post-September 11 counterterrorism strategy are still in their initial stages, and it is too early to assess their effectiveness with any certainty. For their part, Ashcroft and Mueller say they are fairly sure that their recent campaign has prevented other terrorist attacks. But, as Ashcroft conceded in late November, "Frankly, we cannot know which acts of terrorism we have deferred, how many we've prevented." Unless the FBI changes strategy, he probably never will.

UNIT 3
Process of American Politics

Unit Selections

Key Points to Consider

- How "democratic" is the American political system compared with others?

- How do the political views of young people compare and contrast with those of their parents?

- Do you think that our current procedures for choosing the president are good ones? In light of the Florida controversy in the 2000 presidential election, do you think that electoral reforms are necessary? Explain your answer.

 **Links: www.dushkin.com/online/**
These sites are annotated in the World Wide Web pages.

The Henry L. Stimson Center
http://www.stimson.org

Influence at Work
http://www.influenceatwork.com

LSU Department of Political Science Resources
http://www.artsci.lsu.edu/poli/

Marketplace of Political Ideas/University of Houston Library
http://info.lib.uh.edu/politics/markind.htm

NationalJournal.com
http://nationaljournal.com

Poynter Online
http://www.poynter.org

RAND
http://www.rand.org

According to many political scientists, what distinguishes *more* democratic political systems from *less* democratic ones is the degree of control that citizens exercise over government. This unit focuses on the institutions, groups, and processes that are supposed to serve as links between Americans and their government.

Political parties, elections, pressure groups, and news media are all thought to play important roles in communications between people and government in the American political system. Changes that are occurring today in some of these areas may affect American politics for decades to come, and these changes are the focus of many of the readings in this section.

The first and second sections focus on politicians, parties, money, and elections. Violence and controversy relating to the 1968 Democratic nominating convention led to a series of changes in the procedures that both parties use to select their presidential candidates. And one of the legacies of the Watergate scandal of the early 1970s was the passage of new laws to regulate campaign financing, which was followed by extensive debate about the impact of those reforms.

In the 1980s, candidates increasingly used focus groups, political consultants, and public opinion polling to shape expensive advertising campaigns, and many observers thought that negative television advertisements played a particularly prominent role in the 1988 presidential campaign. In 1992 more changes in campaign tactics and techniques appeared, including numerous appearances by presidential candidates on television talk shows and a half dozen or so 30-minute paid "infomercials" by third party candidate Ross Perot. In the 1994 congressional elections, Republicans were generally successful in "nationalizing" the competition for 435 House and 30-odd Senate seats, apparently belying the adage that "all politics is local" and winning control of both houses of Congress for the first time since 1954. In 1996, apparently unprecedented amounts of "soft" money from questionable sources fueled President Clinton's reelection campaign, and campaign finance practices became the target of more and more criticism. The 2000 presidential election, of course, will long be remembered for the unprecedented 5-week controversy over which candidate had won Florida and, in turn, a majority of votes in the Electoral College. All these events and more underlie the selections in the section.

The third section treats the roles of interest groups in the American political process and their impact on what government can and cannot do. While "gridlock" is a term usually applied to inaction resulting from "divided government" in which neither major party controls the presidency and both houses of Congress, it seems that "gridlock"—and perhaps favoritism in policymaking—also results from the interaction of interest groups and various government policymakers. The weakness of parties in the United States, compared to parties in other western democracies, is almost certainly responsible for the great strength of interest groups in the American political system. In turn, one can wonder whether a possible new era of stronger, more disciplined parties in government will contribute to the weakening of interest groups.

The fourth section addresses news and other media, which probably play a more important role in the American political system than their counterparts do in any political system in the world. Television news broadcasts and newspapers are not merely passive transmitters of information. They inevitably shape—or distort—what they report to their audiences. They also greatly affect the behavior of people and organizations in politics. As already noted, in recent years, especially during the 1992 and 1996 presidential campaigns, less traditional media forums have begun to play bigger roles in politics. Radio and television talk shows and 30-minute "infomercials" have entered the political landscape with considerable effect. Selections in the fourth section provide coverage of how media can shape or distort political communication and the behavior of political actors.

RUNNING SCARED

Painfully often the legislation our politicians pass is designed less to solve problems than to protect the politicians from defeat in our never-ending election campaigns. They are, in short, too frightened of us to govern

by ANTHONY KING

To an extent that astonishes a foreigner, modern America is *about* the holding of elections. Americans do not merely have elections on the first Tuesday after the first Monday of November in every year divisible by four. They have elections on the first Tuesday after the first Monday of November in every year divisible by two. In addition, five states have elections in odd-numbered years. Indeed, there is no year in the United States— ever—when a major statewide election is not being held somewhere. To this catalogue of general elections has of course to be added an equally long catalogue of primary elections (for example, forty-three presidential primaries last year). Moreover, not only do elections occur very frequently in the United States but the number of jobs legally required to be filled by them is enormous—from the presidency of the United States to the post of local consumer advocate in New York. It has been estimated that no fewer than half a million elective offices are filled or waiting to be filled in the United States today.

Americans take the existence of their never-ending election campaign for granted. Some like it, some dislike it, and most are simply bored by it. But they are all conscious of it, in the same way that they are conscious of Mobil, McDonald's, *Larry King Live*, Oprah Winfrey, the Dallas Cowboys, the Ford Motor Company, and all other symbols and institutions that make up the rich tapestry of American life.

INDIVIDUALLY AND COLLECTIVELY AMERICAN POLITICIANS ARE MORE VULNERABLE, MORE OF THE TIME, TO THE VICISSITUDES OF ELECTORAL POLITICS THAN ARE THE POLITICIANS OF ANY OTHER DEMOCRATIC COUNTRY.

To a visitor to America's shores, however, the never-ending campaign presents a largely unfamiliar spectacle. In other countries election campaigns have both beginnings and ends, and there are even periods, often prolonged periods,

when no campaigns take place at all. Other features of American elections are also unfamiliar. In few countries do elections and campaigns cost as much as they do in the United States. In no other country is the role of organized political parties so limited.

America's permanent election campaign, together with other aspects of American electoral politics, has one crucial consequence, little noticed but vitally important for the functioning of American democracy. Quite simply, the American electoral system places politicians in a highly vulnerable position. Individually and collectively they are more vulnerable, more of the time, to the vicissitudes of electoral politics than are the politicians of any other democratic country. Because they are more vulnerable, they devote more of their time to electioneering, and their conduct in office is more continuously governed by electoral considerations. I will argue that American politicians' constant and unremitting electoral preoccupations have deleterious consequences for the functioning of the American system. They consume time and scarce resources. Worse, they make it harder than it would otherwise be for the system as a whole to deal with some of America's most pressing problems. Americans often complain that their system is not sufficiently democratic. I will argue that, on the contrary, there is a sense in which the system is too democratic and ought to be made less so.

Although this article is written by a foreigner, a Canadian citizen who happens to live in Great Britain, it is not written in any spirit of moral or intellectual superiority. Americans over the years have had quite enough of Brits and others telling them how to run their affairs. I have no wish to prolong their irritation. What follows is the reflections of a candid friend.

FEAR AND TREMBLING

POLITICS and government in the United States are marked by the fact that U.S. elected officials in many cases have very short terms of office *and* face the prospect of being defeated in primary elections *and* have to run for office more as individuals than as standard-bearers for their party *and* have continually to raise large sums of money in order to finance their own election campaigns. Some of these factors operate in other countries. There is no other country, however, in which all of them operate, and operate simultaneously. The cumulative consequences, as we shall see, are both pervasive and profound.

The U.S. Constitution sets out in one of its very first sentences that "the House of Representatives shall be composed of members chosen every second year by the people of the several states." When the Founding Fathers decided on such a short term of office for House members, they were setting a precedent that has been followed by no other major democratic country. In Great Britain, France, Italy, and Canada the constitutional or legal maximum for the duration of the lower house of the national legislature is five years. In Germany and Japan the equivalent term is four years. Only in Australia and New Zealand, whose institutions are in some limited respects modeled on those of the United States, are the legal maximums as short as three years. In having two-year terms the United States stands alone.

Members of the Senate are, of course, in a quite different position. Their constitutionally prescribed term of office, six years, is long by anyone's standards. But senators' six-year terms are not all they seem. In the first place, so pervasive is the electioneering atmosphere that even newly elected senators begin almost at once to lay plans for their re-election campaigns. Senator Daniel Patrick Moynihan, of New York, recalls that when he first came to the Senate, in 1977, his colleagues when they met over lunch or a drink usually talked about politics and policy. Now they talk about almost nothing but the latest opinion polls. In the second place, the fact that under the Constitution the terms of a third of the Senate end every two years means that even if individual senators do not feel themselves to be under continuing electoral pressure, the Senate as a whole does. Despite the Founders' intentions, the Senate's collective electoral sensibilities increasingly resemble those of the House.

Most Americans seem unaware of the fact, but the direct primary—a government-organized popular election to nominate candidates for public office—is, for better or worse, an institution peculiar to the United States. Neither primary elections nor their functional equivalents exist anywhere else in the democratic world. It goes without saying that their effect is to add a further dimension of uncertainty and unpredictability to the world of American elective politicians.

In most other countries the individual holder of public office, so long as he or she is reasonably conscientious and does not gratuitously offend local or regional party opinion, has no real need to worry about renomination. To be sure, cases of parties refusing to renominate incumbent legislators are not unknown in countries such as France, Germany, and Canada, but they are relatively rare and tend to occur under unusual circumstances. The victims are for the most part old, idle, or alcoholic.

The contrast between the rest of the world and the United States could hardly be more striking. In 1978 no fewer than 104 of the 382 incumbent members of the House of Representatives who sought re-election faced primary opposition. In the following three elections the figures were ninety-three out of 398 (1980), ninety-eight out of 393 (1982), and 130 out of 409 (1984). More recently, in 1994, nearly a third of all House incumbents seeking re-election, 121 out of 386, had to face primary opposition, and in the Senate the proportion was even higher: eleven out of twenty-six. Even those incumbents who did not face opposition could seldom be certain in advance that they were not going to. The influence—and the possibility—of primaries is pervasive. As we shall see, the fact that incumbents usually win is neither here nor there.

To frequent elections and primary elections must be added another factor that contributes powerfully to increasing the electoral vulnerability of U.S. politicians: the relative lack of what we might call "party cover." In most democratic countries the fate of most politicians depends not primarily on their own endeavors but on the fate—locally, regionally, or nationally—of their party. If their party does well in an election, so do they. If not, not. The individual politician's interests and those of his party are bound together.

In contrast, America's elective politicians are on their own—not only in relation to politicians in most other countries but also in absolute terms. Party is still a factor in U.S. electoral politics, but it is less so than anywhere else in the democratic world. As a result, American legislators seeking re-election are forced to raise their own profiles, to make their own records, and to fight their own re-election campaigns.

If politicians are so vulnerable electorally, it may be protested, why aren't more of them defeated? In particular, why aren't more incumbent congressmen and senators defeated? The analysis here would seem to imply a very high rate of turnover in Congress, but in fact the rate—at least among incumbents seeking re-election—is notoriously low. How can this argument and the facts of congressional incumbents' electoral success be reconciled?

This objection has to be taken seriously, because the facts on which it is based are substantially correct. The number of incumbent congressmen and senators defeated in either primary or general elections *is* low. But to say that because incumbent members of Congress are seldom defeated, they are not really vulnerable electorally is to miss two crucial points. The first is that precisely because they are vulnerable, they go to prodigious lengths to protect themselves. Like workers in nuclear-power stations, they take the most extreme safety precautions, and the fact that the precautions are almost entirely successful does not make them any less necessary.

Second, congressmen and senators go to inordinate lengths to secure re-election because, although they may objectively be safe (in the view of journalists and academic political scientists), they do not know they are safe—and even if they think they are, the price of being wrong is enormous. The probability that anything will go seriously wrong with a nuclear-power station may approach zero, but the stations tend nevertheless to be built away from the centers of large cities. A congressman or a senator may believe that he is reasonably safe, but if he wants to be re-elected, he would be a fool to act on that belief.

HOW THEY CAME TO BE VULNERABLE

AMERICAN politicians run scared—and are right to do so. And they run more scared than the politicians of any other democratic country—again rightly. How did this come to be so?

The short answer is that the American people like it that way. They are, and have been for a very long time, the Western world's hyperdemocrats. They are keener on democracy than almost anyone else and are more determined that democratic norms and practices should pervade every aspect of national life. To explore the implications of this central fact about the United States, and to see how it came to be, we need to examine two different interpretations of the term "democracy." Both have been discussed from time to time by political philosophers, but they have never been codified and they certainly cannot be found written down in a constitution or any other formal statement of political principles. Nevertheless, one or the other underpins the political practice of every democratic country—even if, inevitably, the abstract conception and the day-to-day practice are never perfectly matched.

One of these interpretations might be labeled "division of labor." In this view, there are in any democracy two classes of people—the governors and the governed. The function of the governors is to take decisions on the basis of what they believe to be in the country's best interests and to act on those decisions. If public opinion broadly supports the decisions, that is a welcome bonus. If not, too bad. The views of the people at large are merely one datum among a large number of data that need to be considered. They are not accorded any special status. Politicians in countries that operate within this view can frequently be heard using phrases like "the need for strong leadership" and "the need to take tough decisions." They often take a certain pride in doing what they believe to be right even if the opinion of the majority is opposed to it.

The function of the governed in such a system, if it is a genuine democracy, is very important but strictly limited. It is not to determine public policy or to decide what is the right thing to do. Rather, it is to go to the polls from time to time to choose those who will determine public policy and decide what the right thing is: namely, the governors. The deciding of issues by the electorate is secondary to the election of the individuals who are to do the deciding. The analogy is with choosing a doctor. The patient certainly chooses which doctor to see but does not normally decide (or even try to decide) on the detailed course of treatment. The division of labor is informal but clearly understood.

It is probably fair to say that most of the world's major democracies—Great Britain, France, Germany, Japan—operate on this basis. The voters go to the polls every few years, and in between times it is up to the government of the day to get on with governing. Electing a government and governing are two different businesses. Electioneering is, if anything, to be deplored if it gets in the way of governing.

This is a simplified picture, of course. Democratically elected politicians are ultimately dependent on the electorate, and if at the end of the day the electorate does not like what they are doing, they are dead. Nevertheless, the central point remains. The existing division of labor is broadly accepted.

The other interpretation of democracy, the one dominant in America, might be called the "agency" view, and it is wholly different. According to this view, those who govern a country should function as no more than the agents of the people. The job of the governors is not to act independently and to take whatever decisions they believe to be in the national interest but, rather, to reflect in all their actions the views of the majority of the people, whatever those views may be. Governors are not really governors at all; they are representatives, in the very narrow sense of being in office solely to represent the views of those who sent them there.

In the agency view, representative government of the kind common throughout the democratic world can only be second-best. The ideal system would be one in which there were no politicians or middlemen of any kind and the people governed themselves directly; the political system would take the form of more or less continuous town meetings or referenda, perhaps conducted by means of interactive television. Most Americans, at bottom, would still like to see their country governed by a town meeting.

WHY THEIR VULNERABILITY MATTERS

IN this political ethos, finding themselves inhabiting a turbulent and torrid electoral environment, most American elective officials respond as might be expected: in an almost Darwinian way. They adapt their behavior—their roll-call votes, their introduction of bills, their committee assignments, their phone calls, their direct-mail letters, their speeches, their press releases, their sound bites, whom they see, how they spend their time, their trips abroad, their trips back home, and frequently their private and family lives—to their environment: that is, to their primary and overriding need for electoral survival. The effects are felt not only in the lives of individual officeholders and their staffs but also in America's political institutions as a whole and the shape and content of U.S. public policy.

It all begins with officeholders' immediate physical environment: with bricks, mortar, leather, and wood paneling. The number of congressional buildings and the size of congressional staffs have ballooned in recent decades. At the start of the 1960s most members of the House of Representatives contented themselves with a small inner office and an outer office; senators' office suites were not significantly larger. Apart from the Capitol itself, Congress was reasonably comfortably housed in four buildings, known to Washington taxi drivers as the Old and New House and Senate Office Buildings. The designations Old and New cannot be used any longer, however, because there are now so many even newer congressional buildings.

Congressional staffs have grown at roughly the same rate, the new buildings having been built mainly to house the staffs. In 1957 the total number of people employed by members of the House and Senate as personal staff was 3,556. By 1991 the figure had grown to 11,572—a more than threefold increase within the political lifetime of many long-serving members. Last year the total number of people employed by Congress in all capacities, including committee staffs and the staffs of support agencies like the Congressional Research Service, was 32,820, making Congress by far the most heavily staffed legislative branch in the world.

Much of the growth of staff in recent decades has been in response to the growth of national government, to Congress's insistence on strengthening its policymaking role in the aftermath of

Vietnam and Watergate, and to decentralization within Congress, which has led subcommittee chairmen and the subcommittees themselves to acquire their own staffs. But there is no doubt that the increase is also in response to congressional incumbents' ever-increasing electoral exposure. Congress itself has become an integral part of America's veritable "elections industry."

One useful measure of the changes that have taken place—and also an important consequence of the changes—is the increased proportion of staff and staff time devoted to constituent service. As recently as 1972 only 1,189 House employees—22.5 percent of House members' personal staffs—were based in home-district offices. By 1992 the number had more than doubled, to 3,128, and the proportion had nearly doubled, to 42.1 percent. On the Senate side there were only 303 state-based staffers in 1972, making up 12.5 percent of senators' personal staffs, but the number had more than quadrupled by 1992 to 1,368, for fully 31.6 percent of the total. Since a significant proportion of the time of Washington-based congressional staffs is also devoted to constituent service, it is a fair guess that more than half of the time of all congressional staffs is now given over to nursing the district or state rather than to legislation and policymaking.

Much constituent service is undoubtedly altruistic, inspired by politicians' sense of duty (and constituents' understandable frustration with an unresponsive bureaucracy); but at the same time nobody doubts that a large proportion of it is aimed at securing re-election. The statistics on the outgoing mail of members of Congress and their use of the franking privilege point in that direction too. Congressional mailings grew enormously in volume from some 100 million pieces a year in the early 1960s to more than 900 million in 1984—nearly five pieces of congressional mail for every adult American. New restrictions on franking introduced in the 1990s have made substantial inroads into that figure, but not surprisingly the volume of mail emanating from both houses of Congress is still invariably higher in election years.

The monetary costs of these increases in voter-oriented congressional activities are high: in addition to being the most heavily staffed legislative branch in the world, Congress is also the most expensive. But there is another, non-monetary cost: the staffs themselves become one of the congressman's or senator's constituencies, requiring management, taking up time, and always being tempted to go into business for themselves. American scholars who have studied the burgeoning of congressional staffs express concern about their cumulative impact on Congress as a deliberative body in which face-to-face communication between members, and between members and their constituents, facilitates both mutual understanding and an understanding of the issues. Largely in response to the requirements of electioneering, more and more congressional business is conducted through dense networks of staffers.

One familiar effect of American politicians' vulnerability is the power it accords to lobbyists and special-interest groups, especially those that can muster large numbers of votes or have large amounts of money to spend on campaigns. Members of Congress walk the electoral world alone. They can be picked off one by one, they know it, and they adjust their behavior accordingly. The power of the American Association of Retired Persons, the National Rifle Association, the banking industry, and

the various veterans' lobbies is well known. It derives partly from their routine contributions to campaign funds and the quality of their lobbying activities in Washington, but far more from the votes that the organizations may be able to deliver and from congressmen's and senators' calculations of how the positions they take in the present may affect their chances of re-election in the future—a future that rarely is distant. Might a future challenger be able to use that speech against me? Might I be targeted for defeat by one of the powerful lobbying groups?

A second effect is that American politicians are even more likely than those in other countries to engage in symbolic politics: to use words masquerading as deeds, to take actions that purport to be instrumental but are in fact purely rhetorical. A problem exists; the people demand that it be solved; the politicians cannot solve it and know so; they engage in an elaborate pretense of trying to solve it nevertheless, often at great expense to the taxpayers and almost invariably at a high cost in terms of both the truth and the politicians' own reputations for integrity and effectiveness. The politicians lie in most cases not because they are liars or approve of lying but because the potential electoral costs of not lying are too great.

At one extreme, symbolic politics consists of speechmaking and public position-taking in the absence of any real action or any intention of taking action; casting the right vote is more important than achieving the right outcome. At the other extreme, symbolic politics consists of whole government programs that are ostensibly designed to achieve one set of objectives but are actually designed to achieve other objectives (in some cases simply the re-election of the politicians who can claim credit for them).

Take as an example the crime bills passed by Congress in the 1980s and 1990s, with their mandatory-minimum sentences, their three-strikes-and-you're-out provisions, and their extension of the federal death penalty to fifty new crimes. The anti-drug and anti-crime legislation, by the testimony of judges and legal scholars, has been at best useless and at worst wholly pernicious in its effects, in that it has filled prison cells not with violent criminals but with drug users and low-level drug pushers. As for the death penalty, a simple measure of its sheer irrelevance to the federal government's war on crime is easily provided. The last federal offender to be put to death, Victor H. Feguer, a convicted kidnapper, was hanged in March of 1963. By the end of 1995 no federal offender had been executed for more than thirty years, and hardly any offenders were awaiting execution on death row. The ferocious-seeming federal statutes were almost entirely for show.

The way in which the wars on drugs and crime were fought cannot be understood without taking into account the incessant pressure that elected officeholders felt they were under from the electorate. As one former congressman puts it, "Voters were afraid of criminals, and politicians were afraid of voters." This fear reached panic proportions in election years. Seven of the years from 1981 to 1994 were election years nationwide; seven were not. During those fourteen years Congress passed no fewer than seven major crime bills. Of those seven, six were passed in election years (usually late in the year). That is, there was only one election year in which a major crime bill was *not* passed, and only one non-election year in which a major crime bill *was* passed.

Another effect of the extreme vulnerability of American politicians is that it is even harder for them than for democratically elected politicians in other countries to take tough decisions: to court unpopularity, to ask for sacrifices, to impose losses, to fly in the face of conventional wisdom—in short, to act in what they believe to be their constituents' interest and the national interest rather than in their own interest. Timothy J. Penny, a Democrat who left the House of Representatives in 1994, put the point starkly, perhaps even too harshly, in *Common Cents* (1995).

> Voters routinely punish lawmakers who try to do unpopular things, who challenge them to face unpleasant truths about the budget, crime, Social Security, or tax policy. Similarly, voters reward politicians for giving them what they want—more spending for popular programs—even if it means wounding the nation in the long run by creating more debt.

America's enduring budget deficit offers a vivid, almost textbook illustration. For nearly a generation—ever since the early 1980s—American politicians have bemoaned the deficit and exhorted themselves to do something about it. However, they have never done nearly enough, even in their own eyes. Why? Part of the answer undoubtedly lies in genuine ideological differences that make it hard for conservatives and liberals to compromise; but much of the answer also lies in the brute fact that every year in the United States is either an election year or a pre-election year, with primaries and threatened primaries intensifying politicians' electoral concerns. In 1985 Senator Warren Rudman, of New Hampshire, reckoned that he and other senators who had voted for a bold deficit-reduction package had flown a "kamikaze mission." One of his colleagues said they had "jumped off a cliff." Twelve years later, not surprisingly, the federal budget remains in deficit.

MORE DEMOCRACY, MORE DISSATISFACTION

NUMEROUS opinion polls show that millions of Americans are profoundly dissatisfied with the functioning of their political system. Consequently, there is a widespread disposition in the United States—at all levels of society, from the grass roots to the editorial conference and the company boardroom—to want to make American democracy "work better," and concrete proposals abound for achieving this goal.

The proposed reforms can be grouped loosely under four headings. First come those that if implemented would amount to the creation of electronic town meetings, taking advantage of technological developments such as CD-ROM, interactive cable systems, electronic mail, and the Internet. *The Wall Street Journal* referred in this general connection to "arranging a marriage of de Tocqueville and technology."

Second, and related, are proposals for promoting democratic deliberation and citizen participation. The Kettering Foundation and the Public Agenda Foundation already organize National Issues Forums that embrace some 3,000 educational and civic groups across America. David Mathews, the president of the Ket-

tering Foundation, considers these modern forums to be directly linked to America's ancient "town meeting tradition." Benjamin R. Barber, a political philosopher at Rutgers University, would go further and create a nationwide network of neighborhood assemblies that could take actual decisions on strictly local matters and also debate and lobby on broader national questions. James S. Fishkin, a political scientist at the University of Texas, likewise seeks to leap the modern barriers to face-to-face democracy by means of what he calls "deliberative opinion polls" (which have been tried, with considerable success, in England).

The third group of proposed reforms is equally radical but more old-fashioned. This group seeks to complete the work of Progressive Era reformers by extending to the federal level the characteristic state-level reforms that were introduced in that period: the referendum, the initiative, and the recall. The political analyst Kevin Phillips, for example, suggests that "the United States should propose and ratify an amendment to the Constitution setting up a mechanism for holding nationwide referendums to permit the citizenry to supplant Congress and the president in making certain categories of national decisions." He would also like to see congressmen and senators be subject to popular recall once they have been in office for a year. Certainly proposals of this kind have broad public support. Depending on the precise wording of the question, more than 50 percent of Americans support the idea of national referenda and more than 80 percent support both the initiative and the recall.

Finally, many commentators—and the majority of the American public—strongly back the newest and most fashionable item on the "making democracy work better" agenda: the imposition of term limits on both state and federal elected officials, notably members of Congress. But the great majority of those who favor term limits, true to the American democratic tradition, are less concerned with good government and the public interest as such than with the present generation of politicians' alleged lack of responsiveness to the mass of ordinary people. At the center of this argument is the idea that the United States is now governed by an unresponsive, self-perpetuating, and increasingly remote class of professional politicians, a class that ought to be replaced as soon as possible by "citizen legislators"—men and women who will serve the people simply because they *are* the people. As one advocate of term limits puts it, ordinary people—the proposed citizen legislators of the future—"know things about life in America that people who have lived as very self-important figures in Washington for thirty years have no way of knowing or have forgotten."

Some of the items on this four-part shopping list of reforms are intrinsically attractive, or at least a good case can be made for them. Nevertheless, taken as a whole, the mainstream reformist agenda, with its traditional American emphasis on agency democracy and its view of politicians as mere servants of the people's will, rests on extremely tenuous conceptual foundations and, more important, is almost certainly inappropriate as a response to the practical needs of turn-of-the-century America. America's problem of governance is not insufficient responsiveness on the part of its elected leaders. On the contrary, America's problem is their hyper-responsiveness. Politicians do not need to be tied down still further, to be subjected to even more external pressures than they are already. Rather, they need to be given just a little more political leeway, just a little more room for policy maneuver. Reforms should seek to strengthen division-of-labor democracy, not to create a still purer form of American-style agency democracy.

THE USUAL SUSPECTS

IF the reformist prescriptions are bad ones, there may be something wrong with the reformist diagnoses on which they are based. What *are* the principal sources of dissatisfaction with the current state of American democracy?

Many commentators have gotten into the habit of blaming Americans' dissatisfaction, in an almost knee-jerk fashion, on "the Vietnam War and Watergate." It is certainly the case that evidence of widespread dissatisfaction began to appear during and shortly after Vietnam and Watergate. *Post hoc, ergo propter hoc?* Maybe. But in the first place, Vietnam and Watergate led to a flowering of idealism as well as cynicism (and to the election, in 1974, of the "Watergate babies," one of the most idealistic and public-spirited cohorts ever to be elected to Congress). And in the second place, it seems strange to attribute the dissatisfactions of the 1990s to events that took place in the 1960s and early 1970s. That distance in time is roughly that between the two world wars; most of today's college students were not yet born when President Richard Nixon resigned. To be sure, subsequent scandals have undoubtedly (and deservedly) damaged the reputations of the White House and Congress, but at least some of the sleaze of recent years has come about because politicians need such enormous sums to finance their re-election campaigns.

Two other hypotheses can be dismissed, or at least assigned little importance. One is that politicians today are a poor lot compared with the intellectual and moral giants of the past. It probably is the case that having to run scared all the time has tended to drive some able people out of politics and to discourage others from coming in. But the phenomenon is a relatively recent one, and for the time being there is no reason to think that the average congressman or senator is in any way inferior to his or her predecessors. The quality of America's existing political class is at most a small part of the problem.

The same is almost certainly true of the idea that divided government—in which one party controls one or both houses of Congress while the other controls the presidency—is to be preferred. Divided government has characterized America for most of the past thirty years, and it has been associated with some of the more spectacular political and policy failures of that period—the Iran-contra scandal of the 1980s (which arose out of a Republican Administration's desire to circumvent a Democratic Congress), and successive shutdowns of parts of the government as Presidents and Congress have failed to agree on timely taxing and spending measures. Other things being equal, divided government is probably to be regretted.

All the same, it is hard to credit the idea that Americans' disillusionment with their politics would be significantly less today if party control had been mainly undivided over the past thirty years. On the one hand, recent periods in which the government has not been divided (the Carter years, 1977–1980, and the first two Clinton years, 1993–1994) were not notably successful (Carter never surmounted the energy crisis, and Clinton failed to reform America's healthcare system even though that reform had figured prominently in his campaign promises). On the other hand, as David R. Mayhew, a political scientist at Yale University, has shown, periods of divided government have often been extremely productive in legislative terms. On balance, divided government appears to be more of a nuisance and a distraction than a root cause of either the government's difficulties or the public's disillusionment.

The idea that the system suffers from the excessive power of interest groups, however, needs to be taken seriously. Jonathan Rauch, in his recent book *Demosclerosis*, argues persuasively that America's interest groups have become larger, more numerous, and more powerful over the past three decades, to the point that they now have the capacity to prevent the government from doing almost anything that would disadvantage or offend any of the clients they represent—taking in, as it happens, virtually the whole American population.

WHEN AMERICANS BECOME DISSATISFIED WITH GOVERNMENT, THEY CALL FOR MORE DEMOCRACY. THE MORE THEY CALL FOR MORE DEMOCRACY, THE MORE OF IT THEY GET. THE MORE THEY GET, THE MORE DISSATISFIED THEY BECOME.

Rauch is probably right; but one needs to go on to ask, as he himself does, what the power of these pullulating and all-encompassing lobby groups is based on. The answer is straightforward: their power depends ultimately on their money, on their capacity to make trouble for elected officials, on the votes of their members (the AARP has more than 30 million members), and on elective politicians' fear of not being re- elected. The groups' power, in other words, depends on politicians' electoral vulnerability; and America's interest groups are peculiarly powerful in large measure because America's elective politicians are peculiarly vulnerable. It is not quite as simple as that—but almost.

It is also important to note the precise timing of the developments described by Rauch and by almost everyone else who has written on this subject. Nearly all these developments date, almost uncannily, from the past thirty years: the rise in the number of interest groups, the growth in their membership and power, the decline in the public's trust in government officials, and the increased sense among voters that who they are and what they think do not matter to politicians and officials in Washington. In other words, the origins of the present era of democratic discontent can be traced to the end of the 1960s and the beginning of the 1970s. It was then that people began to think something was wrong not with this or that aspect of the system but with the system itself.

THERE IS NO SPECIAL VIRTUE IN A SYSTEM THAT REQUIRES LARGE NUMBERS OF POLITICIANS TO RUN THE RISK OF MARTYRDOM IN ORDER TO ENSURE THAT TOUGH DECISIONS CAN BE TAKEN IN A TIMELY MANNER IN THE NATIONAL INTEREST.

What happened at that time? It is hard to escape the conclusion that the crucial developments, largely provoked by the Vietnam War and Watergate, were the attempts from 1968 onward to open up the American system, to make it more transparent, to make it more accessible, to make it, in a word, more "democratic." These attempts led to an increase in the number of primary elections, to a further weakening of America's already weak political parties, to increases in the already high costs of electoral politics, and to the increasing isolation, in an increasingly hostile environment, of elective officials. In short, the post-Vietnam, post-Watergate reforms led, as they were meant to lead, to increased vulnerability to their electorates on the part of individual American officeholders.

The paradox that has resulted is obvious and easily stated. Recent history suggests that when large numbers of Americans become dissatisfied with the workings of their government, they call for more democracy. The more they call for more democracy, the more of it they get. The more of it they get, the more dissatisfied they become with the workings of their government. The more they become dissatisfied with the workings of their government, the more they call for more democracy. The cycle endlessly repeats itself.

WHAT, IF ANYTHING, MIGHT BE DONE?

PRECISELY because American politicians are so exposed electorally, they probably have to display—and do display—more political courage more often than the politicians of any other democratic country. The number of political saints and martyrs in the United States is unusually large.

There is, however, no special virtue in a political system that requires large numbers of politicians to run the risk of martyrdom in order to ensure that tough decisions can be taken in a timely manner in the national interest. The number of such decisions that need to be taken is always likely to be large; human nature being what it is, the supply of would-be martyrs is always likely to be small. On balance it would seem better not to try to eliminate the electoral risks (it can never be done in a democracy) but to reduce somewhat their scale and intensity. There is no reason why the risks run by American politicians should be so much greater than the risks run by elective politicians in other democratic countries.

How, then, might the risks be reduced? What can be done? A number of reforms to the existing system suggest themselves. It may be that none of them is politically feasible—Americans

hold tight to the idea of agency democracy—but in principle there should be no bar to any of them. One of the simplest would also be the most radical: to lengthen the terms of members of the House of Representatives from two years to four. The proposal is by no means a new one: at least 123 resolutions bearing on the subject were introduced in Congress in the eighty years from 1885 to 1965, and President Lyndon B. Johnson advocated the change in his State of the Union address in January of 1966.

A congressman participating in a Brookings Institution round table held at about the time of Johnson's message supported the change, saying, "I think that the four years would help you to be a braver congressman, and I think what you need is bravery. I think you need courage." Another congressman on the same occasion cited the example of another bill that he believed had the support of a majority in the House. "That bill is not going to come up this year. You know why it is not coming up?... Because four hundred and thirty-five of us have to face election.... If we had a four-year term, I am as confident as I can be the bill would have come to the floor and passed."

A similar case could be made for extending the term of senators to eight years, with half the Senate retiring or running for re-election every four years. If the terms of members of both houses were thus extended and made to coincide, the effect in reducing America's never-ending election campaign would be dramatic.

There is much to be said, too, for all the reasons mentioned so far, for scaling down the number of primary elections. They absorb extravagant amounts of time, energy, and money; they serve little democratic purpose; few people bother to vote in them; and they place additional and unnecessary pressure on incumbent officeholders. Since the main disadvantage of primaries is the adverse effect they have on incumbents, any reforms probably ought to be concerned with protecting incumbents' interests.

At the moment, the primary laws make no distinction between situations in which a seat in the House or the Senate is already occupied and situations in which the incumbent is, for whatever reason, standing down. The current laws provide for a primary to be held in either case. An incumbent is therefore treated as though the seat in question were open and he or she were merely one of the candidates for it. A relatively simple reform would be to distinguish between the two situations. If a seat was open, primaries would be held in both parties, as now; but if the incumbent announced that he or she intended to run for re-election, then a primary in his or her party would be held only if large numbers of party supporters were determined to have one—that is, were determined that the incumbent should be ousted. The obvious way to ascertain whether such determination existed would be by means of a petition supervised by the relevant state government and requiring a considerable number of signatures. The possibility of a primary would thus be left open, but those who wanted one would have to show that they were both numerous and serious. A primary would not be held simply because an ambitious, possibly demented, possibly wealthy individual decided to throw his or her hat into the ring.

Any steps to strengthen the parties as institutions would be desirable on the same grounds. Lack of party cover in the United States means that elective officeholders find it hard to take tough decisions partly because they lack safety in numbers. They can seldom, if ever, say to an aggrieved constituent or a political-action committee out for revenge, "I had to vote that way because my party told me to," or even "I had to vote that way because we in my party all agreed that we would." Lack of party cohesion, together with American voters' disposition to vote for the individual rather than the party, means that congressmen and senators are always in danger of being picked off one by one.

BALLOT FATIGUE

WHAT might be done to give both parties more backbone? Clearly, the parties would be strengthened—and elective office-holders would not need to raise so much money for their own campaigns—if each party organization became a major source of campaign funding. In the unlikely event (against the background of chronic budget deficits) that Congress ever gets around to authorizing the federal funding of congressional election campaigns, a strong case could be made for channeling as much of the money as possible through the parties, and setting aside some of it to cover their administrative and other ongoing costs.

The party organizations and the nexus between parties and their candidates would also be strengthened if it were made easier for ordinary citizens to give money to the parties and for the parties to give money to their candidates. Until 1986, when the program was abolished, tax credits were available for tax-payers who contributed small sums to the political parties. These credits could be restored. Larry J. Sabato, a political scientist at the University of Virginia, has similarly suggested that citizens entitled to a tax refund could be allowed to divert a small part of their refund to the party of their choice. Such measures would not, however, reduce candidates' dependence on donations from wealthy individuals and PACs unless they were accompanied by measures enabling the parties to contribute more generously to their candidates' campaigns. At the moment there are strict legal limits on the amount of money that national or state party organizations can contribute to the campaigns of individual candidates. The limits should be raised (and indexed to inflation). There is even a case for abolishing them altogether.

All that said, there is an even more straightforward way of reducing incumbents' dependence on campaign contributors. At present incumbents have to spend so much time raising funds because the campaigns themselves are so expensive. They could be made cheaper. This, of course, would be one of the effects of making U.S. elections less numerous and less frequent than they are now. Another way to lower the cost of elections would be to provide candidates and parties with free air time on television and radio.

THE CASE FOR SWANS

CLEARLY, the idea of term limits also needs to be taken seriously. After all, if American politicians are excessively vulnerable at the moment, one way of rendering them invulnerable would be to prevent them from running for re-election—no impending election contest, no need to worry overmuch about the voters.

As is evident, much of the actual campaigning in favor of term limits takes the form of ranting—against big government, against Washington, against "them," against taxes, against the deficit. Much of the rhetoric of term-limiters is sulfurous, and their principal motive often seems to be revenge. They claim that members of Congress are insufficiently responsive to their constituents, when the evidence suggests that, on the contrary, they are far too responsive. The term-limits movement is of a piece with previous outbursts of frustrated American populism, including the Know-Nothing movement of the 1850s—an essay, as one historian has put it, in "the politics of impatience."

Nevertheless, there is an alternate case for term limits, based not on American politicians' alleged lack of responsiveness to the voters but on their alleged overresponsiveness to the voters and interest groups in order to secure their own re-election. The most persuasive and subtle advocate of this line of argument is the political commentator George F. Will. His goal, Will says partway through his book *Restoration* (1992), "is deliberative democracy through representatives who function at a constitutional distance from the people." He reiterates the point about distance in his final paragraphs: "Americans must be less demanding of government. They must give to government more constitutional space in which to think, more social distance to facilitate deliberation about the future."

The case for giving American politicians more space and distance is undoubtedly a strong one, but assuming these objectives are desirable, it is still not clear that term limits are a suitable means for achieving them. Three questions arise. Would term limits achieve the desired objectives? Would they do so at an acceptable cost in terms of other American goals and values? Might the desired objectives not be better achieved by other means? The first question is strictly empirical. The other two mix the empirical and the moral.

One way in which term limits might promote deliberation is by causing some incumbent legislators—namely those serving out their final term under term limits—to think, speak, and vote differently from the way they would have thought, spoken, and voted if they had been eligible and running for re-election. In addition, for term limits to affect the behavior not just of certain individuals but of Congress as a whole, it would be necessary for any given Congress to contain a significant number of these final-term members. In other words, congressional lame ducks would have to quack differently from other ducks, and there would have to be a fair number of them on the pond.

It is impossible to be sure, but it seems unlikely that term limits would have significant effects along these lines. In the first place, existing research (along with most human experience) suggests that a final-term congressman or senator, after eleven or twelve years on Capitol Hill, would be unlikely to alter his pattern of behavior in any radical way. He might send out fewer pieces of franked mail and make fewer trips back home, but he would probably not execute many U-turns in the way he spoke and voted. In the second place, although the proportion of senators who would be in their final term under term limits would normally be large (possibly half if senators were restricted to two terms), the proportion of lame-duck congressmen would normally be much smaller (an average of sixty to seventy out of 435 if House members were limited to six terms). The cumulative impact of the lame ducks would thus be much greater in the Senate than in the House, and in both houses it would probably be felt mainly at the margins (though of course the margins can, on occasion, be important).

But those who advocate term limits in fact build very little of their case on the expected future behavior of lame ducks. Rather, they are seeking to create a wholly new class of elected representatives. George Will holds out the prospect that mandatory term limits would have the effect of replacing today's political careerists with noncareerists—in other words, of replacing today's ducks with creatures more closely resembling swans. The new legislators, because they were not careerists, would not be driven by the need to secure re-election, and for that reason they would be more likely to concern themselves with the national interest. Also because they were not political careerists, they would be more likely to have some personal, hands-on understanding of America and its real concerns.

The prospect is undoubtedly attractive. But is it realistic? Would term limits in fact diminish the number of careerists and produce legislators who were more national-minded and disinterested?

The most important difficulties with Will's hypothesis are twofold. One is that modern politics at all levels, local and state as well as national, is an immensely time-consuming, energy-consuming activity that demands enormous commitment from those who are attracted to it. Legislative sessions are long, constituents' demands are exigent, policy problems are increasingly complicated. As a result, politics all over the world, not just in the United States, is becoming professionalized. Men and women in all countries increasingly choose a political career at an early age and then stick with it. It seems likely that even under term limits the great majority of congressmen and senators would be drawn from this professional political class, which has not only the commitment to politics but also the requisite patience, skills, and contacts. To be sure, people's political careers would take a different shape; but they would still be political careers.

The other difficulty is the reverse of the first. Just as politics is becoming more professionalized, so is almost every other occupation. As many women in particular know to their cost, it is becoming harder and harder to take career breaks—those who jump off the ladder in any profession find it increasingly hard to jump back even to the level they were on when they left, let alone the level they would have attained had they stayed. For this reason it is hard to imagine that many upwardly mobile corporate executives or successful professionals or small-business owners would take time off to serve in Congress on a citizen-legislator basis. The citizens who sought to serve on this basis would probably be largely the rich and the old.

VOTER-PROOFING

DESPITE their differences, term limits and the proposals offered here have in common the fact that they seek major changes in America's political institutions—in some cases involving an amendment to the Constitution. But of course America's politicians are free to alter the way they behave in the context of the country's existing institutions. They can try to find alternative ways of insulating at least some aspects of policymaking from the intense campaigning and electioneering pressures they are now under.

Short of taking difficult issues out of electoral politics altogether, there are tactics that could be employed. Most of them are out of keeping with the contemporary American preferences for direct democracy, high levels of political participation, and the maximum exposure of all political processes to the public gaze; but that is precisely their strength. Bismarck is reputed to have said that there are two things one should never watch being made: sausages and laws. Both should be judged more by the end result than by the precise circumstances of their manufacture.

One available tactic might be called "the collusion of the elites." There may be occasions on which the great majority of America's politicians, in both the executive and legislative branches, are able to agree that an issue is of such overriding importance to the nation that it must be dealt with at almost any cost; that the politicians involved must therefore be prepared to set aside their ideological and other differences in the interests of finding a workable solution; and that having found a solution, they must stick together in presenting it to what may well be a disgruntled or even hostile electorate. In order to be successful, the collusion-of-elites tactic requires not only a substantial degree of bipartisanship (or, better still, nonpartisanship) but also unusually small teams of negotiators, complete secrecy (not a single ray of "sunshine" must penetrate the proceedings), and the presentation to Congress and the public of a comprehensive, all-or-nothing, take-it-or-leave-it proposal.

The number of occasions on which politicians will be prepared to set aside their ideological differences and pool their political risks in this fashion will inevitably be small. There were no signs that such a spirit might prevail when President Clinton and the Republican majorities in Congress wrangled over how to cut the budget deficit last winter. But there have been instances of the successful collusion of elites, even in relatively recent times.

One of them occurred in 1983, when representatives of President Reagan and the two party leaderships on Capitol Hill colluded to save the Social Security system, which at that time was in imminent danger of bankruptcy. Paul Light's classic account of the 1983 Social Security reform, *Artful Work* (1985), is in effect a case study of how to conduct collusion-of-elites politics and of the circumstances in which it may succeed. The so-called Gang of Seventeen that was originally put together to hammer out a deal (and was later reduced to a Gang of Nine) excluded all the more-extreme ideologues and met in circumstances of great secrecy, even using, according to one participant, "unmarked limos."

Of the Gang of Seventeen's activities, Light writes,

> The meetings seemed to inaugurate a new form of presidential-congressional government. The meetings were secret. There were no minutes or transcripts. All conversations were strictly off the record. The gang was free to discuss all of the options without fear of

political retaliation. It… [existed] completely outside of the constitutional system.

Ultimately, as Light relates, the "secret gang built a compromise, wrapped it in a bipartisan flag, and rammed it through Congress. There was no other way to move. It was government by fait accompli." It was also successful government—and none of the participants suffered electoral damage.

Another possible tactic, with many similarities to the collusion of elites, might be called "putting it into commission." If taking tough decisions is too risky politically, then get someone else to take them. If someone else cannot be found to take them, then make someone else *appear* to take them. The someone else need not be but usually will be a bipartisan or nonpartisan commission of some kind.

Such a commission, the National Commission on Social Security Reform, played a role in the passage of the 1983 act, but an even better example was the procedure adopted by Congress in 1990 for closing redundant military bases. Earlier practice had been almost a caricature of Congress's traditional decision-making process. The Secretary of Defense would propose a program of base closures. Senators and congressmen would immediately leap to the defense of targeted bases in their home states or districts. They of course had the support of their colleagues, who were threatened with or feared base closures in *their* home states or districts. Almost never did anyone manage to close any bases.

Realizing that the process was absurd and that huge sums of taxpayers' money were being wasted in keeping redundant bases open, Congress decided to protect itself from itself. It established the Defense Base Closure and Realignment Commission, which employed an extraordinarily simple formula. The Defense Secretary every two years published a list of the bases he proposed to close, together with a statement of criteria he had used in compiling his list. The commission then examined the list in light of the criteria, held public hearings, and recommended a modified list (with additions as well as deletions) to the President. The President was obliged to accept the commission's list as a whole or reject it as a whole. If, as invariably happened, he accepted it, Congress could intervene only if within forty-five legislative days it passed a bill overriding the President's decision and rejecting the whole list. This it never did.

The formula was a near miracle of voter-proofing. Members of Congress were left free to protest the closure of bases in their home districts or states, but the decision was ultimately taken by the President, who could nonetheless ascribe all blame to the commission, and all Congress had to do for the President's decision to take effect was to do nothing. In the event, hundreds of bases were closed and millions of dollars saved, but no member of Congress ever had to vote—and be seen by his constituents to be voting—in favor of closing a base near home. Beyond any question the results were in America's national interest.

It is not wholly fantastic to suppose that the President in odd-numbered years might, on the basis of advice received from a bipartisan commission, announce a list of "program eliminations," which Congress could countermand only by voting to reject the list as a whole. Presidents would probably prefer to put forward such lists at the beginning of their first term in office—or at any time during their second term—when they, at least, were not up for re-election.

A final tactic, which could also be adopted without major institutional change, might be described as "thinking big." Proposals that are put forward on a piecemeal basis can also be opposed, and in all probability defeated, on a piecemeal basis. In contrast, large-scale, broad-based proposals may have a better chance of success simply by virtue of their comprehensiveness. They can provide something for everyone—conservatives as well as liberals, deficit cutters as well as program defenders, residents of the Sun Belt as well as of the Rust Belt. Gains as well as losses can be broadcast widely. The 1983 Social Security reform and the 1986 tax reform were certainly "big thoughts" of this general type. So, in its way, was the recent base-closure program.

Tactics like these—the collusion of elites, putting issues into commission, and thinking big—all have their virtues, but they also suffer from being tactics in the pejorative as well as the descriptive sense. At bottom they are somewhat cynical devices for getting around the real difficulty, which is the hyper-responsiveness of American politicians that is induced by their having to run scared so much of the time. Although it would be harder, it would be better over the long term to confront this problem directly and try to bring about at least some of the fundamental institutional changes proposed here. The American people cannot govern themselves. They therefore need to find appropriate means of choosing representatives who can do a decent job of governing on their behalf, and that means giving the people's representatives space, time, and freedom in which to take decisions, knowing that if they get them wrong, they will be punished by the voters. In twentieth-century America the airy myths of agency democracy are precisely that: myths. What America needs today, though it does not seem to know it, is a more realistic and down-to-earth form of division-of-labor democracy.

Anthony King, a political scientist who teaches at the University of Essex, and an elections analyst for the British Broadcasting Corporation, is a regular contributor to *The Economist*.

From *The Atlantic Monthly*, January 1997, pp. 41-44, 46-48, 52-54, 56-58, 60-61. Adapted from *Running Scared: Why America's Politicians Campaign Too Much and Govern Too Little* by Anthony King. © 1997 by Free Press. Reprinted by permission of Simon & Schuster.

Family Tree, Party Roots

THE ODYSSEY OF THE REPUBLICAN PARTY CAN BE TRACED THROUGH THE PHILOSOPHICAL AND GEOGRAPHICAL TRAVELS OF THE BUSH CLAN.

BY CARL M. CANNON

Nearly five decades ago, on a cool night in late October, a political neophyte running for a vacant U.S. Senate seat in Connecticut appeared at a rally in Bridgeport with a fiery conservative from Wisconsin who drew red-meat Republican crowds wherever he went.

DYNASTY-BUILDING:
Prescott Bush, a self-described "moderate progressive," rode Ike's coattails into the Senate in 1952. His son George threw in his lot with Reagan and the conservatives from the West.

The Connecticut Yankee was a Yale man and a New York investment banker with money, social status, and a regal bearing. His name was Prescott Bush. The imported political talent—and the headliner at the event—was an ardent anti-Communist crusader and World War II veteran with nothing but rough edges. His name was Joseph McCarthy.

McCarthy was in Bridgeport to raise Bush's profile, contribute financially to his campaign, and galvanize Republican voters. So what did Bush do? He welcomed "Tailgunner Joe" to his state, then added this caveat: "But I must in all candor say that some of us, while we admire his objectives in this fight against Communism, we have very considerable reservations, sometimes, concerning the methods which he employs." It was a gutsy thing to

do, and in an oral history that he made before he died in 1972, Bush recalled what happened next: "And with that, the roof went off, with boos and hisses and catcalls and 'Throw him out.'"

Bush, however, had already aligned himself with Dwight D. Eisenhower, a Republican vastly more popular than McCarthy, and on Election Day 1952, Bush rode Ike's coattails into the Senate.

In his younger days, Prescott Bush was a loyal Herbert Hoover conservative, which implied a belief in limiting government spending and involvements in foreign affairs. But the Depression and World War II made that an untenable ground from which to fashion a national majority. Five consecutive Democratic victories in the race for the White House, meanwhile, leached the ideological purity out of many party activists, who chose Eisenhower over the conservative establishment's candidate, Robert Taft of Ohio. Prescott Bush described himself then as a "moderate progressive."

Although nothing unifies a political party as effectively as two successive landslide victories by its presidential candidate, Eisenhower made little attempt to reshape the Republican Party in his own image. Nonetheless, the party took its cues from Ike, and from 1952 onward, the GOP housed liberals, moderates, and conservatives, even as the issues changed. It was not until 1980, when Ronald Reagan emerged as the unquestioned leader of the Republican Party, that the GOP's conservative wing reasserted itself over Prescott Bush's "moderate progressives."

And it is not just a historical footnote that Reagan's running mate in 1980 was Prescott Bush's son George. A better way to look at it is through a history of the Bushes:

The evolution of the Republican Party during the past 50 years can be traced in their family tree—specifically, through the political careers of Prescott Bush and his son and grandson, both named George and both elected President.

In exploring the genealogy of the GOP during the latter half of the 20th century, it must be stressed that the conservatives who helped lead Reagan to victory two decades ago are in no way a monolithic force. This fact became plain in 1989 the moment Reagan flew back to California and into the sunset of his life. And even throughout his presidency, there was within the conservative firmament a built-in tension over what it meant to be a true Reaganite. Was the genuine article the live-and-let-live kind of conservative predominant in the sprawling American West, whose passion was to resist the scope and sweep of government? Or were the true keepers of the flame the religious conservatives, so influential in the South, who saw their primary mission as stopping America's moral decay?

OLYMPIA SNOWE:
Jefford's defection revealed a problem that "the party has been trying to suppress."

That question has not yet been answered, and likely never can be. The reason is that the two great branches of conservatism are, in some ways, fundamentally at odds in how they view the proper use of government power. But in the first months of his presidency, before he even had a chance to try to fill Reagan's role as a unifier of the two branches, George W. Bush was hit with a bracing message. That message, delivered in the form of Sen. James M. Jefford's resentful departure from the Republican Party, is that a third force survives within the GOP. It is the liberal wing known a generation ago as "Rockefeller Republicans," whose stronghold remains in New York and New England. It is an atrophied and shrinking wing, but as the Senator from Vermont proved, it remains an indispensable part of the Republican coalition.

JIM JEFFORDS:
Fifty years ago, Prescott Bush was what Jeffords is today: a New England maverick.

"Jim's departure is a manifestation of a larger problem that I think the party has been trying to suppress," observes Sen. Olympia Snowe of Maine, the Republican closest to Jeffords personally and politically. "We really do have to come to grips with how we are going to incorporate the views of those who might not share the opinions and perspectives of those who represent the South and the West."

If Bush was surprised by Jefford's defection, he shouldn't have been. Fifty years ago, his own grandfather was what Jeffords is today: a maverick Senator from New England who bucked the conservative establishment of his own party. In Prescott Bush's day, that establishment was based in the Midwest and was personified by Taft. In the time of Prescott's son, George H.W. Bush, the home base of the GOP was "Reagan Country"—Southern California. Today, the Republican base begins in the South, in the upscale Republican suburbs of Atlanta, Charlotte, N.C., and Jacksonville, Fla., and runs through the Bible Belt to the wealthy white neighborhoods of Dallas and Houston, where George W. Bush's political career was launched.

In other words, the odyssey of the Republican Party over the past half-century can be traced through the travels—philosophical and geographical—of the Bush clan itself.

PRESCOTT BUSH'S 'PARTY OF LINCOLN'

When Jim Jeffords made his fateful announcement in Burlington, Vt., on May 24, he invoked the illustrious list of Vermont's other 20th-century Republican Senators. "The party I grew up in was the party of George Aiken, Ernest Gibson, Ralph Flanders, Winston Prouty, and Bob Stafford," Jeffords said. "I became a Republican, not because I was born into the party, but because of the kind of fundamental principles that these and many Republicans stood for: moderation, tolerance, fiscal responsibility. Their party—our party—was the party of Lincoln."

Jefford's comparisons may have been self-serving, but the flinty, independent-minded, and socially progressive Vermont Republicans he invoked were real enough. George D. Aiken, a Vermont governor and U.S. Senator, was famous for asking why America couldn't just declare victory in Vietnam and go home. For many years, he was the senior Republican in the Senate, where he helped secure funding for sweeping capital projects such as the rural electrification program and the building of the St. Lawrence Seaway. Aiken was also the principal architect of the food stamp program.

Jeffords could have gone beyond Vermont's borders with his list. Liberal lions from New England and New York once constituted the very face of the national Republican Party. He could have pointed out that, with the New England delegation in the lead, 82 percent of Senate Republicans (a higher percentage than among Democrats) voted for the Civil Rights Act of 1964. Or that in 1966, Massachusetts voters sent the first African-American to the U.S. Senate since Reconstruction—and that he was a Republican, Edward W. Brooke.

Another Bay Stater, Rep. Joseph William Martin Jr., was the last Republican to serve as House Speaker until Newt Gingrich claimed that honor 40 years later, in 1995. "Uncle Joe" Martin is remembered for his collegial relationship with his Democratic counterpart, Sam Rayburn. The precedent was conspicuously rejected by Gingrich, who noted that Martin's Republicans lost control of the chamber after only two years. Gingrich believed that in order to keep the House, Republicans needed to define themselves as distinct from Democrats. Gingrich's vision has been vindicated, but the bill came due in the Senate, when the Republicans lost control of that chamber following Jeffords's defection. The ideological descendants of Prescott Bush's GOP, as it turns out, are still around—and hold the balance of power on Capitol Hill: in the Senate, Maine's two moderate Republicans, Snowe and Susan Collins, along with Rhode Island's Lincoln D. Chafee and Pennsylvania's Arlen Specter; in the House, Nancy L. Johnson and Christopher Shays of Connecticut and Amo Houghton of New York, among others; in the states, Connecticut Gov. John G. Rowland and Rhode Island Gov. Lincoln Almond.

"They are certainly not close to the party's ideological center of gravity, as they were in the heyday of Tom Dewey and the Eastern Establishment," says John P. Burke, a professor of political science at the University of Vermont. "But if anything, they are increasingly critical to the GOP's ability to hold the White House and Congress. I think the GOP really faces something of a predicament in looking at the Electoral College map. They have maxed out on states where a conservative message alone will work. Nor are there any more Southern or border states to be had."

The New Englanders have made this very case to the party's conservative leaders, adding that in their regions, they are utterly mainstream Republicans. "We're very vital at the local level, in local government, because we're harmonious with the traditions of New England," Johnson said in an interview. Those traditions include striving for racial justice and gender equality; protecting the environment; and deferring to decisions made at the local level.

Other characteristics are at play as well, some of them the result of New England's forbidding climate and geography. In *The Nine Nations of North America*, demographer and author Joel Garreau explains that the rocky soil and short growing season in New England helped forge a personality type that is to this day hardy, thrifty, pragmatic—and amenable to government assistance. "Historically, the poorest state in the union was not Mississippi, but Maine," Garreau says. "In the region that imports home heating oil from Texas, the equation of whether government is part of the problem or part of the solution just doesn't come up."

The region's Ivy League schools and other colleges—coupled with liberal media influences from New York City and Boston—keep generating new progressive ideas. While much of the rest of the country is still debating abortion rights, New England—Vermont especially—is pushing new social frontiers in the area of gay and lesbian unions. "Abortion and those kinds of issues are seen as one's personal beliefs in our part of the country," says Johnson. "And not something the government should have a hand in."

That a goodly number of these New England Republicans are women is also no coincidence. Prescott Bush's distancing of himself from McCarthy was made easier for him by the courageous act of Margaret Chase Smith of Maine. A Republican House member and later Senator—the first woman elected to the Senate without being first appointed to the job—Smith earned her place in American history on June 1, 1950, when she went to the well of the Senate to make a 15-minute "Declaration of Conscience." Although she did not mention McCarthy by name, Smith issued a frontal attack on McCarthyism, protesting that the Senate debate had been "debased to the level of a forum of hate and character assassination shielded by the shelter of congressional immunity." She was the first Senator from either party to make such a statement.

This, then, was the branch of the party that produced Jim Jeffords and the family political legacy of George Herbert Walker Bush, the 41st President.

In 1989, the first President Bush awarded Margaret Chase Smith the nation's highest civilian award, the Presidential Medal of Freedom. But this gesture was a throwback, or perhaps an example of the famous Bush manners, more than a political statement. For between the decade of the 1950s and 1989, a great deal had happened to the Republican Party—and to the Bushes.

GEORGE BUSH IN REAGAN COUNTRY

George H.W. Bush launched his quest for national office in 1979 as a rival to the conservatives' darling, Ronald Wilson Reagan. By the time he left Washington 13 years later, Bush had embraced the entire Reagan agenda, served two terms as Reagan's Vice President, and spent another four years as President in what many conservatives fancied as "Reagan's third term."

Reagan's own political launch began while he was trying to elect someone else. The spark was struck, fittingly, in a Los Angeles television studio on October 27, 1964, when Reagan, then a 53-year-old retired movie actor, gave a nationally televised address called "A Time for Choosing." The speech was a paid political message in which Reagan outlined the reasons Americans should choose Republican presidential nominee Barry Goldwater over Democratic President Johnson.

"You and I have a rendezvous with destiny," Reagan said, borrowing a phrase from Franklin D. Roosevelt. "We can preserve for our children this last, best hope of man on Earth, or we can sentence them to take the first step into a thousand years of darkness."

But if Reagan relied—as he did to the end of his career—on the evocative wordplay of his boyhood hero, FDR (who was not only a Democrat, but a New Yorker), "A Time for Choosing" was also a speech written by someone with the sensibilities, and grievances, of a conservative from the West.

"Already the hour is late," Reagan proclaimed. "Government has laid its hand on health, housing, farming, industry, commerce, education, and to an ever-increasing degree interferes with the people's right to know.... Either we accept the responsibility for our own destiny, or we abandon the American Revolution and confess that an intellectual belief in a far-distant capital can plan our lives for us better than we can plan them ourselves."

WESTERN WING:
Reagan set his own destiny in motion by assuming the Goldwater mantle.

Ronald Reagan couldn't save the doomed Republican ticket, but he assumed the Goldwater mantle and set his own destiny in motion. The day after the 1964 election, "Republicans for Reagan" committees sprang up around the country, including one in Owosso, Mich., the hometown of two-time GOP presidential nominee Thomas E. Dewey, the epitome of the Eastern Establishment and a Bush family friend.

Unlike the Bush clan, Reagan had voted Democratic well into middle age. He stumped for Harry S. Truman against Dewey in 1948 and went for liberal Democratic senatorial candidate Helen Gahagan Douglas of California (against Richard Nixon) in 1950. But Reagan joined many New Deal Democrats of his generation when he crossed party lines in 1952 to support Eisenhower, just as "Reagan Democrats" would do in 1980 when they voted for him. Reagan's biographers have plumbed the many reasons Reagan switched parties: his first-hand observation of duplicitous Communist Party members in Hollywood while he was president of the Screen Actors Guild; his marriage to Nancy Davis, whose father, Loyal Davis, was an ardent conservative; his hosting of *General Electric Theatre*, a successful eight-year gig in the new medium of television that also entailed his speaking at General Electric plants around the country.

But perhaps most important was the issue of taxes. When Reagan was at the peak of his earning power as an actor, the top income tax bracket was 90 percent. To Reagan, this was emblematic of a culture in Washington that treated Americans' income as the government's money. Reagan's conviction struck a chord with voters, even those who would never see a dime of their income taxed at the top rate. When he made taxes the centerpiece of his appeal, he moved the Republican Party away from the noblesse oblige attitudes of the GOP gentry, which included Prescott Bush. According to *Boston Globe* political writer Michael Kranish, who examined Bush's early career, Sen. Prescott Bush called on Congress to "have the courage to raise the required revenues by approving whatever levels of taxation may be necessary" to pay for such things as defense, science, and education.

Reagan's own rhetoric had gone from blaming Big Business for the problems of everyday Americans to identifying Big Government as the villain. After being elected governor of California in 1966, Reagan joined a small but growing fraternity of like-minded Republican conservatives from the West, including Goldwater, Sen. Paul Laxalt of Nevada, and a Goldwater friend in Arizona named Sandra Day O'Connor.

"He was an outsider who talked common sense to people," recalls former Attorney General Edwin Meese, who first went to work for Reagan in Sacramento. "California's a little different today, but at that time, people there were excited by the freshness of his message. It was a reasonable, straightforward approach you didn't get from either party. A frontier approach, you might say—a Western approach."

Westerners of this stripe mistrusted central government, whether it was in Moscow or in Washington. In time, Western conservatives, some of them Democrats, would launch the "sagebrush rebellion," which had as its aims nothing less radical than the repatriation of federal lands in the West to the states—or even outright secession.

Because these Westerners were suspicious of government, they tended not to focus on the part of the conservative agenda that would help bring the government into the bedroom. Although by 1980 they would make common purpose with religious conservatives, these Westerners and their constituencies were not animated by such cultural issues as school prayer and opposition to abortion and homosexual rights. In his first term as California governor, Reagan actually signed a bill liberalizing abortion law. O'Connor, as a state legislator in Arizona, was a member of the local board of Planned Parenthood. Laxalt, who hailed from a pro-gambling state, once owned a casino.

On the issue of race, probably the best thing that can be said of these economic conservatives is that their mistrust of government led them astray. Goldwater and Reagan, for instance, opposed the landmark Civil Rights Act of 1964. Along with their defenders, the two men always bristled at the suggestion they might have racist impulses, but it is simply undeniable that their suspicion of the courts and of federal power in general landed them on the wrong side of history during one of the great moral crusades of the 20th century.

George H.W. Bush wrestled with these questions as well. In fact, on race as well as on the issues of crucial importance to Western conservatives—especially environmental policy and taxes—Bush made a long, painful attempt to reconcile the Republicanism of his youth, his family, and his home region of New England with the conservative party he wound up leading. It wasn't an easy transition, but in the end, Bush proved himself as an economic conservative.

It started, for Bush, when he physically left New England. In one of the more memorable lines of her storied career, Texas writer Molly Ivins insisted that Bush would never truly be accepted in the Lone Star State, because "real Texans do not use the word *summer* as a verb… and do not wear blue slacks with little green whales all over them." Be that as it may, Bush did move his family to West Texas in 1948—and started a company in the oil business. "He could have stayed in the beautiful confines of Connecticut and done well. But he wanted to do it on his own. Not be Daddy's boy," Lance Tarrance, a Houston-based GOP pollster, once observed. "There's excitement about not wanting to fit into the old patterns. So he came to Odessa, Texas."

He may have gone a little too native. In 1964, Bush sought a Senate seat held by liberal Democratic Sen. Ralph Yarborough. He won the Republican primary, but not before coming out against the civil rights legislation "on constitutional grounds." During the general election, Bush criticized the nuclear test-ban treaty negotiated by President Kennedy; said the United States should withdraw from the United Nations if "Red China" were to be admitted; termed Medicare "socialized medicine"; and expressed support for expanding the war in Vietnam, even to the point of considering the use of nuclear weapons if "militarily prudent." At least this was more genteel than Goldwater's memorable quip about wanting to "lob one into the men's room in the Kremlin."

In subsequent years, Bush didn't talk much about this campaign (he lost badly). But in 1966, the Republican establishment in Texas carved out a safe seat for Bush in a posh Houston area, and he won easily. Bush was in Congress when the civil rights act of 1968, with its controversial open-housing provisions, came up for a vote. It has often been reported that Bush earned the wrath of some in his district by voting aye on this bill, but what is not remembered is that on the key procedural vote that day, April 10, 1968, Bush sided against the liberals, who won a 229–195 vote to beat back the conservatives' gambit to send the open-housing provisions of the bill back to committee.

In 1970, Bush ran for the Senate again and lost to Democrat Lloyd Bentsen. He spent the next decade as Republican Party chief, CIA director, and ambassador to China. In 1979, as the GOP prepared to get out of Richard Nixon's shadow, Bush ran for President, emerging as the moderate alternative to Reagan. The primaries were a mismatch, but at the end of the process, Reagan confounded conservatives by choosing Bush as his running mate. Bush had famously referred to the proposed Reagan tax cut and the "supply-side" theory that undergirded it as "voodoo economics." But Reagan wanted to win, and

he was persuaded by a survey, done by his adviser and pollster Richard Wirthlin, that showed Bush as the most popular choice for Vice President.

Whatever Prescott Bush's views had been, his son over the next four years came to adopt the Westerners' convictions on low taxes and limited government involvement in the economy. The "voodoo economics" crack was eventually replaced, in the public memory, with the famous "Read my lips: No new taxes!" pledge made at the 1988 GOP convention.

Today, movement conservatives sometimes disparage Bush over his 1990 tax deal, but Bush probably paid a higher political price for his Western-style laissez-faire response to recession than for anything he did with taxes. It was moderates and Perotians who deserted Bush in droves in 1992, not conservatives. And they did so, in large part, because Bush seemed uninterested in the nation's sluggish economic performance during the last half of his presidency. In truth, Bush wasn't unconcerned. It was just that by then he was a staunch economic conservative—one of the Westerners—who was convinced that anything government tried to do would make things worse.

In the 1980s, Reagan had such a firm hold on the GOP that only one House Republican voted against his 1981 tax cuts. His name was Jim Jeffords. What is less-often remembered is that in 1983, five GOP moderates in the Senate, three of them from New England, called on the President to delay implementation of the final part of his tax cut. The five were Robert T. Stafford of Vermont, John H. Chafee of Rhode Island, Mark O. Hatfield of Oregon, Charles Mathias Jr. of Maryland, and Lowell P. Weicker Jr. of Connecticut.

A year before, the White House had stood blandly, but hopefully, on the sidelines as an untested Connecticut conservative had tried unsuccessfully to wrest the Republican senatorial nomination away from Weicker. The challenger was George H.W. Bush's brother and Prescott Bush's namesake. It wasn't that surprising, really: Prescott Bush Jr., and the entire Bush family, had changed—along with their party.

GEORGE W., SON OF THE SOUTH

History will record that cutting taxes was George W. Bush's first major initiative as President. His grandfather may have seen raising taxes as a sign of political courage, but on this question the 43rd President took his cue from the 40th. In the aftermath of Jeffords's departure from the GOP, many pundits pointed their fingers at movement conservatives such as Stephen Moore, president of the conservative Club for Growth, which ran ads targeting the liberal Republicans who initially opposed Bush's original $1.6 trillion tax cut. But Moore points right back: "For a political party to survive and to thrive, it must stand grandly and unwaveringly for something," he says. "Tax cuts are a signature issue for the Republican Party.

If liberals in the party don't want to cut taxes, then why are they Republicans?"

It's a legitimate question, and one with some potency. Jeffords himself—on the very day he was deciding to leave the Republican Party—voted for Bush's scaled-down $1.35 trillion tax cut, apparently believing that it was in his interest, and Vermont's, to support it. And out in Arizona, Republican Sen. John McCain, after years of bucking party elders, found himself facing a recall effort from grassroots conservatives who criticized his vote against the tax cut as one maverick step too far.

If lowering taxes is the issue that binds Republicans, abortion may be the one that divides them. It is not well remembered, but when Reagan chose O'Connor to be the first woman on the Supreme Court, New Right leaders such as Virginians Richard Viguerie and the Rev. Jerry Falwell were initially critical because of her limited support of abortion rights. This fight pitted Westerners against Southerners. "Good Christians" should be concerned about the choice of O'Connor, Falwell said. Goldwater shot back: "Every good Christian ought to kick Falwell right in the ass." He also said at the time, "I don't like the New Right. What they're talking about is not conservatism."

But if such tensions between the two great branches of conservatism exist in Arizona and California, or in the onetime Bush stronghold of New England, they decidedly do not in the South, the region that produced George W. Bush.

POLITICS AND PRAYER:
Bush's evangelical brand of Christianity is the Southern piece of his political persona.

At the Democrats' 1988 convention in Atlanta, Texas state Treasurer Ann Richards derided Vice President Bush as someone who "was born on third base and thinks he hit a triple." The idea was to paint him as a rich Easterner, and not a Texan at all. Citing the same Andover-Yale connections, some Democrats tried that last year with George W.—and met with even less success. The reason is that he is the real Texas deal, brought to that state when he was 2. George W. grew up in the Odessa-Midland region of West Texas and in Houston, and even his fiercest, most liberal Texas critics concede that Bush talks, walks, looks—and thinks—like a Texan.

"He's so goddamn dumb about it, he's coming back to Texas *for the month of August*," said Molly Ivins in mock horror. Reached at her home in Austin, Ivins recalls without prompting the "mean" thing she wrote about Bush's father and using the word *summer* as a verb. "For all the time Big George spent here, he remained a classic, refined, New England-type WASP person. But George W.

clearly identifies with Texas and its mores." If Ivins finds it noteworthy that George W. prefers his Crawford ranch to the Bush family compound in Kennebunkport, Maine, New Englanders have noticed, too. "His father was perceived to be more of an Easterner, more moderate Republican, and this President is a Texas Republican," Rep. Tom Allen, D-Maine, said recently. "He prefers his ranch in Texas, and it's a different climate—and it's a different *political* climate."

It is often said that Texas is part West, part South. With his anti-lawyer, and low-tax pro-business sensibilities, Bush certainly reflects the Western branch of conservatism. But with George W. Bush—as with the state of Texas—the Southern part of the equation is always there, too. Bush's evangelical brand of Christianity is not the religion of his father and grandfather, but of the Old South. His embrace of "faith-based" government programs for fighting poverty comes out of existing programs he was shown while governor of Texas.

In Texas and the rest of the South, Republicans are not tripped up by issues that hurt GOP conservatives elsewhere. Prominent Western Republican Dan Lungren realized this three years ago when he ran for governor of California. Lungren is a devout Catholic opposed to abortion in all cases. When polls showed that this stance was hurting Lungren in California, his wife called Laura Bush, whom she knew, and asked how she had handled the abortion question when speaking on her husband's behalf. Dan Lungren recalled Laura Bush responding, "It just doesn't come up." Lungren, relating this story, says simply: "That's the difference between California and Texas."

But if different regions of the country shape the attitudes of the people who live there, it's also true that regional attitudes are altered by influxes of pilgrims. In recent years, college-educated professionals and middle managers born and educated in the Midwest and the East have migrated south to work in burgeoning companies such as Federal Express and Bank of America Corp. The running gag in Cary, N.C., is that the name of the town stands for "Containment Area for Relocated Yankees."

Although these immigrants may not be Prescott Bush-type "Yankees," they nevertheless bring in new attitudes. They may not have made the South more overtly liberal in terms of voting patterns, but they have made it more modern. These new Southerners are more likely to subscribe to *Southern Living* magazine than to *Southern Partisan*, for instance. And they have blurred some of the old distinctions between "country club" Republicans and fundamentalists. These white professionals attend such churches as the sprawling nondenominational Calvary Church outside Charlotte, N.C. Funeral services were held there for auto-racing legend Dale Earnhardt, but the Old South is not much in evidence inside that church: This past Easter Sunday, one of the pastors leading services was African-American; two others spoke with Northern accents. Many of these congregants are evangelical Christians *and* avid golfers, who have joined one of Mecklenburg County's many country clubs.

This, says Republican pollster Frank Luntz, is George W. Bush country.

Bush himself, however, has demonstrated an awareness that even if all three branches of the GOP were acting in concert—and they aren't—the Republican Party can't be a majority party unless it broadens its ethnic appeal. In California, the GOP has seen its support crater in the Hispanic community after party leaders took a series of stances seen as anti-immigration, and even anti-Latino. But in Texas, the Spanish-speaking Bush embraced the idea of immigration, and celebrated the contributions of Mexican immigrants—and in November, he held his own with Mexican-American voters. As President, he is now working on a plan to grant legal residency to some 3 million Mexican immigrants already here.

This is not to suggest that the future holds a magic bullet for the Republicans. What it does hold, most likely, is a Bush. One of them who has already shown star quality is George P. Bush. He's Jeb's kid, and is both a Southerner *and* a Latino, or at least half-Latino. At 25, he's already better at speaking off the cuff than his uncle, the President. And he's as handsome as his great-grandfather. Come to think of it, he's named after him. Yes, the P. stands for Prescott.

Staff Correspondent James A. Barnes and Reporter Gia Fenoglio contributed to this article.

The Politics of Welfare Reform

Republicans with Hearts Give Democrats Hope

by Tom Downey

As a charter member of the Democratic left, my view has always been that welfare reform has two goals: helping people get work and eliminating poverty. We haven't had a discussion about ending poverty in a long time. But I think we may be ready for one.

I've got a long history as a mock sparring partner preparing Democrats for the televised presidential campaign debates. In the 1996 campaign, I played Jack Kemp. In 2000, I was Bill Bradley—another professional athlete but otherwise quite a contrast. Last fall, my preparations to play George W. Bush ended abruptly when I got a package in the mail that included his debate material and a videotape of him debating. But before that happened, I had spent two months studying everything that Bush had done on the issue of poverty and welfare, everything he'd said. I was probably his web site's most frequent visitor.

As the campaign unfolded, I began to have a certain amount of partisan unease, I must say. I knew it was going to be a close election. But Bush was doing some-thing that Republicans have historically just not done. Prosperity with a purpose. Compassionate conservatism. Stealing the phrase of the Children's Defense Fund—leave no child behind.

These are important statements and phrases. They mean something when they're repeated as often as they have been. I was uneasy because I have always felt that Republicans with hearts—thankfully, there are not a lot of them—are pretty potent and pretty effective politically. I was afraid that Bush was a Republican with a heart and that he was going to be real trouble for us. Well, while I personally think we won the election last fall, he was certainly trouble.

From now on, part of the welfare debate has to be focused on what George Bush wants to do and how he is going to do it. And here, there are some intriguing suggestions.

First of all, Bush named Governor Tommy Thompson to be his health and human services secretary. During Thompson's confirmation, Senator John Edwards (D-NC) asked him, "Do you save money doing welfare reform?" And Thompson said, "I've been preaching about this forever. Welfare reform is not about saving money. It's about getting people to work and getting them started." Frankly, while I'm not always excited by some of Secretary Thompson's rhetoric on the subject, I think that if all the states in the union did what Wisconsin does to help people get work and to help provide quality day care and wage supplements, we'd be a lot better country.

Then there is President Bush's inaugural address, a couple of passages from which are well worth noting:

"In the quiet of American conscience, we know that a deep persistent poverty is unworthy of our nation's promise. And whatever our views of its cause, we can agree that children at risk are not at fault; abandonment and abuse are not acts of God, they are failures of love.

"Where there is suffering, there is duty. Americans in need are not strangers. They are citizens. Not problems, but priorities. And all of us are diminished when they are hopeless.

"Many in our country do not know the pain of poverty. But we can listen to those who do. And I pledge our nation to a goal. When we see that wounded traveler on the road to Jericho, we will not pass to the other side."

Now, my friend Al Gore may not like for me to say it, but this was a beautiful inaugural address. And these particular words were the first words of President Bush espousing the deep principles of his presidency. So the question in the weeks and months ahead will be: do these words have meaning?

Democrats will be watching closely. Congressman George Miller (D-CA), an unlikely supporter of President Bush, said to me recently that he believes Bush is going to do some important work in educating the disadvantaged. Maybe Bush will do other important work that would make an enormous difference to people who are still suffering from poverty, as—make no mistake about it—many are, and grievously.

Last December, a report by the Catholic Charities noted that the number of people receiving emergency assistance at their shelters had increased 22 percent. The number of people receiving emergency food assistance from soup kitchens, food banks, and other food services had surged 32 percent. Emergency cash assistance, which helps people pay for rent, utilities, and medicine, had risen 29 percent to $80 million. The number of people receiving utility assistance had increased 15 percent. Clothing assistance had gone up 9 percent. Homelessness had also gone up.

These disturbing trends are also mirrored in reports by the League of Cities. And as Peter Edelman has eloquently pointed out in his book, *Searching for America's Heart*, many, many people have left the welfare rolls, but have not found jobs. The incidence of real grinding poverty—that is, income less than half the poverty level—has been pretty persistent and consistent.

What can happen? President Bush can say, "I'm going to do more for early childhood education. I'm going to expand Head Start for three- and four-year-olds. I want to make it a reading program and I want to make it much bigger." A lot of Democrats will be happily applauding on the sidelines. Bush can say he wants to expand the school day and the school year. We'll cheer him every step of the way and give him large majorities when it comes time to vote.

The president wants to increase the child tax credit from $500 to $1,000. That's a good idea, too—but not quite good enough unless it's partially refundable so that it can go to some of the people who really need the help. We can also expand the earned income tax credit—not only to eliminate its marriage penalty, but also to account for a third child. That's expensive, but it's the right thing to do. And we can expand the Child Health Insurance Program.

I'm frankly a lot more optimistic about the prospects for all these initiatives than I might have been right after last November's election. I think some of the signs are good. We might not see a lot of changes in the welfare reform law. It's going to be hard to undo the time limits, though maybe we can change the way the clock starts in some parts of the country. And we also must face the painful reality that about a third of the folks who have received public assistance over the years are just not going to get to work. And we'd better be damned concerned about what happens to their kids.

On some of these issues, the president has spoken eloquently. Now it's up to him to show us the money.

Tom Downey, chairman of Downey McGrath Group, represented the second district of New York in the U.S. House of Representatives for 18 years. He was acting chairman of the House Ways and Means Subcommittee on Human Resources for five years and one of the chief House architects of the 1988 Family Support Act.

WHO NEEDS POLITICAL PARTIES?

BY RICHARD M. VALELLY

As the major political parties convene this summer, with all the usual noise, pomp, and expense, Americans can be counted on to let out a collective yawn, or maybe a grimace. But not so for political scientists. Academic experts see a lot to like—or at least a lot to study—in the American two-party system. In their considered view, a competitive party system ensures the legitimacy of opposition to government, promotes public debate about policy options, and gets citizens involved in the public sphere. The two-party system never does these things perfectly, but it does them well enough. Without it our system would collapse overnight, leaving gridlock and hyperpluralism—or so most political scientists think.

But if one looks closely at the views of those who are researching, thinking about, and writing about political parties, one finds an interesting division of opinion. One school of thought is that parties are in decline and, consequently, that we have a major problem. The public is right to be irritated. A second view holds that parties have changed dramatically but that they are just as strong as they used to be. The public ought to get used to the transformation and stop griping. A third school, best articulated by David Mayhew of Yale University, is that political scientists have attributed too much importance to party dynamics. They matter, but less so than the professional literature has suggested. In this light, the public's gripes are beside the point.

To make sense of the disagreement, we must first sift through the ruins of realignment theory. For about 20 years, American government students were instructed in this line of thinking. Its concepts still echo in political punditry. But the theory died a decade ago when it became clear it wasn't explaining with any precision the events of the actual political world.

Without political parties, our system would collapse overnight, leaving the branches of government tangled and frozen.

Still, it was an elegant idea. Realignment theory held that not all elections were the same. In certain highly charged elections or in a string of two or three such elections, big and lasting shifts occurred in how voters behaved. A new voter coalition would assert control over our system, determining policy outcomes for a generation. Walter Dean Burnham, the theory's best-known proponent, suggested such elections might be a uniquely American surrogate for political revolution. Before realignment, there might be a third-party challenge, protests, and even civil disorder. Eventually, ambitious politicians would pick up the pressing issues and make them their own.

With the image of periodic political renewal, there was a soothing message in all this. Realignments allowed the political system to adjust to social and political stress, and to bring those citizens who might otherwise be absorbed in personal concerns into political action. The party system periodically restored its own vitality and that of the system as a whole.

Burnham explicitly warned, however, that the party system's capacity for "peaceful revolution" was not automatic. If and when the party system lost its ability to adapt, the branches of government would lock up. Governmental remedy as both an ideal and a practice would wither. Gradually, a propensity toward broad-based oligarchy would set in. After all, the wealthy are best protected by government that is deadlocked. Simultaneously, a huge class of unmobilized people would emerge as a "party of nonvoters." Their influence on the system would necessarily be weaker.

Scholars in the "party decline" school have inherited Burnham's worry. They agree that as a party system weakens it tends to pull the rest of the order down with it. Sidney Milkis of the University of Virginia, who is close in spirit to Burnham, makes such a case in *Political Parties and Constitutional Government*, a study of the rise and development of political parties since the founding. While Milkis does not share Burnham's open distaste for markets, capitalism, and social inequalities, he does adopt Burnham's democratic nationalism. For Milkis the weakening of parties has promoted broad discontent with American government and has generated an anemic civic culture.

In Milkis's account—and this is what makes his work so provocative—the cause of party decline, and thus of public cynicism, is not the depoliticizing force of market values, as Burnham has long argued. Instead, it is the particular development of the presidency. To put Milkis's claim bluntly, FDR killed the parties when he built a government competent enough to run a welfare state. In doing that, he changed the constitutional balance that had been supported by the parties since the time of Madison, Jackson, and Van Buren. Subsequent presidents failed to reverse Roosevelt's legacy.

Party competition first emerged, Milkis argues, when James Madison and Thomas Jefferson sought to develop a political opposition to Alexander Hamilton, John Adams, and the Federalist legatees of George Washington's two-term presidency. Madison, in particular, feared for the future of federalism and the separation of powers if Hamilton's economic nationalism were left politically unchecked. Milkis takes pains to point out that there was a second Madison, one less well-known but just as important as the more familiar Madison who framed the Constitution. The first disliked parties and factions; the second had no trouble embracing them in order to save his overall institutional design. Happily for Madison, the party system that he helped to launch evolved (thanks to the genius of Martin Van Buren) into a stable contest between two large confederations of state and local parties. And happily for the system as a whole, Milkis says, the parties won the political loyalties of voters scattered across a vast geographic expanse.

Americans came to appreciate the full range of national, state, and local institutions contemplated by the founders. Voters liked their town and county governments; they valued their state institutions; and they came to treasure not only the presidency but the Senate, the House, and the Supreme Court. America's elaborate mix of national, state, and local jurisdictions and offices might never have taken hold without the early development of decentralized but nationally competitive parties. This accomplishment helps to explain the persistence of the Constitution of 1787 despite the extraordinary events of the Civil War and the Reconstruction, and the huge expansion of the republic's size.

But our party system and institutions were never particularly well-suited for strong, positive government, Milkis argues. They were good for participation and office-seeking, but not for supple macroeconomic management or the competent bureaucratic delivery of social benefits, such as old-age income security or work relief. Here Milkis carries forward a long line of thinking about party politics and public administration that dates to the work of Herbert Croly and other progressives in the early decades of the 1900s.

FDR was the first president, in Milkis's view, who was forced to cope with the lack of fit between the institutional forms given to him and new executive tasks. He keenly understood the limits of the party system he inherited, and sought briefly to do something about them, through the ill-fated 1938 "Roosevelt purge" in which New Deal liberals were encouraged to run against reactionary and conservative Democratic incumbents in Congress. He hoped to transform his party into a programmatic, responsible organization. He failed miserably.

FDR did not try again, opting instead for the independent regulatory commissions, new bureaucracies, court-packing, and executive reorganization that he or congressional liberals had already launched or planned before the purge effort.

Roosevelt grasped that he could, and probably should, soft-pedal his party as an instrument of executive governance. It was too loaded with southern conservatives and stand-pat careerists. Time was short, and there was much work to be done to save liberal capitalism from its enemies within and without.

But there was a hidden price for this understandable decision. The cost to the polity, one that was not immediately obvious, was reduced voter involvement. As Kennedy, Johnson, and Nixon perfected the New Deal state, they did so on the backs of social movements, professors, experts, and government executives and lawyers. Their mission was not to revitalize the remnants of the urban machines or to reform the conservative state parties and party factions that they scorned. They made the same choice Roosevelt did. So the decentralized system of confederated parties—imagined by Madison and perfected by Van Buren—collapsed, as one ward club or county committee after another (with the notable exception of Chicago) died on the liberal vine. These local institutions were the vital foundation of voter involvement; without them voter turnout began its long decline.

Not all political scientists are alarmed by such developments. In his important 1995 work, *Why Parties?*, John H. Aldrich responds to the passing of the ward heelers by saying, in effect, "so what?" He wants us to face up to a stark proposition: The forms of parties are going to change. As he notes, trenchantly, "The major political party is the creature of the politicians.... These politicians do not have partisan goals per se, and the party is only the instrument for achieving them." Politicians run the parties, and they will inevitably change the ways in which parties help them to be politicians.

Aldrich is no iconoclast, to be sure. His book is deeply thoughtful, gently argued, and quite rigorous.

At the heart of Aldrich's case lies an extended comparison between two party systems: the system that emerged in the North during the 1820s and 1830s and that lasted until the Civil War, and the more familiar two-party system that has structured our politics since the 1960s. The first was intensely mobilizing and generated sharp increases in voter turnout until it reached extraordinary, indeed uniquely high levels. This was also a period of "team parties," in which politicians subordinated their individual identities to the corporate identity of their party since the path to power lay through making that trade-off.

Today's parties, in contrast, are service-providing organizations. They resemble a franchise for entrepreneurs. The individual candidates of the two parties meet certain programmatic requirements related to party ideology, but in terms of campaigning they act as free-lancers. They have no trouble behaving as highly competitive teams within government, particularly within the House of Representatives, but they do not cooperate with each other to rally voters. Stimulating turnout is up to an individual candidate if he or she chooses.

The point of Aldrich's contrast is not that there has been decline relative to some golden age. Instead, these are fundamentally different systems. Juxtaposed to this claim is a lucid demonstration of the central tendency of any competitive party system, regardless of differences in the campaign styles of politicians. Using simple modeling, Aldrich posits that a party system will solve pathologies that would otherwise plague politicians. Without a competitive party system, politicians could not cooperate around mutual policy gains, which can only come through repeated interaction and binding commitments that hold up across time. They would instead treat all their interactions with each other as one-shot games and thus fall prey to the noncooperative trap epitomized by the "prisoner's dilemma."

Second, without parties' resources and their capacity to stimulate, motivate, and inform voters, politicians could never solve a major dilemma facing voters, i.e., the propensity to avoid voting and to instead "free ride" on those who take the trouble to vote out of an irrationally strong sense of civic duty. If most of us were freeriders, there could be no genuinely popular electoral system.

Third, without the partisan organization of legislatures and government, politicians could never efficiently restrict the agenda of conflict and debate to a basic set of important issues. They would instead stumble in and out of fragile log-rolls that would incorporate many unrelated items. The result would be policy immobility, rendering deliberation and participation beside the point.

Professional politicians in a democracy obviously need parties to satisfy their policy and office-seeking ambitions. But the rest of us also need parties. No parties, no "positive externalities" (in the language of welfare economics)—no streams of consistent and related policies, no agenda for public debate, and little prospect of even a modicum of voter attachment to the polity and its concerns. Thus, our current party system provides essentially the same "positive externalities," Aldrich is saying, as the earlier party system.

But a somewhat different take on the same facts is offered by Steven Schier in *By Invitation Only*. During the golden age of party politics, roughly the period from 1830 to 1890, we had something approaching a genuinely participatory democracy in this country. Today we have, in its place, a vast congeries of professionally managed "activation," that is, the stimulation and enlistment of thousands of small subsets of the citizenry in service of the ambition of an interest group or a candidate. Several kinds of professional consultancies are available to

the well-heeled or the well-organized to accomplish their preferred strategy of activation: pollsters, media consultants, fundraisers, gatherers of demographic data, opposition and issue researchers, speechwriters, schedulers, and so forth. Schier catalogues them all succinctly.

The basic idea here is that parties now compete in a broad marketplace of service providers for the politically ambitious. Their historic monopoly on access to office and influence disappeared with the rise of primaries, referenda, campaign finance regulation, and a privately operated system of broadcast communications.

The loser in the shift toward a competitive market in political techniques is the mass of ordinary citizens. Following politics and getting involved in it is up to them. If they do not have the education, confidence, partisan-ship, or time to do so, no one will ask them. Expending resources to activate the already motivated voters is cost-effective. It is less cost-effective to pursue those who are not listed in the databases of the consultants.

In this way, the political system is a bit like the medical system: technologically advanced, expensive, and replete with a variety of coverages and exclusions. As a nation, we spend a huge amount of money on electoral politics and employ all the latest campaign techniques, but we do not get much average-voter turnout in return.

Schier's final chapter offers an exceptionally thoughtful treatment of possible cures for this state of affairs. The bottom line for reform, he suggests, is making party affiliation more salient to political candidates than it currently is. In response, politicians might have stronger incentives to cooperate with one another in mobilizing voters, rather than worrying only about their own constituency.

We should reorganize campaign finance so that parties control more resources than they do now. And the states could provide ballots that are organized as party slates. More states could do what Maine and Nebraska do, which is to allocate votes in the electoral college to whomever carries a congressional district and give the "Senate votes" to the state-wide winner. These are among the most plausible reforms of the many that Schier discusses.

Could it be that such reforms overemphasize the importance of political parties to democracy? David Mayhew is the one leader of the political science profession who has consistently resisted such enthusiasms. In the course of his career, he has helped to show that political parties have little to do with whether Congress works well, that states with weak parties are not necessarily less generous with social policies (and are sometimes more generous), and that from 1947 to 1990 divided government at the national level simply had no effect on the production of important public policy, budgetary balance, or the frequency or disruptiveness of congressional investigations of the White House or the executive bureaucracies.

It could also be the case that the party system, as Aldrich says, is not in decline but simply has acquired new forms. One might retort that the earlier system made for more active citizens. But cross-national survey research does not show that countries with party systems more like our earlier system have citizens more satisfied with how their democracy works than ours.

Nonetheless, Walter Dean Burnham was right to think as long and as hard as he did about cycles of decline and renewal in American party politics. Perhaps critical realignments never really existed, but political decline and renewal are hardly fanciful inventions of Burnham's towering intellect. They are the oldest and most important issues of political thought, going back to Aristotle.

For all their faults, political parties have been the essential foundation of both citizen involvement and citizen awareness of the issues facing a democratic polity. Perhaps nothing will come of letting our two-party system continue to become just one among many channels for citizen involvement, rather than the premier channel. It is more likely, though, that good things would come from trying, as Schier suggests, to make our party system more salient for voters and politicians than it currently is.

RICHARD M. VALELLY is a professor of political science at Swarthmore College.

Making Every Vote Count

LANI GUINIER

For years many of us have called for a national conversation about what it means to be a multiracial democracy. We have enumerated the glaring flaws inherent in our winner-take-all form of voting, which has produced a steady decline in voter participation, underrepresentation of racial minorities in office, lack of meaningful competition and choice in most elections, and the general failure of politics to mobilize, inform and inspire half the eligible electorate. But nothing changed. Democracy was an asterisk in political debate, typically encompassed in a vague reference to "campaign finance reform." Enter Florida.

The fiasco there provides a rare opportunity to rethink and improve our voting practices in a way that reflects our professed desire to have "every vote count." This conversation has already begun, as several highly educated communities in Palm Beach experienced the same sense of systematic disfranchisement that beset the area's poorer and less-educated communities of color. "It felt like Birmingham last night," Mari Castellanos, a Latina activist in Miami, wrote in an e-mail describing a mammoth

rally at the 14,000-member New Birth Baptist Church, a primarily African-American congregation in Miami. "The sanctuary was standing room only. So were the overflow rooms and the school hall, where congregants connected via large TV screens. The people sang and prayed and listened. Story after story was told of voters being turned away at the polls, of ballots being destroyed, of NAACP election literature being discarded at the main post office, of Spanish-speaking poll workers being sent to Creole precincts and vice-versa.... Union leaders, civil rights activists, Black elected officials, ministers, rabbis and an incredibly passionate and inspiring Marlene Bastiene—president of the Haitian women's organization—spoke for two or three minutes each, reminding the assembly of the price their communities had paid for the right to vote and vowing not to be disfranchised ever again."

We must not let this once-in-a-generation moment pass without addressing the basic questions these impassioned citizens are raising: Who votes, how do they vote, whom do they vote for, how are their votes

counted and what happens after the voting? These questions go to the very legitimacy of our democratic procedures, not just in Florida but nationwide—and the answers could lead to profound but eminently achievable reforms.

§ *Who votes—and doesn't?* As with the rest of the nation, in Florida only about half of all adults vote, about the same as the national average. Even more disturbing, nonvoters are increasingly low-income, young and less educated. This trend persists despite the Voting Rights Act, which since 1970 has banned literacy tests nationwide as prerequisites for voting—a ban enacted by Congress and unanimously upheld by the Supreme Court.

We are a democracy that supposedly believes in universal suffrage, and yet the differential turnout between high-income and low-income voters is far greater than in Europe, where it ranges from 5 to 10 percent. More than two-thirds of people in America with incomes greater than $50,000 vote, compared with one-third of those with incomes under $10,000. Those convicted of a felony are permanently banned from voting in Florida and twelve other states. In

149

Florida alone, this year more than 400,000 ex-felons, about half of them black, were denied the opportunity to vote. Canada, on the other hand, takes special steps to register former prisoners and bring them into full citizenship.

§ *How do they vote?* Florida now abounds with stories of long poll lines, confusing ballots and strict limitations on how long voters could spend in the voting booth. The shocking number of invalid ballots—more ballots were "spoiled" in the presidential race than were cast for "spoiler" Ralph Nader—are a direct result of antiquated voting mechanics that would shame any nation, let alone one of the world's oldest democracies. Even the better-educated older voters of Palm Beach found, to their surprise, how much they had in common with more frequently disfranchised populations. Given how many decisions voters are expected to make in less than five minutes in the polling booth, it is common sense that the polls should be open over a weekend, or at least for twenty-four hours, and that Election Day should be a national holiday. By highlighting our wretched record on voting practices, Florida raises the obvious question: Do we really want large voter participation?

§ *Whom do they vote for?* Obviously, Florida voters chose among Al Gore, George Bush and a handful of minor-party candidates who, given their status as unlikely to win, were generally ignored and at best chastised as spoilers. But as many voters are now realizing, in the presidential race they were voting not for the candidates whose name they selected (or attempted to select) but for "electors" to that opaque institution, the Electoral College. Our constitutional framers did some things well—chiefly dulling the edge of winner-take-all elections through institutions that demand coalition-building, compromise and recognition of certain minority voices—but the Electoral College was created on illegitimate grounds and has no place in a modern democracy.

As Yale law professor Akhil Reed Amar argues, the Electoral College was established as a device to boost the power of Southern states in the election of the President. The same "compromise" that gave Southern states more House members by counting slaves as three-fifths of a person for purposes of apportioning representation (while giving them none of the privileges of citizenship) gave those states Electoral College votes in proportion to their Congressional delegation. This hypocrisy enhanced the Southern states' Electoral College percentage, and as a result, Virginia slaveowners controlled the presidency for thirty-two of our first thirty-six years.

Its immoral origins notwithstanding, the Electoral College was soon justified as a deliberative body that would choose among several candidates and assure the voice of small geographic areas. But under the Electoral College, voters in small states have more than just a voice; indeed their say often exceeds that of voters in big states. In Wyoming one vote in the Electoral College corresponds to 71,000 voters; in Florida, one electoral vote corresponds to 238,000 voters. At minimum we should eliminate the extra bias that adding electors for each of two senators gives our smallest states. As Robert Naiman of the Center for Economic and Policy Research reports, allowing each state only as many electors as it has members in the House of Representatives would mean, for example, that even if Bush won Oregon and Florida, he would have 216 and Gore would have 220 electoral votes.

Today its backers still argue that the Electoral College is necessary to insure that small states are not ignored by the presidential candidates. Yet the many states—including small ones—that weren't close in this election were neglected by both campaigns. Some of the nation's biggest states, with the most people of color, saw very little presidential campaigning and get-out-the-vote activity. Given their lopsided results

this year, we can expect California, Illinois, New York, Texas and nearly all Southern states to be shunned in the 2004 campaign.

§ *How are their votes counted?* The presidency rests on a handful of votes in Florida because allocation of electoral votes is winner-take-all—if Gore wins by ten votes out of 6 million, he will win 100 percent of the state's twenty-five electoral votes. The ballots cast for a losing candidate are always "invalid" for the purposes of representation; only those cast for the winner actually "count." Thus winner-take-all elections underrepresent the voice of the minority and exaggerate the power of one state's razor-thin majority. Winner-take-all is the great barrier to representation of political and racial minorities at both the federal and the state level. No blacks or Latinos serve in the US Senate or in any governor's mansion. Third-party candidates did not win a single state legislature race except for a handful in Vermont.

Given the national questioning of the Electoral College sparked by the anomalous gap between the popular vote and the college's vote in the presidential election, those committed to real representative democracy now have a chance to shine a spotlight on the glaring flaws and disfranchisement inherent in winner-take-all practices and to propose important reforms.

What we need are election rules that encourage voter turnout rather than suppress it. A system of proportional representation—which would allocate seats to parties based on their proportion of the total vote—would more fairly reflect intense feeling within the electorate, mobilize more people to participate and even encourage those who do participate to do so beyond just the single act of voting on Election Day. Most democracies around the world have some form of proportional voting and manage to engage a much greater percentage of their citizens in elections. Proportional representation in South Africa, for example, allows the white Afrikaner parties and the ANC to gain seats in the national legislature commensurate with the total number of votes cast for each party. Under this system, third parties are a plausible alternative. Moreover, to allow third parties to run presidential candidates without being "spoilers," some advocate instant-runoff elections in which voters would rank their choices for President. That way, even voters whose top choice loses the election could influence the race among the other candidates.

Winner-take-all elections, by contrast, encourage the two major parties to concentrate primarily on the "undecideds" and to take tens of millions of dollars of corporate and special-interest contributions to broadcast ads on the public airwaves appealing to the center of the political spectrum. Winner-take-all incentives discourage either of the two major parties from trying to learn, through organizing and door-knocking, how to mobilize the vast numbers of disengaged poor and working-class voters. Rather than develop a vision, they produce a product and fail to build political capacity from the ground up.

§ *What happens after the voting?* Our nation is more focused on elections now than it has been for decades; yet on any given Sunday, more people will watch professional football than voted this November. What democracy demands is a system of elections that enables minor parties to gain a voice in the legislature and encourages the development of local political organizations that educate and mobilize voters.

Between elections, grassroots organizations could play an important monitoring role now unfulfilled by the two major parties. If the Bush campaign is right that large numbers of ballots using the same butterfly format were thrown out in previous elections in Palm Beach, then something is wrong with more than the ballot. For those Democratic senior citizens in Palm Beach, it was not enough that their election supervisor was a Democrat. They needed a vibrant local organization that could have served as a watchdog, alerting voters and election officials that there were problems with the ballot. No one should inadvertently vote for two candidates; the same watchdog organizations should require ballot-counting machines like those in some states that notify the voter of such problems before he or she leaves the booth. Voters should be asked, as on the popular TV quiz show, "Is that your final answer?" And surely we cannot claim to be a functioning democracy when voters are turned away from the polls or denied assistance in violation of both state and federal law.

Before the lessons of Florida are forgotten, let us use this window of opportunity to forge a strong pro-democracy coalition to rally around "one vote, one value." The value of a vote depends on its being fairly counted but also on its counting toward the election of the person the voter chose as her representative. This can happen only if we recognize the excesses of winner-take-all voting and stop exaggerating the power of the winner by denying the loser any voice at all.

Lani Guinier is a professor of law at Harvard Law School. Her latest book is the forthcoming The Miner's Canary: Rethinking Race and Power *(Harvard). Rob Richie of the Center for Voting and Democracy (www.fairvote.org) provided invaluable assistance in the preparation of this essay.*

FOLLOW THE MONEY

Why campaigns should be publicly financed

Jay Mandle

What would happen if the United States funded the Defense Department through private contributions? Would those sections of the country that contribute more to defense be better protected than those that gave less? If the interstate highway system were paid for by the donations of private citizens, how likely is it that the nation's transportation system would serve the entire country and not just those who foot the bill?

The answers to such questions are obvious. Few would doubt that if these services were privately financed, their benefits would be biased toward the funders. The interests of the rest of the population would at best be an afterthought. Damaging as such a system would be, what then is to be said about a political system in which the wealthy provide the bulk of campaign financing? Certainly it would not be a stretch to say that a political system paid for by the affluent is one that will be disproportionately responsive to the well-off and less attentive to the needs of the rest of the population.

Funding for elections in a democracy should not depend on an economic elite. When the rich pay for electoral campaigns, the substance of politics is confined to the issues and policies that wealthy funders approve of. To be sure, the electorate gets to vote. But the choices presented to voters are, at best, those that are acceptable to the wealthy. At worst, of course, such a system is simply corrupt.

Almost all economically developed democracies have tried to reduce the importance of private money in elections. A study by the Center for a New Democracy and the Center for Responsive Politics showed that only the United States, Ireland, and Switzerland do not either provide public financing for candidates to the national legislature, or restrict the expenditures of such candidates. Further, the United States is alone in not providing free media time to office seekers. Presidential candidates in this country do have the option of funding their campaigns with public money (Albert Gore chose public funding, while George W. Bush relied exclusively on private donations). In addition, four states offer significant public financing for state offices and several cities do the same for local races. Nevertheless, the United States lags behind virtually all of the developed world in the effort to democratize elections.

The dominance of the rich is now so blatant that even politicians who benefit from it are ashamed. The McCain-Feingold Bill (Shays-Meehan in the House of Representatives) is a well-intentioned effort at reform. This legislation imposes a ban on "soft money" payments to national parties, and restricts "issue advocacy" by unions, corporations, and other interest groups. It is not hard to understand what motivates these limitations. Unregulated donations made for "party building" easily find their way into electoral campaigns. Similarly, issue-advocacy ads have become an only slightly disguised means of circumventing current campaign contribution limits.

There are elements of McCain-Feingold, however, that raise concerns. The first and most obvious is that, as passed by the Senate, the legislation doubles the permitted level of "hard money" contributions. Obviously this provision—perhaps necessary to secure Senate passage—is a concession that chips away at the principle that private money in elections should be curtailed. Two other aspects of the legislation are also worrisome. First, its passage is likely to result in increased, not decreased, public cynicism because, in the end, the legislation's restrictions will not do very much to rid the system of its pro-wealth bias. News reports have already appeared detailing how the major political parties plan to circumvent the law's intent. The prevailing view is that with the banning of soft money, political action committees (PACs) will once again serve as the conduit of choice for the wealthy. Finding other loopholes in the law has already begun.

The second matter of concern is the impact of McCain-Feingold on the political parties. Parties are vehicles for political mobilization and expression. Depriving them of funds tends to weaken an important mechanism by which opinion is expressed. The banning of issue-advocacy advertisements does the same. It narrows the scope of political discussion without creating an alternative outlet for public debate.

This argument is used by critics of campaign finance reform, such as Bradley A. Smith who, in his recent book, *Unfree Speech* (Princeton), plausibly maintains that legislation such as McCain-Feingold will reduce political debate. Smith, a member of the Federal Elections Commission, also contends, in this case unconvincingly, that campaign contributions play only a minimal role in shaping policies and legislation. But even he does not totally deny the problems associated with privately financed campaigns. Rather, Smith argues that the unintended consequence of limiting private financing will do more harm than good.

What about a reform that does not limit contributions, instead making public money available to candidates? Public financing would provide funds directly to viable candidates, enabling them to present their ideas and policies without considering the effect on potential contributors. With public financing, there would be no need to be concerned with the inevitable loopholes that will be found in any effort to regulate political contributions.

In this case Smith reverses course and argues against reform not on principle, but because of political expediency. Smith concedes the advantages associated with public financing of elections: increased electoral competitiveness and accountability; a better flow of information to voters; and an increase in the number of well-qualified candidates. Nevertheless Smith opposes this kind of reform. In this case, however, it is not because of a lack of intrinsic merit, but because it is an approach that is "off the charts politically."

Voters have to be persuaded that the electoral system is just as important to the health—in this case the democratic health— of the nation as the defense budget, airports, highways, schools, and law enforcement.

Taken at face value, Smith's argument constitutes a case for grass-roots organizing. Polls show that the American people overwhelmingly support reforming the electoral system but shy away from full public financing as a remedy. What is at issue here is the antipathy of the American people to government social programs. The criticism made by opponents of reform that public financ-

ing presents "welfare for politicians" brilliantly taps into this hostility. Therefore, this attitude must change if we are to democratize our electoral system.

To persuade the American people to support the public financing of elections it will be necessary to convince them that elections are a "public good." Public goods are services that by their nature tend to be shared not only by those who pay but also by those who do not pay. Their use by one person generally does not preclude their use by others. Because of the collective way they are consumed, it is logical that they be purchased socially. If there is an attempt to have public goods privately funded, their availability becomes inadequate and their use distorted. If we tried to have our roads paid for privately we would wind up with a patchwork of toll roads located where users dictate instead of a network that links the whole society together. The same is true of policing. If based on private consumption, police would work to ensure the safety of those willing to pay, while the rest would go unprotected. As a consequence the society would be deprived of any hope of a consistent and fair administration of justice.

Many of the same attributes that make the nation's defense or highway system public goods are present in the electoral system. The outcome of elections affects all the people of the country, whether or not they contribute financially to campaigns. In politics, of course, the problem is not that campaigns are underfinanced—the deep pockets of wealthy special interests ensure that that is not the case. But the generosity of private funders does corrupt and distort the electoral process. Just as we would not want the highway system to serve private, as opposed to public, needs, or the police to protect one group of citizens but not another, we should not be satisfied when every election is little more than an exercise in which the wealthy seek access and influence by contributing to the campaign war chests of politicians. The solution is for the community as a whole to foot the bill.

Voters have to be persuaded that the electoral system is just as important to the health—in this case the democratic health—of the nation as the defense budget, airports, highways, schools, and law enforcement. The costs of electoral campaigns should be paid for out of tax revenues. Doing so would ensure that each outcome reflects the interests of all, not just the privileged few.

Obviously it will take much educational and political work to persuade voters to look at elections in this way. But until that is done, we will not be able to alter the reality that the private funding of electoral campaigns is the means by which the affluent set the political agenda. For reform to happen, grass-roots pressure is required. In its absence not much will change. Politicians have too great a stake in the current system. In short, campaign finance reform is a cause in need of a social movement.

There is reason for hope in this regard. Recent experience has convinced at least some activists that solving global economic and environmental problems must begin with domestic U.S. politics. For example, the Kyoto global environmental accord has been subverted by the refusal of the United States to accede to its terms. The United States has also failed to ratify the International Labor Organization's core labor standards, thus providing a license to anti-union efforts in poor countries. And the International Monetary Fund's notorious structural adjustment programs, depriving the poor of assistance and education, are in place because the United States, the country with the single largest influence in that organization, insists that what poor countries need is minimalist government. In all of this there is encouragement to be drawn from the fact that people in the movements addressing these issues increasingly recognize that the roadblock to progress is the role of private wealth in our politics.

A second source of hope has been the democratizing of the electoral process in cities and states around the country. In Maine, Arizona, and Massachusetts "clean money, clean elections" campaigns have won, and the option of full public funding of elections has been implemented. In cities such as New York and Long Beach and Oakland in California, partial public funding of elections has been adopted. These initiatives are the result of dedicated local organizers working far outside the glare of national publicity. Organizers know that triumphs at the state and local levels are critical in the struggle for national reform. Indeed, the history of progressive politics in the United States suggests that the momentum for federal legislation must bubble up from the grass roots. There would be no national civil rights, women's rights, or environmental legislation if it were not for such local groundwork.

The campaign-finance reform movement desperately needs an infusion of energy and enthusiasm. Advocates of reform have not been well served by the "Beltway" mentality. There are far too many lobbyists and lawyers tinkering with the details of reform legislation, and not nearly enough student and community activists holding politicians' feet to the fire. Democracy Matters, a campus-based organization with which I am associated, is attempting to reorient campaign-finance reform efforts. Our strategy anticipates that students working with diverse communities will find an outlet with a real possibility for political success. At the same time, community activists working with students will gain much-needed help in carrying out their efforts. Such a coalition can stimulate a rethinking of the way political campaigns should be financed.

Success will ultimately depend on whether these two wings of activism—students and local communities—join together. United States global and domestic policy will remain a private preserve of the rich and corporate interests as long as politics remain in thrall to the wealthy. Those who advocate change in America—and the world—cannot win until our elections are publicly financed.

Jay Mandle *is the W. Branford Wiley Professor of Economics at Colgate University. He is also director of development for Democracy Matters (www.democracymatters.org).*

From *Commonweal*, July 13, 2001, pp. 12-17. © 2001 by Commonweal Foundation. For Subscriptions, call toll-free: 1-888-495-6755. Reprinted by permission.

NO NEED TO REPEAL THE ELECTORAL COLLEGE

Before we wipe out the entire electoral college, there are some changes we can make to improve the entire election system.

By Norman Ornstein

Until this November, the Electoral College was a vague remembrance from high school civics classes, a subject to master for SATs (and then forget immediately afterward) or an occasional final Jeopardy category. Not any more.

The election controversy of 2000, the first of any major magnitude since 1876, has put the Electoral College right in front of Americans' faces, on their television screens and in daily conversations in barber shops, coffee houses, at office water coolers and the dinner table.

Of course, if the Electoral College was civics trivia for most citizens, it has been a matter of great disagreement and concern to lawmakers and other opinion leaders since its inception. It was, after all, a compromise born of a struggle at the Constitutional Convention between small states and large states, or more accurately, between confederalists, who wanted to incorporate most of the Articles of Confederation, and those who wanted a large, national republic. As the late political theorist Martin Diamond has written, the confederalists wanted the president to be chosen directly by state legislatures. James Madison, James Wilson and Gouverneur Morris preferred a direct popular vote. That option was vehemently rejected by the confederalists. So Madison and his allies hit upon the Electoral College as a way to keep the states involved, but retain a role for the people. The state legislatures would choose electors, but they would be guided by the popular vote.

Their compromise did not stop the controversy. Actually, nothing has. The EC was changed early on (in 1804) via the 12th Amendment to the Constitution, creating separate votes by electors for president and vice president to avoid the problem of a president elected from one party and a vice president from the other. (Until then, the candidate with the most electoral votes became president and the runner up became vice president). The EC was changed again via legislation in states in the 19th century, as they responded to the democracy movement and went to having the electors selected via direct popular vote within the states (almost always on a winner-take-all basis).

1,028 PROPOSALS TO CHANGE THE SYSTEM

But those adjustments have not erased the broader debate. The Congressional Research Service has uncovered 1,028 legislative proposals for changing the system since the First Congress. Between 1889 and 1946, 109 constitutional amendments to reform the Electoral College were introduced in Congress, with another 265 between 1947 and 1968. In 1967, an American Bar Association commission recommended that the Electoral College be scrapped and replaced by direct popular vote for the president, with a provision for a runoff if no candidate achieved the threshold of 40 percent of the votes. The ABA plan, introduced by Indiana Senator Birch Bayh and endorsed by the Nixon White House, passed the House 338-70, but died on a filibuster in the Senate led by North Carolina Senator Sam Ervin.

Since 1969, there have been at least 113 reform proposals introduced in Congress—with many more certain to come next year. Most of the proposals call directly for abolition of the EC, and its replacement by direct popular vote. Others call for retaining the EC, but mandating that states divide their electoral votes by congressional district (as is now done voluntarily in Nebraska and Maine), or by proportion of popular votes cast in each state. A small number call simply for the elimination of electors—the real-live, flesh-and-blood people who go to their state capitols in mid-December to cast the electoral votes—and their replacement by an automatic system.

CHOOSING PRESIDENTIAL ELECTORS—THE DISTRICT SYSTEM VS. THE AT-LARGE SYSTEM

The states currently employ two methods for selecting presidential electors through popular election—the district and the at-large system. Most of the states use the at-large system, which awards all of the state's electoral votes to the candidate who wins the highest number of popular votes.

Two states, Maine and Nebraska, use the district system. One elector is chosen based on the popular vote in each congressional district, and two are assigned to the candidate who wins the most votes in the state. Under this system, it's possible for the state's electors to be divided among more than one candidate. For instance, the Republican candidate might carry the majority in one of Maine's two congressional districts, while the Democratic candidate wins in the second congressional district and also statewide. If that were to occur, Maine would select one Republican elector and three Democrats.

Maine adopted the district system in 1972, Nebraska in 1991. While they are the only two states that currently use the district system, it used to be more common. In the 1800s, Illinois, Kentucky, Maryland, Massachusetts, Missouri, New York, North Carolina and Tennessee all used the district system at one time or another. By 1836, all of these states had switched to the at-large system.

—*Jennie Drage, NCSL*

WHY REFORM?

Why the insistent calls for reform, mostly via elimination? The main reason is the broader cultural and societal impetus for more and more "democracy"—the same impetus that has extended the vote to women, minorities and young people, and that has generated the movement to direct democracy via initiatives and referendums.

Another reason is the trend to nationalization of politics in America—the sense that an emphasis on states is archaic for a modern rational government. A third reason is the fear of an election outcome that would be viewed as illegitimate—especially one where a presidential candidate wins a majority of the national popular vote but still loses the presidency to a candidate who prevails in the Electoral College.

America has certainly had its electoral crises related to the Electoral College: in 1800, when an EC tie between Thomas Jefferson and Aaron Burr required the House to select the president, taking 36 ballots and ending up with Jefferson winning and his foe Burr serving as vice president; in 1824, when a four-way race left no candidate with a majority of electoral votes, and House maneuvering made John Quincy Adams, who led neither in popular nor electoral votes, the winner; in 1876, when disputed electoral slates in three states (including Florida) had to be sorted out by an electoral commission. In addition, in 1888, we had the dreaded result of a president (Grover Cleveland) elected without a popular vote majority or plurality (albeit with little evident national controversy or disagreement.)

But three (or four) crises out of more than 50 presidential elections is remarkably small. And the drive for reform, based on the actual crises or the threat of another precipitated by the Electoral College, tends to ignore the crises that could be generated by direct national popular vote for the president.

The calls for reform accelerated with the 2000 presidential vote count, which started as a bad dream and ended up as a recurring nightmare—kind of like the movies *Groundhog Day* and *Friday the 13th* combined. The subsequent calls for repeal of the Electoral College were led by Senator-elect Hillary Rodham Clinton.

IRON LAW OF UNINTENDED CONSEQUENCES

It is only natural, of course, when a problem emerges, to seek a way to solve that problem. But the impulse to do so also brings with it what many have called "The Iron Law of Unintended Consequences." This election snarl provides a perfect example. As an exercise, let's look at this election through the lens of Frank Capra's *It's a Wonderful Life*: What would have happened if there were no Electoral College?

For one thing, we would have had no quick and clean resolution of the election. On the morning after the election, Al Gore led George W. Bush by around 200,000 votes, or about 0.2 percent. That on the surface might seem substantial enough. But there were approximately 3 million absentee and vote-by-mail ballots *yet to be counted*, including well over 1 million in California, and several hundred thousand each in Oregon and Washington. It took more than three full weeks for all those absentee and vote-by-mail ballots to be tallied, with doubt remaining over the final leader for nearly all that period.

The almost-final difference between the candidates was 333,576 votes, roughly 0.3 percent. That is well below the number that triggers an automatic recount in Florida and many other states (some use 0.5 percent, some 0.33 percent, and so on.) Can anyone doubt that a hard-fought presidential campaign ending with a cloud over the counts in a number of counties and precincts around the country would call for a recount?

But that would not be a recount like Florida—confined to 67 counties, each with its own clear-cut partisan power structure and administration. Instead we would have a *nationwide* recount, taking place in thousands of election units, some counties, some cities, some precincts, depending on individual states. All the ballot boxes in the country would have to be impounded. Instead of the

REFORMING THE ELECTORAL COLLEGE

Nebraska was the last state to reform its process for selecting presidential electors with its switch to the district system in 1991. Ways in which the states could choose to reform the system include:

- Abolishing the Electoral College—The legislatures of two-thirds of the states can petition Congress to convene a constitutional convention. At that, any part of the Constitution could be amended; action is not restricted to the sections governing the electoral college or any other part of the Constitution. Any proposed amendment would have to be ratified by three-fourths of the states. Pennsylvania and Ohio considered, but did not pass, measures on this in 1999.

- Switching to the district system—More states could switch from the at-large system to the district system for selecting presidential electors. A bill considered in New York in 1999 proposed this change, and lawmakers in a number of states are considering such legislation for 2001. On the other hand, a 1999 bill was introduced in Nebraska proposing that it stop using the district system and switch back to the at-large system. That bill failed.

- Switching to a proportional system—In 1999, the Washington Legislatures considered a measure that would have allocated the presidential electors according to their proportional share of the statewide popular vote. It did not pass.

—*Jennie Drage, NCSL*

PROBLEMS WITH ABSENTEES

But there are huge problems with absentee voting, starting with the fact that more and more people are voting weeks before the campaign ends, before they know what happens or how the candidates react under the intense pressure of the final days of the process.

Imagine if a 15-round heavyweight championship fight had the judges vote on a winner after the 12th round. The staggered voting has sharply increased the costs of campaigning, and has actually increased the amount of negative campaign advertising; instead of saving their firepower until the final two weeks, when most voters begin to pay attention, candidates and parties in heavy absentee states have been forced to advertise much sooner for the early voters, and then spend more to target the later ones.

More significant for the purposes of evaluating the Electoral College, absentee votes and vote-by-mail have other important characteristics: one, they are more laborious to count—envelopes have to be opened individually, signatures checked, ballots certified and searches done to be sure citizens vote only once, and counts taken. Oregon's self-vaunted all vote-by-mail system was a national embarrassment; the state only included ballots that arrived by the close-of-business Election Day, but it couldn't come up with any counts for days thereafter.

Of course, in most states, a large share of the absentee ballots don't arrive by Election Day. Many states are like Florida, allowing 10 days after an election for overseas and other ballots postmarked by Election Day to come in and be counted. In Washington, any ballot postmarked Election Day is counted no matter when it arrives, adding to potential delays. So brace yourselves: Eliminate the Electoral College, and it will be a rare presidential election where we know the outcome even a week after!

Proponents of the repeal of the Electoral College might argue that this scenario is not a great brief in favor of it. If both the EC and direct popular vote have even equal potential built in for nightmares, why not opt for the more directly democratic process?

The answer is that there are many other powerful arguments in favor of the Electoral College. The EC tends to produce larger and more decisive margins for wins when the popular vote is very close, leading to a more definitive judgment of victory, and giving presidents some greater sense of legitimacy and mandate—a necessity in a system of checks and balances where a president relies heavily on intangibles like credibility.

John F. Kennedy's 1960 popular vote margin over Richard Nixon was 118,000 votes, or just over 0.1 percent, one vote per precinct. But Kennedy won 303 electoral votes, 56 percent of them, a cushion large enough to discourage a challenge from Nixon and enough to give him some running room as president.

The factor is even more important when there is a three-way race for president and the winner ends up well below 50 percent of the popular vote. In 1968, with

squadron of lawyers who have descended on Florida to oversee, sue and kibitz about the recounts, we would have armies of lawyers, exceeding the troops massed for the D-Day invasion, fanning out across the country to argue, bicker and litigate.

This horrific nightmare would not likely be a one-time thing if the Electoral College was abolished. There has been a sharp trend in the country toward absentee ballots and vote-by-mail. The parties have encouraged it, because it is easier and cheaper to get out the vote by targeting voters and getting commitments in advance, fulfilled just by filling out a ballot and mailing it in. The states have moved in that direction because it can increase turnout and reduce their costs of keeping polling places open and filled with workers. California has up to a third of its voters going absentee, Washington about 60 percent, and Oregon went to a total vote-by-mail system this time. In 1996, the Census Bureau calculated that 20 percent of voters nationwide voted absentee; the number from this election will approach 30 percent.

ELECTORAL COLLEGE— THE ROLE OF THE LEGISLATURE

Although the presidential electors have been chosen by popular elections for many years, that's not the way it always worked. In fact, when the Florida Legislature appointed electors, it wasn't the first time a legislature has done so. The U.S. Constitution clearly puts the power for deciding how electors are chosen in the hands of the state legislatures. Section 1 of Article II states, "Each State shall appoint, in such Manner as the Legislature thereof may direct, a Number of Electors, equal to the whole Number of Senators and Representatives to which the State may be entitled in the Congress…"

In the country's early years, it was common for legislatures to appoint the electors. In the early 1800s, about half the states appointed their electors through the legislature, and the other half did it through popular elections. Gradually, the legislatures handed over the responsibility for choosing electors to the people through a popular vote. By 1836, South Carolina was the only state that selected its electors through the legislature. By the 1864 election, South Carolina had switched to a popular vote system, as well.

The only other states that have selected their presidential electors through the legislature since 1836 are Massachusetts, Colorado and, surprise!, Florida. In 1848, the Massachusetts General Court was forced to choose the electors when none of the three slates on the ballot won a majority of the popular vote. Massachusetts had a statute that required the legislature to choose the electors if no slate won a majority. The Florida Legislature chose the electors in 1868. Colorado was a brand new state and had just held its first statewide elections in August of that year, and didn't want to hold another statewide election to choose electors so soon afterward.

Even though it has not been uncommon throughout history for a state legislature to choose presidential electors, it has not been done in modern times. The Florida Legislature was poised to make history this year when it met in special session to name presidential electors as a precaution against the possibility that court challenges would leave the state out when the Electoral College met on Dec. 18. It would have been the first time a legislature has stepped in to settle a contested election for presidential electors.

—*Jennie Drage, NCSL*

lar advantage over Democrat Hubert Humphrey. But even though Wallace siphoned off 46 electoral votes that year, Nixon still received 301 electoral votes, 31 over the majority necessary, 120 more than Humphrey and enough to give him some sense of mandate in a difficult, divisive and bitter year.

In 1992, with H. Ross Perot running as an independent, Bill Clinton received just over 43 percent of the popular votes—but won with a near-landslide 370 electoral votes, 69 percent of the total.

CLOUT FOR SMALL STATES

The EC was designed originally to give states both large and small some role in presidential contests. It has done just that, while also encouraging candidates to campaign in small states and sparsely populated regions and to do retail, face-to-face campaigning instead of just television air wars targeting the large cities and other populous areas.

Large states, partly because they have all retained their winner-take-all electoral vote formula, have remained important, although the importance of one-party dominant large states would clearly increase with direct popular vote (hence Senator-elect Clinton's position.) But smaller states have clearly greater importance than they would have without the EC; indeed, in most elections, small states would be largely irrelevant without their electoral votes as lures.

Because of the obvious clout the EC gives to small states, the chances of Electoral College repeal remain small. They are smaller yet because of the public reaction to the November (or should we say December) 2000 results—the clear prospect after this election that a George W. Bush presidency would come with Al Gore having won the national popular vote caused not the slightest hint of public outrage.

So what will happen—and what should happen—in the aftermath of this election? One constitutional amendment would make some sense: the elimination of electors themselves and their replacement with automatic votes. Any concept of electors as actual deliberators disappeared in the early 19th century. Even though real examples of "faithless" electors are rare, the prospect is always there of rogue or faithless electors changing their votes, reneging on their pledges or being swayed by inducements, and especially with a very close election.

It also makes sense to remind states that they do not need a constitutional amendment to change the distribution of their electoral votes, perhaps joining Maine and Nebraska and dividing them by congressional district. In small one-party states, especially, this can give them more clout by dangling for the opposite party the prospect of winning one or two electoral votes out of the four or five because of a congressional district or two with different political leanings than the overall state. (In large states, on the other hand, division by congressional district could dilute their power and add to the confusion

George Wallace running as an independent, Richard Nixon received only 43.4 percent of the popular vote, a precarious margin overall and with only a slender popu-

and close results in a tight election.) Remember too, that if large states like California allocated their electors by congressional district, it would create opportunities for more third and fourth party candidates like Ralph Nader to run for president, pick off a handful of districts (and electors), and perhaps throw the election into the House of Representatives.

But there is more that should happen now than direct reform or change in the Electoral College itself. This November, Americans learned as vividly as one can imagine that in our elections, every vote counts. Unfortunately, they have also learned, just as vividly, that not every vote is counted—not even close. For all except a handful of election aficionados, the messy, sloppy, underfunded, undermanned, sometimes incompetent and occasionally corrupt administration of our elections, in a process more decentralized than any area other than garbage collection, has come as a shock.

ELECTION REFORM

It demands reform—major, swift and comprehensive—in the way Americans run our elections. Elections are woefully underfunded, resulting in outdated equipment, misaligned machines, poorly trained and inadequate personnel, out-of-date voter registration information at the polling places, poorly designed ballots and huge voter errors.

The first step to reform is more money. And the money—probably $250 million, a small sum in the context of a nearly $2 trillion federal budget, but huge for local officials—becomes the key to substantive reform. States should consider their own reform programs, providing grants to election districts. And Congress should pass a bill providing the money in the form of matching grants (like the Highway Trust Fund, with a 90 percent to 10 percent ratio) to localities that agree to implement the following substantive reforms:

• **Uniform ballots for federal elections.** No more "butterfly" ballots or other comparable monstrosities; all voters should confront the same, simple and easy-to-use ballot, with clearly defined and directed choices.

• **Uniform use of modern "touch-screen" technology.** In many jurisdictions in the country, including Baltimore city for example, voting is done by touch screens similar to ATM machines that most Americans are familiar with. The capital investment in new equipment is significant, but because of the costs of printing paper ballots, maintaining the old machines and hiring the personnel to count the paper ballots, the long-term costs of using modern technology are actually lower.

• **Updating and upgrading voter registration data.** Many legally registered voters went to the polls on Nov. 7 only to be told that their names were not on the registra-

tion printout lists. Some lists had not been updated or synchronized; some had not been transferred from motor vehicle offices. It is an affront to democracy to prevent people who want to vote and have complied with the rules from doing so. Money and effort can fix the problem.

• **Use of local area networks (LANs) so that voters can cast their ballots either near their homes or their workplaces.** Voting by Internet would exacerbate the problems listed below with absentee balloting. But information technology can make it easier for people with difficult work schedules to vote, and have the vote count in their home precincts.

• **Weekend, 24-hour voting, with uniform poll-closing times.** It is time to move the system from elections on the first Tuesday following the first Monday in November to elections that run from, say, 8 a.m. Saturday morning to 8 a.m. Sunday morning. Opening and closing times should be staggered across the time zones so that all the polls close at the same time. This might make election eve less dramatic for viewers and for networks, but it would enhance turnout, and make for fewer media muffs.

• **Discouragement of runaway absentee voting.** Absentee ballots used to be for military personnel and those unavoidably away from home. Now voting by mail has become an easy tool of convenience—convenience for election officials who can ease the burden and cost at polls on Election Day; for parties, who can more easily target voters in their get-out-the-vote drives; and for voters who can avoid the hassle of voting at the polls. But those voters also lose the protection of privacy of the closed curtain in the polling place, and the importance of the collective act of gathering to exercise the sacred franchise. Absentee voting also raises the prospect of widespread corruption, a fact in many areas, with widespread use of absentee voting. Absentee voting should be for absentees—period. Make voting at the polls easier, but stop the trend of voting by mail.

The Electoral College will always remain controversial. The controversy may grow in the Information Age, with individual empowerment and the drive for direct democracy ascendant. But this "archaic" device is not anti-democratic—any more than a World Series that picks a winner by best-of-seven games, instead of by the overall number of runs scored, is wrong or illegitimate. As the data and arguments above suggest, the EC has legs—it continues to provide major benefits to American democracy. We need reform, and we need it now—in election administration and campaign finance. We do not need repeal of the Electoral College.

Norman Ornstein is a resident scholar at the American Enterprise Institute for Public Policy Research in Washington, D.C.

From the *State Legislatures,* February 2001, pp. 12-16. © 2001 by the National Conference of State Legislatures. Reprinted by permission.

Soft Money Unleashed

By Brody Mullins and Charlie Mitchell

It was the political equivalent of the arms race. During the 1999–2000 election cycle, big business and big labor nearly doubled their "soft-money" contributions to the Republican and Democratic parties from four years earlier.

A *National Journal* analysis shows that in the just-completed election cycle, the two major parties raked in $440.1 million in soft money, the unlimited political contributions donated for party-building activities. That was an 83 percent increase over the $240 million that the parties received during the 1995–96 election cycle.

These final spending figures dramatize soft money's growing influence on elections. The data, compiled by Votenet Solutions, a nonpartisan group, come a month before the Senate is set to debate legislation by Sens. John McCain, R-Ariz., Russell Feingold, D-Wis., and Thad Cochran, R-Miss., to ban soft-money donations.

Business interests this past election cycle shoveled a total of $227 million in soft money to the parties, a 50 percent increase over the previous period. But a bigger story involved the labor movement, which gave a total of $29.9 million in soft money. Seven different unions moved into the top 20 of all soft-money contributors. The American Federation of State, County and Municipal Employees, for example, earned the No. 1 slot in the rankings by virtue of its $5.91 million soft-money contribution, a 418 percent increase over its 1995–96 total. (*See chart*)

Other unions also saw dramatic increases. The Service Employees International Union shot from No. 80 in the rankings four years ago to No. 2 this time by giving $3.9 million, an increase of 1,014 percent over 1995–96. The United Brotherhood of Carpenters and Joiners of America went from No. 253 to No. 4 by putting together a 1,618 percent increase to $2.92 million.

But the labor movement's contributions represented just 7 percent of all soft money raised this cycle, a total still far below its corporate rivals. (Contributions from well-heeled individuals, single-issue groups, ideological organizations, and so-called leadership PACs comprised the balance of the total giving. These will be featured in a forthcoming story.)

The story on labor is complicated by the fact that many in the union movement are seeking a détente on soft-money giving.

"We support the goals of the Democratic Party, but there is only so much money we have and would be willing to give to party committees," said Larry Gold, the AFL-CIO's associate general counsel. "We wouldn't want to see it continue to climb like this."

The problem for unions is that they have proved very successful at mobilizing small "hard-money" contributions from their rank and file; soft dollars, by contrast, come from each organization's general treasury. And the general treasuries of corporations typically outstrip those of unions.

"We really don't have a treasury that supports soft-dollar contributions," one labor official said. "We're made up of small-donor contributors," he said. "It's 10 cents a week from each [union member] if you broke it down. The people who run the locals may give $5 or $10 a week. We believe that hard dollars is the money that should be used in campaigns. We're for abolishing soft dollars."

Corporations take a completely different tack. Gregory S. Casey, president of the Business-Industry Political Action Committee, says soft money is a critical part of the way "business plays in the political arena." Casey, a former Senate sergeant at arms, insists that business must learn to compete with labor at the grass-roots level. But in the meantime, he said, business shouldn't lay down its soft-money weapons.

Many big-name companies took that opinion to heart. AT&T, the most generous corporate contributor, was No. 3 among the top-20 soft-money contributors. It gave $3.58 million in donations, a 265 percent increase over the previous cycle. At the same time, AT&T slashed its hard-money donations in half. Another example is Freddie Mac, which earned the No. 5 slot in the rankings by contributing $2.4 million in 1999–2000, a 329 percent increase over 1995–96. Freddie Mac does not operate a PAC, which is required for hard-money donations.

Microsoft Corp., at No. 11 in the rankings, is an interesting story. It dished out $1.67 million in soft money this

Top Corporate and Labor Soft-Money Contributors

Rank, Company	1999-2000	1995-1996	% INCREASE
1. AFSCME	$5.91 million	$1.14 million	+418%
2. Service Employees Int'l Union	$3.9	$350,000	+ 1,014
3. AT&T	$3.58	$980,000	+ 265
4. United Brotherhood of Carpenters and Joiners	$2.92	$170,000	+ 1,618
5. Freddie Mac	$2.4	$560,000	+ 329
6. Communications Workers of America	$2.36	$1.15 million	+ 105
7. Philip Morris	$2.3	$3 million	-23
8. United Food & Commercial Workers Int'l Union	$2.15	$780,000	+ 176
9. SBC Communications	$1.77	$790,000	+ 124
10. Int'l Brotherhood of Electrical Workers	$1.73	$330,000	+ 424
11. Microsoft Corp.	$1.67	$77,000	+ 2,069
12. Pfizer	$1.54	$490,000	+ 214
13. American Federation of Teachers	$1.53	$540,000	+ 183
14. Bristol-Myers Squibb Co.	$1.51	$490,000	+ 208
15. National Rifle Association	$1.46	$88,000	+ 1,559
16. Verizon Communications	$1.45	$1.1 million	+ 32
17. United Parcel Service	$1.31	$190,000	+ 589
18. Federal Express	$1.28	$1.1 million	+ 15
19. Citigroup	$1.27	$570,000	+ 123
20. Sheet Metal Workers Int'l Assn.	$1.24	$240,000	+ 417
TOTAL	**$43.27 million**	**$14.13 million**	**+ 206**

time, compared with just $77,000 in 1995–96, a 2,069 percent increase. Sources familiar with Microsoft's strategy say the company's huge soft-money investment is "proportionate" with the company's expanded efforts in lobbying, grass-roots activities, and hard-dollar PAC contributions. Until recently, Microsoft had not been keen on playing the Washington political game. But since coming in, the company has deployed every tool at its disposal.

BILL GATES: In for a dime... in for $1.7 million. His company has jumped into the soft-money game with both feet.

Verizon Communications offers a more telling example of today's soft-money race. In 1995–96, when Verizon was Bell Atlantic, the company gave $1.1 million and finished No. 8 in the rankings of soft-money contributors. In 1999–2000, it boosted soft-money giving by nearly one-third, to $1.45 million, but finished at No. 16.

Philip Morris—the soft-money leader in 1995–96 at $3 million—dropped to No. 7 this cycle with $2.3 million in donations, a 23 percent decrease. RJR Nabisco, the second-ranked contributor in the previous cycle, trimmed $1 million from its soft-money budget and dropped to No. 184, while Walt Disney fell from No. 3 to No. 66 after a 45 percent decrease in contributions. Atlantic Richfield dropped from No. 4 to No. 67 following a 41 percent decrease in its soft-money contributions.

Meanwhile, a handful of other corporations have begun to bow out altogether from the soft-money race. General Motors and Time Warner (before its merger with AOL) have mostly stopped giving soft money. "We haven't seen a negative downside," GM spokesman William Noack says. "We have so many plants in so many congressional districts. I don't know if the political parties respected our decision, but they stopped knocking on our door asking for soft money."

Some of the biggest soft-money givers of 1996 slowed soft-money giving this cycle...

Rank, Company	1999-2000	1995-96	% DECREASE	'95-'96 RANK
66. Walt Disney	$740,000	$1.34 million	- 45%	3
67. Atlantic Richfield	$740,000	$1.26 million	- 41	4
70. MCI WorldCom	$730,000	$1.06 million	- 31	9
72. Joseph A. Seagram & Son	$710,000	$1.02 million	- 30	10
184. RJR Nabisco	$410,000	$1.44 million	- 72	2
323. General Electric	$260,000	$830,000	- 69	12
* Time Warner	$232,000	$640,000	- 64	27
* General Motors	$50,000	$400,000	- 88	69

...While other companies dipped in the rankings despite writing more checks

RANK, COMPANY	1999-2000	1995-96	% INCREASE	'95-96 RANK
16. Verizon Communications	$1.45 million	$1.1 million	+ 32%	8
34. Assn. of Trial Lawyers of America	$980,000	$810,000	+ 21	13
35. Anheuser-Busch Cos.	$970,000	$770,000	+ 26	17

* Not ranked among the top 400

Some in the business community are taking up the call on behalf of the McCain-Feingold-Cochran legislation. The Committee for Economic Development, a public policy organization of corporate executives and university presidents, sponsored Sen. McCain's Feb. 12 Chicago town hall rally for campaign finance reform. The group says it intends to sponsor at least one more event in the coming weeks to promote a soft-money ban. CED President Charles E. M. Kolb, who served in both the Reagan and elder Bush Administrations, argues that soft money is a bad deal for business. "I hadn't thought much about it… but the more I studied it, the more I decided I didn't want the political process to be the equivalent of a nuclear arms race."

Kolb said Sen. Mitch McConnell, R-Ky., the former chairman of the GOP's Senate campaign committee, "attacked us and tried to get our board members to quit on this issue. We were grateful for the attention, but it highlights the problem: 'If you don't play our game, we won't play with you.'"

Kolb describes himself as a conservative Republican—and "a great admirer of Sen. McConnell." But, he warns: "There are people in the business world who don't believe you have to pay to play."

That may be fine for Kolb, but Casey at the Business-Industry PAC says corporate America has to stick with soft money.

"I'm telling my guys," Casey said, "'Understand the [McCain-Feingold-Cochran approach] in its entirety.' It's not just a blanket injunction on soft money. It has a lot of impacts…. There's no reason to believe the next few election cycles won't be as close as the last one, so get-out-the-vote efforts are going to be the most important element. On the Republican side, that's been a party function [heavily] financed by soft money."

Charles Mitchell is senior editor and Brody Mullins is a reporter for National Journal's CongressDaily.

Government's End

THE REFORMERS IN THE '80S AND '90S TRIED TO PULL THE FEDERAL GOVERNMENT TO THE RIGHT OR THE LEFT. BUT, IN THE END, THEY DID NOT REMAKE GOVERNMENT. IT REMADE THEM.

By Jonathan Rauch

Since 1980, three waves of reformers have sought to transform American government. None succeeded. What went wrong? And what does it mean? In his new book Government's End: Why Washington Stopped Working—*extensively revised since its first publication in 1994 as* Demosclerosis— National Journal *senior writer Jonathan Rauch suggests an answer: The American public, having accepted limits on government's ability to change society, must now also accept equally exacting limits on society's ability to change government. An adapted excerpt follows.*

To look back upon the 1980s and 1990s is to see what appears to be, at first blush, a period of quietude following the social and political storms of the 1960s and 1970s. The Reagan and Clinton years brought fiscal wars over deficits and culture wars over abortion and political correctness, but no Vietnam, no stagflation, no dogs and fire hoses in Alabama, and no chilling confrontations between democracy and totalitarianism. Intellectuals often complained that the Reagan period was complacent and vacuous, and that the Clinton years brought the abandonment of the activist spirit that once had energized American liberalism. The appearance, though, was partly deceiving. If American society was calmer after the 1970s, American government decidedly was not, for discontent with society had been displaced by discontent with government.

The era beginning in 1981 and ending, perhaps, in 1996 marks the most concentrated period of governmental reformism since the Progressives swept to power in Washington and in the cities nearly a century earlier. There was, however, a difference. The Progressives largely succeeded in breaking the old cronyist machines and replacing them with a class of professional administrators and a "clean government" ethic (with mixed effects, by the way). The reformers in the Reagan-to-Clinton years failed. They did not remake government; it remade them.

For the Progressives, the problem had been corruption and greed and the heavy hands of the bosses, who favored friends and shut out adversaries and thereby (in the view of the day) created political monopolies as damaging to the public good as were the great economic trusts. More openness, more access, and above all more professionalism were the answers. By 1981, when President Reagan took office, the Progressive formula had been turned on its head, although at that point few people realized the extent of the change. America's government was easily among the cleanest in the world or, indeed, in history. Endless safeguards of bureaucratic procedure and legal due process ensured that any decision that was deemed arbitrary or unfair could be challenged, first in administrative rulemaking, then in court, and finally in Congress. The civil service had been professionalized— and so, more recently and probably more importantly, had been the political class. It was now not only possible but common to be a full-time, professional lobbyist or political consultant.

And access? It was copious, redundant—so copious and redundant as to transform Washington itself into the site of a bidding war. With the old congressional seniority system weakened by the post-Watergate reformers of the 1970s, Congress now consisted of 535 individual entrepreneurs, each member chosen independently of party and president, each member a canny survivalist who could be asked to follow where the committee chairman or whip led but who could not be required to do so. For the (now) countless thousands of groups that professionally worked Washington, this meant that what you did not get from one member of Congress you could seek from another. The relationship worked the other way, too. When the politicians came calling on the lobbies for campaign money, as they did with growing brazenness, each group knew there were plenty of other lobbies, often competitors and adversaries, eager to help. If the Banking Committee chairman did not get what he wanted from the American Bankers Association, why, the credit union people or S&L people or insurance people or securities people were only too willing to step into the breach. The culture of government, by 1981, was honest and professional and astonishingly transparent; no one hid anything. But the economics of government, by then, was that of a piranha pool, with thousands of small but sharp-toothed and very strongly motivated actors determined not to be the loser at the end of the day. Every actor's activity, of course, drew in yet more actors. The Maryland state lottery, once ran an ad campaign on the theme "If you don't play, you can't win." By the 1980s, Washington had become a kind of demented casino, whose slogan was "If you don't play, you can't win—but boy, can you lose!" Not surprisingly, everybody played.

PUSH, PULL:
With his ambitious health reform plan, Bill Clinton tried to move government to the left. With his Contract With America, Newt Gingrich tried to move it to the right. Both failed.

The public, of course, was angry and disillusioned by 1981. The "trust in government" barometer had collapsed since the early 1960s. Confidence in government had been replaced with cynicism and suspicion. Among conservatives, a reform movement had arisen, in tandem with the change in the government itself. The movement was not progressivism so much as regressivism, but it was equipped with a powerful and sweeping critique of government and with a grand architecture of reform. Some liberals, too, dreamed of sweeping change. Ironically, however, although the liberal reformers and conservative reformers vied to pull Washington in opposite directions, they would soon discover they were trapped together like antagonistic prisoners thrown into the same cell. Both were mostly helpless.

If you view Washington's problems as superficial and transitory—the result of having elected this or that president, or of divided partisan control of government, or

what have you—then the answer should be to elect some new leader or to consolidate power. If you think the problem is that the politicians are all the same, all empty suits wedded to the status quo, then the solution should be to elect some revolutionaries who will shake things up. If you think the problem is that reform in one direction simply goes the wrong way, then the right approach should be to try reform in the opposite direction.

As it turned out, the era of reform proved to be a uniquely useful natural laboratory for diagnosing government's condition, because many of the available permutations were tried. First the Republicans enjoyed effective control of both Congress and the White House, then the Democrats controlled both branches, and then control was divided. Far from electing empty suits, the voters on three occasions brought in strikingly fresh and energetic leaders, leaders who fervently believed in reform and who spared no effort to make it happen. And far from standing pat in moderation, the reform efforts lurched in two opposite directions. Reagan and House Speaker Newt Gingrich had pulled to the right, and had mostly failed (with a few important exceptions, such as Reagan's tax reform and Gingrich's welfare reform); Bill Clinton, with his sweeping health-care reform, had pulled to the left, but fared no better.

Yet, by the end of the 1990s, the reform era had subsided into exhaustion. The voters seemed to have given up, and there was no viable reform movement anywhere in sight. The battlefield was empty, the Bastille untaken, and the adversary little more than inconvenienced. In fact, the Washington establishment was fatter and happier than ever.

A Revolutionary's Blueprint

Of the reformers, none showed more energy and promise than Newt Gingrich. In hindsight (always the most discerning kind of vision), Gingrich seems to have been an overweening idealist who pushed his luck too far. But defeat appears inevitable only after the war. Gingrich did not enter office as House speaker without a plan. He explained it in January 1995, and it was not a stupid plan.

Gingrich was no newcomer. He went in with his eyes wide open. The power structure on Capitol Hill, he told *The Washington Times* as he assumed the speakership, had "ossified into a straitjacket. That is not partisan or ideological—these guys and their staffs had networks of power and networks of relationships and habits and things that they weren't going to break for a mere president. They'd ignored Nixon, Ford, Carter. They had blocked Reagan and beaten Bush." Moreover, "every time you mention something which ought to be shrunk or zeroed, twenty-five people who are making money off of it jump up to explain why it is a wonderful institution and they should continue to make money off it."

Gingrich's response, his battle plan, is instructive, because on paper it was plausible. First, he would mobilize his supporters, the fiery voters who had demolished Democrats and tossed out a reigning House speaker to put Gingrich and his reformers in charge. "The point we're going to make to people is, you'd better call your representative and tell them you want them to help pass the constitutional amendment to require a balanced budget—with a tax-increase limit. We're going to use every bully pulpit we have.... And we're going to tell every conservative group in the country and every group that wants smaller government, you'd better talk to your representatives." The intensity of the government reformers was high, Gingrich knew, so they could mobilize some of the same merciless spot pressure as the interest groups.

As for the Democrats, the 1994 election had thrown them into disarray. The president sounded chagrined, humbled, the wind knocked out of him. "I agree with much of what the electorate said yesterday," he said the day after the election. "They still believe that government is more often the problem than the solution. They don't want any party to be the party of government. They don't want the presumption to be that people in Washington know what's best.... I accept responsibility for not delivering to whatever extent it's my fault we haven't delivered." This humbled president would still wield a veto, but he would be presented with a stream of bills passed on the Republicans' terms in the wake of an election that had given them a mandate. If he refused to deal, he would risk seeming obstructive and deaf to the voters' demands. Anyway (said the Republicans to themselves), this was not a president who had shown a lot of backbone.

The lobbies, of course, could be counted upon to try to block or emasculate everything. Gingrich's response: swamp them. Attack so many programs at once that the Democrats and liberals and establishmentarians would have to choose the programs they wanted to save. The rest, the Republicans would knock off. The Democrats would have to "figure out which fights to stay and fight," Gingrich said. Gingrich was hoping to invert the usual Washington pattern, in which reformers were required to focus their energies on a few programs and let the rest of their agenda slide away. By attacking on a broad front, he would force the *defenders* to concentrate their fire. The Republicans would not get everything, but they would get a great deal.

Finally, Gingrich knew that at each stage of the process—House deliberations, Senate deliberations, House-Senate conferences, negotiations with the White House, presidential vetoes—he would lose bits and pieces of his agenda. A month or a year wouldn't be enough, a point he went out of his way to emphasize. Instead, he would start in 1995, running a flying wedge through the Washington power structure, and then come back again and again after that, widening the breach. There could be no "Mao-style revolution," he said. "I want to get to a dramatically smaller federal government. I think you do that

one step at a time, but you insist on steps every year.... The reason I keep telling people to study FDR is if you take fourteen steps successfully you're a lot farther down the road than this guy next to you if he's trying to get all fourteen steps in one jump."

The trouble was, of course, that he never got to the second step. Why?

The Paradox Of Particulars

Voters in the polling booth vote for "change" in the abstract. But presidents and members of Congress can't. "In Congress, we don't get to vote on the abstraction," Republican Rep. Vin Weber of Minnesota told Time Magazine in 1992, shortly before retiring from office. "We have to vote for or against actual programs." That means confronting actual constituencies. Gingrich's hope to invert this equation foundered on the fact that in the case of any *particular* program or subsidy or perquisite of whatever sort, there is almost always far more energy on the defensive side than on the offensive side.

Say someone in Gingrich's position as a House leader hoped to reform or abolish a thousand programs. No one of those programs is essential to his effort. If he must, he can always drop twenty or thirty or even a hundred or two. There is no overwhelming incentive to go after any particular constituency. To the defender of the subsidy for left-handed screwdrivers, however, only *one* program matters: his own. He will spare no effort. For that defender, and for each of the others, it's life or death.

TRUE TO FORM:
The public wants the government to be leaner, but not at the expense of students, farmers, bankers, workers, veterans, retirees.

Gingrich understood this but thought he could count on his zealous Republicans to hold the line across a broad front. The discipline he was expecting, however, was superhuman. The temptation to help out this one group, or that one, was not Democratic or liberal; it was universal. After all, the clients understood that if one congressman would not help them, another might. Every congressman understood this, too. Why let someone else do the rescuing and take the credit? And every congressman also understood that every other congressman understood. And so, at every stage in the process, Democrats *and* Republicans demanded that this or that program be let off the hook. "I'd love to support you, Mr. Speaker, but I tell you, I am just taking a beating from those left-handed screwdriver people in my district—you've got to cut me a break." Facing this inevitable onslaught, Gingrich found that it was he and his reformers, not the Democrats or liberals, who were swamped.

HARRY AND LOUISE:
With their narrow focus, lobbies are adept at defending themselves with "red alert" mailings and scary television ads.

David Stockman, Reagan's reformist budget director, had run into the same problem, and had reacted with contempt for the gutless Republicans who were all for cutting government except the bits they wanted to save. Stockman, however, missed the point: Given the calculus of the game, the gutless Republicans were doing the only rational thing. The same sort of calculus had wrecked Clinton's health-care package in 1994. In fact, what was remarkable in 1995, arguably, was not how much the reform package was watered down in Gingrich's House (with significant program terminations shrinking by a factor of ten) but how large a tattered remnant actually survived.

Gingrich understood the importance of public mobilization. He counted on it to push his program past the Democrats and Clinton. In Gingrich's case, and also in Stockman's and Clinton's, the reformers depended on the public to rally around when political hackery began to prevail over the spirit of reform. And, sure enough, the public always did rally—but *to the wrong side*.

It turns out to be surprisingly easy for the protectors of programs to spook the public by screaming bloody murder. The public wants the government to be leaner, but not at the expense of students, farmers, bankers, workers, veterans, retirees, homeowners, artists, teachers, train riders, or cats and dogs. The people cannot abide the ghoulish shrieks and moans that are heard the moment the reformers' scalpel comes out. The same narrow focus and intense commitment that make lobbies so adept at defending themselves on Capitol Hill also make them good at alarming the public with "red alert" mailings and scary television ads (as with "Harry and Louise"). When all else fails, there is the old "Don't hurt our children" ploy. In 1993, when Congress managed to abolish the wool and mohair subsidy, the reformers were all the more courageous for having faced down pleas like the one from Nelda Corbell, whose parents raised mohair in Texas: "I am eight years old and I want to know why the government wants to take away our living." What kind of monster would hurt little Nelda?

Now and then, politicians manage to turn public opinion against a particular lobby, or at least they manage to exploit a change in public opinion, as the tobacco lobby found out. But usually they can't even do that. In his 1996 presidential campaign, when Bob Dole tried to mobilize public sentiment against the teachers' unions, he was judged quixotic. The public is nervous, often rightly, when politicians try to demonize some faction or other. Public nervousness makes the climate of opinion flammable; all that remains is to light a spark.

CHOP, CHOP:
With the help of Stockman, Reagan tried to cut government programs, but encountered GOP resistance.

Rational Paranoia

In May 1981, President Reagan, on Stockman's advice, proposed a package of modest reductions in Social Security: reduced benefits for early retirees, a three-month delay in the cost-of-living adjustment, and so forth. The result was what Congressional Quarterly described as a "tempest in Congress." The Democrats until then had been helpless against Stockman, but they knew that this time he had stumbled onto vulnerable ground. The House Democratic caucus promptly and unanimously passed a resolution denouncing Reagan's "unconscionable breach of faith" and swearing not to "destroy the program or a generation of retirees." Democrats in the Senate promised to use "every rule in the book" to stop the proposal. "Democrats waged their assault with obvious glee," said Congressional Quarterly, and they kept waging it through the 1982 elections, when they gained twenty-six seats in the House and regained effective control there. Painting Reagan and the Republicans as scourges of Social Security received a good deal of the credit (the economic recession received most of the rest).

In 1995, Newt Gingrich's Republicans, responsibly and courageously, undertook to propose some modest but significant reforms of the Medicare program for the elderly. That the program's finances were in trouble, and that reductions would have to be made one way or another, were facts known to everybody in Washington, including President Clinton. He proposed reducing the growth of Medicare's costs from more than 4 percent a year for six years to 2.7 percent. The Republican plan, in not exactly sharp contrast, proposed reducing the growth path to 1.5 percent, with some larger structural reforms than Clinton preferred. In dollars, the difference between the plans was about 7 percent in the last year, 2002. But that was enough for the Democrats. Through the 1996 campaigns, they hammered the Republicans for "cutting" Medicare. "The Republicans are wrong to want to cut

Medicare benefits," a voice-over intoned in one Democratic ad, as the faces of Bob Dole and Newt Gingrich danced on the screen. "And President Clinton is right to protect Medicare, right to defend our decision as a nation to do what's moral, good, and right by our elderly." The campaign became known as Mediscare, and it was accounted a great success. The public was quite willing to believe that Gingrich and his crew were out to gut Medicare. Despite their pleas of innocence, the Republicans never recovered.

In 1993, Bill Clinton proposed his health-care reform package. In 1994 came the "Harry and Louise" ads and plenty of others like them. Again, opponents had little trouble arousing public hostility to reform. So the trick works for both parties.

It works, you may say, because the public is ignorant and easily frightened. That explanation is right, to some extent. But it fails to give the public quite enough credit, because the public's suspicions were rational in each case. When the Gingrichites tried to make changes in Medicare, they plausibly argued that the (small) pain they were imposing on one group would be more than offset by the benefits to everybody from lower deficits, lower taxes, and a solvent Medicare program. But at that stage, the Democrats and the lobbies, acting as a swing vote, did exactly as the playbook suggests. They recast the debate as group versus group rather than as group versus nation. They stood on a box with a megaphone and warned: "Don't believe those Republicans! They're not going to give anything back to you once they've cut Medicare. They're financing tax cuts for the rich! They're just taking from you to give to their friends!"

Most Americans will sacrifice for a larger public good, but few will sacrifice for a competing group. The larger public loses interest in reducing Medicare, or in reducing anything else, if it believes that the only result will be to shift resources from one group to another. By kindling suspicions that the Republicans were acting in the interests of their favorite clients rather than of the nation as a whole, the Democrats and their allied lobbies had no trouble sinking the Republicans' Medicare deal. On health reform, the Republicans and the plan's other opponents used the same tactic against Clinton and the Democrats. "This plan doesn't mean more care at lower prices," they said. "It means poorer care for you and better care for other people, with huge new bureaucracies in the bargain."

Alas, this trick of kindling mistrust can almost always be used by somebody, because the charges, though overdrawn and often misleading, are usually plausible and partly true. The Republicans *were* trying to cut Medicare while also reducing taxes for better-off citizens. The Democrats *were* relying on bureaucratic controls to constrain choices for the middle class and expand health access for the poor. In 1981, the Reagan administration *was* trying to use Social Security reductions to help pay for upper-class tax cuts. In a democracy, parties do not get things done

(or win elections) unless they favor their supporters, which means that the other side of any argument can always cry foul. And the voters' cynicism, which admittedly is often justified, makes them quick to believe charges that the system will double-cross them. The cynicism, of course, is self-fulfilling.

So here is the conundrum of collective political action. If you assume that everyone else will act in his rational self-interest, you have every reason to support politicians who put dollars or benefits or protections in your pocket, and little or no reason to support politicians who remove them. Although it is certainly possible to neutralize the opposition party and divide the lobbies and win the public's support, no sensible politician or voter ought to expect it to happen. Far more likely is the fate of the reformers of the 1980s and 1990s, who found themselves, after starting out well, suddenly staring at a coalition of opponents that comprised the opposition party, the lobbies, and the broad public. Against that array of forces, there is simply no hope. Reformers are crushed.

ON GUARD:
Lobbyists have been succesful in perpetuating a stalemate. The borders of the jungle are more or less set.

In the movie *The African Queen*, a famous scene has the protagonists' boat hopelessly stuck in a marsh—only a few yards, it turns out, from open water. Today's government is in a similar plight. Dissatisfaction ought, by rights, to open the path to comprehensive change. But it does not. The *African Queen* was lifted from the quagmire by the tide. But in the case of the American government, the boat cannot be lifted. The government is, of its nature, inseparable and inalienable from the million commitments it has made and the million interest groups it has spawned. They now form its environment. It cannot lift itself above them. With the replacement of Carter with Reagan, Bush with Clinton, and Clinton (for a while) with Gingrich, the restive electorate outside Washington showed that it could still radicalize politics, at least temporarily, and shake the very ground of the capital. Notwithstanding all the little gray groups and politicians and lobbyists and claques that occupy and ossify the government, the broad electorate proved more than able to coil itself and strike back. What was lacking in the system was not energy or leadership but the ability to focus reformist energy on any *particular* program of reform. Converting the electorate's shuddering waves of discontent into the hundreds or thousands of alterations to programs affecting specific groups is like converting earthquake energy into steam power: possible in theory but elusive in practice.

Borders of the Jungle

In ideological terms, conservatives see government as properly a guarantor of individual rights, and possibly also as a watchman for the interests of enterprise. For 150 years or so, American government conformed largely to their vision. By today's standards, it was very small and very weak, and the country's many associations were of the voluntary, nonlobbying kind that were familiar to Alexis de Tocqueville in the 1830s.

Liberals see government as properly a solver of national problems, and possibly also as a builder of a more nearly ideal society. For thirty or forty or fifty years, beginning around the time of the New Deal, the liberals had their day: The government was ambitious, undertook all sorts of commitments to pensioners and veterans and students and consumers, and seemed often successful in meeting them. But with the growth of the programs came the dense jungle of modern Washington, with all its burrowing and flying and stinging creatures; and with the growing perception of the failure—with farmers being paid not to grow food, the welfare culture expanding, the tax code becoming spaghetti, lawyers and lobbyists overrunning Washington, inflation, deficits, bureaucracies—came the backlash and the era of reform.

And now, at last, comes this, what you see around you: the perpetual stalemate of evolutionary equilibrium, in which the clients and the calculus of collective action will not allow the government to become much smaller or to reorganize its basic functions, while the taxpayers will not suffer it to grow much bigger. The borders of the jungle are more or less as they will be. From a distance, in macrocosm, the jungle seems an immovable mass, unchanging from year to year and impenetrably dense, whereas up very close, in microcosm, it is a constant turmoil of digging and scurrying and eating and mating. But it exists primarily to survive from year to year and to feed its clients. Its clients—we—draw sustenance from it but yield control.

In the end, it is not the conservative vision of government or the liberal vision that prevailed. It is no vision at all that prevailed. The client groups prevailed. And that is the end of government. To see the future, look around.

ASSOCIATIONS WITHOUT MEMBERS

BY THEDA SKOCPOL

In just a third of a century, Americans have dramatically changed their style of civic and political association. A civic world once centered in locally rooted and nationally active membership associations is a relic. Today, Americans volunteer for causes and projects, but only rarely as ongoing members. They send checks to service and advocacy groups run by professionals, often funded by foundations or professional fundraisers. Prime-time airways echo with debates among their spokespersons: the National Abortion Rights Action League debates the National Right to Life Committee; the Concord Coalition takes on the American Association of Retired Persons; and the Environmental Defense Fund counters business groups. Entertained or bemused, disengaged viewers watch as polarized advocates debate.

The largest membership groups of the 1950s were old-line and well-established, with founding dates ranging from 1733 for the Masons to 1939 for the Woman's Division of Christian Service (a Methodist women's association formed from "missionary" societies with nineteenth-century roots). Like most large membership associations throughout American history, most 1950s associations recruited members across class lines. They held regular local meetings and convened periodic assemblies of elected leaders and delegates at the state, regional, or national levels. Engaged in multiple rather than narrowly specialized pursuits, many associations combined social or ritual activities with community service, mutual aid, and involvement in national affairs. Patriotism was a leitmotif; during and after World War II, a passionate and victorious national endeavor, these associations sharply expanded their memberships and renewed the vigor of their local and national activities.

To be sure, very large associations were not the only membership federations that mattered in postwar America. Also prominent were somewhat smaller, elite-dominated civic groups—including male service groups like Rotary, Lions, and Kiwanis, and longstanding female groups like the American Association of University Women and the League of Women Voters. Dozens of ethnically based fraternal and cultural associations flourished, as did African-American fraternal groups like the Prince Hall Masons and the Improved Benevolent and Protective Order of Elks of the World.

For many membership federations, this was a golden era of national as well as community impact. Popularly rooted membership federations rivaled professional and business associations for influence in policy debates. The AFL-CIO was in the thick of struggles about economic and social policies; the American Legion and the Veterans of Foreign Wars advanced veterans' programs; the American Farm Bureau Federation (AFBF) joined other farmers' associations to influence national and state agricultural policies; and the National Congress of Parents and Teachers (PTA) and the General Federation of Women's Clubs were influential on educational, health, and family issues. The results could be decisive, as exemplified by the pivotal role of the American Legion in drafting and lobbying for the GI Bill of 1944.

Then, suddenly, old-line membership federations seemed passé. Upheavals shook America during "the long 1960s," stretching from the mid-1950s through the mid-1970s. The southern Civil Rights movement challenged white racial domination and spurred legislation to enforce legal equality and voting rights for African Americans. Inspired by Civil Rights achievements, additional "rights" movements exploded, promoting equality for women, dignity for homosexuals, the unionization of farm workers, and the mobilization of other nonwhite ethnic minorities. Movements arose to oppose U.S. involvement in the war in Vietnam, champion a new environmentalism, and further other public causes. At the forefront of these groundswells were younger Americans, especially from the growing ranks of college students and university graduates.

The great social movements of the long 1960s were propelled by combinations of grassroots protest, activist radicalism, and professionally led efforts to lobby government and educate the public. Some older membership associations ended up participating and expanding their bases of support, yet the groups that sparked movements were more agile and flexibly structured than pre-existing membership federations.

The model of civic effectiveness has been upended since the 1960s. Activist groups no longer need actual members.

The upheavals of the 1960s could have left behind a reconfigured civic world, in which some old-line membership associations had declined but others had reoriented and reenergized themselves. Within each great social movement, memberships could have consolidated and groups coalesced into new omnibus federations able to link the grass roots to state, regional, and national leaderships, allowing longstanding American civic traditions to continue in new ways.

But this is not what happened. Instead, the 1960s, 1970s, and 1980s brought extraordinary organizational proliferation and professionalization. At the national level alone, the *Encyclopedia of Associations* listed approximately 6,500 associations in 1958. This total grew by 1990 to almost 23,000. Within the expanding group universe, moreover, new kinds of associations came to the fore: relatively centralized and professionally led organizations focused on policy lobbying and public education.

Another wave of the advocacy explosion involved "public interest" or "citizens'" groups seeking to shape public opinion and influence legislation. Citizens' advocacy groups espouse "causes" ranging from environmental protection (for example, the Sierra Club and the Environmental Defense Fund), to the well-being of poor children (the Children's Defense Fund), to reforming politics (Common Cause) and cutting public entitlements (the Concord Coalition).

THE FORTUNES OF MEMBERSHIP ASSOCIATIONS

As the associational explosions of 1960 to 1990 took off, America's once large and confident membership federations were not only bypassed in national politics; they also dwindled as locally rooted participant groups. To be sure, some membership associations have been founded or expanded in recent decades. By far the largest is the American Association of Retired Persons (AARP), which now boasts more than 33 million adherents, about one-half of all Americans aged 50 or older. But AARP is not a democratically controlled organization. Launched in 1958 with backing from a teachers' retirement group and an insurance company, the AARP grew rapidly in the 1970s and 1980s by offering commercial discounts to members and establishing a Washington headquarters to monitor and lobby about federal legislation affecting seniors. The AARP has a legislative and policy staff of 165 people, 28 registered lobbyists, and more than 1,200 staff members in the field. After recent efforts to expand its regional and local infrastructure, the AARP involves about 5 to 10 percent of its members in (undemocratic) membership chapters. But for the most part, the AARP national office—covering an entire city block with its own zip code—deals with masses of individual adherents through the mail.

Four additional recently expanded membership associations use modern mass recruitment methods, yet are also rooted in local and state units. Interestingly, these groups are heavily involved in partisan electoral politics. Two recently launched groups are the National Right to Life Committee (founded in 1973) and the Christian Coalition (founded in 1989). They bridge from church congregations, through which they recruit members and activists, to the conservative wing of the Republican Party, through which they exercise political influence. Two old-line membership federations—the National Education Association (founded in 1857) and the National Rifle Association (founded in 1871)—experienced explosive growth after reorienting themselves to take part in partisan politics. The NRA expanded in the 1970s, when right-wing activists opposed to gun control changed what had traditionally been a network of marksmen's clubs into a conservative, Republican-leaning advocacy group fiercely opposed to gun control legislation. During the same period, the NEA burgeoned from a relatively elitist association of public educators into a quasi-union for public school teachers and a stalwart in local, state, and national Democratic Party politics.

Although they fall short of enrolling 1 percent of the adult population, some additional chapter-based membership associations were fueled by the social movements of the 1960s and 1970s. From 1960 to 1990, the Sierra Club (originally created in 1892) ballooned from some 15,000 members to 565,000 members meeting in 378 "local groups." And the National Audubon Society (founded in 1905) went from 30,000 members and 330 chapters in 1958 to about 600,000 members and more than 500 chapters in the 1990s. The National Organization for Women (NOW) reached 1,122 members and 14 chapters within a year of its founding in 1966, and spread across all 50 states with some 125,000 members meeting in 700 chapters by 1978. But notice that these "1960s" movement associations do not match the organizational scope of old-line membership federations. At its post-World War II high point in 1955, for example, the General Federation of Women's Clubs boasted more than 826,000 members meeting in 15,168 local clubs, themselves divided into representative networks within each of the 50 states plus the District of Columbia. By contrast, at its high point in 1993, NOW reported some 280,000 members and 800 chapters, with no intermediate tier of representative governance between the national center and local chapters. These membership associations certainly matter, but mainly as counterexamples to dominant associational trends—of organizations without members.

After nearly a century of civic life rooted in nation-spanning membership federations, why was America's associational universe so transformed? A variety of factors have contributed, including racial and gender change; shifts in the political opportunity structure; new techniques and models for building organizations; and recent transformations in U.S. class relations. Taken together, I suggest, these account for civic America's abrupt and momentous transition from membership to advocacy.

SOCIETY DECOMPARTMENTALIZED

Until recent times, most American membership associations enrolled business and professional people together with white-collar folks, farmers, and craft or industrial workers. There was a degree of fellowship across class lines—yet at the price of other kinds of exclusions. With only a few exceptions, old-line associations enrolled either men or women, not both together (although male-only fraternal and veterans' groups often had ties to ladies' auxiliaries). Racial separation was also the rule. Although African Americans did manage to create and greatly expand fraternal associations of their own, they unquestionably resented exclusion by the parallel white fraternals.

> The styles of civic involvement have changed, especially for women—much to the disadvantage of associations trying to hold regular meetings.

Given the pervasiveness of gender and racial separation in classic civic America, established voluntary associations were bound to be shaken after the 1950s. Moreover, changing gender roles and identities blended with other changing values to undercut not just membership appeals but long-standing routes to associational leadership. For example, values of patriotism, brotherhood, and sacrifice had been celebrated by all fraternal groups. During and after each war, the Masons, Knights of Pythias, Elks, Knights of Columbus, Moose, Eagles, and scores of other fraternal groups celebrated and memorialized the contributions of their soldier-members. So did women's auxiliaries, not to mention men's service clubs and trade union "brotherhoods." But "manly" ideals of military service faded after the early 1960s as America's bitter experiences during the war in Vietnam disrupted the intergenerational continuity of male identification with martial brotherliness.

In the past third of a century, female civic leadership has changed as much or more than male leadership. Historically, U.S. women's associations—ranging from female auxiliaries of male groups to independent groups like the General Federation of Women's Clubs, the PTA, and church-connected associations—benefited from the activism of educated wives and mothers. Although a tiny fraction of all U.S. females, higher-educated women were a surprisingly substantial and widespread presence—because the United States was a pioneer in the schooling of girls and the higher education of women. By 1880, some 40,000 American women constituted a third of all students in U.S. institutions of higher learning; women's share rose to nearly half at the early twentieth-century peak in 1920, when some 283,000 women were enrolled in institutions of higher learning. Many higher-educated women of the late 1800s and early 1900s married immediately and stayed out of the paid labor force. Others taught for a time in primary and secondary schools, then got married and stopped teaching (either voluntarily or because school systems would not employ married women). Former teachers accumulated in every community. With skills to make connections within and across communities—and some time on their hands as their children grew older—former teachers and other educated women became mainstays of classic U.S. voluntary life.

Of course, more American women than ever before are now college-educated. But contemporary educated women face new opportunities and constraints. Paid work and family responsibilities are no longer separate spheres, and the occupational structure is less sex-segregated at all levels. Today, even married women with children are very likely to be employed, at least part-time. Despite new time pressures, educated and employed women have certainly not dropped out of civic life. Women employed part-time are more likely to be members of groups or volunteers than housewives; and fully employed women are often drawn into associations or civic projects through work. Yet styles of civic involvement have changed—much to the disadvantage of broad-gauged associations trying to hold regular meetings.

THE LURE OF WASHINGTON, D.C.

The centralization of political change in Washington, D.C. also affected the associational universe. Consider the odyssey of civil rights lawyer Marian Wright Edelman. Fresh from grass-roots struggles in Mississippi, she arrived in Washington, D.C. in the late 1960s to lobby for Mississippi's Head Start program. She soon realized that arguing on behalf of children might be the best way to influence legislation and sway public sympathy in favor of the poor, including African Americans. So between 1968 and 1973 Edelman obtained funding from major foundations and developed a new advocacy and policy research association, the Children's Defense Fund (CDF). With a skillful staff, a small national network of individual supporters, ties to social service agencies and foundations, and excellent relationships with the national media, the CDF has been a determined proponent of federal antipoverty programs ever since. The CDF has also worked with Democrats and other liberal advocacy groups to expand such efforts; and during periods of conservative Republican ascendancy, the CDF has been a fierce (if not always successful) defender of federal social programs.

Activists, in short, have gone where the action is. In this same period, congressional committees and their staffs subdivided and multiplied. During the later 1970s and 1980s, the process of group formation became self-reinforcing—not only because groups arose to counter other groups, but also because groups begot more groups. Because businesses and citizens use advocacy groups to influence government outside of parties and between elections, it is not surprising that the contemporary group explosion coincides with waning voter loyalty to the two major political parties. As late as the 1950s, U.S. political parties were networks of local and state organizations through which party officials often brokered nominations, cooperated with locally rooted membership associations, and sometimes directly mobilized voters. The party structure and the associational structure were mutually reinforcing.

> In the new electoral arena, where political parties consist largely of direct mailings and fundraisers, advocacy groups can play an influential role.

Then, demographic shifts, reapportionment struggles, and the social upheavals of the 1960s disrupted old party organizations; and changes in party rules led to nomination elections that favored activists and candidate-centered efforts over backroom brokering by party insiders. Such "reforms" were meant to enhance grassroots participation, but in practice have furthered oligarchical ways of running elections. No longer the preserve of party organizations, U.S. campaigns are now managed by coteries of media consultants, pollsters, direct mail specialists, and—above all—fundraisers. In this revamped electoral arena, advocacy groups have much to offer, hoping to get access to elected officials in return for helping candidates. In low-turnout battles to win party nominations, even groups with modest mail

memberships may be able to field enough (paid or unpaid) activists to make a difference. At all stages of the electoral process, advocacy groups with or without members can provide endorsements that may be useful in media or direct mail efforts. And PACs pushing business interests or public interest causes can help candidates raise the huge amounts of money they need to compete.

A NEW MODEL OF ASSOCIATION-BUILDING

Classic American association-builders took it for granted that the best way to gain national influence, moral or political, was to knit together national, state, and local groups that met regularly and engaged in a degree of representative governance. Leaders who desired to speak on behalf of masses of Americans found it natural to proceed by recruiting self-renewing mass memberships and spreading a network of interactive groups. After the start-up phase, associational budgets usually depended heavily on membership dues and on sales of newsletters or supplies to members and local groups. Supporters had to be continuously recruited through social networks and person-to-person contacts. And if leverage over government was desired, an association had to be able to influence legislators, citizens, and newspapers across many districts. For all of these reasons, classic civic entrepreneurs with national ambitions moved quickly to recruit activists and members in every state and across as many towns and cities as possible within each state.

Today, nationally ambitious civic entrepreneurs proceed in quite different ways. When Marian Wright Edelman launched a new advocacy and research group to lobby for the needs of children and the poor, she turned to private foundations for funding and then recruited an expert staff of researchers and lobbyists. In the early 1970s, when John Gardner launched Common Cause as a "national citizens lobby" demanding governmental reforms, he arranged for start-up contributions from several wealthy friends, contacted reporters in the national media, and purchased mailing lists to solicit masses of members giving modest monetary contributions. Patron grants, direct mail techniques, and the capacity to convey images and messages through the mass media have changed the realities of organization building and maintenance.

The very model of civic effectiveness has been upended since the 1960s. No longer do civic entrepreneurs think of constructing vast federations and recruiting interactive citizen-members. When a new cause (or tactic) arises, activists envisage opening a national office and managing association-building as well as national projects from the center. Even a group aiming to speak for large numbers of Americans does not absolutely need members. And if mass adherents are recruited through the mail, why hold meetings? From a managerial point of view, interactions with groups of members may be downright inefficient. In the old-time membership federations, annual elections of leaders and a modicum of representative governance went hand in hand with membership dues and interactive meetings. But for the professional executives of today's advocacy organizations, direct mail members can be more appealing because, as Kenneth Godwin and Robert Cameron Mitchell explain, "they contribute without 'meddling'" and "do not take part in leadership selection or policy discussions." This does not mean the new advocacy groups are malevolent; they are just responding rationally to the environment in which they find themselves.

ASSOCIATIONAL CHANGE AND DEMOCRACY

This brings us, finally, to what may be the most civically consequential change in late-twentieth-century America: the rise of a very large, highly educated upper middle class in which "expert" professionals are prominent along with businesspeople and managers. When U.S. professionals were a tiny, geographically dispersed stratum, they understood themselves as "trustees of community," in the terminology of Stephen Brint. Working closely with and for nonprofessional fellow citizens in thousands of towns and cities, lawyers, doctors, ministers, and teachers once found it quite natural to join—and eventually help to lead—locally rooted, cross-class voluntary associations. But today's professionals are more likely to see themselves as expert individuals who can best contribute to national well-being by working with other specialists to tackle complex technical or social problems.

Cause-oriented advocacy groups offer busy, privileged Americans a rich menu of opportunities to, in effect, hire other professionals and managers to represent their values and interests in public life. Why should highly trained and economically well-off elites spend years working their way up the leadership ladders of traditional membership federations when they can take leading staff roles at the top, or express their preferences by writing a check?

If America has experienced a great civic transformation from membership to advocacy—so what? Most traditional associations were racially exclusive and gender segregated; and their policy efforts were not always broad-minded. More than a few observers suggest that recent civic reorganizations may be for the best. American public life has been rejuvenated, say the optimists, by social movements and advocacy groups fighting for social rights and an enlarged understanding of the public good.

Local community organizations, neighborhood groups, and grassroots protest movements nowadays tap popular energies and involve people otherwise left out of organized politics. And social interchanges live on in small support groups and occasional volunteering. According to the research of Robert Wuthnow, about 75 million men and women, a remarkable 40 percent of the adult population, report taking part in "a small group that meets regularly and provides caring and support for those who participate in it." Wuthnow estimates that there may be some 3 million such groups, including Bible study groups, 12-step self-help groups, book discussion clubs, singles groups, hobby groups, and disease support groups. Individuals find community, spiritual connection, introspection, and personal gratification in small support groups. Meanwhile, people reach

out through volunteering. As many as half of all Americans give time to the community this way, their efforts often coordinated by paid social service professionals. Contemporary volunteering can be intermittent and flexibly structured, an intense one-shot effort or spending "an evening a week on an activity for a few months as time permits, rather than having to make a long-term commitment to an organization."

In the optimistic view, the good civic things Americans once did are still being done—in new ways and in new settings. But if we look at U.S. democracy in its entirety and bring issues of power and social leverage to the fore, then optimists are surely overlooking the downsides of our recently reorganized civic life. Too many valuable aspects of the old civic America are not being reproduced or reinvented in the new public world of memberless organizations.

Despite the multiplicity of voices raised within it, America's new civic universe is remarkably oligarchical. Because today's advocacy groups are staff-heavy and focused on lobbying, research, and media projects, they are managed from the top with few opportunities for member leverage from below. Even when they have hundreds of thousands of adherents, contemporary associations are heavily tilted toward upper-middle-class constituencies. Whether we are talking about memberless advocacy groups, advocacy groups with some chapters, mailing-list associations, or nonprofit institutions, it is hard to escape the conclusion that the wealthiest and best-educated Americans are much more privileged in the new civic world than their (less numerous) counterparts were in the pre-1960s civic world of cross-class membership federations.

Mostly, they involve people in "doing for" others—feeding the needy at a church soup kitchen; tutoring children at an after-school clinic; or guiding visitors at a museum exhibit—rather than in "doing with" fellow citizens. Important as such volunteering may be, it cannot substitute for the central citizenship functions that membership federations performed.

A top-heavy civic world not only encourages "doing for" rather than "doing with." It also distorts national politics and public policymaking. Imagine for a moment what might have happened if the GI Bill of 1944 had been debated and legislated in a civic world configured more like the one that prevailed during the 1993–1994 debates over the national health insurance proposal put forward by the first administration of President Bill Clinton. This is not an entirely fanciful comparison, because goals supported by the vast majority of Americans were at issue in both periods: in the 1940s, care and opportunity for millions of military veterans returning from World War II; in the 1990s, access for all Americans to a modicum of health insurance coverage. Back in the 1940s, moreover, there were elite actors—university presidents, liberal intellectuals, and conservative congressmen—who could have condemned the GI Bill to the same fate as the 1990s health security plan. University presidents and liberal New Dealers initially favored versions of the GI Bill that would have been bureaucratically complicated, niggardly with public expenditures, and extraordinarily limited in veterans' access to subsidized higher education.

But in the actual civic circumstances of the 1940s, elites did not retain control of public debates or legislative initiatives. Instead, a vast voluntary membership federation, the American Legion, stepped in and drafted a bill to guarantee every one of the returning veterans up to four years of post–high school education, along with family and employment benefits, business loans, and home mortgages. Not only did the Legion draft one of the most generous pieces of social legislation in American history, thousands of local Legion posts and dozens of state organizations mounted a massive public education and lobbying campaign to ensure that even conservative congressional representatives would vote for the new legislation.

Half a century later, the 1990s health security episode played out in a transformed civic universe dominated by advocacy groups, pollsters, and big-money media campaigns. Top-heavy advocacy groups did not mobilize mass support for a sensible reform plan. Hundreds of business and professional groups influenced the Clinton administration's complex policy schemes, and then used a combination of congressional lobbying and media campaigns to block new legislation. Both the artificial polarization and the elitism of today's organized civic universe may help to explain why increasing numbers of Americans are turned off by and pulling back from public life. Large majorities say that wealthy "special interests" dominate the federal government, and many Americans express cynicism about the chances for regular people to make a difference. People may be entertained by advocacy clashes on television, but they are also ignoring many public debates and withdrawing into privatism. Voting less and less, American citizens increasingly act—and claim to feel—like mere spectators in a polity where all the sig-nificant action seems to go on above their heads, with their views ignored by pundits and clashing partisans.

From the nineteenth through the mid-twentieth century, American democracy flourished within a unique matrix of state and society. Not only was America the world's first manhood democracy and the first nation in the world to establish mass public education. It also had a uniquely balanced civic life, in which markets expanded but could not subsume civil society, in which governments at multiple levels deliberately and indirectly encouraged federated voluntary associations. National elites had to pay attention to the values and interests of millions of ordinary Americans.

Over the past third of a century, the old civic America has been bypassed and shoved to the side by a gaggle of professionally dominated advocacy groups and nonprofit institutions rarely attached to memberships worthy of the name. Ideals of shared citizenship and possibilities for democratic leverage have been compromised in the process. Since the 1960s, many good things have happened in America. New voices are now heard, and there have been invaluable gains in equality and liberty. But vital links in the nation's associational life have frayed, and we may need to find creative ways to repair those links if America is to avoid becoming a country of detached spectators. There is no going back to the civic world we have lost. But we Americans can and should look for ways to recreate the best of our civic past in new forms suited to a renewed democratic future.

The World According to AARP

Horace Deets's organization is bigger than ever, but is it losing its edge as a force for the elderly?

By STEVEN A. HOLMES

WASHINGTON

EVERY day, across the country, the letters arrive with the inevitability of taxes and death—which is just what some recipients think of when they open them.

"Dear friend," comes the greeting. "The enclosed AARP card has never been more valuable to you than it is today." Some who get the letter view it with dread or with humor, but since all recipients have just turned 50, they cannot help but see it as a symbol: they have just crossed a Rubicon.

The humorist Bill Geist once wrote that with the end of the draft and the arrest of the Unabomber, the AARP letter is the most feared piece of mail a person can get.

Yet the organization that mails nine million of these letters each month—and last year sent one to Mark Spitz, Stevie Wonder, Morgan Fairchild and David Cassidy, among others—is famous for more than just reminding people of something they would rather forget. Over the years, AARP—formerly known as the American Association of Retired Persons—has become the older American's 800-pound gorilla, known for its sheer size and political muscle. Its membership, 33.4 million, is bigger than the population of Canada, and represents 45 percent of Americans 50 and older. Those letters may cause some resentment, but they are effective.

AARP's annual budget of $435 million is about three times the size of the National Rifle Association's. For the last three years it has topped Fortune magazine's survey as the most effective lobbying organization in Washington.

And this behemoth may be about to grow bigger. The huge post-World War II cohort of baby boomers is starting to swell AARP's ranks. Americans are turning 50 at the rate of 1 every 7.6 seconds; in the next 30 years, the number of people aged 65 or older will double, to 20 percent of the population.

"The demographics are on our side," Horace B. Deets, the group's executive director, once told an interviewer.

But even as Mr. Deets, 62, prepares to step down later this year, there are signs that all has not been well with the organization he has headed since 1988. Membership grew at 20 percent a year in the 12 years before Mr. Deets took over, powered partly by AARP's lowering the eligibility age to 50 from 55 in 1984. Membership growth slowed to 1 percent a year during his tenure. From 1996 to 1999, the last year for which complete financial data are available, revenue from dues, which makes up 32 percent of AARP's income, was relatively flat.

And there has been a series of embarrassments. In 1994, AARP, a nonprofit group, agreed to pay the Internal Revenue Service $135 million to resolve a dispute over its business income from 1985 through 1993. The group paid $15 million in lieu of back taxes in 1994 and 1995, and another $52 million two years ago. And it had to spin off a commercial subsidiary that sold insurance and other services to its members. Two years ago, the Postal Service fined AARP $5.6 million, citing it for illegally mailing millions of solicitations for commercial insurance. The Postal Service said that AARP should have been paying a commercial rate for postage rather than the cheaper rate charged to nonprofit agencies.

This is not the worst of it. Notwithstanding the Fortune designation, some Congressional staff members and dispassionate observers say AARP, once in the forefront of legislative battles like the fight over cutting Social Security cost-of-living increases, has lost its lobbying edge, adopting a more cautious approach out of fear that a strident tone might alienate some of its members, once largely Democratic but now roughly divided between Democrats and Republicans.

"I've almost stopped thinking of them as a lobby," said a House Democratic staff member familiar with the group's work on Capitol Hill. "They have all kinds of valuable member services and do really good research work. But in terms of being a tough lobby, they're not what they used to be."

Yet of all the challenges that AARP faces, perhaps the greatest is keeping a cohesive purpose and sense of direction with a membership that is split by an age gap and a sense of identity. The organization may be poised to achieve explosive growth, but it also has to figure out how to appeal to people who are 50 to 65 and still working, while remaining relevant to older retirees. How, for example, will AARP ultimately come down on the issue of privatizing Social Security, which many

175

younger members might favor, when retirees fear such a move might lead to a cut in their benefits?

John Rother, AARP's chief lobbyist in Washington, responded to these concerns. "Part of the Social Security debate that everyone would expect us to be prominent in would be to protect current beneficiaries," he said. "And if we were just a membership organization for people 65 and above, maybe that's where we would spend most of our energy.

"But because we're putting so much focus now on the younger group, it pushes us to think much longer-term," Mr. Rother continued. "So we're putting just as much emphasis on pensions and savings that people can do in their working years as we are on the traditional Social Security system itself."

Those intellectual, marketing and lobbying strains will only intensify in the future. Sixty percent of AARP's membership is currently 65 and over; 40 percent is between 50 and 65. With the baby boomers, those proportions may change. And if the differences between the two groups sunder AARP's mission and outlook—there is no guarantee that it will—then its size could turn from an asset to a liability.

The challenges of bigness are nothing new for AARP. The group was founded in 1958 by Dr. Ethel Andrus, a retired educator who as head of the National Retired Teachers Association was concerned that many of her members could not obtain health insurance. Dr. Andrus struck up a partnership with Colonial Penn Life Insurance, whose marketing of insurance through the association helped increase the group's appeal.

The association's explosive growth came under Cyril F. Brickfield, a back-slapping hail fellow who took over in 1967 when the group had about one million members. By the time Mr. Brickfield stepped down in 1987, membership was 28 million.

He was followed by Jack Carlson, a former chief economist at the Office of Management and Budget in the Nixon administration. Mr. Carlson lasted only 15 weeks before being forced out. Association officials said he and the group's directors did not agree on his desire to restructure the group's businesses to make each operation pay for itself. Mr. Carlson accused the group of slovenly management.

If Mr. Brickfield, the group's most famous leader, was a man about Washington, Mr. Deets, who became executive director in 1988, is about as low-key as they come. At a time when the heads of interest groups are media stars, Mr. Deets prefers to work in the background. To many in Washington his name seems to be Horace Who?

Though his penchant is for strategic thinking and management reforms, Mr. Deets has spent much of his time putting out brush fires. Not long after he took over, the association was criticized for supporting legislation that set up a catastrophic health insurance plan in Medicare.

The measure, the biggest expansion of Medicare since its inception in 1965, provided insurance for elderly people beset by huge medical bills for major illnesses. But some seniors with higher incomes objected to the plan's $60-a-year increase in Medicare premiums and its annual surtax that ran as high as $800.

Howls from a group of higher-income older people prompted Congress to repeal the program in 1989. But some turned their scorn on the AARP. Mr. Deets, who still defends the group's support for catastrophic care, estimated that 12,000 to 14,000 members resigned in protest. For a group with nearly 30 million members, the loss was minuscule. But the experience was searing.

"We learned some tough lessons out of that repeal," Mr. Rother said. "One thing we learned was that it wasn't sufficient to just do the policy analysis here in Washington. You really had to lay the groundwork all across the country."

The setback helped spur AARP to open more state offices, an idea that had been resisted by AARP leadership, which feared it would lead to fragmentation. But with so many government functions devolving to the states, establishing a stronger grass-roots network has taken on an importance beyond setting up structures that communicate what the group is doing in Washington.

"So much of what is done that affects the audience we serve is either funded, regulated or delivered at the state level," Mr. Deets said. "If you're going to be effective in serving your members' needs, you have to be a player at the state level."

In 1988, the group had 10 regional offices and one state office. By the end of this year, it will have 53 offices, one in every state and major territory. AARP employs about 1,900 people and enlists about 3.4 million volunteers.

AARP may have learned something else from the travails of catastrophic health insurance—political caution. "This was considered a major blunder by the Washington operation in that they got out ahead of their members," said a Democratic Congressional staff member. "They haven't gotten over it yet."

Since then, the knock on AARP has been that it has tried to maintain a middle ground so it would not be closely identified with either party. This was further sharpened by the Republicans' capture of Congress in 1994, and the wafer-thin margins that now divide the House and the Senate. With AARP's membership evenly divided politically, the leadership has felt the need to cling to the middle so as not to jeopardize either the $141 million it gets from dues or the $161 million in royalties from the sale of goods and services like insurance and prescription drugs that carry the AARP imprimatur. Or so the argument goes.

In addition to lobbying, AARP researches issues important to older people and organizes volunteers for community projects. For $12 a year, members receive discounts on prescription drugs, travel, car rentals and other services, including advice on financial planning and health.

"They don't want to lose membership, because membership feeds into all their products," said Robert Binstock, a professor of aging, health and society at Case Western Reserve University in Cleveland. "I think that's what they are trying to do—do enough advocacy for the aging so it seems like they're doing the right thing, but not enough to seem radical."

Curiously, AARP officials do not disagree with this assessment, though they say the part about being primarily motivated by money is overstated.

"AARP has developed a certain lobbying position," said William Novelli, an associate executive director of the organization and a possible successor to Mr. Deets. "What it boils down to is, don't get way out in front of your membership. We're not Planned Parenthood. Try to work with both sides, bring them together, keep raising the bar in terms of what you want. When you represent 34 1/2 million people, the majority of whom vote, you don't have to smack people in the head with a stick."

Mr. Novelli promised that in the future, AARP would take more of a leadership role in lobbying efforts, would build its grass roots into a more potent force and would become more forceful on issues like pensions. But do not expect it to become a strident voice identifying strongly with one side or the other on Capitol Hill.

"If you come down hard on somebody, you're going to rile up a certain percent of your own members," Mr. Novelli said. "Of course, then they'll go to your membership and try to turn them against you."

These days AARP is trying not only to make sure no one turns its members against it but also to enroll more baby boomers.

The organization is in the middle of a five-year effort to figure how to attract younger members. It has started a $100 million campaign to erase its image as an organization for old people. In 1998, it changed its name, dropping the periods in its acronym, along with its dowdy title.

Earlier this year AARP started a magazine, My Generation, which is offered to younger members instead of Modern Maturity, which will continue to go to older members. "We've known for several years that we had to start reaching out for a younger audience," said Martha Ramsey, the director of publications. The premier issue, with the actor Ed Harris on the cover, featured articles on subjects like technology and gadgets, financial planning and camps offering trapeze lessons.

Whether all this will attract the baby boomers, and whether these new members can keep the organization together, Mr. Deets and the AARP leaders are determined that if the organization goes the way of the dinosaur, it will not be out of complacency.

Recently Mr. Deets read a book by Peter Drucker that contained these words, " 'Those whom the gods would destroy are first granted 40 years of business success.'"

AARP is 43 years old.

From the *New York Times,* March 21, 2001, pp. D1, D8. © 2001 by The New York Times Company. Reprinted by permission.

JOURNALISM & DEMOCRACY

ON THE IMPORTANCE OF BEING A 'PUBLIC NUISANCE'

by BILL MOYERS

Hi. My name is Bill, and I'm a recovering Unimpeachable Source. I understand "Unimpeachable Source" is now an oxymoron in Washington, as in "McCain Republican" or "Democratic Party." But once upon a time in a far away place—Washington in the 1960s—I was one. Deep Backgrounders and Unattributable Tips were my drugs of choice. Just go to Austin and listen to me on those tapes LBJ secretly recorded. That's the sound of a young man getting high… without inhaling. I swore off thirty-four years ago last month, and I'm here to tell you, it hasn't been easy to stay clean. I can't even watch *The West Wing* without breaking into a sweat. A C-SPAN briefing by Ari Fleischer pushes me right to the edge. But I know one shot—just one—and I could wind up like my friend David Gergen, in and out of revolving doors and needing to go on *The NewsHour* for a fix between Presidents.

But I'm not here to talk about my time in the White House. I haven't talked much about it at all, though I do plan to write about it someday soon. During the past three and a half decades, I have learned that the job of trying to tell the truth about people whose job it is to hide the truth is almost as complicated and difficult as trying to hide it in the first place. Unless you're willing to fight and refight the same battles until you go blue in the face, to drive the people you work with nuts going over every last detail to make certain you've got it right, and then to take hit after unfair hit accusing you of having a "bias," or these days even a point of view, there's no use even in trying. You have to love it, and I do.

I always have. Journalism is what I wanted to do since I was a kid. Fifty years ago, on my 16th birthday, I went to work at the *Marshall News Messenger*. The daily newspaper in a small Texas town seemed like the best place in the world to be a cub reporter. It was small enough to navigate but big enough to keep me busy, happy and learning something new every day. I was lucky. Some of the old-timers were out sick or on vacation and I got assigned to cover the Housewives' Rebellion. Fifteen women in Marshall refused to pay the new Social Security withholding tax for their domestic workers. The rebels argued that Social Security was unconstitutional, that imposing it was taxa-

tion without representation, and that—here's my favorite part—"requiring us to collect [the tax] is no different from requiring us to collect the garbage." They hired themselves a lawyer—Martin Dies, the ex-Congressman best known (or worst known) for his work as head of the House Committee on Un-American Activities in the 1930s and 1940s. Eventually the women wound up paying the tax—while holding their noses. The stories I wrote for the *News Messenger* were picked up and moved on the Associated Press wire. And I was hooked.

Two years later, as a sophomore in college, I decided I wanted to become a political journalist and figured experience in Washington would show me the ropes. I wrote a man I had never met, a United States senator named Lyndon Johnson, and asked him for a summer job. Lucky again, I got it. And at summer's end LBJ and Lady Bird offered me a job on their television station in Austin for $100 a week. Looking back on all that followed—seminary, the Peace Corps, the White House, *Newsday*, PBS, CBS and PBS again—I often think of what Joseph Lelyveld, the executive editor of the *New York Times*, told some aspiring young journalists. "You can never know how a life in journalism will turn out," he said.

> *It took me awhile to learn that what's important in journalism is not how close you are to power but how close you are to reality.*

It took me awhile after the White House to learn that what's important in journalism is not how close you are to power but how close you are to reality. Journalism took me there: to famine in Africa, war in Central America, into the complex world of inner-city families in Newark and to working-class families in Milwaukee struggling to survive the good times. My life in journalism has been a continuing course in adult education. From colleagues—from producers like Sherry Jones—I keep learning about journalism as storytelling. Sherry and I have been collaborating off and on for a quarter of a century, from the time we did the very first documentary ever about political action committees. I can still see the final scene in that film—yard after yard of computer printout listing campaign contributions unfurled like toilet paper stretching all the way across the Capitol grounds.

That one infuriated just about everyone, including friends of public television. PBS took the heat and didn't melt. When Sherry and I reported the truth behind the news of the Iran/*contra* scandal for a *Frontline* documentary called "High Crimes and Misdemeanors," the right-wing Taliban in town went running to their ayatollahs in Congress, who decried the fact that public television was committing—horrors—journalism. The Clinton White House didn't like it a bit, either, when Sherry and I reported on Washington's Other Scandal, about the Democrats' unbridled and illegal fundraising of 1996.

If PBS didn't flinch, neither did my corporate underwriter for ten years now, Mutual of America Life Insurance Company. Before Mutual of America I had lost at least three corporate underwriters, who were happy as long as we didn't make anyone else unhappy. Losing your underwriting will keep the yellow light of caution flickering in a journalist's unconscious. I found myself—and I could kick myself for this—not even proposing controversial subjects to potential underwriters because I had told myself, convinced myself: "Nah, not a chance!" Then Mutual of America came along and the yellow light flickers no more. This confluence of good fortune and good colleagues has made it possible for us to do programs that the networks dare not contemplate.

Commercial television has changed since the days when I was hired as chief correspondent for CBS Reports, the documentary unit. A big part of the problem is ratings. It's not easy, as John Dewey said, to interest the public in the public interest. In fact, I'd say that apart from all the technology, the biggest change in my thirty years in broadcasting has been the shift of content from news about government to consumer-driven information and celebrity features. The Project for Excellence in Journalism conducted a study of the front pages of the *New York Times* and the *Los Angeles Times*, the nightly news programs of ABC, CBS and NBC, and *Time* and *Newsweek*. They found that from 1977 to 1997 the number of stories about government dropped from one in three to one in five, while the number of stories about celebrities rose from one in every fifty stories to one in every fourteen.

Does it matter? Well, as we learned in the 1960s but seem to have forgotten, government is about who wins and who loses in the vast bazaar of democracy. Government can send us to war, pick our pockets, slap us in jail, run a highway through our garden, look the other way as polluters do their dirty work, take care of the people who are already well cared for at the expense of those who can't afford lawyers, lobbyists or time to be vigilant. It matters who's pulling the strings. It also matters who defines the news and decides what to cover. It matters whether we're over at the Puffy Combs trial, checking out what Jennifer Lopez was wearing the night she ditched him, or whether we're on the Hill, seeing who's writing the new bankruptcy law, or overturning workplace safety rules, or buying back standards for allowable levels of arsenic in our drinking water.

Big money and big business, corporations and commerce, are again the undisputed overlords of politics and government.

I need to declare a bias here. It's true that I worked for two Democratic Presidents, John Kennedy and Lyndon Johnson. But I did so more for reasons of opportunity than ideology. My worldview was really shaped by Theodore Roosevelt, who got it right about power in America. Roosevelt thought the central fact of his era was that economic power had become so centralized and dominant it could chew up democracy and spit it out. The power of corporations, he said, had to be balanced in the interest of the general public. Otherwise, America would undergo a class war, the rich would win it, and we wouldn't recognize our country anymore. Shades of déjà vu. Big money and big business, corporations and commerce, are again the undisputed overlords of politics and government. The White House, the Congress and, increasingly, the judiciary reflect their interests. We appear to have a government run by remote control from the US Chamber of Commerce, the National Association of Manufacturers and the American Petroleum Institute. To hell with everyone else.

What's the role of journalism in all this? The founders of our nation were pretty explicit on this point. The First Amendment is the first for a reason. It's needed to keep our leaders honest and to arm the powerless with the information they need to protect themselves against the tyranny of the powerful, whether that tyranny is political or commercial. At least that's my bias. A college student once asked the journalist Richard Reeves to define "real news." He answered: "The news you and I need to keep our freedoms." Senator John McCain echoed this in an interview I did with him a couple of years ago for a documentary called "Free Speech for Sale." It was about the Telecommunications Act of 1996, when some of America's most powerful corporations were picking the taxpayers' pocket of $70 billion. That's the estimated value of the digital spectrum that Congress was giving away to the big media giants.

Senator McCain said on the Senate floor during the debate, referring to the major media, "You will not see this story on any television or hear it on any radio broadcast because it directly affects them." And, in our interview, he added, "The average American does not know what digital spectrum is. They just don't know. But here in Washington their assets that they own were being given away, and the coverage was minuscule." Sure enough, the Telecommunications Act was introduced around May of 1995 and was finally passed in early February of 1996. During those nine months, the three major network news shows aired a sum total of only nineteen minutes on the legislation, and none of the nineteen minutes included a single mention of debate over whether the broadcasters should pay for use of the digital spectrum.

The Founders didn't count on the rise of mega-media. They didn't count on huge private corporations that would own not only the means of journalism but also vast swaths of the territory that journalism should be covering. According to a recent study done by the Pew Research Center for the People and the Press for the *Columbia Journalism Review*, more than a quarter of journalists polled said they had avoided pursuing some newsworthy stories that might conflict with the financial interests of their news organizations or advertisers. And many thought that complexity or lack of audience appeal causes newsworthy stories not to be pursued in the first place.

I don't mean to suggest there was a Golden Age of journalism. I told you earlier about covering the Housewives' Rebellion in Marshall, Texas, fifty years ago. What I didn't tell you is that it was the white housewives who made news with their boycotts of Social Security, not the domestic workers themselves. They were black; I wasn't sent to interview them, and it didn't occur to me that I should have. Marshall was 50 percent black, 50 percent white, and the official view of reality was that only white people made news. I could kick myself for the half-blindness that has afflicted me through the years—from the times at the White House when I admonished journalists for going beyond the official view of reality in Vietnam to the times I have let the flickering yellow light turn red in my own mind on worthy journalistic projects.

I'm sure that growing up a Southerner and serving in the White House turned me into a fanatic—at least into a public nuisance—about what journalism should be doing in our democracy. In the South the truth about slavery was driven from our pulpits, our newsrooms and our classrooms, and it took the Civil War to bring the truth home. Then the truth about Jim Crow was censored, too, and it took another hundred years to produce the justice that should have followed Appomattox. In the White House we circled the wagons, grew intolerant of news that didn't comfort us and, if we could have, we would have declared illegal the sting of the bee. So I sympathize with my friends in commercial broadcasting who don't cover the ocean they're swimming in. But I don't envy them. Having all those resources—without the freedom to use them to do the kinds of stories that are begging to be done—seems to me more a curse than a blessing. It reminds me of Bruce Springsteen's great line, "It's like eating caviar and dirt."

But I am not here to hold myself up as some sort of beacon. I've made my own compromises and benefited from the special circumstances of my own good luck. But the fact that I have been so lucky shows that it can be done. All that is required is for journalists to act like journalists, and their sponsors—public or private—to back them up when the going gets a little rough.

Because when you are dealing with powerful interests, be they in government or private industry, and bringing to light what has been hidden, the going does—inevitably—get a little rough.

Let me give you a couple of examples of what I mean—why the battle is never-ending: Some years ago my colleague Marty Koughan was looking into the subject of pesticides and food when he learned about a National Academy of Sciences study in progress on the effects of pesticide residuals on children. With David Fanning of *Frontline* as an ally, we set about a documentary. Four to six weeks before we were finished the industry somehow purloined a copy of our rough script—we still aren't certain how—and mounted a sophisticated and expensive campaign to discredit the documentary before it aired. They flooded television reviewers and the editorial pages of newspapers with propaganda. A *Washington Post* columnist took a dig at the broadcast on the morning of the day it aired—without even having seen it—and later admitted to me that the dig had been supplied to him by a top lobbyist in town. Some station managers were so unnerved that they protested the documentary with letters that had been prepared by industry. Several station managers later apologized to me for having been suckered.

Here's what most perplexed us: Eight days before the broadcast, the American Cancer Society—a fine organization that in no way figured in our story—sent to its 3,000 local chapters a "critique" of the unfinished documentary claiming, wrongly, that it exaggerated the dangers of pesticides in food. We were puzzled: Why was the American Cancer Society taking the unusual step of criticizing a documentary that it hadn't seen, that hadn't aired and that didn't claim what the society alleged? An enterprising reporter in town named Sheila Kaplan later looked into this question for *Legal Times*, which headlined her story: "Porter/Novelli Plays All Sides." It turns out that the Porter/Novelli public relations firm, which has worked for several chemical companies, also did pro bono work for the American Cancer Society. Kaplan found that the firm was able to cash in some of the goodwill from that pro bono work to persuade the compliant communications staff at the society to distribute some harsh talking points about the documentary that had been supplied by, but not attributed to, Porter/Novelli.

Others used the society's good name to discredit the documentary, including the right-wing polemicist Reed Irvine. His screed against what he called "Junk Science on PBS" called on Congress to pull the plug on public broadcasting. PBS stood firm. The report aired, the journalism held up (in contrast to the disinformation about it) and the National Academy of Sciences was liberated to release the study that the industry had tried to cripple.

But there's always the next round. PBS broadcast our documentary on "Trade Secrets." It's a two-hour investigative special based on the chemical industry's own archives, on documents that make clear, in the industry's own words, what the industry didn't tell us about toxic chemicals, why they didn't tell us and why we still don't know what we have the right to know. These internal industry documents are a fact. They exist. They are not a matter of opinion or point of view.

They state what the industry knew, when they knew it and what they decided to do.

The public policy implications of our broadcast are profound. We live today under a regulatory system designed by the industry itself. The truth is, if the public, media, independent scientists and government regulators had known what the industry knew about the health risks of its products—when the industry knew it—America's laws and regulations governing chemical manufacturing would be far more protective of human health than they are today. But the industry didn't want us to know. That's the message of the documents. That's the story.

The spokesman for the American Chemistry Council assured me that contrary to rumors, the chemical industry was not pressuring stations to reject the broadcast. I believed him; the controversy would only have increased the audience. But I wasn't sure for a while. The first person to contact us from the industry was a public relations firm here in Washington noted for hiring private detectives and former CIA, FBI and drug enforcement officers to do investigations for corporations. One of the founders of the company is on record as saying that sometimes corporations need to resort to unconventional resources, and some of those resources "include using deceit." No wonder Sherry and I kept looking over our shoulders. To complicate things, the single biggest recipient of campaign contributions from the chemical industry over the past twenty years in the House has been the very member of Congress whose committee has responsibility for public broadcasting's appropriations. Now you know why we don't take public funds for reports like this!

For all the pressures, America, nonetheless, is a utopia for journalists. In many parts of the world assassins have learned that they can kill reporters with impunity; journalists are hunted down and murdered because of their reporting. Thirty-four in Colombia alone over the past decade. And here? Well, Don Hewitt of *60 Minutes* said to me recently that "the 1990s were a terrible time for journalism in this country but a wonderful time for journalists; we're living like [GE CEO] Jack Welch." Perhaps that's why we aren't asking tough questions of Jack Welch.

I don't want to claim too much for our craft, but I don't want to claim too little, either. The late Martha Gellhorn spent half a century observing war and politicians and journalists, too. By the end she had lost her faith that journalism could, by itself, change the world. But she had found a different sort of comfort. For journalists, she said, "victory and defeat are both passing moments. There is no end; there are only means. Journalism is a means, and I now think that the act of keeping the record straight is valuable in itself. Serious, careful, honest journalism is essential, not because it is a guiding light but because it is a form of honorable behavior, involving the reporter and the reader." And, one hopes, the viewer, too.

Editors' Postscript: This article is adapted from Moyers's speech to the National Press Club on March 22, hosted by PBS to observe his thirtieth year as a broadcast journalist. The chemical industry's trade association did attempt to discredit the March 26 documentary, "Trade Secrets" (see "The Times *v. Moyers," April 16), accusing Moyers and Jones of "journalistic malpractice" for inviting industry participation only during the last half-hour of the broadcast. Moyers replied that investigative journalism is not a collaboration between the journalist and the subject.*

Bill Moyers is executive editor of Public Affairs Television, the independent production company he founded in 1986.

From *The Nation*, May 7, 2001, pp. 11-13, 15,17. © 2001 by The Nation. Reprinted by permission.

THE MEDIA AND POLITICS:
It's More Than the News

"… We cannot afford to ignore the overwhelming evidence that the media— old and new combined—is dramatically changing the democratic process."

BY STEVE BELL

To PARAPHRASE the old Bill Clinton political commercial, "It's the media, stupid!" In fact, it's almost conventional wisdom now that the media played a pivotal role in Campaign 2000. Pregnant chads aside, there never before has been a campaign in which the media—and not just the news media—so dominated the attention, and many say dictated the behavior, of both the voters and the candidates.

On election night, the news media played the kind of role that inspires the public to think the worst of the messenger. When the networks "called" Florida for Al Gore early in the evening, it might have affected voter turnout in the Florida Panhandle and further west across the country. Partisans of George W. Bush certainly think so.

Consider that, at the same time, well before polls were closed beyond the eastern time zone, the networks also were projecting that Gore had won Pennsylvania and Michigan. These reports had the appearance of indicating a Gore victory in the election itself, thus reducing the incentive for Bush supporters to bother going to the polls. Did that tip the scales for Gore in what turned out to be razor-thin outcomes in several states in the Midwest and West? Who knows?

Much later on election night, the same networks called Bush the winner in Florida. Although they retracted the call a short time later, many Gore partisans believe that second miscall gave the Bush claim of victory a "sense of legitimacy." After all, Gore had to place a second call to Bush withdrawing his concession statement, and from then on he seemed to be fighting the perception that he was the one trying to "manipulate" the Florida vote count.

If anything, media coverage of the postelection contest was just as suspect in the minds of partisans on both sides. The challenge and contest phases featured some outstanding reporting and commentary. Nevertheless, more often than not, it appeared to be a contest of "talking heads" being packaged in the most contentious and incendiary way possible.

If there was an argument to be made that politics and perfidy were at work, it often found both print and electronic platforms, magnifying the bitterness and suspicion on both sides. Only on the night Gore made his generous concession speech, and Bush responded in kind, did a theme of moderation and search for consensus prevail.

In truth, no one knows the impact of the media-inspired events on Election Day, or the aftermath. Still, a growing number of

Americans are convinced that something is wrong with the entire election process, and they have the media in their crosshairs.

What is becoming increasingly clear is that "the media" needs to be defined in terms that go far beyond the news media. Less than 20 years ago, members of the establishment news media were the dominant "gatekeepers" when it came to election information flow. True, there were campaign commercials, some of them clearly influential in shaping voter perceptions. Candidates for president also produced their own audience-participation programs, carefully controlled to get out only the message they intended.

However, when it came to the daily drumbeat of campaign coverage and candidate messages, the flow was regulated primarily by journalists representing a relatively few newspapers, magazines, and the three commercial networks. What they defined as "news" was pretty much what was available to the American public.

This was not so in Campaign 2000. During the campaign, voters had far more information and opinion options than ever before. There were 24-hour news and talk options, with many of the talking heads competing for shock-value soundbites. For the first time, more Americans got election news from the cable networks than from

ABC, NBC, and CBS. The Internet offered literally hundreds of additional options, many of them reflecting partisan points of view that ranged from the outrageous to the slanderous. Then, there were the late-night comedy routines.

There is considerable evidence that the traditional news media were not even the most influential source when it came to voter information, and especially voter perceptions. Certainly, the candidates saw it that way, when they often "stiffed" hard-nosed reporters like Tim Russert and Sam Donaldson in favor of Oprah Winfrey, Jay Leno, and David Letterman.

Twenty years ago, you could argue that presidential candidates were "used" by the news media to make election coverage a dramatic story. Today, it more often seems to be the candidates who "use" the entire media spectrum to get out their messages, picking and choosing from a media smorgasbord.

When you look for the catalyst for this seminal change in candidate use of the media, look at Bill Clinton. Yes, Ronald Reagan was a master of the media, but his options were primarily within the traditional framework. Clinton and independent candidate Ross Perot, on the other hand, were the first to take advantage of the nontraditional media during the 1992 presidential campaign as a less risky option for getting out their messages. One can argue that Clinton's "Monicagate" scandal put a focus on "character" and personality during Campaign 2000 that led the candidates to the talk-show and late-night venues.

Before looking deeper into Campaign 2000, it's worth looking back briefly at the 1992 campaign. One can easily argue that, by turning to the talk-show circuit and other nontraditional media forms, Perot created his campaign for president almost from scratch and that Clinton saved his Democratic nomination.

Perot used talk-show appearances, especially on the "Larry King Show," to put himself into the public spotlight and recruit followers for his party. Clinton used an even wider variety of programs to deal with his image problems. Remember, Clinton was almost forced out of the 1992 primary race by allegations of a sexual relationship with Gennifer Flowers, controversy over his anti-Vietnam War activities and efforts to avoid the draft, and his claim that he "never inhaled" while experimenting with marijuana.

To stay alive in the race, Clinton turned to the talk-show circuit as well as a memo-rable appearance on CBS's "60 Minutes" with his wife Hillary. The talk-show format was the perfect vehicle for Clinton to project sincerity and even create sympathy without being held to short sound bites or being grilled sharply by reporters on the Sunday-morning political talk programs.

Whether it was the Don Imus radio show (which influenced the critical New York primary) or on Phil Donahue, Clinton was in his element. During one Donahue appearance, Clinton even had the audience cheering his attacks on the host for persisting in questions about Flowers.

It is also worth noting that, during the presidential debates in 1992, both Perot and Clinton were far more comfortable than incumbent George Bush with the first debate format to feature questions from a live studio audience. Clinton, in particular, projected empathy and understanding, while the President was caught looking at his watch and misunderstanding a question from a young woman in the audience.

In 1996, this fundamental shift in the way candidates could bypass the traditional news media tended to get little attention. After all, it was Clinton, the incumbent president and favorite, who had the skills, not challenger Bob Dole.

Campaign 2000 was different. Although Clinton wasn't running, Gore found himself trying to run away from the public revulsion over Clinton's personal behavior while, at the same time, trying to share credit for the healthy economy of the Clinton-Gore years. It turned out to be a daunting task.

Through much of the campaign, Gore made every effort to keep the focus on his version of "the issues," but the Bush campaign wasn't cooperating. From the very beginning, George W. Bush projected himself as a different kind of Republican, one who subscribed to "compassionate conservatism."

For the record, Bush did articulate positions on issues that were both innovative and controversial. Nevertheless, he and his advisors wanted the campaign to be about "character" and image, sensing that they had Gore caught in the Clinton dilemma.

It's at this point that "using" the media, traditional and otherwise, came into play. By the time the Democrats held their convention in Los Angeles, Gore had a problem. The Republicans had done a masterful job of utilizing their Philadelphia convention to create a campaign in which "image is everything." The roster of speakers was diverse, and the message was one of reconciliation and "healing the wounds" from the contentious relationship between the Clinton Administration and the partisan Republican Congress.

As the Democrats gathered in Los Angeles, Gore was trailing in the polls by double-digit figures. Worse yet, he needed to shore up support from the hard-core, liberal Democrats who wanted to hear a populist "us against them" message.

Enter "the kiss." Was it premeditated? Skeptics think not, but whatever the motivation, to go along with his acceptance speech, Gore planted a passionate kiss on wife Tipper that became a kind of symbolic message heard round the country, if not the world.

It's not possible to assign percentages to the impact of "the kiss," but Gore came out of the convention with a surprising lead, and many voters, especially women, told pollsters the candidate's moment of passion had given him an entire new—and much more positive—image.

Enter the Oprah show. It had not been lost on both campaigns that the personal images of the candidates and the public perceptions of their character and "like-ability" were a key to election victory. In this new age of media influence, Oprah Winfrey is queen, and both candidates wanted to be her "king for a day."

According to a Pew Research Center survey, Oprah and Regis Philbin reach about 22,000,000 viewers, 80% of them women. Furthermore, 14% of those polled said they would be influenced to vote for a candidate publicly supported by Oprah.

Gore got the first appearance with Oprah, and he was a hit. In that kind of an often-joshing, one-on-one setting, Gore can be both funny and appealing. (It helps to have good writers.) Gore forgot to kiss Oprah, though, and Bush didn't. At a time when he was trailing in the polls, Bush not only held his own with humor and repartee (he, too, has good writers), he gave Oprah a kiss on the cheek that became its own breathless headline.

Wait a minute; are we really serious here? Is this really the substance of presidential politics 2000? Enter the late-night comedy circuit. According to the Pew survey, more than 50% of younger voters in America get the largest part of their information about politics from late-night comedians.

Jon Stewart, the host of Comedy Central's "The Daily Show" rode Campaign 2000 from the fringe of the popular culture to the "mainstream," according to television researcher Robert Thompson of Syracuse University. Withering parodies on

NBC's "Saturday Night Live" are credited, or blamed, by some for prompting Gore to change his persona from one presidential debate to the next.

In that context, it is not so surprising that both candidates were ready to trade on-camera barbs as well as substantive commentary with the late-night comics. For Bush, however there was a problem. While the candidates could, and did, choose among talk-show hosts for the right tone and treatment, on the comedy front, it was hard to find "Bush country."

Throughout the campaign, comedians got most of their Gore laugh lines by caricaturing him as someone who was stiff and programmed. Bush, on the other hand, was the target of jokes that questioned his intelligence. In an article in The *New York Times Magazine* titled "The Stiff and the Dumb Guy," Marshall Sella pointed out that, while both caricatures are negative, being "dumb" is potentially lethal for a presidential candidate.

After extensive interviews with New York and Hollywood comedians and comedy writers, Sella concluded that they are overwhelmingly liberals, and their material reflects their bias. On the other hand, Bush may have benefited from low expectations by being far more interesting and intelligent than expected during his appearances.

Suffice it to say, such non-news programming had an important, if nonmeasurable, impact on Campaign 2000. *Newsweek* caught the significance with an article titled, "The Talk-Show Primary… How Bush and Gore are fighting for the Oprah-Regis-Leno audiences—women and young voters who make a difference."

Richard Nixon may have helped parody himself years ago on "Laugh-in" and Clinton may have played the saxophone on "Arsenio Hall," but in 2000, this was serious. Both candidates clearly recognized the new media playing field and often proved more accessible to the gabbers and comedians than to the hard news types.

Is this all bad? In a quote in the *American Journalism Review*, media critic Danny Schechter observes that "comedy to some degree humanizes the process." Others feel such appearances trivialize the candidates and obscure the issues. For better or worse, no one is overlooking the fact that, after his appearances with Oprah and Regis, Bush's ratings in the polls went up among the exact demographic groups known to be loyal watchers of the programs.

Yet another form of "new media" that obviously had impact on Campaign 2000 is the Internet. A survey by the Pew Internet and American Life Project found that 18% of Americans used the Internet to keep up with the campaign, four times as many as in 1996. The candidates had sophisticated websites, and so did a host of special-interest groups.

As for Web journalism, it remains an emerging form. Still, most observers agree that the Bush-Gore campaign variety tended to be more shrill and "edgy" than print and broadcast journalism. The Internet also allowed more and more sources to put stories "in play" that might have been otherwise ignored by the mainstream media.

Despite the role and power of non-news programs, no one is dismissing the importance of traditional news coverage and its impact on voters. That, in turn, raises the recurring issue of news media bias.

Without question, more journalists working at the national level are liberal than conservative. A 1992 Roper poll found that 89% of Washington bureau chiefs and correspondents had voted for Clinton, compared to seven percent for George Bush. Are these personal views reflected in their reporting to the point where it seriously impacts the electoral process itself?

Also in 1992, when incumbent Bush was upset by Clinton, the conservative Mediawatch group found the networks guilty of unfair "labeling" during the two party conventions. After monitoring coverage, Mediawatch charged that the networks "never ever once referred to anybody at the Democratic convention as being far left or hard left," not even Jesse Jackson or other outspoken liberals. Yet, at the Republican convention, Pat Buchanan and others were described as "far right extremists."

In Campaign 2000, there were similar charges, but this time they came from both sides. Charles Cook, of the highly regarded *National Journal*, felt he saw too many reporters "larding their stories with their own ideological biases" in favor of Gore. An *Editor and Publisher* poll found that more than half of all Bush supporters felt the news media was biased against their candidate.

Yet, surveys by The Committee of Concerned Journalists revealed that, during key weeks in September and October, 2000, "Gore's coverage was decidedly more negative, more focused on the internal politics of campaigning and had less to do with citizens than did his Republican rival." One of the weeks surveyed fell during the presidential debates, and the committee concluded that Gore, the more experienced debater and the one expected to do the best, may have suffered from the press "playing the expectations game."

The Committee of Concerned Journalists did not include in its survey results, however, the last week of the campaign, when a story suddenly broke that Bush had been convicted of drunk driving more than 20 years ago. Although polls vary on the impact of the story, the percentage of voters who said they were "influenced" by the story was more than enough to have affected such a close election. Since Democratic partisans were identified as the source of the story, it raised again the question of how and when journalists allow themselves to be "used" by politicians, especially during the final days of a heated campaign.

If there is a consensus about news media bias, it focuses on accusations of a "negative bias." Ever since the Vietnam/Watergate era, critics have charged that journalists are guilty of cynicism and sensationalism, always looking for the worst at the expense of the best. As former *New York Times* columnist Tom Wicker described it, journalists have traded the traditional "ethic of objectivity for an ethic of disclosure."

Harvard University professor Thomas Patterson has documented a clear tilt toward the negative in campaign reporting. He found that, in 1960, the majority of coverage received by both Nixon and John F. Kennedy was positive, but that it has evolved to the point where all candidates receive negative coverage. Patterson worries that this kind of coverage contributes to public cynicism toward the political process.

Whether one calls it bias or not, news coverage during Campaign 2000 raised another issue involving "pack journalism" and what motivates it. Howard Kurtz, media reporter for the *Washington Post*, was among those documenting a clear pattern of what he calls "the media's swinging with the polls." After his convention "bounce" in the polls, the majority of news reports gave Bush a positive spin. However, when Gore (and his kiss) got a similar bounce, the tone of reporting was reversed. As *Newsweek* correspondent Howard Fineman put it, "We all respond like Pavlov's dog to the polls."

Finally, there is one other area in which today's media, especially the electronic media, is a major player in politics—campaign advertising. Political candidates and their consultants are absolutely convinced that those 20- and 30-second commercials "sell." Many of them, though, add to the negative tone of campaigns.

Because so much money must be raised to pay for commercials, campaign finance reform has become a national issue. There is widespread concern that candidates are being compromised by the pressures of fund-raising and that the whole process is undermining voter confidence in our political system.

Further complicating the issue, many of the Campaign 2000 ads were financed by so-called "soft money," raised by political parties and special-interest groups. Many of the most controversial ads came from such sources, and the money to pay for them falls outside current campaign spending laws and reporting requirements. Whatever the impact, broadcasters—both local and network—are making huge profits from campaign spending, and they are resisting any suggestions that they give free airtime to candidates.

Is there any way to assess accurately the impact of the media on Campaign 2000? Because of its diversity, the answer clearly would seem to be "no." There may be surveys and polls to assess one area or another, but how do you weigh the various media influences one against another?

No matter how elusive the answers, we cannot afford to ignore the overwhelming evidence that the media—old and new combined—is dramatically changing the democratic process. Where freedom of speech is involved, new laws are not likely to be the answer. Instead, we may need a new consensus on what is "proper"—both for the candidates and for the media practitioners who cover them and provide them with a means of communication.

Steve Bell, professor of telecommunications, Ball State University, Muncie, Ind., is a former ABC News correspondent.

THE MAKING OF A MOVEMENT:
GETTING SERIOUS ABOUT MEDIA REFORM

BY ROBERT W. McCHESNEY AND JOHN NICHOLS

No one should be surprised by the polls showing that close to 90 percent of Americans are satisfied with the performance of their selected President, or that close to 80 percent of the citizenry applaud his Administration's seat-of-the-pants management of an undeclared war. After all, most Americans get their information from media that have pledged to give the American people only the President's side of the story. CNN chief Walter Isaacson distributed a memo effectively instructing the network's domestic newscasts to be sugarcoated in order to maintain popular support for the President and his war. Fox News anchors got into a surreal competition to see who could wear the largest American flag lapel pin. Dan Rather, the man who occupies the seat Walter Cronkite once used to tell Lyndon Johnson the Vietnam War was unwinnable, now says, "George Bush is the President.... he wants me to line up, just tell me where."

No, we should not be surprised that a "just tell me where" press has managed to undermine debate at precisely the time America needs it most—but we should be angry. The role that US newsmedia have played in narrowing and warping the public discourse since September 11 provides dramatic evidence of the severe limitations of contemporary American journalism, and this nation's media system, when it comes to nurturing a viable democratic and humane society. It is now time to act upon that anger to forge a broader, bolder and more politically engaged movement to reform American media.

The base from which such a movement could spring has already been built. Indeed, the current crisis comes at a critical moment for media reform politics. Since the middle 1980s, when inept and disingenuous reporting on US interventions in Central America provoked tens of thousands of Americans to question the role media were playing in manufacturing consent,

media activism has had a small but respectable place on the progressive agenda. The critique has gone well beyond complaints about shoddy journalism to broad expressions of concern about hypercommercial, corporate-directed culture and the corruption of communications policy-making by special-interest lobbies and pliable legislators.

Crucial organizations such as Fairness & Accuracy In Reporting (FAIR), the Institute for Public Accuracy, the Media-Channel, Media Alliance and the Media Education Foundation have emerged over the past two decades. Acting as mainstream media watchdogs while pointing engaged Americans toward valuable alternative fare, these groups have raised awareness that any democratic reform in the United States must include media reform. Although it is hardly universal even among progressives, there is increasing recognition that media reform can no longer be dismissed as a "dependent variable" that will fall into place once the more important struggles have been won. People are beginning to understand that unless we make headway with the media, the more important struggles will never be won.

On the advocacy front, Citizens for Independent Public Broadcasting and People for Better TV are pushing to improve public broadcasting and to tighten regulation of commercial broadcasting. Commercial Alert organizes campaigns against the commercialization of culture, from sports and museums to literature and media. The Center for Digital Democracy and the Media Access Project both work the corridors of power in Washington to win recognition of public-interest values under extremely difficult circumstances. These groups have won some important battles, particularly on Internet privacy issues.

Something Old, Something New

Media Policy in the Digital Age

JEFFREY CHESTER AND GARY O. LARSON

It's become commonplace to divide the media into "old" and "new," neatly corresponding to analog and digital technology. Under this handy dichotomy the old media (print and broadcast especially) represent mass marketing and mediocrity; conglomerate ownership and economies of scale have produced mainstream, profit-driven programming. Variations occur at the margins, certainly, but even their collective impact pales before the market share of newspaper chains, publishing empires and the assorted television, cable and entertainment giants. In contrast to these old-media oligopolies, the new, digital media—fueled by desktop production and driven by global, networked distribution— seem wildly democratic. So out with the old and in with the new; the World Wide Web awaits!

If only it were that simple. First, the old media aren't going anywhere, and their dominance in our lives—radio and TV usage still outstrip the Internet by a factor of 20–1—will continue for years. Second, the old media giants have made their presence felt online, too, establishing digital beachheads that might not be making much money (yet) but that are certainly attracting their share of online traffic. This is particularly true of the hybrid (and hydra-headed) AOL Time Warner, whose multimedia reach extends to more than 70 percent of all online users in the United States, and fully a third of all time spent online. Thus, even if the long-touted media convergence has been slow in arriving, the distinction between old media and new—particularly with regard to the impact of conglomerate culture—is largely a false one.

That's why the public-policy battles now being waged to rein in the power of the old media (many of them last-ditch efforts to limit further ownership consolidation and to make the media more publicly accountable) are important to the future of the new media as well—particularly in the areas of ownership limits, spectrum management and noncommercial programming.

A combination of successful court challenges and the ascendant deregulatory spirit in Washington has put the existing cable-ownership limits—currently 30 percent of all cable households nationwide—at risk. As a result, we now face the specter of a single company controlling access to more than half of all households. Broadcast networks and station groups (two of which have already throttled commercial radio) are also poised to tighten their grip on key TV markets by acquiring more stations, far exceeding the current 35 percent national audience limit and further eroding local news and public-affairs programming. Perhaps most alarming, the old prohibitions against one company owning both a TV station and a newspaper, or a cable system and a TV station and a newspaper, or a cable system and a TV station, in the same community are also under threat. In all these instances, the public's fundamental right to "the widest possible dissemination of information from diverse and antagonistic sources" (in the words of the Supreme Court) will be jettisoned in favor of lowest-common-denominator shows assembled by the conglomerate multimedia stables.

There are more media outlets than ever before, but this numerical growth, as Consumers Union has pointed out, "has not been accompanied by a comparable growth of independent, diversely owned competitive communications services and media voices."

On one level, spectrum management—literally, the organization and oversight of the radio frequencies that make broadcast and other wireless transmissions possible—is dauntingly complex. But the current battle over spectrum is distressingly simple: In 1996, the nation's 1,600 TV stations were lent additional spectrum (a six-megahertz slice equal to that over which they've been transmitting analog signals for years). According to the FCC's original timetable, all stations were to be broadcasting digitally by 2003, and by 2006 they were to return their old spectrum (which could then be auctioned off by the government and used for other purposes). For a variety of reasons, the digital TV transition has progressed slowly; in the interim, industry lobbyists have been pressing for stations to be allowed to retain their additional spectrum and put it to various commercial uses, like data transmission, or auction it off themselves. As appalling as that may sound,, it is not such a farfetched scheme, given the lobby's clout and Washington's belief in finding "marketplace solutions."

But this kind of corporate welfare is no solution at all. Not only should the spectrum be returned in a timely fashion but a portion of the subsequent auction proceeds should be devoted to noncommercial, public-interest content. Such programming, largely entrusted in the past to the Corporation for Public Broadcasting and its PBS grantees, needs a much broader mandate in the digital future. And here, too, old and new media converge. For perhaps now, with the additional capacity that digital broadcasting affords, and with funding derived from the spectrum auctions, we can finally realize the original vision for public-service broadcasting, updated for the digital age. As the Carnegie Commission on Educational Television wrote back in 1967, "We seek for the artist, the technician, the journalist, the scholar, and the public servant freedom to create, freedom to innovate, freedom to be heard in this most far-reaching medium. We seek for the citizen freedom to view, to see programs that the present system, by its incompleteness, denies him."

The emerging broadband networks, which promise to bring broadcast and online technologies together in a platform that fosters interactivity and exchange, has the potential finally to realize that vision—but only if public-interest policies are in place insuring that the old-media giants won't be able to stifle competition and diversity in the new-media environment, too.

Jeffrey Chester is executive director of the Center for Digital Democracy (www.democraticmedia.org), a Washington-based nonprofit organization dedicated to maintaining the diversity and openness of the new broadband communications systems. Gary O. Larson manages CDD's "Dot-Commons" project.

In addition, local media watch groups have surfaced across the nation. Citizens' organizations do battle to limit billboards in public places and to combat the rise of advertising in schools—fighting often successfully to keep Channel One ads, corporate-sponsored texts and fast-food promotions out of classrooms and cafeterias. Innovative lawsuits challenging the worst excesses of media monopoly are being developed by regional groups such as Rocky Mountain Media Watch and a national consortium of civic organizations, lawyers and academics that has drawn support from Unitarian Universalist organizations. Media activists in Honolulu and San Francisco have joined with unions and community groups to prevent the closure of daily newspapers that provided a measure of competition and debate in those cities.

Despite its successes, the media reform movement is at something of a standstill. The sheer corruption of US politics is one obstacle.

Despite all these achievements, however, the media reform movement remains at something of a standstill. The sheer corruption of US politics is itself a daunting obstacle. The Center for Public Integrity in 2000 issued "Off the Record: What Media Corporations Don't Tell You About Their Legislative Agendas"—an alarming exposé of the huge lobbying machines employed by the largest communications corporations and their trade associations, as well as the considerable campaign contributions they make. According to the center, the fifty largest media companies and four of their trade associations spent $111.3 million between 1996 and mid-2000 to lobby Congress and the executive branch. Between 1993 and mid-2000, the center determined, media corporations and their employees have given $75 million in campaign contributions to candidates for federal office and to the two major political parties. Regulators and politicians tend therefore to be in the pockets of big-spending corporate communications lobbies, and—surprise, surprise—the corporate newsmedia rarely cover media policy debates. Notwithstanding all the good work by media activists, the "range" of communications policy debate in Washington still tends to run all the way from GE to GM, to borrow a line from FAIR's Jeff Cohen.

At this very moment, for example, the FCC is considering the elimination of the remaining restrictions on media consolidation, including bans on cross-ownership by a single firm of TV stations and newspapers in the same community, and limits on the number of TV stations and cable TV systems a single corporation may own nationwide. The corporate media lobbying superstars are putting a full-court press on the FCC—which, with George W. Bush's imprint now firmly on its membership, is now even more pro-corporate than during the Clinton years. The proposed scrapping of these regulations will increase the shareholder value of numerous media firms dramatically, and will undoubtedly inspire a massive wave of mergers and acquisitions. If the lessons of past ownership deregulation—particularly the 1996 relaxation of radio ownership rules—are any

guide, we can expect even less funding for journalism and more commercialism. All of this takes place without scrutiny from major media, and therefore is unknown to all but a handful of Americans.

The immensity of the economic and political barriers to democratic action has contributed to demoralization about the prospects for structural media reform and an understandable turn to that which progressives *can* hope to control: their own media. So it has been that much energy has gone into the struggle over the future of the Pacifica radio chain, which looks at long last to be heading toward a viable resolution. The Independent Press Association has grown dramatically to nurture scores of usually small, struggling nonprofit periodicals, which are mostly progressive in orientation. And dozens of local Independent Media Centers have mushroomed on the Internet over the past two years. These Indy Media Centers take advantage of new technology to provide dissident and alternative news stories and commentary; some, by focusing on local issues, have become a genuine alternative to established media at a level where that alternative can and does shift the dialogue. We have seen the positive impact of the IMC movement firsthand—in Seattle, in Washington, at the 2000 Democratic and Republican national conventions, at the three lamentable presidential debates later that year, during the Florida recount and in the aftermath of September 11 in New York and other cities. It is vital that this and other alternative media movements grow in scope and professionalism.

Yet, as important as this work is, there are inherent limits to what can be done with independent media, even with access to the Internet. Too often, the alternative media remain on the margins, seeming to confirm that the dominant structures are the natural domain of the massive media conglomerates that supposedly "give the people what they want."

The trouble with this disconnect between an engaged and vital alternative media and a disengaged and stenographic dominant media is that it suggests a natural order in which corporate media have mastered the marketplace on the basis of their wit and wisdom. In fact, our media system is not predominantly the result of free-market competition. Huge promotional budgets and continual rehashing of tried and true formulas play their role in drawing viewers, listeners and readers to dominant print and broadcast media. But their dominance is still made possible, in large part, by explicit government policies and subsidies that permit the creation of large and profitable conglomerates. When the government grants free monopoly rights to TV spectrum, for example, it is not setting the terms of competition; it is picking the winner of the competition. Such policies amount to an annual grant of corporate welfare that economist Dean Baker values in the tens of billions of dollars. These decisions have been made in the public's name, but without the public's informed consent. We must not accept such massive subsidies for wealthy corporations, nor should we content ourselves with the "freedom" to forge an alternative that occupies the margins. Our task is to return "informed consent" to media policy-making and to generate a diverse media system that serves our democratic needs.

Isolated and impoverished, groups are forced to defend against new corporate initiatives rather than advance positive proposals.

In our view, what's needed to begin the job is now crystal clear—a national media reform coalition that can play quarterback for the media reform movement. The necessity argument takes two forms.

First, the immense job of organizing media reform requires that our scarce resources be used efficiently, and that the various components of a media reform movement cooperate strategically. The problem is that the whole of the current media reform movement is significantly less than the sum of its parts. Isolated and impoverished, groups are forced to defend against new corporate initiatives rather than advance positive reform proposals. When they do get around to proposing reforms, activists have occasionally worked on competing agendas; such schisms dissipate energy, squander resources and guarantee defeat. More important, they are avoidable. Organizers of this new coalition could begin by convening a gathering of all the groups now struggling for reform, as well as the foundations and nonprofits willing to support their work. "All the issues we talk about are interlinked. We are fighting against a lot of the same corporations. The corporations, while they supposedly compete with one another, actually work together very well when it comes to lobbying," explains Jeffrey Chester of the Center for Digital Democracy. "We need to link up the activists and start to work together as well as the corporations do for the other side." Will every possible member organization get on the same media reform page? No. But after years of working with these groups in various settings, we have no doubt that most will.

Second, a coherent, focused and well-coordinated movement will be needed to launch a massive outreach effort to popularize the issue. That outreach can, and should, be guided by Saul Alinsky's maxim that the only way to beat organized money is with organized people. If the media reform movement stays within the Beltway, we know that we will always lose. Yet, so far, outreach beyond the core community of media activists has been done on a piecemeal basis by various reform groups and critics with very limited budgets. The results have, by and large, been predictably disappointing. As a result, says Representative Jesse Jackson Jr., "the case for media reform is not being heard in Washington now. It is not easy to make the case heard for any reform these days. That's why we need to do more. I hear people everywhere around the country complaining about the media, but we have yet to figure out how to translate those complaints into some kind of activist agenda that can begin to move Congress. There has to be more pressure from outside Washington for specific reforms. Members have to start hearing in their home districts that people want specific reforms of the media."

That will only happen if a concerted campaign organized around core democratic values takes the message of media reform to every college and university, every union hall, every convention and every church, synagogue and mosque in the land. To build a mass movement, the new coalition must link up with organized groups that currently engage in little activity in the way of media reform but that are seriously hampered by the current media system. Organized labor, educators, progressive religious groups, journalists, artists, feminists, environmental organizations and civil rights groups are obvious candidates.

These groups will not simply fall into place as coalition partners, however. Media corporations do not just lobby Congress; they lobby a lot of the groups that suffer under the current system. Some of those groups have been bought off by contributions from foundations associated with AOL, Verizon and other communications conglomerates; others—particularly large sections of organized labor—have been convinced that they have a vested interest in maintaining a status quo that consistently kicks them in the teeth. Building a broad coalition will require a tremendous amount of education and old-fashioned organizing that will inevitably involve pressure from the grassroots on major institutions and unions in order to get the national leadership of those organizations to engage. Movement-building will require that able organizers like Chester, Cohen, FAIR's Janine Jackson and Media Alliance executive director Jeff Perlstein—who have already been engaged in the struggle—be provided with the resources to travel, organize and educate.

All the organizing in the world won't amount to a hill of beans, however, unless there is something tangible to fight for, and to win. That's why we need reform proposals that can be advocated, promoted and discussed. Media reform needs its equivalent of the Voting Rights Act or the Equal Rights Amendment—simple, basic reforms that grassroots activists can understand, embrace and advocate in union halls, church basements and school assemblies. And there has to be legislation to give the activism a sense of focus and possibility.

Fortunately, there are several members of Congress who are already engaged on these issues: Senator Fritz Hollings has emerged as a thoughtful critic of many of the excesses of media monopolies; Senator John McCain has questioned the giveaway of public airwaves to communications conglomerates; Representative John Conyers Jr., the ranking Democrat on the House Judiciary Committee, has been outspoken in criticizing the loss of diversity in media ownership and the failure of the FCC to battle monopolization and homogenization; Representative Louise Slaughter has introduced legislation mandating free airtime for political candidates; Senator Paul Wellstone has expressed an interest in legislation that would reassert standards for children's programming and perhaps adopt the approaches of other countries that regulate advertising directed at young children; and Jesse Jackson Jr. has expressed a willingness to introduce legislation aimed at broadening access to diverse media, along with a wide range of other media reform proposals. If an organized movement demands it, there are people in Congress with the courage and the awareness to provide it with a legislative focus.

Ultimately, we believe, the movement's legislative agenda must include proposals to:

- Apply existing antimonopoly laws to the media and, where necessary, expand the reach of those laws to restrict ownership of radio stations to one or two per owner. Legislators should also consider steps to address monopolization of TV-station ownership and move to break the lock of newspaper chains on entire regions.
- Initiate a formal, federally funded study and hearings to identify reasonable media ownership regulations across all sectors.
- Establish a full tier of low-power, noncommercial radio and television stations across the nation.
- Revamp and invest in public broadcasting to eliminate commercial pressures, reduce immediate political pressures and serve communities without significant disposable incomes.
- Allow every taxpayer a $200 tax credit to apply to any non-profit medium, as long as it meets IRS criteria.
- Lower mailing costs for nonprofit and significantly noncommercial publications.
- Eliminate political candidate advertising as a condition of a broadcast license, or require that if a station runs a paid political ad by a candidate it must run free ads of similar length from all the other candidates on the ballot immediately afterward.
- Reduce or eliminate TV advertising directed at children under 12.
- Decommercialize local TV news with regulations that require stations to grant journalists an hour daily of commercial-free news time, and set budget guidelines for those newscasts based on a percentage of the station's revenues.

We know from experience that many of these ideas are popular with Americans—when they get a chance to hear about them. Moreover, the enthusiasm tends to cross the political spectrum. Much of our optimism regarding a media reform movement is based on our research that shows how assiduously the corporate media lobbies work to keep their operations in Washington out of public view. They suspect the same thing we do: When people hear about the corruption of communications policy-making, they will be appalled. When people understand that it is their democratic right to reform this system, millions of them will be inclined to exercise that right.

A broad coalition could stand outside political parties and pressure all of them to take up the mantle of democratic media reform.

What media policy-making needs is to be bathed in democracy. The coalition we envision will have its similarities to the civil rights movement or the women's movement—as it should, since access to information ought to be seen as a fundamental human right. It will stand outside political parties and encourage all of them to take up the mantle of democratic media reform, much as Britain's impressive Campaign for Press and Broad-

casting Freedom has done. Although its initial funding may well come from large grants, this reform coalition ultimately must be broad-based and member-funded, like Greenpeace or, dare we say it, the National Rifle Association. Activists must feel a sense of ownership and attachment to a citizen lobby if it is to have real impact. We understand that success will depend, over the long term, upon a rejuvenation of popular politics and, accordingly, a decrease in corporate political and economic power. At the same time, we are certain that a movement that expands the range of legitimate debate will ultimately change not just the debate but the current system. "I am convinced that when people start talking about these big issues, these fundamental issues, when they start to understand that they have the power as citizens in a democracy to take on the powers that be and change how things are done, then change becomes inevitable," says Jackson. "The challenge, of course, is to get people to recognize that they have that power."

Even before it gets down to the serious business of reforming existing media systems, the coalition we propose can lead an organized resistance to corporate welfare schemes like the proposed FCC deregulation. And it might even be able to prevent the complete corporatization of the Internet [see Jeffrey Chester and Gary O. Larson, "Something Old, Something New," *The Nation,* January 7/14, 2002]. The key is to have a network of informed organizations and individuals who are already up to speed on media issues and can swing into action on short notice. Currently that network does not exist. The heroic public-interest groups that now lead the fight to oppose corporate domination of FCC policies find themselves without sufficient popular awareness or support, and therefore without the leverage they need to prevail. The movement we propose will be all about increasing leverage over the FCC and Congress in the near term, with an eye toward structural reform down the road.

But is it really possible that such a coalition can take shape in the months and years to come and begin to shift the debate? History tells us that the possibility is real. At times of popular political resurgence throughout the twentieth century, media activism surfaced as a significant force. It was most intense in the Progressive Era, when the rise of the modern capitalist media system was met with sustained Progressive and radical criticism from the likes of Upton Sinclair, Eugene Victor Debs and Robert La Follette. In the 1930s a heterogeneous movement arose to battle commercial broadcasting, and a feisty consumer movement organized to limit advertising in our society. In the postwar years, the Congress of Industrial Organizations attempted to establish a national FM radio network, one of the first casualties of the war on independent labor and the left that marked that period. In the 1960s and '70s the underground press provided vital underpinning for the civil rights, antiwar and feminist movements.

In short, we are building on a long tradition. And there is considerable momentum at present to coalesce. In November some thirty-five media activists from all over the nation met for a day in New York to begin coordinating some of their activities on a range of issues, from local and national policy matters to creating alternative media. Leading media scholars and educators are forming a new national progressive media literacy organization, one that will remain independent of the media conglomerates that bankroll existing groups. We are excited by speculation that Bill Moyers, who has done so much to drum up funding for reform initiatives, will in 2002 use his considerable influence to convince progressive foundations to make a genuine commitment to this fundamental democratic initiative.

The bottom line is clear. Until reformers come together, until we create a formal campaign to democratize our communications policy-making and to blast open our media system, we will continue to see special issues of *The Nation* like this one lamenting our situation. We need no more proof than the current moment to tell us that the time to build a broad coalition for media reform has arrived.

Robert W. McChesney, who teaches at the University of Illinois at Urbana, Champaign, is the author of Rich Media, Poor Democracy *(The New Press), and co-editor of* Monthly Review. *John Nichols is* The Nation's *Washington correspondent and the author of* Jews for Buchanan: Did You Hear the One About the Theft of the American Presidency? *(The New Press). Together, they are the authors of* It's the Media, Stupid! *(Seven Stories).*

From *The Nation,* January 7/14, 2002, pp. 11, 13, 16-17. © 2002 by The Nation. Reprinted by permission.

Echo Chamber of Horrors

BY SCOTT STOSSEL

Let's get one thing straight right from the get-go. We would rather be last in reporting returns than be wrong.... If we say somebody has carried a state, you can pretty much take it to the bank, book it that that's true.

—DAN RATHER, CBS News,
early evening, November 7

We've always said, you know, this is not an exact science. It's an imperfect art at best. And one of the things I think we could do better is to underscore more often with people that while we believe we were right in making these calls... they can be wrong.

—DAN RATHER on CNN's *Reliable Sources*,
November 11

It is not long past 4:00 a.m., Eastern Standard Time, on the morning of November 8, and Brit Hume and the rest of the Fox News commentators have lapsed into silence for what seems like a full 20 seconds, an eternity in television time. A quiet moment of contrition, perhaps, for the series of prognosticatory debacles that has preceded? A humble recognition of the fact that by this point—with the presidency effectively having been granted to and rescinded from each candidate over the course of six hours—there is nothing left to say?

If only.

No, the Fox News folks are quiet because they are watching CNN. Fox is at this moment broadcasting live video from War Memorial Plaza in Nashville, where thousands of Al Gore supporters stand in the rain, waiting for the vice president to appear and bring dramatic closure to the evening. People have been watching the stage with an acute sense of anticipation for hours, enduring a cold drizzle that, as the night drags on, has begun to feel unhappily appropriate. By this time in the morning, they—along with the millions of us watching television at home—have been subjected to a full range of results and emotions. Florida, and with it the election, has been given to them (7:49 P.M.), taken away from them (9:54 P.M.), given to George W. Bush (2:16 A.M.), and taken away from him (3:50 A.M.). Special graphics saying "George Bush, President-elect" and "George Bush, 43rd President" have

appeared and then vanished. The vice president, the networks report, has called the governor to concede (2:30 A.M.) and then unconcede (3:45 A.M.). The crowd on War Memorial Plaza—and the viewers at home—are dazed and stupefied.

This is also a fair description of the network news anchors. Peter Jennings and Tom Brokaw appear pained and enervated; Dan Rather, though apologetic, seems oddly energized, growing loopier as the hour grows later. "We've lived by the crystal ball; we're eating so much broken glass. We're in critical condition," he says. "We don't just have egg on our face; we have an omelet," Brokaw says. "If you're disgusted with us, frankly, I don't blame you," says Rather. Jennings, glancing despairingly around the studio for direction that is not forthcoming, admits he honestly doesn't know what to do next. It's not just Jennings: No one does.

This may be the best explanation for how it is that at this moment, circa 4:00 a.m. on November 8, the Fox News team (Brit Hume, *The Weekly Standard*'s Fred Barnes and Bill Kristol, and National Public Radio's Mara Liasson) has come to be watching CNN. As Hume comments in his desultory way on the scene in Nashville, he stops to survey the live video feed and then to listen to what sound like official announcements in the background. Except it turns out that these announcements are emanating from the giant video screen overhanging the plaza like a JumboTron at a rock concert: CNN correspondent John King is describing in authoritative tones what he knows about what is happening at the War Memorial, which is effectively nothing. Yet Hume and gang, apparently mesmerized by the prospect of some real information—is Gore about to appear?—strain to listen. And 10, 15—could it even have been 20?—seconds pass without comment from the Fox studio. All that can be heard are the murmur of the crowd and the strains of CNN. Mara Liasson finally breaks in with an embarrassed, "Well, enough of that. Our coverage is better than that," and Hume quickly concurs with a chuckle.

What makes this tableau even more weirdly postmodern is that the people on the plaza are gleaning most of their information from the television networks, which are being broadcast on the large screen looming over the crowd. (A similar screen is set up by the capitol building in Austin, where throngs of Bush supporters are gathered.) And what the networks are broadcasting, of course, is the scene at Nashville's War Memorial Plaza—so what the people on the plaza are seeing on the network broadcasts is… themselves, watching themselves watching themselves (and so on) on the huge TV above. Which means, in effect, that they are gleaning information from themselves—except, of course, they don't know anything. It makes your head spin.

This moment is as emblematic of the evening's TV follies as any: Network A publicly reduced to watching Network B for information while Network B, in turn, watches itself. Can there be any more apt a symbol for the infinite feedback loop that television news has become? (Actually, maybe so: At one point, CNN's Judy Woodruff asks correspondent John King, "What's that noise in the background?" King, grinning sheepishly, responds, "Um, that's me. They've got CNN broadcasting on the big screen, so there's an echo." As you hear King's words reverberating a split second later in the background, the crowd on the plaza breaks into laughter and applause.)

TOM BROKAW: *Doris, Doris, Doris…*
DORIS KEARNS GOODWIN, historian-turned-TV analyst: *Uh oh, something has happened.*
   —NBC News, November 8, 2:18 A.M.

There is no underestimating the psychological impact of the unanimous network calls for Bush. For anyone born since 1940—and for pretty much everyone else, too—television is truth. Yes, everyone knows that advertisements are full of distortions and exaggerations, that pundits are full of hot air, that sitcoms and dramas and even "reality TV" are not real. But in a matter as weighty as this, the presidency of the United States, television is simply not wrong. Television, for most of us, is reality.

Even presidents and would-be presidents get their reality from TV, which is why Gore conceded in response to the 2:16 a.m. network call. When Tom Brokaw said, "George Bush is the president-elect of the United States," television was not just reporting an external reality. It was declaring reality. Hundreds of thousands of votes remained to be counted in Florida and elsewhere. But with the network calls for Bush, the election was—as the mammoth TV screen outside the capitol in Austin blared while displaying a video montage of George W. at work and play—signed, sealed, delivered to the Texas governor. This despite the fact that, based on the vote count then current, he hadn't actually won.

Television cannot be blamed for butterfly ballots, hanging chads, or the oddity of the Florida vote count's falling within the statistical margin of error, but it can be blamed for the erroneous impression that the election was won by Bush and then stolen by Gore. Bush may yet, through courts and counts, legitimately win this election.

But if he doesn't, there will be the lingering feeling that his rightful election-night victory was yanked away from him unfairly. And depending on the outcome, Gore will look like either a sore loser or an illegitimate winner. While it is demonstrably false that a Bush victory was clear on the morning of November 8, the power of television is such that the impression many people had on Wednesday morning was that a victory by Bush (the television said he won!) was stolen by Gore. This is not a trivial misunderstanding; the media, through faulty news coverage, may have robbed a Gore presidency of whatever fragile legitimacy it might have had. And having declared Bush the winner, the networks had, however subconsciously, a stake in continuing to depict Gore as a sore loser.

The networks giveth and the networks taketh away.
   —TOM BROKAW, NBC News,
   late evening, November 7

How could the networks (all of them!) have screwed up something so important (twice!) as a presidential election call, briefly coronating the wrong candidate?

For a satisfactory answer to this question, we have to go back to 1934, when passage of the Federal Communications Act established licensed broadcasters' responsibility to serve "the public interest, convenience, and necessity." The act was supposed to ensure that, since the government was basically giving away part of the public domain, the commercial licensees would produce at least some programming that served the public interest and not just a broadcaster's bottom line.

At the dawn of television, news rarely made money, and it wasn't expected to do so. Though the very first television news show—*Camel Newsreel Theatre*, which premiered in 1948 on NBC—was designed as a fundamentally commercial enterprise (its sponsorship contract stipulated that there must always be a Camel cigarette burning visibly in an ashtray on the news desk), subsequent news programs like *The Huntley-Brinkley Report* (which premiered in 1956) and the *CBS Evening News with Walter Cronkite* (which premiered in 1963) were aimed at generating prestige but not necessarily profits for the networks. Broadcasters could generate quality news programming and serve the public interest without being overly concerned with commercial imperatives.

CBS's *60 Minutes* changed that. Premiering in 1968, *60 Minutes* was almost a decade old before it became the ratings hit that it remains today. But when it did, as one of its creators, Don Hewitt, said years later, "it single-handedly ruined television." Before *60 Minutes*, news shows were seen as a public service; after its great success, they were seen as potential profit centers.

For a few years, news divisions managed to hold the line, albeit feebly, against eroding quality, even in the new profit-maximizing environment. The legacy of network news was still a proud one, and the diversity of ownership produced healthy competition among network news divisions for talent and stories. But as conglomerates came into power—like General Electric (which bought NBC), a product manufacturer and defense subcontractor; Westinghouse (which bought CBS), a manufacturer and defense contractor with insurance and banking interests; and Disney, a media-entertainment complex (which bought ABC)—the emphasis on the bottom line intensified. News division budgets were sometimes cut deeply.

After the dismal 1988 election (Michael Dukakis versus George H.W. Bush) drew poor ratings, the corporate bosses at GE and Westinghouse pointed to the $17 million it cost to do polling and data collection for each of the news divisions and asked whether that figure couldn't be reduced. Until this point, each network had its own armada of statisticians, pollsters, and political scientists, who would collect data in the field and oversee the decision making process on election night, making sure calls were made accurately and not prematurely. In this way, each network served as a check and balance on all the others: As soon as, say, ABC had declared so-and-so the winner in Florida, then NBC and CBS would be checking their own, independently collected numbers to see whether they felt comfortable following suit. Yes, the networks competed hard to be first; but they were very careful because if they were wrong they would be shown up quickly.

But in 1990, under pressure from corporate headquarters, the Big Three networks joined with CNN and the Associated Press to establish the Voter News Service (VNS). The VNS pooled survey and polling data for all the news organizations, saving them each up to $10 million per election. This also had the advantage of relieving the individual networks of the responsibility to make election projections. Instead, VNS would make the call on a given state or election and then make that call available to all the networks and news services at the same time. But while this saved money, it removed the system of checks in place under the old regime, since VNS had become the sole source of data.

Compounding this problem, ABC News decided in 1994 to set up, more or less clandestinely, its own decision desk to interpret and extrapolate from VNS data. Drawing on VNS data but making its own predictions, ABC successfully called George Pataki's gubernatorial defeat of Mario Cuomo in New York, Chuck Robb's senatorial defeat of Oliver North in Virginia, and George W. Bush's defeat of Ann Richards in Texas before VNS did—and therefore before any of the other networks did. It was, according to Richard Morin, director of polling for *The Washington Post*, "the polling equivalent of Pearl Harbor." By 1996 all the networks had their own decision desks for processing VNS data.

This has brought us to the current arrangement—the worst of all possible worlds. With everyone drawing on the same VNS data pool, there's no opportunity for independent corroboration (or disputing) of results. Yet with each network hoping to have its predictions be the first, there's enormous competitive pressure to make calls prematurely, before VNS has called an election or a state. This is why we had the spectacle on election night of states and congressional elections being pulled back and forth willy-nilly. And it's why we are now treated to the bizarre spectacle of networks crowing not about who was right first but who was wrong last. (We also get to see network executives trying to hide behind VNS—as if VNS were other than a creation of the networks!)

This is where we appear to be, folks. The CBS New— News has now, for the second time tonight, pulled back Florida.
—DAN RATHER, around 3:50 a.m., November 8

The most malodorous product of this execrable system in the 2000 election was the botched Florida call. When Florida was declared the first time, all the networks and VNS gave the state to Gore at about the same time. They also all retracted around the same time, within a 20-minute period. But here's a telling point, little noted in press reports to date: VNS never called Florida for Bush. The numbers it was producing around 2:15 A.M. were trending that way, but not definitively enough for them to make the call. It was reportedly Fox decision desk staffer John Ellis—who, as has widely been reported (originally by Jane Mayer in *The New Yorker*), is a first cousin of George W. and Jeb Bush and had been on the phone with them all night—who called Florida, and thus the election, for Bush that night. The other networks, under pressure from their corporate chieftains not to get badly beaten by the upstart Fox, quickly followed suit over the next two minutes. It's impossible to put too fine a point on this: The outcome of a very close presidential election was nearly decided by George Bush's first cousin—who had quit his job as a columnist for *The Boston Globe* because, he said, his loyalty to his cousin would trump his commitment to objective journalism. If that doesn't indicate a problem with the system as currently constituted, what does?

We ought not to speculate on a Bush presidency yet. And I think you're right. Should we speculate on a Gore presidency? I mean, someone has got to be president.
—SAM DONALDSON, ABC News correspondent, late evening, November 7

The problems afflicting television news (PBS's *NewsHour with Jim Lehrer* is an admirable exception to most of what follows here) go broader and deeper than incorrect election calls, serious as those may be. The list of negative indicators is long and familiar. The evening network news audience has dropped from 40 million to 20 million over the past 10 years, with viewers defecting to CNN or the Internet or simply tuning out. In the 1960s, the average candidate sound bite on television was 45 seconds; today it's less than eight seconds. According to the Hess Report, a project of the Brookings Institution funded by Pew Charitable Trusts, nightly news shows are devoting less and less time to campaign coverage. The last eight weeks of this election (before November 7, that is) saw 670 fewer minutes of coverage than the comparable period in 1992. And the percentage of that time dedicated to "horse race coverage," as opposed to exploration of substantive policy issues, keeps increasing; it comprised 71 percent of all campaign coverage between Labor Day and the end of October this year. Horse race coverage bleeds quickly into wanton speculation. CNN may have been the first network to institutionalize speculation-as-news—the art of reporting on something not just as or after it happens, but before. Now all of the networks have caught on.

The most urgent challenge of all may be how to minimize what I'll call the Ellis effect: the danger that TV media will cross the line from reporting an event to affecting it. To some extent, there's an inevitable Heisenberg principle at work in all reporting. No media rendering of events is completely transparent, and such basic decisions as what to cover and how to cover it can always have an impact on an audience's perception of reality, which may then affect how the audience reacts to it. But surely there is something to be done about the more tangible problems of "changing" reality by making erroneous election calls, or of suppressing turnout by making early (even if correct) election calls. Republican Congressmen Billy Tauzin of Louisiana, Christopher Cox of California, and Cliff Stearns of Florida held a press conference on November 17 to demand hearings on the effects of early calls by the networks, especially in Democratic states. While Tauzin was engaging in partisan gamesmanship, this is a bipartisan complaint.

I would rather walk through a furnace in a gasoline suit than be wrong about anything.
    —DAN RATHER on *Reliable Sources*

I did not enjoy looking like a fool.
    —CBS political analyst BOB SCHIEFFER to radio-TV-personality Don Imus on November 8

Other than momentary embarrassment, the networks have suffered no ill effects from their dreadful election-night performance. Quite the opposite. At 11:00 p.m. on November 7, CNN had nearly eight million viewers, its highest total since the day of the Columbine murders. For the three days after the election, the cable networks CNN, MSNBC, and Fox News drew ratings 500 percent greater than their average third-quarter numbers. And the total election-night audience for broadcast and cable combined was 61.6 million viewers, a 70 percent increase from 1996,

when Bill Clinton clobbered Bob Dole. In fact, while ratings were higher in the 1960 and 1976 elections because the overall U.S. population was smaller, the 2000 election drew more households than any election in television history. What's more, advertisers are banging down the door to buy slots on the election-controversy broadcasts. Larry Goodman, CNN's president of ad sales and marketing, has reported that clients have come to him saying, "Get me on the air and keep me on the air for as long as this thing stays hot." And trade publications report that some networks are selling special "breaking news" packages to advertisers. It is clear that, given the perverse logic of the news industry whereby bad news is good for ratings and profits, the networks can financially afford to address some of their problems.

A straightforward solution to the Heisenberg-Ellis problem would be a proscription on calling elections before all votes are cast. Legislators on both sides of the aisle have expressed an interest in some kind of regulation along this line, and a recent Pew Research Center poll found that 87 percent of respondents thought networks should wait until all votes are counted before announcing election results.

An easy remedy for the problem of VNS being the lone data source is to establish competitors who will also collect exit poll data and early returns. The hard part is finding the funding to bankroll such competitors. (Currently, the *Los Angeles Times* has the only other national-election-data service.) But this remedy addresses the most extreme symptom of the debasement of public-service programming by television.

Curtis Gans of the Committee for the Study of the American Electorate proposes a regulation that correlates the size of a local broadcaster's market share with the size of its mandated public-service obligation, as a way of ensuring that primary-election debates, for example, get more television coverage. Robert Lichter, head of the Center for Media and Public Affairs, proposes outlawing paid campaign commercials outright and replacing them with free prime-time slots (in chunks of 15 minutes and longer) to candidates from parties who have polled more than 5 percent in the previous election.

But such proposals seem, one way or another, politically unrealistic: too utopian, too naive about the broadcasters' lobbying clout, too cavalier about abrogating the First Amendment. What's more, an occupational flaw of the civic-minded media critic is the chronic underestimation of the human appetite for fluff over substance. An effective reform plan must take this foible into account. More important, such a plan must one way or another win network news divisions enough distance from commercial demands that they have the freedom and the resources necessary to produce good news programming.

I said earlier that the most apt symbols of the election-night follies were those that signified the closed-loop nature of the network news media. But perhaps a still better symbol of television news today is George Stephanopoulos's beard. As November 7 turned to November 8, viewers could watch as the ABC commentator's beard grew visibly darker—remarkably so, like something in a time-lapse photography series.

What the gradual darkening of George's beard suggests to me—he stayed on the air for 14 hours straight—is that the relationship between time and the news has changed. No longer, the former Clinton aide's face seemed to be saying, is the news a fixed point in time. News, in other words, used to be presented for the most part in discrete increments, with the arrival of the morning and evening newspapers or the broadcast of the nightly news. News was not simply information, an endless supply of data, but, rather, perspective, something you could take the time to digest. Of course, in reality, events never stopped long enough for the morning paper or the evening newscast to fix them in place; after all, the

conceit that we ever knew the "latest" from Israel or Tallahassee just because we read the morning paper was always arrogant. And the new, continuous-flow definition of news more nearly approximates the flow of life itself. Still, news in the days when the news cycle remained a once-per-24-hour-period proposition was certainly different—not to say better—in that it gave more time both to viewers and to news broadcasters, who could produce real stories, place them in their proper context, and explain them, rather than simply provide running commentary on a live video feed. What we see when we watch CNN or MSNBC, or news on the networks that is constantly "breaking" (as with O.J. or impeachment or JonBenet or, now, the 2000 election) is not news in the classic sense but, as media expert Bob Lichter has put it, the "news-gathering process. You're watching reporters gathering items. Some turn out to be right; some turn out to be wrong; some are propaganda spinning from the campaigns." We would do well to remember this.

The Two-Bucks-a-Minute Democracy

By handing out millions of dollars' worth of Web TV's, two political scientists at Stanford have gathered the most perfect sample of Americans in the history of polling and persuaded them to answer survey after survey, week after week, year after year. It's a marketer's dream. And it just might change how we think about democracy.

By Michael Lewis

Earlier this year, a truly weird and possibly inspired company founded by a pair of Stanford political scientists, Norman Nie and Doug Rivers, finished spending tens of millions of dollars to install Web television sets in 40,000 American homes. The company, called Knowledge Networks, was trying to address the single greatest problem in polling—getting a random sample of Americans to answer questions—by paying a random sample of Americans for their time. In the summer of 1999, Rivers sent out 40,000 letters, most of them containing $10 bills. The money was the teaser for the big offer: spend 10 minutes each week answering his questions over the Internet, and Rivers would give you a free Web TV, free Internet access and a raft of prizes doled out in various contests and raffles. If you were uneasy with new gadgets, Rivers promised to give you not only the TV and the Internet access but also to send an engineer to install the stuff. An astonishing 56 percent of the people they set out to contact took the offer—compared with the roughly 15 percent now willing to answer questions from a stranger over the telephone.

One of those people was Marion Frost. When she received the letter from Rivers, she had just turned 80, which meant she was gold to any pollster looking to build a random sample of Americans. Along with Americans who earn more than $150,000 a year, Americans who have less than an eighth-grade education and Americans who don't speak English, Americans over 75 tend to elude pollsters. Frost has lived in the same quaint cottage for 46 years, nestled in a middle-class Silicon Valley neighborhood doing its best to avoid being overrun by property developers. The only hint of frailty about her was the cast on her left wrist, which she had broken, absurdly, on her way back from the D.M.V., where she had gone to obtain a handicapped parking sticker. The only sign that she found it odd for a complete stranger to show up at her house to watch her watch television was that she had invited a friend over to join us. The three of us—me, Frost and her friend, Yvette Reyes—settled down to a spread of pizza, cookies and coffee in a living room that doubled as a shrine to bygone values. The furniture would be familiar to anyone who had grandparents in the 1960's; the television was one of those giant oak cabinets with chrome dials that they stopped making back in the 1970's. "My husband died 18 years ago," Frost said, "and we bought the TV at least 15 years before that." The single anomaly in the place was the black Web TV box on top of the television cabinet. With its infrared ports, flashing lights and miniature keyboard, the thing was as incongruous as a Martian.

It was the night of the second Bush-Gore debate, and CBS was using Knowledge Networks—and by extension Marion Frost—to conduct two kinds of polls. One, which Dan Rather was calling "a snap poll," would measure who won the debate. The other, which Dan Rather would never mention, since CBS was still testing it, would seek to understand *why* he won. Twenty minutes before the debate, the red light on top of Frost's black box began to flash, its way of saying that it was waiting for her to switch on her TV and answer a few questions from Knowledge Networks.

Among the many things I was curious to know was why Rivers had been so successful at luring Americans into being the rats in his massive laboratory experiment. I assumed that in all cases he had appealed to the rats' insatiable lust for money and freebies. I was wrong.

"How did these people talk you into taking their surveys?" I asked Frost.

"They just called me out of the blue," she said. She sat toward the edge of her chair, her arm in a dark blue sling. All around her were photographs of children. She had reared three of her own, adopted another and taken in seven foster children.

"But you got their letter with the $10 in it?"

"They never sent me a letter with $10 in it," she said. "I got a letter from Doug Rivers but no $10." Yvette chuckled softly on the sofa beside me. "You come cheap, Marion," she said.

I motioned to her $249 Web TV. The box enabled Knowledge Networks to send polls and surveys to her over the Internet, which then could be displayed on her TV screen. Once each week, the red light flashed to tell Frost that questions awaited her answers whenever she had 10 minutes to spare. Tonight's poll was an exception in that it required Frost's presence at an appointed time. "So," I said, "what do you use that for?"

A hint of discomfort flashed across her impossibly sweet face. "The truth is, I haven't figured out how to use it."

"Then how do you take the surveys?"

"Oh," she said, "I do all the surveys. When the light comes on, I call Robert, and he comes over and turns it on and feeds in the information." Robert is Frost's 45-year-old son.

"When I get the cast off, I think I'll learn how to use it," Frost added, trying and failing to raise her broken arm.

"But you still answer the surveys?" I said.

"Oh, yes," she said, brightening. "Mostly all the questions are about products. Juice. One I remember was the different kinds of juice. They wanted to know what was my opinion of cranberry juice. Would I mix it in with other juices. I don't know. I figure they want to dilute the cranberry juice with other juices. I told them my opinion."

No $10 bill, no interest in the Web TV or the free Internet access or the raffles and contests. No sense whatsoever that she was being paid to answer questions.

"I don't understand," I said. "Why did you agree to be in this survey?"

She was at a loss for an answer, which was O.K., since Yvette wasn't. "Because," she said, with a tone that put an end to further questions, "she's a good person."

On that note, we settled back and waited for Knowledge Networks to begin measuring Marion Frost's opinions.

EVER SINCE THE INTERNET WENT BOOM, PEOPLE HAVE BEEN trying to figure out how to use it to open a window on the American mind. One curious subplot of this year's presidential campaign has been huge, inexplicable swings in the polls. There are a number of possible reasons for these—inept pollsters, fickle voters—but the most persuasive is the growing reluctance of Americans to take calls from pollsters. In the past decade, the response rate to telephone polls has fallen from as high as 40 percent to 15 percent. If the 15 percent of our population still willing to be polite to people who interrupt their dinners were representative, this trend would not be a problem for pollsters. But they aren't, so it is.

> Anyone with anything to mass-market longs for more detailed portraits of the consumer. A network of tens of thousands of Web TV's represents not just a statistical improvement. It creates a new genre of portraiture.

Onto this scene, the Internet seems to have arrived just in time. It gives new hope to people who believe that human behavior can be studied and explained scientifically. Internet polling enjoys several obvious advantages over old-fashioned survey techniques: it's potentially more scientific than chasing down people in shopping malls, it's less blatantly intrusive than phoning people at dinner and it carries video to those polled so that ads, movie trailers and product designs can be tested directly. But maybe as important as all these combined is the ease with which an Internet pollster can create a new kind of dialogue with the people he polls. In what Doug Rivers calls "a virtual conversation," the pollster with easy, steady access to a cross-section of the population can unspool a detailed story about the population's tastes and habits.

But the Internet has one huge disadvantage for pollsters: not quite half the U. S. population uses it. In the summer of 1998, Rivers and his Stanford colleague, Nie, both of whom had made distinguished careers studying polling techniques, discovered that they shared an outrage at the sham polls of the "general population" conducted on the Internet. They got to talking about ways that the Internet might be used to poll properly, short of waiting the years it would take for the technology to trickle down. They decided to go out and identify a random sample of Americans and persuade them to go online, for free.

Of course, it costs a fortune to dole out tens of thousands of Web TV's. So Rivers, who wound up running the business, was forced to neglect his original interest in political polling and acquire an interest in market research. Corporate America spends $5 billion a year for market surveys. Companies pay roughly $2 for every minute that randomly selected Americans spend answering questions of people who pester them at dinner time. The reason you are worth $120 an hour while you scratch yourself and talk on the phone to a pollster is that pretty much anyone with anything to mass-market—packaged goods, media come-ons, financial products—longs for detailed portraits of the consumer. A network of tens of thousands of Web TV's randomly distributed across the population would represent not just a statistical improvement. It would create a new genre of portraiture.

Typically, the relationship between the American Observer and the American Observed has been a one-night stand. A pollster calls and insists on pawing you a bit, and then you never hear from him again. Knowledge Networks was after something more. Its Web TV's would follow the same people, easily and cheaply, and measure not just their responses to surveys but also their behavior on the Internet. And it would be able to divine patterns in that behavior that companies could then exploit. As Knowledge Networks expanded, it would become possible to poll random samples of tiny populations—people who drank expensive tequila, say, or voted for Pat Buchanan. "Try finding a random sample of Jews by phone," Rivers says. "Jews are 2 percent of the population. Do you know how many randomly generated phone numbers you need to call to find 400 Jews?"

Interestingly, all parties to this new and seemingly intrusive relationship shared a financial interest in it becoming ever more intrusive. There might be people like Marion Frost who don't think of their time as money, but they are a rare breed. By enriching the information he mined from the brains of his random sample, Rivers raised the value of those who spent time answering his questions. The more their time was worth, the more goodies they got, and the more goodies they got, the more willing they would be to answer questions.

It took Rivers just three days to raise the first $6 million he needed from Silicon Valley venture capitalists. The only question they had was why Rivers was sending $10 to people before they agreed to his deal. "The V.C.'s said things like, 'If you sent that to me, I'd just keep the money and not do the surveys,'" Rivers says. "I had to tell them that most people weren't like venture capitalists." Once Rivers had proved to his backers that his system worked in a few hundred homes, he went back and asked for another $36 million so he could install many, many more Web TV's. The V.C.'s promptly handed that over too.

By the spring of this year, 100,000 Americans were spending 10 minutes each week answering Rivers's questions, often e-mailing him with extra ideas and comments and news about their lives. ("Mr. Rivers," wrote one, "Terrence cannot answer the questions this week because he is in jail.") By the end of the summer, the system was running at full capacity. So Rivers has gone back once

again to the venture capitalists for as much as $60 million more to install another 60,000 black boxes. By the end of next year, 250,000 Americans will be engaged in Knowledge Networks' virtual conversation—the fastest, biggest and quite possibly most accurate tracking poll ever conducted. Each person will remain in the sample for three years, at which point they are considered too overexposed to polls to be accurately polled.

Even by Silicon Valley standards, this is a fairly sensational financial story. Among other things, it tells you a great deal about what might be called the public opinion of public opinion. Between 1876, when the last new polling technology, the telephone, was invented, and the 1960's, when the phone was sufficiently widespread to allow for random sampling, it occurred to no one to go out and install 100,000 telephones in American homes. The telephone didn't become a polling device until it had spread on its own into every nook and cranny of American life. But the world is no longer willing to wait for a more accurate self-portrait. Offered even the slightest chance to, as Rivers puts it, "get inside people's minds and find out what's there," investors have proved willing to pay whatever it cost.

The ever-evolving relationship between American consumers and producers inevitably spills over into American politics, which is why a Stanford political scientist has wound up, at least for the moment, testing cranberry juice cocktails for a living. A better view of the public opinion of juice soon becomes a better view of the public opinion of issues and ads and phrases and candidates. Once investors had poured in tens of millions of dollars to create an elaborate mechanism designed to obtain a "360-degree picture of the mind of the American consumer," Rivers knew it wouldn't be long before some enterprising political consultant used it to enter the mind of the American voter. "But the thing we've found," he says, "is that the political people are slower on the uptake than the businesspeople. In part, it's because they don't have the same money to spend. But it's also that the sort of people who become pollsters to presidential campaigns don't like to hear the answers to honest polls. They're believers in a cause."

He is able to say this with detached amusement rather than despair because he assumes that the political people will come around—and how could they not? Politics is a competitive market. Better polls give politicians who follow them an edge. Those who don't will wind up being put out of business by those who do.

PEOPLE WHO BOTHER TO IMAGINE HOW THE INTERNET might change democracy usually assume it will take power away from politicians and give it to the people. It's easy to see how the Internet might lead inexorably to the same extreme form of democracy that has evolved in California, where the big issues often are put directly to the people for a vote. Sooner or later, it will be possible to vote online. And sooner or later, it will be possible to collect signatures online. Together, these changes might well lead to a boomlet in direct democracy, at least in states like California where citizens can call votes on an issue simply by gathering enough signatures on its behalf. At which point someone asks, Why can't we do the same thing in Washington? One constitutional amendment later and—poof—we're all voting directly to decide important national questions rather than voting for politicians and leaving the decisions up to them.

This line of futurology has history on its side. Every step taken by American democracy has been in an egalitarian direction. The direct elections of U.S. senators, the extension of the vote to blacks, women and adolescents, the adoption of initiative and referendum in the vast majority of states, the rise of public opinion polling—all of this pushes democracy in the same direction. It forces politicians to be more informed of, and responsive to, majority opinion. It nudges American democracy ever so slightly away from its original elitist conception and moves it toward something else.

The Knowledge Networks poll offers a glimpse of what that something else might be, a world in which politicians become so well informed about public opinion that there is no need for direct democracy.

It was with something like this in mind that George Gallup began his campaign in the 1930's to make political polling scientifically respectable. Gallup thought that democracy worked better the better-informed politicians were of majority opinion. Rivers does not exactly share this view. He created Knowledge Networks because he believed that inaccurate polls are a danger to democracy and an insult to good social science—but that is a long way from Gallup's original utopian vision. Rivers says he believes that Internet polling is inevitable, so that it might as well be done honestly. But he also believes that his faster and cheaper opinion-gathering machine will provide politicians with a more detailed snapshot of public opinion, and thus give rise to an even more constipated politics. The more perfectly informed politicians are about public opinion, the more they are chained to it. "The problem right now isn't that politicians in Washington are out of touch," Rivers says. "The problem is that they're too closely in touch. And this will make the problem worse." In short, you may believe that politicians could not be more automated than they are now. Just wait.

But it isn't just the politicians who are changed by the technology. The more perfectly watched that voters are, the less they have to pay attention to politics. After all, there's no point in anyone but a revolutionary participating in a system of majority rule when the will of the majority is always, and automatically, known.

OF COURSE, IT TAKES A WHILE FOR AN ENTIRE CULTURE TO get used to the idea that there is no point in participating in democracy unless you are paid to do so. It takes even

longer for it to figure out that its participation is worth two bucks a minute. For old ideas to die, the people who hold them must die first. And Marion Frost wasn't quite ready for that. Fifteen minutes before the second presidential debate began, her doorbell rang. It was a young man from Knowledge Networks, who had driven an hour to switch on her Web TV. (Frost's son was traveling, and I couldn't figure it out.) The screen, previously given over to Dan Rather's face, went blue. Onto it came a message: "Please try to have fun while being as serious about this test as possible."

It went on to ask several long, pro-forma questions, which Frost insisted on reading aloud before turning her attention to the alien keyboard. Yvette sighed. "This is going to be a long night, Marion." This was my cue to take her son's place at the keyboard. When we had finished with their questions, the picture came back on the screen, with a long measuring rod at the bottom of it. The rod had a plus sign on one end and a minus sign on the other. Frost was meant to signal what she thought of whatever Bush and Gore said, as they said it, by moving a tiny rectangle back and forth between the two. Instead, she told me what she thought, and I moved the rectangle for her. Her stream of opinions would flow into a river through Knowledge Networks' computers and into CBS studios in New York.

The debate started. I waited for Marion Frost's first command. "I like that Jim Lehrer," she said.

Lehrer had asked Bush a question about foreign policy, and Bush talked for as long as he could on the subject, then did his best to think up some more words to fill the time. Frost said nothing. The little rectangle didn't budge.

"I don't know about Bush," she finally said, "but I'm glad Jim Lehrer's going to be there." Al Gore then went off on his usual relentless quest for a gold star, and Frost listened to all of what he said intently, but again failed to respond. She seemed to want to think about what he said, but the new technology didn't want thought. It wanted quick.

"I don't know," she finally said, as Bush took over. "I'm confused. I think they're both right on some areas." She was growing ever so slightly distressed at her inability to give the black box what it wanted. Finally, Bush said something that caused Frost to say: "I like that. Go ahead and make it positive." But it was as much out of a concern for the little rectangle than actual deep feeling. In any case, her reflex was too slow to hit its mark; by the time I'd moved the rectangle, Gore had again butted in. This didn't seem to bother Frost. She was too busy trying to make sense out of the arguments Bush had made about the I.M.F. "That's the International Monetary Fund," she said—for my benefit, I think.

Yvette sighed and headed for the kitchen. "I get to take a break," she said. "You two can't move."

Frost looked at me with concern and asked, "Would you like a cookie?" The debate heated up again. Gore began to attack Bush's record on health care. Frost became irritated.

"'I believe he has a good heart,' what kind of statement is that?" she said. Hearts were something she knew about. The implications for the rectangle were unclear.

"Should I make it negative?"

"A little," she said.

On this went for an hour and a half, much like the debate itself, defying any possibility of the reflection or deliberation that Frost was intent on supplying. The joy of watching her with her Web TV was her insistence on layering old and dying habits of mind onto the new, supercharged process. Her opinions were being monitored as closely as political opinions have ever been monitored, and yet she didn't really allow the monitoring to interfere with her idea of how to watch a political debate. She avoided making snap judgments just as she had somehow avoided getting paid for offering them. She watched without much interest Dan Rather announce that Bush had won the snap poll—52 percent to 48 percent. She just did what she did because she entertained some notion of her social obligations above and beyond her economic interests. Either that, or she simply could not believe that a citizen is meant to be paid for her services.

Michael Lewis is a contributing writer for the magazine. He is the author, most recently, of "The New New Thing."

UNIT 4

Products of American Politics

Unit Selections

Key Points to Consider

- What do you think is the single most important social welfare or economic policy issue facing the American political system today? The single most important national security or diplomatic issue? What do you think ought to be done about them?

- What factors increasingly blur the distinction between foreign and domestic policy issues? How does "homeland security" fit into this context?

- How would you compare President George W. Bush's performance in the areas of social welfare and economic policies with the way he has handled national security and diplomatic affairs? What changes has he tried to make in each of these areas? What about President George W. Bush?

- What policy issues currently viewed as minor matters seem likely to develop into crisis situations?

- What do you think is the most significant policy failure of American national government today? The most significant policy success?

- What do you think about the idea of devolution, which means giving state and local governments *more* responsibility for policy making and policy implementation and the national government *less*? What reasons are there to expect that state and local governments will do a better—or worse—job than the national government in such areas as welfare and health care benefits for the old and the poor?

- What short-term and long-term effects did the events of September 11 have on the U.S. policy process and the content of U.S. government policies?

 **Links: www.dushkin.com/online/**
These sites are annotated in the World Wide Web pages.

American Diplomacy
http://www.unc.edu/depts/diplomat/

Cato Institute
http://www.cato.org/research/ss_prjct.html

Foreign Affairs
http://www.foreignaffairs.org

The Gallup Organization
http://www.gallup.com

International Information Programs
http://usinfo.state.gov

STAT-USA
http://www.stat-usa.gov/stat-usa.html

Tax Foundation
http://www.taxfoundation.org/index.html

"**P**roducts" refers to the government policies that the American political system produces. The first three units of this book have paved the way for this fourth unit, because the products of American politics are very much the consequences of the rest of the political system.

Dilemmas and difficulties in one policy area are often reflected in others. Indeed, tensions between fundamental values lie at the heart of much public policy making in all spheres: equality versus freedom, reliance on the public sector versus reliance on the private sector, collectivism versus individualism, internationalism versus isolationism, and so forth.

The health of the American economy is always a prominent policy issue in the American political system. One of the most remarkable consequences of 12 years (1981–1993) under President Reagan and the first President Bush was enormous growth in budget deficits and in the national debt. During the Clinton presidency the country enjoyed the longest period of continuous economic growth in U.S. history, accompanied by relatively low unemployment and inflation rates. Indeed, a healthy economy was the foundation of President Clinton's popularity in public opinion polls and of his successful reelection campaign in 1996. Continuing economic growth increased tax revenues to such an extent that the long-sought goal of a balanced budget was reached in 1998 amidst predictions that the entire national debt would be eliminated within a decade or so. In the last months of the Clinton administration, however, some signs of an economic slowdown appeared and the country entered a recession in the second half of President George W. Bush's first year in office. The terrorist attacks on September 11 doubtless accelerated the economic downturn.

Domestic public policy usually involves "trade-offs" among competing uses of scarce resources. During his 1992 campaign, Bill Clinton called attention to many such trade-offs in the area of health care. For example, are we as a nation content to spend a greater proportion of our national income on health care than any other industrialized country? If not, are we willing to limit medical spending when that may mean that sophisticated and sometimes life-saving treatments become less available to middle-class and poor Americans? Do we want to extend medical insurance to those millions of less affluent Americans currently uninsured, even though this might result in higher costs and/or less medical treatment for those who are already insured? As president, Clinton introduced a comprehensive health care reform proposal late in 1993. Congress never voted on that proposal, and, while various minor changes were made in the nation's health care delivery system during the Clinton administration, no comprehensive overhaul was ever achieved.

Other domestic policy areas also involve trade-offs. To what extent should we make the unemployed who are receiving welfare payments work, and what responsibility should the government take for preparing such citizens for work and for ensuring that jobs are available? (The landmark 1996 welform reform act, the result of a compromise between President Clinton and House Speaker Newt Gingrich, addressed several of these issues in fairly direct ways.) How much are cleaner air and other environmental goals worth in terms of economic productivity, unemployment, and so forth? How much of a role should the national government play in financing and shaping elementary and secondary schooling? Explicit and implicit trade-offs underlie debate about specific tax policies, social welfare programs, immigration policies, environmental problems, education policies, and the like.

For at least three decades, the United States and the Soviet Union each had the capacity to end human existence as we know it. Not surprisingly, the threat of nuclear war often dominated American diplomacy and national security policy making. Since World War II, however, the United States has used conventional military forces in a number of places such as Korea, Vietnam, Grenada, Panama, the Persian Gulf area, and Afghanistan. In 1991, the Soviet Union dissolved into 15 independent republics. The demise of the Soviet Union left the United States as the world's only remaining superpower and has greatly affected world politics and U.S. foreign policy ever since. Questions about the appropriateness of U.S. intervention in disparate places such as Bosnia-Herzegovina, Somalia, Haiti, Iraq, Kosovo, and even Russia were at the forefront of foreign policy concerns during the Clinton administration.

The foreign and defense policy process in the United States raises a host of related issues, including the struggle between legislative and executive branches for control of foreign and defense policy. Conflict between the branches sometimes takes place today in the context of the War Powers Resolution Act of 1973, which is itself a legacy of the Vietnam War. In 1991, Congress authorized war with Iraq, which was the first time since World War II that there has been explicit and formal congressional approval prior to commencement of military hostilities by the United States. In late 1995, President Clinton committed the United States to sending troops to Bosnia-Herzegovina as part of a multinational peacekeeping force. Despite some opposition in Congress, resolutions supporting the troops were passed. Toward the end of 1997, President Saddam Hussein of Iraq obstructed UN weapons inspection teams in his country. President Clinton responded by increasing the readiness of U.S. military forces in the Persian Gulf. In late 1998, in response to what the United States considered further provocation, there were several days of U.S. air strikes on Iraq. In the aftermath of the terrorist attacks in 2001, Congress supported President George W. Bush in pursuing the perpetrators and launching an assault on Al Qaeda sites in Afghanistan. Yet certain decisions taken by the Bush administration on the domestic scene and in connection with the treatment of individuals captured in Afghanistan soon led to criticism and controversy on Capitol Hill and in the country more generally.

The traditional distinction between domestic and foreign policy is becoming more and more difficult to maintain, since so many contemporary policy decisions (for example, passage of NAFTA in 1993) seem to have important implications for both the foreign and domestic scenes. President Clinton's emphasis on the connection between domestic and international economic issues in maintaining what he called national economic security reinforced this point. Similarly, President George W. Bush repeatedly noted the connection between military activities in faraway places like Afghanistan and "homeland security" in the post–September 11 era.

What Next for Welfare Reform?

A Vision for Assisting Families

by Wendell Primus

When I joined the Clinton administration at the Department of Health and Human Services in 1993, non-Social Security budget deficits were projected to be about $5 trillion over the next 10 years. Today, those same projections yield surpluses of about $3 trillion. This fiscal situation offers an unparalleled opportunity to build on the successes of welfare reform, to ensure that the working poor have a livable income, to reduce child poverty, and to provide health insurance to a greater share of low-income working parents and their children. As we applaud the achievements of welfare reform, we need to keep in mind its shortcomings as well—and to take steps to mend them.

Results So Far

Although one crucial feature of the 1996 welfare reform law—time limits—has still not been fully implemented, the results of reform thus far are striking. Since the law terminated the Aid to Families with Dependent Children program and replaced it with Temporary Assistance for Needy Families, welfare caseloads have fallen dramatically. Single mothers are working more and earning more. In 1992, about one-third of single mothers with young children were working. By 1999, the share had grown to more than half. Official child poverty rates have declined, and under a comprehensive measure of poverty that includes government benefits and taxes, the child poverty rate fell to 12.9 percent in 1999, the all-time low since this measure became available in 1979.

Not all these changes can be ascribed to the new welfare law. A strong economy and public policies that "make work pay" must also be credited. Welfare reform coincided with the longest-running economic expansion in U.S. history—a time when hourly wage rates for the lowest-paid workers began to rise after falling for two consecutive decades.

Among the most important "make work pay" policy steps of the 1990s was expanding the earned income tax credit. The credit, available only to low-wage workers with children, is refundable and can have as much value as a $2 per-hour raise. One leading study found that EITC expansions between 1984 and 1996 were responsible for more than half the increase in employment among single mothers during that time. Other such policies include expanded public health insurance for low-income children not receiving cash assistance, increased spending on child care subsidies, and increased earned income "disregards" that allow welfare recipients to keep more of their earnings when they work while remaining on welfare.

One would expect earnings to rise and child poverty to fall under these conditions. Yet some families are still floundering. On average, the inflation-adjusted disposable incomes of the poorest fifth of single mothers (about 1.8 million families) fell 4 percent between 1995 and 1999.

Another worrisome indicator is the "poverty gap," which has scarcely budged in recent years despite the falling poverty rate. The poverty gap—the number of dollars required to bring all low-income people up to the poverty line—takes into account not only the breadth of poverty, but also its depth.

Table 1. Poverty Gap for Families with Children, 1993-99

Billions of 1999 inflation-adjusted dollars

	Poverty Gap			Change in Poverty Gap	
	1993	**1995**	**1999**	**1993-1995**	**1995-1999**
Before taxes and transfers	85.0	73.0	55.9	-12.0	-17.1
After taxes and transfers	32.0	24.8	22.5	-7.2	-2.3

Source: Current Population Survey.

As shown in Table 1, during 1995–99, the increased earnings of low-income families with children reduced the pre-transfer poverty gap (the gap before government benefits and taxes) an impressive $17 billion. Yet once all government benefits and taxes are included, the gap fell only about $2 billion—only one-third of the reduction between 1993 and 1995, when the drop in the pretransfer poverty gap was considerably smaller.

Changes in the income of single-mother families reflect this same trend. The poorest 40 percent of single-mother families increased their inflation-adjusted earnings about $2,300 per family on average between 1995 and 1999. But their (inflation-adjusted) disposable income increased on average only $292. The increased earnings are not translating into greater disposable income because many of these families are losing ancillary benefits, such as food stamps, for which they remain eligible.

These data about disposable income are significant—and troubling—in light of a recent survey of the results of five separate studies covering 11 different welfare reform programs. The survey found that increased parental employment did not by itself significantly improve the lives of the parents' children. Only in programs where the parents increased both their employment and their income did the survey note positive effects—such as higher school achievement—for elementary school-aged children.

Supporting Working Poor Families

Because their disposable income has grown so little of late, the key issue for working-poor families who are no longer on welfare is their low participation in work support programs. These families should be able to get food stamps, child care, and health insurance readily, ideally from one place and through a relatively simple joint application. States should be allowed to simplify the transitional Medicaid program and provide transitional food stamp benefits for families going to work. Community-based groups, including faith-based ones, should help eligible families get these benefits.

Several changes in food stamp policy could boost participation among the working poor. The federal quality control system, for example, should be modified, for it has led many states to take administrative actions that have cut participation among working families. The food stamp program itself should be simplified. Asset tests, in particular,

should be revisited, for current tests make the program hard to administer and make too many low-income working families ineligible. The adequacy of the food stamp benefit structure also warrants reexamination, particularly in light of the cuts in benefits enacted in 1996.

Some changes in health insurance are also needed. In the typical (or median) state, a parent in a family of three loses Medicaid eligibility when her income surpasses 67 percent of the poverty line. Research has shown that expanding state Medicaid programs to cover parents also increases the number of low-income children protected by health insurance. We should expand funding for the State Children's Health Insurance Program (State-CHIP) and allow states to use the funds to extend coverage (through Medicaid or state programs) to low-income working parents (including noncustodial parents who pay child support) along with their children.

Employed immigrants are twice as likely to be poor as employed natives, and children in immigrant families make up one-quarter of all children below the poverty line. The 1996 welfare law eliminated much of the federal safety net for legal immigrants, including food stamps, Medicaid, and CHIP. Though aimed at immigrants, the impact of these restrictions falls also on children who are U.S. citizens. The children themselves and some immigrant parents remain eligible for benefits, but confusion about eligibility and concerns about the immigration consequences of receiving benefits have lowered participation. Congress should allow states to provide Medicaid, CHIP, and TANF benefits to working-poor immigrants and restore food stamp benefits for those who were made ineligible by the welfare law.

Finally, several changes in the federal tax code would benefit low-income working families. The EITC could be expanded for larger families and for families in targeted income ranges to reduce the high marginal tax rates that many such families face. And the child tax credit could be made partially refundable for low-income working families.

Focusing TANF on Poverty Reduction

When TANF is reauthorized in 2002, the first step toward improving it will be to shift its focus from reducing caseloads to reducing poverty. A principal purpose of welfare should be to reduce child and family poverty. Over the next 10 years, Prime Minister Tony Blair has committed his government to cutting UK child poverty rates—which are similar to our own—in half. The United States should follow suit.

Since Congress reformed welfare in 1996, a key impediment to measuring progress against poverty has been the lack of accurate state data on poverty rates and poverty gaps among families with children. The Census Bureau's new American Community Survey will be able to provide this data after the law is reauthorized. States that cut poverty the most, by emphasizing both work and the work support programs described above, should be rewarded.

Recognizing Special Needs of Certain Families

According to one study, 44 percent of TANF recipients reported at least two significant obstacles to work, such as low education, no recent work experience, language barriers, mental or physical health problems and disabilities, and lack of transportation or child care. The share of recipients reporting no work activity increased steadily with the number of significant obstacles. Research also indicates that families that fail to meet work requirements (and have their welfare benefit reduced as a result) have greater barriers to employment than other families receiving welfare. Providing services and accommodations appropriate to their greater needs should enable more of these parents to succeed in the workplace. Some states have been able to help many families that initially fail to comply with work requirements, rather than simply sanctioning them and setting them adrift. All states should be encouraged to follow their lead.

The five-year lifetime limit on federally funded welfare receipt also should be revisited. Work requirements and earnings disregards encourage welfare recipients to make the transition to work by combining earnings from work with a wage supplement in the form of small cash assistance payments. But recipients who make this transition and receive these wage supplements risk hitting the time limit and becoming ineligible for benefits when they may need them in the future. States should be able to use federal TANF dollars to provide wage supplements to families that are working but not earning enough to support themselves.

The share of participating families that states may exempt from time limits—now 20 percent of current caseload—should also be increased. Today the exemption covers many fewer people than was envisioned when the law was passed because current caseload size is much smaller than anyone expected.

Supporting Noncustodial Parents

Noncustodial parents (most of whom are fathers) should be encouraged to provide for their children both financially and emotionally. Child support, for poor families that receive it, is the second largest part of their family budget—more than one-quar-

ter of income on average. But many eligible families do not receive child support or receive it only irregularly. For children in families that have ever been on welfare, the government keeps much of the support that noncustodial parents pay as reimbursement for public welfare costs. Ending the "cost recovery" focus of the current child support system would remove a major disincentive for fathers to pay child support and allow children to benefit directly from their fathers' contributions. States could go further and build on the proven success and cost-effectiveness of the EITC by creating similar financial incentives for payment of child support. For example, a state could match low-income fathers' child support payments.

States also could increase the capacity of low-income noncustodial parents to pay child support by providing employment services and work supports. One reason why many such parents do not pay child support regularly is that they are un-or under-employed and have only a limited income from which to pay child support. Welfare reform encouraged more low-income mothers to enter the workplace so they could better support their children. The next steps are to help low-income noncustodial parents get jobs and to address some of their difficulties With the child support system (including child support orders that are high relative to their income, large accumulated child support debts owed to states, and economic disincentives to pay child support) so that they can take more financial and emotional responsibility for their children.

Keeping Fragile Families Together

According to recent research, about half of children born to single parents live with both biological parents at birth. As time goes by, however, these fragile families tend to separate. Policymakers need to find ways to help fragile families stay together. A welfare study in Minnesota found that two-parent working-poor families receiving cash assistance benefits and work supports were more likely to wed or stay married. Because two-parent families participate in food stamps, Medicaid, and cash welfare assistance at a lower rate than single-parent families, even when their incomes are similar, states should eliminate any remaining barriers or eligibility restrictions that apply to them. States should also actively seek to serve larger proportions of eligible two-parent families.

Increase TANF Funding

To better accomplish the goals of TANF and to reduce child poverty, both the TANF and child care block grants should be increased when the welfare law is reauthorized. At the same time, states must be more accountable for how they use their TANF block grant funds.

The TANF block grant should be indexed for inflation so that the resources do not erode and states can maintain services. The cost of child care, work programs, and other supports funded by TANF will rise with time. States also may need more funds to accomplish the multiple goals of TANF including serving families with multiple barriers to employment, fragile families, and noncustodial parents, as well as providing more child support to these families.

More money will also be necessary to reduce huge disparities in TANF resources available to states. Today wealthier states receive about $1,778 in TANF dollars per poor child, while poorer states, which have higher child poverty rates and lower fiscal capacity, receive $733. Recognizing these disparities, the 1996 law established supplemental grants for the poorer states to begin to move toward greater parity. These grants, scheduled to expire after 2001, should be extended.

Finally, because TANF provides a fixed amount of funding, states will not have additional resources when caseloads increase during an economic downturn. It is widely agreed that the TANF "contingency fund"—which is supposed to provide states additional funds in a recession—will be ineffective. States will need a measure that works.

The Next Round of Reform

Welfare reform has improved the prospects of many current and former recipients, but has had adverse effects on some. When TANF is reauthorized, policymakers should build on its successes, supporting those families who have left welfare for work, helping them climb the economic ladder to a more livable income, and reducing child poverty significantly, while providing additional resources and opportunities to those families left behind by the first round of welfare reform.

Wendell Primus is director of income security at the Center for Budget and Policy Priorities.

SOCIAL SECURITY

The liberal case for partial privatization

By Maya MacGuineas

Democrats are already lining up in opposition to the President's plan to reform Social Security. Bush has put forth only an outline of what he proposes to do—allow workers to use part of their payroll tax to fund private investment accounts, which, upon retirement, would be used to help augment Social Security benefits. Beyond that, the President intends to leave the specifics up to a bipartisan commission. But bipartisan commission or not, it appears that the President is in for one hell of a fight.

To liberals, privatization appears, at best, a risky gamble that would leave unsophisticated investors vulnerable to the perils of the turbulent stock market. At worst, it's a plot by anti-government radicals to entirely dismantle the Social Security system. Mainstream moderates who support privatization have tried to diffuse the visceral responses to the idea by developing friendlier labels. Still, whether it's "privatizing," "personalizing," or "capitalizing," most Democrats aren't buying it.

Certainly, many of liberals' concerns are legitimate. As Vice President Gore never hesitated to point out, investing in the stock market is risky. Many workers are unfamiliar with investing. The stock market does indeed seem like a dangerous place to park retirement benefits. For the many Americans who care about preserving a strong social safety net, risking the promise of a secure retirement is precisely the wrong way to go about reforming Social Security. Bush's pronouncement that he "trusts Americans to make their own decisions and manage their own money," does little to ease their minds.

But the types of reforms many liberals favor instead, from means-testing benefits to lifting the cap on payroll taxes to increasing the retirement age, if taken alone, would not create a fully viable reform package. For one, support for the communal retirement system will erode if it is transformed into an overly redistributive welfare program. Second, when Social Security began, it was a tremendously good deal for earlier participants. People got out far more than they paid in. But the returns participants receive on what they pay into Social Security have de-

clined precipitously and are now expected to be roughly one to two percent; for many, they will actually be negative. Increasing what is paid into the program or decreasing what is paid out, will only exacerbate the problems of the discouragingly low returns—increasing the generational inequities and tensions that already exist. Finally, even a package of benefit cuts and tax increases large enough to return the system to solvency in the short run would not do so in the long-run. It would simply postpone the problem.

Assuming certain concessions from Republicans, Democrats should embrace private investment accounts, combining the idea with traditional Democratic proposals. By recognizing the benefits private accounts have to offer, while structuring them to ensure that the risks are mitigated and the neediest retirees are protected, Democrats can, in fact, create a plan that would tackle not only the problem of the Social Security funding shortfall but that of declining returns head on. Republicans, at the same time, should be structuring their privatization plans to retain the progressivity so important to giving all the elderly security.

Searching for Compromise

The existing political standoff between the two parties does nothing to change the financial and demographic realities facing Social Security. According to our best estimates, because of the upcoming retirement of the baby boomers and growing life expectancies, the dedicated payroll tax used to fund the intergenerational transfer system will no longer provide enough money to cover promised benefits starting in 2015. By 2037, the program will be running annual deficits of $300 billion in today's dollars; it will take an infusion of $4 trillion to pay full benefits between now and when today's 30 year-olds retire. And the problems will grow rapidly thereafter.

An undertaking as financially challenging and politically explosive as reforming Social Security will demand compromise. One obvious approach would be for President Bush to back off from the contentious private investment component of his plan and to work with Democrats on developing other options. But the alternatives are, frankly, quite bleak. The only two remaining approaches to keeping the system liquid are cutting benefits or increasing revenues, either from increasing taxes, diverting money from the rest of the budget, or borrowing through deficit spending.

To keep the program solvent for 75 years, the amount of time program actuaries use to judge its financial health, Congress will in the future have to slash benefits across the board by one-third, leaving Social Security a tattered remnant of what it is today. Although such a drastic cut would not harm wealthier retirees, it would be devastating to those who depend on Social Security for a substantial part of their income.

Alternatively, we could increase the payroll tax that funds the system to cover compromised benefits. That would take an unpalatable 50-percent increase over time, and that's not counting the portion of the tax used to pay for Medicare. Since financial planners estimate individuals need to save roughly seven percent of their pre-retirement income to retire comfortably, the resulting 18 percent payroll tax would be clearly excessive, even considering the additional disability and survivor benefits the program offers.

Or taxes could remain unchanged and the money to pay for Social Security, which already consumes almost a quarter of the federal budget, could be taken from other areas of the government's spending. For instance, cutting the entire federal budgets for defense, science, the environment, and education would do the trick.

The final option, borrowing, would make the deficits of the past look microscopic compared to those we would run in the future, and it would drain the economy of savings, thus dragging down economic growth and incomes.

The difficulty of creating comprehensive reform plans that exclude private accounts is the reason there are no realistic alternatives floating around. A few years back, the Clinton administration, pledging to put Social Security first, proposed channeling new money out of general revenues into Social Security to be invested by the government in the stock market. Acknowledging the need to increase the program's returns, few Democrats voiced fears about the stock market then. In fact, at a 1999 White House conference on Social Security, Vice President Gore pointed out that "over any 10-year period in American history, returns on equities are just significantly higher than these other returns."

But while the stock market itself was not seen as a threat, the notion that the government would oversee the investment decisions was received about as warmly as the Presidential pardon of Marc Rich. Most politicians who initially flirted with the plan later recoiled from it in light of the inherent risks in intertwining financial markets and politics, not to mention the difficulties of the government investing a multi-trillion dollar fund without adversely affecting Wall Street.

Clinton quickly dropped the idea and, as *The New York Times* reported, Gore determined that "The magnitude of the government's stock ownership would be such that it would at least raise the question of whether or not we had begun to change the fundamental nature of our economy."

Generational Risk

While critics regularly refer to the market risks that would exist in an investment program, they ignore the risks in the current system, those spread between generations rather than portfolios.

Members of smaller generations have to pay far more in taxes to support larger, older generations, greatly reducing the returns they get from Social Security. Because these generational risks are less transparent, they tend to be overlooked in discussions about fairness and risk. But ignoring these risks promises to unravel support for the program from young workers on the wrong end of what has become simply a bad deal.

By allowing workers to invest a portion of their payroll taxes, they would, for the first time through Social Security, be able to save and invest and benefit from compounding returns. Assuming average returns of only five percent, lifetime workers could expect accounts with assets of anywhere from $100,000 to $600,000. Once the accounts had time to grow, they would be able to more than offset the benefit reductions needed to keep the program solvent.

Addressing the Risks

There are legitimate concerns about the risks of pursuing higher returns, and a new system needs to be structured accordingly. For instance, partial privatization could present an opportunity for unscrupulous money managers to take advantage of unsophisticated investors, churning their accounts or robbing them of their assets the way many subprime mortgage companies fleece elderly homeowners.

Clearly, Social Security must not be turned into a free-wheeling laissez-faire system with workers trusting their friend's second cousin to invest in commodity futures or currency swaps. Instead, the privatized part of the system should be structured like an employer-sponsored pension system, with workers choosing from a variety of government-regulated, well diversified, professionally managed stock and bond funds. Few decry these types of savings opportunities as too risky; in fact, Democrats and Republicans alike encourage their expansion as a way to increase personal savings and wealth.

Government regulations can protect workers against charlatan money managers, but what about the roller-coaster stock market? Annual returns have ranged from negative 12 percent to positive 32 percent over the past twenty years. But while markets are rocky, diversified investments—as the Social Security investment options would be—have always been the best method to combat risk.

Furthermore, the perpetual year-to-year fluctuations are irrelevant. Market returns over one's working lifetime really count. The U.S. stock market has never failed to provide positive returns for any 20-year period going back to and including the Great Depression; the average return on the S&P 500 over that period was 12 percent.

The pronounced risk of recent years to workers who couldn't afford to save, (due in no small part to the payroll tax) has been far greater than anything the stock market has dished out. They missed the opportunity to build wealth while a booming economy doled out profits to those on the upper half of the income spectrum. Declaring the stock market too risky for the least well off mainly ossifies existing wealth inequities.

While regulations will be instrumental in mitigating risk, no one should insist on regulating out all selection in investment choices. Workers will have a long time horizon over which to save, with different investments appropriate at different stages of life. Young workers would be more likely to choose higher-yielding equity-fund options, while those approaching retirement would be more likely to switch into safer bond funds. People shouldn't be forced to shoulder more risk than they choose. By making government bond and money market funds available, they wouldn't have to.

Investment vehicles structured particularly for retirement, such as funds that guarantee minimum returns, allowing participants to lock in their gains and guard against unwanted risk, like today's system, should also be included as investment options.

We should partially privatize Social Security, but it should not be turned into a freewheeling laissez-faire system with workers trusting their friend's second cousin to invest in currency swaps.

Additionally, Social Security's fundamental purpose—to ensure a decent retirement—should not only be preserved, it should be strengthened. A base benefit should be set to guarantee that the lowest-level benefits would still be higher than what today's system offers. Under the plans being considered to partially privatize Social Security, the bulk of funding would continue to finance traditional benefits, not private accounts. Gradually folding in an investment component, initially using, for instance, only four percent of the payroll tax, would leave the other 8.4 percent of the tax to finance additional benefits for retirees, as well as disability and survivors' benefits. The traditional retirement benefit could be structured to provide a base level benefit for all retirees or, better yet, a more generous one for those who needed them most.

Making Privatization Progressive

Liberals should insist that any privatization system remain progressive. Because private accounts would partly offset the current Social Security benefit, some of the progressivity built into the current benefit structure—where lower-earning workers

receive larger benefits relative to their earnings—would be lost. The purpose of privatization reform plans should be to increase the efficiency of the system, not to lessen the progressivity.

Under a simple privatization plan saving four percent of earnings, workers earning $20,000 could expect to accumulate roughly $150,000 by the time they were 67, but someone earning $65,000 might have $500,000. The low-income workers' savings would certainly be higher than what they would be without the program, but they would still be far more dependent on the rest of their Social Security benefit to supplement their personal savings.

A better option would be a progressive privatization plan, with low-income workers' savings matched by the government. The savings of low-income workers could be matched by say 2-to-1, scaling down as income increased. Under this scenario, a $20,000 earner would retire with closer to $300,000. While government matches would cost more initially, decreasing poorer workers' reliance on the government-guaranteed portion of the system would more than make up for the cost over time. Some Republicans, notably Congressman Kolbe of Arizona, have developed bipartisan plans structured to help low-income workers that could serve as blueprints for compromise.

To be fair, partial privatization is not the panacea some claim. Mending a system running out of money is never easy. Even with the prospect of private accounts providing new funds and higher returns over time, additional measures will be necessary to keep the program solvent. It will take time to build up private accounts, and in the meantime, part of the payroll tax used to fund the current system will be diverted into investment accounts. Social Security surpluses can provide some of the money to fund both the current system and private accounts, but once the surpluses have abated, the system will need either benefit cuts or new revenues sources.

The Road Less Traveled

Though politicians on both sides of the aisle have promised to protect current Social Security benefits at all costs, it makes no sense to take changing the benefit structure off the table. If current beneficiaries are exempt from any adjustments needed to keep Social Security liquid, the entire responsibility will be shifted onto younger workers and future generations regardless of their economic situation—who already face a far worse deal in Social Security than do current beneficiaries.

Of course, scaling back benefits should not be done through an across-the-board benefit cut, which would rip away benefits from the 60 percent of retirees who depend on the program for at least half their income. But means-testing benefits, or lowering payments for the wealthiest seniors, can easily be structured to protect the less affluent. This would spread the costs of reform among those who can afford them regardless of age.

Secondly, what every politician knows but few are willing to acknowledge is that we need to increase the retirement age. When Social Security began, life expectancies for 65-year-olds were for another 12 years; today they live for another 18. It is absurd for people to be living longer but still retiring at the same age as their grandparents. While the retirement age is gradually increasing to 67, it needs to be increased faster and then indexed to life expectancies. Disability benefits would still be available to anyone forced to stop working before the retirement age.

Critics will no doubt decry these changes as draconian and unfair. But without private investment accounts to fill in much of the funding gap over time, the changes will in fact, have to be much larger. Plans that don't include an investment component inevitably fall out of balance and run huge deficits in the long run.

Finally, the budget surpluses present a unique opportunity to ease the pain of keeping Social Security in the black. If the surpluses materialize as projected, the government will run out of publicly held debt to repurchase and have to pursue the discredited idea of becoming a massive owner of stocks and bonds. Avoiding this quagmire has become one of the newest justifications for large tax cuts. But using the surpluses for tax cuts, stimulating consumption, ignores the reason for reducing the debt in the first place: to increase national savings.

By using the surpluses instead to jump-start private investment accounts and to fund the progressive matches for low-income workers, we would have enough money to cover benefits and build new investment accounts. Moreover, we would ensure that the surplus dollars would still be saved, adhering to the successful fiscal discipline of the past decade.

To give this story a happy ending, Republicans and Democrats will have to cast aside their suspicions and recognize that neither side's concerns are misplaced. Partial privatization—if done right—can achieve liberal goals of equity and conservative goals of efficiency alike. There's plenty of room for compromise. Politicians will look for excuses to delay because there will always be hard choices involved, but the choices will only get harder with time.

MAYA MACGUINEAS *is a Fellow at the non-partisan New America Foundation in Washington, D.C.*

Reprinted with permission from *The Washington Monthly,* April 2001, pp. 23-26. © 2001 by Washington Monthly Publishing, LLC, 733 15th St. NW, Suite 1000, Washington DC 20005; 202-393-5155; *www.washingtonmonthly.com.*

Now Do You Believe We Need a Draft?

We're in a new kind of war. Time for a new kind of draft.

BY CHARLES MOSKOS AND PAUL GLASTRIS

PRESIDENT BUSH HAS SAID THAT THE new war against terrorism will be "a different kind of conflict." He is more right than he knows. Not only are we facing a uniquely shadowy enemy, one committed to inflicting mass civilian casualties on U.S. soil. But for the first time in our history we are entering a war of significant size and probable duration (administration officials have said it may last for "years") without drafting young men to fight the threat.

Not only are we not drafting our young men. We are not even planning to draft them. Elected leaders are not even talking about the possibility of drafting them. That terrorists might poison municipal water supplies, spray anthrax from crop dusters, or suicidally infect themselves with small pox and stroll through busy city streets, is no longer considered farfetched. That we might need to draft some of our people to counter these threats—now *that's* considered farfetched, to the extent that it's considered at all.

America needs to wake up. We're at war. We need a draft. But because this is a new kind of conflict, we need a new kind of draft. A 21st century draft would be less focused on preparing men for conventional combat—which probably won't be that extensive in this war—than on the arguably more daunting task of guarding against and responding to terrorism at home and abroad. If structured right, this new draft might not be as tough to sell as you would think.

Churchill famously said that America could be counted on to do the right thing, after exhausting all other possibilities. On the subject of the draft, we are rapidly reaching that point of exhaustion. A draft might be avoidable if enough Americans were volunteering to serve. But we're not. Soon after the events of September 11, newspapers reported that the phones in military recruitment offices were ringing off the hook. Follow up with

stories showed that all that clamor had brought virtually no new recruits. So far, our patriotism, though sincerely felt, has largely amounted to flag-waving and coat holding.

Perhaps we could get by without a draft if our all-volunteer military had more than enough troops on hand. But it doesn't. The actions so far taken in Afghanistan, and the buildup to support those actions, have been relatively modest. Yet with personnel cut by a third since the end of the Cold War, the services were hard-pressed to meet ongoing missions even before September 11. There is already talk of pulling U.S. forces out of the Balkans, something the Bush administration wanted to do anyway. But it will not please our NATO allies, whose long-term support we will need in the fight against terrorism, and who will have to fill the gap with more troops of their own.

We are calling up large numbers of reservists, but because so many of them work as police officers, firefighters, and emergency medical technicians, our municipalities are being drained of precisely the people we will need if (when) the terrorists return.

Indeed, it seems clear that we are going to need thousands more men and women in uniform to deal with terrorist threats here at home. The president has appointed former Pennsylvania Governor Tom Ridge as his new homeland security "czar." The federal government will be taking over airport security, either providing the services directly or supervising private firms providing it. However the restructuring shakes out, we are clearly going to need more federal armed personnel to guard dams, nuclear power plants, sports complexes, and U.S. embassies abroad; more border patrol and customs agents to keep terrorists and their weapons from entering the country; more INS agents to track down immigrants who have overstayed their visas; more coast guard personnel to inspect ships; more air marshals to ride on passenger jets; and more FBI agents to uncover terrorist cells still operating within and outside our borders.

Where are all these brave men and women going to come from? Certainly, America is rich enough, and the need vital enough, that we could afford to offer significant salaries to lure candidates. But even in a weak economy, there is a finite number of competent people willing to choose a career that requires wearing a uniform, performing often dull work, such as guard duty, with alertness, and being ready at any moment to risk one's life for others. A whole range of government agencies and private firms, from the U.S. Army to Brinks to local police departments, must compete for this limited labor pool. And the pool is probably not expanding.

Consider this: Between 1980 and 2000, surveys showed that the number of young people saying they would definitely not serve in the military rose from 40 to 64 percent. The only reason this change of attitude did not destroy military recruiting efforts is that the need for new recruits plummeted with the end of the Cold War. But the military is feeling the pinch nonetheless. The armed services have had to double starting pay to recruit half as many enlistees, and the quality of new recruits is not what it should be. The number of enlistees scoring in the top half of the armed forces qualification tests has dropped by a third since the mid-1990s. In fiscal year 2000, the Army took in some 380 recruits with felony arrest records, double the number in 1998. Desertions are also on the rise. Most telling, over one-third of those entering the military fail to complete their enlistments. Contrast this with the one in ten of draftees who did not complete his two-year obligation during the Cold War. Much better to have a soldier serve a short term honorably than to be discharged for cause.

No Peeling Potatoes

Reinstituting the draft is the obvious way to meet the suddenly increased manpower needs for military and homeland security. This fact would have seemed obvious to previous generations of Americans. That today we aren't even talking about a draft is a measure of the deep psychological resistance Americans have developed to anything that smacks of the state compelling anyone to do anything. Ideology plays a role here. In general, the left doesn't like the military, and the right doesn't like anything that interferes with the marketplace. When it comes to national needs, the left believes in something for nothing, the right in every man for himself.

The psychological resistance also gains comfort from arguments made by the opponents of the draft and by the military hierarchy, which also resists a return to conscription. (The military resists the draft largely because it resists all change; it opposed *ending* the draft in 1973).

One argument is that today's military requires professional soldiers, especially for overseas missions. Let's leave aside the fact that in World War II, Korea, and Vietnam, most combat soldiers had only six months of training before being sent to war. Let's also grant that because of today's high-tech weapons and complex war-fighting strategies, the actual combat must be

left to professional soldiers (though there is some reason for skepticism here). Still, there are hundreds of thousands of vital military jobs—not peeling potatoes—that could be filled with short-term draftees.

One example is peacekeeping. From experience with U.S. deployments in Bosnia and Kosovo, we know that combat troops tend to chafe at peacekeeping duty when they are stuck on bases with nothing to do and little opportunity to train with their weapons. But it's also clear that military police thrive on such assignments, because they get to perform the jobs they are trained for—patrolling neighborhoods, arresting troublemakers, intervening in disputes with a minimum of force. Military police work doesn't require that many special skills. After two months of basic and four months of special police training, new recruits are shipped off to places like Tuzla, and they do just fine. The average tour of duty in Bosnia or Kosovo: about 6 months. Short-term draftees, in other words, could easily do these M.P. jobs, and many others besides. This would free up more professional soldiers to fight the war on terrorism without requiring that the U.S. abandon other commitments.

Draftees would not have to be offered the relatively high wages and benefits that it takes to lure voluntary recruits (an increasing number of whom are married with families). This would leave more funds available to raise pay for the kinds of personnel that the military is having a terribly hard time holding on to, such as computer specialists, mid-level officers, and master sergeants. To put it baldly, we now have overpaid recruits and underpaid sergeants. In the draft era, the pay ratio between a master sergeant and a private was seven to one; today it is less than three to one. Restoring something like the old balance is the best way to upgrade retention in hard-to-fill skills and leadership positions.

All these arguments apply equally to the homeland security front. There is no reason why conscripts, with professional supervision, can't work as border guards, customs agents, anthrax inoculators, or disaster-relief specialists. Federal law enforcement agencies and unions will deny this with all their bureaucratic might, but it's true. It takes less than five months to train someone to be a border guard. The FBI turns applicants with law or accounting degrees into fully-fledged agents after only four months of training.

Other developed nations that have retained the draft typically use conscripts for homeland security. In Israel, draftees serve in both the regular military and as lightly armed "guard police" along the Gaza Strip. They also man the "home command," which provides security and other services in the country's cities during emergencies, such as the scud missile attacks during the Gulf War. In France, which finally abandoned its draft last year (believing that threats to its security had diminished), conscripts worked alongside professional police in the *Gendarmerie* and provided emergency airport security when terrorists set off bombs in the Paris Metro in 1995. In Germany, most draft-age men choose to serve either in the military or in some form of civilian service, such as working with the elderly. But about one in ten chooses to work in a state or federal police force, providing such things as border security, or they train as volunteer firefighters and serve part-time for seven years.

One can imagine a similar three-tiered system of youth service in America, with 18-month terms of duty for all citizens age 18 to 25. In this new-style draft, conscripts would have what all Americans now demand: choice. They could choose to serve in the military, in homeland security, or in a civilian national service program like AmeriCorps (there's no reason women couldn't be drafted for the latter two categories). In return, draftees would get GI-bill-style college scholarships, with higher awards for those who accept more dangerous duty.

Back in Vietnam days, opting to fulfill your draft requirement stateside in, say, the National Guard, was considered a way to save your skin. That won't be so true in the new war on terrorism. As we saw with the deaths of firefighters in New York, homeland security duty can be dangerous.

The Sucker Factor

That brings up the second argument against the draft: that the sons of the elite will find ways to avoid service. Of course, that's even truer in an age of all-volunteer forces. But it's fair to ask: How can a draft be made equitable?

The best way would be to require all young people to serve. One reason more young people don't serve now is the fear that while they're wearing the uniform, their peers will be out having fun and getting a leg up in their careers. If everyone were required to serve, no one would feel like a sucker. They might even enjoy the experience; surveys show that most former draftees look back on their time in the service with fondness and pride.

It's possible, however, that the country won't have the need for every eligible young person to serve. What then? One answer is a lottery with no student deferments. (Under Selective Service rules established after Vietnam, college deferments are no longer allowed.)

Part of what makes Americans dubious of conscription is our memory of how the class-biased draft of the Vietnam War-era helped drive America apart. We tend to forget that the more eq-uitable draft that existed during World War II and for 20 years afterwards helped bring the country together. During the peaceful years of the 1950s—a time not unlike our own, when the threat of mass destruction hung in the air—most Ivy League men had to spend two years in uniform, before or after college, working and bunking with others of very different backgrounds and races (the military, remember, was about the only racially integrated institution at the time).

This shared experience helped instill in those who served, as in the national culture generally, a sense of unity and moral seriousness that we would not see again—until after September 11, 2001. It's a shame that it has taken terrorist attacks to awaken us to the reality of our shared national fate. We should use this moment to rebuild institutions like the draft that will keep us awake to this reality even as the memory of the attacks fade.

A 21st century draft might be more welcome than most of us realize, especially among young people whose lives will be affected by it. While national leaders and pundits have avoided the subject, a potential return of the draft has been a hot topic of conversation among young people since September 11. "If it's something they want us to do for our country to keep us safe, then go for it," Ryan Aaron, a senior at U.S. Grant High School in Oklahoma City, told *National Journal*. Another young man, Julian Medina, a day laborer cleaning up office buildings near the still-smoldering World Trade Center, told *The Washington Post*: "If I have to, I'd fight to catch the man who did this." Not all young people are so gung ho; many, in fact, hate the idea. But at least they're talking about it. If their views can move from news pages to the editorial pages, and ultimately to the floors of Congress, then we could be on our way to a more secure and more unified America.

CHARLES MOSKOS, *a former draftee, is Professor of Sociology at Northwestern University.* PAUL GLASTRIS *is editor in chief of* The Washington Monthly *and a senior fellow at the Western Policy Center.*

Reprinted with permission from *The Washington Monthly,* November 2001, pp. 9-11. © 2001 by Washington Monthly Publishing, LLC, 733 15th St. NW, Suite 1000, Washington DC 20005; 202-393-5155; *www.washingtonmonthly.com.*

Immigration and Terrorism

The issues have become blurred and entangled

BY ROBERT McCHESNEY

THE MONSTROUS TERRORIST ATTACKS of Sept. 11 have prodded the nation to reexamine itself. As America races to combat agents of global terrorism, particularly fundamentalist Islamic extremists, decision makers should proceed prudently so as to build the requisite broad coalition at home and abroad. A key homeland front, however, will be the many federal detention centers and local jails where noncitizens are held by the Immigration and Naturalization Service. The scope and terms of such detention are one of the sticking points in the antiterrorism legislation before Congress. Attorney General John Ashcroft favors broad powers to detain indefinitely and remove people from the United States, while civil liberties advocates on both sides of the aisle urge a more calibrated approach.

The audacity and carnage of the attacks are unprecedented, but we have been here before. Five years ago last month, America decided to go after terrorists by clamping down on immigrants and asylum-seekers. On Sept. 30, 1996, Congress passed the Illegal Immigration Reform and Immigrant Responsibility Act (IIRIRA), which subsequently spawned the nation's fastest growing segment of the incarcerated population and led to record levels of deportation. There are important lessons to be learned from this history.

The Origins of the Illegal Immigration Reform Act

In the early 1990's the U.S. economy had been stagnant. As economic indicators improved, however, the nation was shocked by a series of highly publicized terrorist crimes and incidents of border violation. On Jan. 25, 1993, a lone gunman ambushed motorists waiting at a red light outside the main entrance to the Central Intelligence Agency headquarters in Langley, Va. Two C.I.A. employees were killed, and three other people were wounded as they sat innocently in their cars. The following month a 28-year-old Pakistani immigrant by the name of Mir Aimal Kansi was charged with capital murder, subsequently found guilty and sentenced to death. As it turned out, he had come to the United States in March of 1991 on a business visa and eventually was issued a work permit. He perpetrated the terrible crime while awaiting disposition of his application for political asylum.

One month after the C.I.A. murders, an explosion rocked the World Trade Center in New York City, killing six people, wounding more than a thousand and sowing widespread fear. The following year, four Muslim fundamentalists were convicted of the crime. Each was sentenced to 240 years in prison. One had applied for political asylum, while another perpetrator had overstayed a student visa.

Still later in 1993, an old cargo steamer ran aground on a sandbar in the surf off New York City. The Golden Venture dumped her human cargo of 286 undocumented Chinese into the water. They swam the last few hundred yards to shore, then were arrested and detained. The Golden Venture quickly became the national news obsession of the day. Every television station in the country played and replayed scenes of what some tabloids described as a "sea invasion of illegals." An already nervous public mainstream was now confronted with stark images of drenched Chinese nationals huddling under blankets on a windy New York beach, staring in confusion at the television cameras.

After three major incidents within six months, unscrupulous elements of the press found increasing profit in sensationalizing a story of immigrant hordes and terrorists breaching permeable borders to attack the fabric of American society. The immigration and criminal terrorist story lines blurred and became conflated. Popular discourse was virulent and fearful, and politicians took notice. The solution seemed all too obvious: close the borders to "illegals" and imprison or deport those already here.

Perhaps the most infamous event of this period occurred on April 19, 1995, when a Ryder truck parked outside the Murrah Federal Building in Oklahoma City exploded. The potent mix of fertilizer and fuel oil blew half the nine-story building into oblivion, killing 168 innocent people, including 19 children, and injuring another 500. According to initial press reports, "Middle-Easterners" were reportedly seen in the vicinity of the crime and were initially regarded as possible suspects. Two days after the blast, however, a Caucasian U.S. military veteran, Timothy McVeigh, was picked up and subsequently convicted of the heinous capital crime.

Legislative reaction to the sluggish economy and high-profile crimes and incidents had begun at the state level. In November of 1994 California passed Proposition 187, which placed onerous restrictions on legal and illegal immigrants. The courts subsequently overturned the initiative, but its popular political resonance remained potent.

In Washington, the newly elected 104th Congress saw a hot-button issue. After 40 years in the minority, Newt Gingrich had led the Republican Party to power in 1994. Citing polls that showed more than 70 percent of Americans wanted tighter restrictions placed on immigration, crime and terrorism, Congressional Republicans promised strict, "tough-on-crime" policy solutions as part of their Contract With America.

Mr. Gingrich interpreted Proposition 187 as the expression of a national public consensus on immigration. Even liberal Democrats were getting on the bandwagon. To maximize the political momentum after Oklahoma City, the Immigration Reform Act and a related bill, the Anti-Terrorism and Effective Death Penalty Act, were considered simultaneously. The latter, also enacted in 1996, suspended several traditional constitutional rights that had previously been granted to noncitizens. The juxtaposition of these two laws reflected the press and pundit sound bites, which loosely associated immigrants with terrorists and criminals.

President Bill Clinton, facing re-election and reading the same polls as the Republicans, signed IIRIRA on Sept. 30. Though a dubious product of the Republican Congress, it arguably represented the bipartisan national political consensus of the mid-1990's. This uncritical association of immigrants with terrorists remains today the most troubling aspect of the national conversation on how to respond to the tragic events of Sept. 11 and can lead only to tragic social consequences and misguided governmental decisions.

Assessing the 1996 Legislation

The result of such loose thinking has a human face. The I.N.S. now holds over 20,000 noncitizens in detention ev-

ery day—more than three times the 1996 number—under the legislated system of mandatory detention. The average length of incarceration is relatively short because many are deported rapidly, but a significant percentage are held for over a year. More than 200,000 are detained annually, at a cost of $1 billion. A large number of those deported hold green cards as legal permanent residents, and can demonstrate significant equities in the community as job holders and property owners. One critic has called the 1996 laws the most extreme punitive outbreak of civil-liberties xenophobia since the Japanese internment camps of World War II.

The I.N.S. annually detains an additional 5,000 unaccompanied minors. None receives the celebrity attention afforded the Cuban boy and press darling, Elián González. Many are placed in isolated juvenile detention centers alongside U.S.-citizen minors with criminal histories, though most children under I.N.S. jurisdiction do not come from such a background. The trauma can be severe.

The 1996 laws provide a variety of strong tools by which to fight terrorism, and some now need to be further strengthened. But churches, community groups and civil liberties proponents have concluded that the 1996 legislation was indiscriminate in the wide net it cast. Both IIRIRA and the antiterrorism bill are blunt instruments that continue to punish many immigrants and their citizen families who have nothing to do with terrorism.

Last June, two Supreme Court decisions served notice that the judiciary, too, is concerned about excesses in the 1996 legislation. Both were favorable to the rights of detained immigrants, specifically to those of so-called "criminal aliens": typically legal permanent residents who have been in the United States a long time. The issue is that these people were never naturalized and were convicted of a crime—often a relatively minor, nonviolent offense for which they served their time. Some never served any time at all in prison because their sentences were suspended. Many are married to citizen spouses and have citizen children. Immigrant advocates argue that "criminal aliens" are neither. But thousands have been deported, and thousands more remain in detention facing deportation.

The Supreme Court was particularly troubled about the practice of indefinite detention and the lack of access for detainees to judicial review. Last summer's decisions put Congress and the administration on notice that any new detention policies and procedures for noncitizens must pass constitutional muster.

In the present debate over new antiterrorist legislation, Congress seems determined not to repeat the mistakes it made in 1996. The ranking member of the House Judiciary Committee, Representative John Conyers, Democrat of Michigan, has addressed the issue squarely: "Legislation that began in good faith as an effort to fine-tune our anti-terrorism laws turned into a legislative race to the bottom.... I sat through the hearings on this legislation and did not hear a single shred of evidence that proved that a single terrorist act could be prevented… by denying immigrants their due process rights." Senator Patrick Leahy, Democrat of Vermont, chairman of the Senate Judiciary Committee, noted in a recent interview with The Los Angeles Times that the nation "must deport people who are intent on harming the United States, and that may require amending our immigration laws." He warned, however, that "we should not brand legal permanent residents as terrorists and detain them indefinitely without giving them the chance to clear their names before a court."

Securing the Detention Front

No one should doubt that the nation faces a dire emergency and that other terrorist incidents may occur. It is also clear that there are many holes in U.S. immigration policy. In the wake of the appalling events of Sept. 11, noncitizen detention will become further institutionalized. Can this be done in a way that is compatible with the best American and ethical values? To fight justly it will be essential at home, as abroad, to target the enemy and not innocent victims, and to do so as humanely as possible. The federal government should address two areas expeditiously.

First, the federal government must provide better oversight for the system it inaugurated in 1996. There are nearly 300 facilities throughout the country housing immigrants and asylum-seekers. City and county jails profit handsomely from such federal contracts. The number of detainees will presumably grow in the near future. Immigrant advocates have complained that there is no adequate I.N.S. system of regulation and evaluation to govern the disposition of this population, despite the availability of a good working model at the federal Bureau of Prisons. This is a recipe for religious bigotry, shameful abuse and denial of basic human rights.

The I.N.S. has shown itself willing to listen. After an extensive dialogue with the American Bar Association and other nongovernmental partners, the agency recently began implementing a set of minimum standards for every facility holding noncitizen detainees under the 1996 legislation. The plan is to monitor and inspect all such facilities by the end of 2002. Unfortunately, the standards are not legally enforceable, and are only as useful as their implementation allows them to be. Presently the I.N.S. detention system relies on local self-reporting from the facilities themselves. When the agency asked for funding for up to 80 new inspectors to better monitor and enforce the standards from Washington, the Office of Management and Budget opposed the request.

Second, the I.N.S. must establish and integrate salaried chaplains into the system. Groundwork has been laid through the Jesuit Refugee Service's Immigration Detention Program, a national Jesuit ministry that has made its personnel and expertise available to jump-start solutions. Working from the ground up at facilities in El Paso, Los Angeles and New York/New Jersey and coordinated through its national office in Washington, J.R.S. has served thousands of detainees and developed positive working relationships with local and national I.N.S. officials.

But the government has been woefully slow to extend systematically to noncitizen detainees the same level of religious care it requires for federal prisoners who are citizens. Together with an interfaith coalition in Washington, the J.R.S. national office has argued that the I.N.S. should establish salaried chaplaincies in its major facilities and integrate them into daily administration. Senior I.N.S. officials in Washington report that they have in fact requested funding for such a national chaplaincy program, but that the response has been negative.

The federal government should act quickly to institutionalize chaplaincy services, based on the successful federal Bureau of Prisons model. Incidents of religious bigotry toward Muslims abound, particularly in the local jails and county facilities where the I.N.S. houses the majority of noncitizen detainees.

Last fall, J.R.S. encountered a particularly troubling incident. When a 17-year-old Muslim from a south Asian country was detained in a Los Angeles County Probation facility, J.R.S./Los Angeles Minors Coordinator Alice Linsmeier began to assist him. She found volunteers who spoke Rajiv's language and eventually a Muslim religious volunteer to minister to him. The youth spoke openly about his Muslim faith and interacted well with staff and other detainees. After several months in Los Angeles, however, the I.N.S. moved Rajiv to a remote county juvenile facility several hours' travel distance to the north. There he experienced religious, linguistic and cultural isolation. In collaboration with the local Catholic diocese, Ms. Linsmeier attempted to arrange for pastoral visits by local Catholic sisters who spoke his language, but the facility chaplain, a fundamentalist Christian, objected.

J.R.S. then inquired about what was required to gain access to the juvenile facility, and was given two documents by the chaplain. "Qualifications for a Volunteer in the Jail Ministry" states at the outset: "Must have experienced God's saving grace and forgiving love through a personal relationship with Christ as his/her Savior." The second document, "Instructions to Volunteer Applicant," reads in part: "The applicant must keep in mind that this is an inter-denominational Christian ministry and our primary purpose is to lead individuals to a saving knowledge of Jesus Christ, instruct them in a knowledge of the Bible, and teach them how to live the Christian faith."

Only religious volunteers approved by the chaplain under these requirements were allowed regular access to the Muslim youth. Within months his condition deteriorated; he became suicidal, was placed in isolation and fitted with a straightjacket. Ms. Linsmeier was able to visit with him, accompanied by the translator from Los Angeles. Rajiv somewhat incoherently began to criticize Islam as "wrong" and said that he had been told the Koran was "a piece of _____." He said he was afraid he was going to die and "burn in hell." The facility social worker confirmed that the youth had developed conflicts of a religious nature.

Now, more than ever, the federal government should act decisively to institutionalize and monitor the freedom of religious expression of detained noncitizens. This reflects what is best about the national heritage. Furthermore, positive engagement with moderate American Muslims and Arabs may be crucial to the long-term defeat of Islamic terrorists and extremist ideologues. Stories of religious bigotry inside the walls may reinforce those who seek another "crusade" and undermine cooperation with law enforcement officials by potential allies. People like Rajiv have Muslim family and friends in the United States as well as their country of origin. The nation must get tougher on terrorism, but should also be smart and fair toward immigration.

ROBERT W. MCCHESNEY, S.J., is the director of the Jesuit Refugee Service Immigration Detention Program in Los Angeles and serves as Immigration Detention Coordinator for the Archdiocese of Los Angeles.

Index

Index

Test Your Knowledge Form

We encourage you to photocopy and use this page as a tool to assess how the articles in *Annual Editions* expand on the information in your textbook. By reflecting on the articles you will gain enhanced text information. You can also access this useful form on a product's book support Web site at *http://www.dushkin.com/online/*.

NAME:

DATE:

TITLE AND NUMBER OF ARTICLE:

BRIEFLY STATE THE MAIN IDEA OF THIS ARTICLE:

LIST THREE IMPORTANT FACTS THAT THE AUTHOR USES TO SUPPORT THE MAIN IDEA:

WHAT INFORMATION OR IDEAS DISCUSSED IN THIS ARTICLE ARE ALSO DISCUSSED IN YOUR TEXTBOOK OR OTHER READINGS THAT YOU HAVE DONE? LIST THE TEXTBOOK CHAPTERS AND PAGE NUMBERS:

LIST ANY EXAMPLES OF BIAS OR FAULTY REASONING THAT YOU FOUND IN THE ARTICLE:

LIST ANY NEW TERMS/CONCEPTS THAT WERE DISCUSSED IN THE ARTICLE, AND WRITE A SHORT DEFINITION:

We Want Your Advice

ANNUAL EDITIONS revisions depend on two major opinion sources: one is our Advisory Board, listed in the front of this volume, which works with us in scanning the thousands of articles published in the public press each year; the other is you—the person a ctually using the book. Please help us and the users of the next edition by completing the prepaid article rating form on this page and returning it to us. Thank you for your help!

ANNUAL EDITIONS: American Government 02/03

ARTICLE RATING FORM

Here is an opportunity for you to have direct input into the next revision of this volume.
We would like you to rate each of the articles listed below, using the following scale:

1. **Excellent: should definitely be retained**
2. **Above average: should probably be retained**
3. **Below average: should probably be deleted**
4. **Poor: should definitely be deleted**

Your ratings will play a vital part in the next revision.
Please mail this prepaid form to us as soon as possible.
Thanks for your help!

RATING	ARTICLE	RATING	ARTICLE
	1. The Declaration of Independence, 1776		38. Who Needs Political Parties?
	2. The Constitution of the United States, 1787		39. Making Every Vote Count
	3. The Size and Variety of the Union as a Check on Faction		40. Follow the Money
	4. Checks and Balances		41. No Need to Repeal the Electoral College
	5. Why Don't They Like Us?		42. Soft Money Unleashed
	6. Which America Will We Be Now?		43. Government's End
	7. "We"—Not "Me"		44. Associations Without Members
	8. America's Ignorant Voters		45. The World According to AARP
	9. The Black-White Wealth Gap		46. Journalism and Democracy
	10. Don't Treat Innocent People Like Criminals		47. The Media and Politics: It's More Than the News
	11. Speech Isn't Cheap		48. The Making of a Movement: Getting Serious About Media Reform
	12. Insurance Against the Once Unthinkable		49. Echo Chamber of Horrors
	13. Overruling the Court		50. The Two-Bucks-a-Minute Democracy
	14. The 28th Amendment		51. What Next for Welfare Reform?
	15. Immigrants for President		52. Social Security
	16. Guns and Tobacco: Government by Litigation		53. *Now* Do You Believe We Need a Draft?
	17. Gone Are the Giants		54. Immigration and Terrorism
	18. Hooked on Polls		
	19. When Presidents Speak		
	20. The Imperial Presidency		
	21. The Art of Compromise		
	22. Leakproof?		
	23. Fixing the Appointment Process		
	24. Crackup of the Committees		
	25. Can It Be Done?		
	26. Feingold's Crusade		
	27. John Dingell's Staying Power		
	28. Of Judges and Senators		
	29. Uninsured Americans Linger on Congress' Waiting List		
	30. A Judge Speaks Out		
	31. Reconsidering "Bush v. Gore"		
	32. Turkey Farm		
	33. Reforming U.S. Intelligence After the Terrorist Attack		
	34. Police Blotter		
	35. Running Scared		
	36. Family Tree, Party Roots		
	37. The Politics of Welfare Reform		

(Continued on next page)

BUSINESS REPLY MAIL
FIRST-CLASS MAIL PERMIT NO. 84 GUILFORD CT

POSTAGE WILL BE PAID BY ADDRESSEE

McGraw-Hill/Dushkin
530 Old Whitfield Street
Guilford, Ct 06437-9989

- -

ABOUT YOU

Name _____ Date _____

Are you a teacher? ☐   A student? ☐
Your school's name
_____

Department
_____

Address _____ City _____ State _____ Zip _____

School telephone # _____

YOUR COMMENTS ARE IMPORTANT TO US!

Please fill in the following information:
For which course did you use this book?
_____

Did you use a text with this ANNUAL EDITION?   ☐ yes ☐ no
What was the title of the text?
_____

What are your general reactions to the *Annual Editions* concept?
_____

Have you read any pertinent articles recently that you think should be included in the next edition? Explain.
_____

Are there any articles that you feel should be replaced in the next edition? Why?
_____

Are there any World Wide Web sites that you feel should be included in the next edition? Please annotate.
_____

May we contact you for editorial input?   ☐ yes ☐ no
May we quote your comments? ☐ yes ☐ no